Management of Organizations

In A Modern World

Edited by: Dean Cleavenger

University of Central Florida

Kendall Hunt
publishing company

Cover image provided by Dean Cleavenger.

Kendall Hunt
publishing company

www.kendallhunt.com
Send all inquiries to:
4050 Westmark Drive
Dubuque, IA 52004-1840

Contents

Introducing Management

CHAPTER OUTLINE

From *John R. Schermerhorn, Jr. Management,*10th Edition, 2009. Reprinted by permission of
John Wiley & Sons, Inc.

We live and work in very complex times. Financial turmoil, great resource and environmental challenges, uncertainties of international relations, the economics of globalization, and complexities of balancing work and personal lives are just some of the forces and trends that are having an undeniable impact on our society. The dynamics of ever-present change extend into the workplace and raise for all of us a host of new career challenges. There is no better time than now to commit your energies and intellect to continuous learning and personal development. Indeed, your future depends on it.

We are dealing with a new workplace, one in which everyone must adapt to a rapidly changing society with constantly shifting demands and opportunities. Learning and speed are in; habit and complacency are out. Organizations are fast changing, as is the nature of work itself. The economy is global, driven by innovation and technology. Even the concept of success, personal and organizational, is evolving as careers are transformed. Can there be any doubt that this is a time when smart people and smart organizations create their own futures?

In the quest for the future, the best employers share an important commitment—they value people! They are extremely good at attracting and retaining talented employees, and they excel at creating high-performance settings in which talented people achieve great results—individually and collectively. In their book *The New American Workplace*, James O'Toole and Edward E. Lawler, III, call such employers "high involvement" organizations and describe them as creating challenging and enriched jobs, allowing employee input in decisions, and avoiding layoffs and excessive turnover.

What often sets great organizations apart today is that they offer creative and inspiring leadership and supportive work environments that reward and respect people, allowing their talents to be fully utilized. The themes of the day are "respect," "participation," "empowerment," "involvement," "teamwork," and "self-management." They are designed to introduce you to the concepts, themes, and directions that are consistent with career success and organizational leadership in the high-performance settings of today's new workplace.

WORKING TODAY

Expectations for organizations and their members are very high. Organizations are expected to continuously excel on performance criteria that include concerns for ethics and social responsibilities, innovativeness, and employee development, as well as more traditional measures of profitability and investment value. When they fail, customers, investors, and employees are quick to let them know. For individuals, there are no guarantees of long-term employment. Jobs are increasingly earned and re-earned every day through one's performance accomplishments. Careers are being redefined in terms of "flexibility," "free agency," "skill portfolios," and "entrepreneurship." Career success takes lots of initiative and discipline, as well as continuous learning.

Talent

If you follow the news you'll find many examples of great organizations, and there should be many right in your local community. One that often makes the management news is Herman Miller, an innovative manufacturer of designer furniture. Respect for employees is a rule of thumb at the firm, whose core values include this statement: "Our greatest assets as a corporation are the gifts, talents and abilities of our employee-owners. . . . When we as a corporation invest in developing people, we are investing in our future." Former CEO Max DePree says, "We talk about the difference between being successful and being exceptional. Being successful is meeting goals in a good way—being exceptional is reaching your potential."

Herman Miller seems to fit O'Toole and Lawler's notion of a high-involvement organization. It also seems consistent with results from a study of high-performing companies by management scholars Charles O'Reilly and Jeffrey Pfeffer. They concluded that high performers achieve success because they are better than their competitors at getting extraordinary results from the people working for them.

"These companies have won the war for talent," they say, "not just by being great places to work—although they are that—but by figuring out how to get the best out of all of their people, every day."

The point of these examples is that people and their talents—what they know, what they learn, and what they do with it—are the ultimate foundations of organizational performance. They represent what managers call **intellectual capital**, the collective brainpower or shared knowledge of a workforce that can be used to create value. Indeed, the ultimate elegance of any organization is its ability to combine the talents of many people, sometimes thousands of them, to achieve unique and significant results.

Consider this intellectual capital equation as a way of personalizing this discussion. If you want a successful career, you must be a source of intellectual capital for employers. You must be someone willing to reach for the heights of personal competency and accomplishment. This means being a self-starter willing to continuously learn from experience. And it means becoming a valued **knowledge worker**—someone whose mind is a critical asset to employers and adds to the intellectual capital of the organization. The late management guru Peter Drucker once said: "Knowledge workers have many options and should be treated as volunteers. They're interested in personal achievement and personal responsibility. They expect continuous learning and training. They will respect and want authority. Give it to them."

Diversity

The term **workforce diversity** describes the composition of a workforce in terms of differences among people on gender, age, race, ethnicity, religion, sexual orientation, and able-bodiedness. The diversity trends of changing demographics are well recognized: more seniors, women, minorities, and immigrants are in the workforce. The U.S. Census Bureau predicts that by 2042 whites will be in the minority and the combined populations of African American, American Indians, Asians and Hispanics will be the majority. Hispanics are now the largest minority group and the fastest growing. And while aging baby boomers are a growing proportion of the population, more of them are postponing retirement.

Even though our society is diverse, diversity issues in employment are not always handled very well. How, for example, can we explain research in which résumés with white-sounding first names, such as Brett, received 50% more responses from potential employers than those with black-sounding first names, such as Kareem? The fact that these résumés were created with equal credentials suggests diversity bias, whether unconscious or deliberate.

Prejudice, or the holding of negative, irrational opinions and attitudes regarding members of diverse populations, sets the stage for diversity bias. It becomes active **discrimination** when minority members are unfairly treated and denied the full benefits of organizational membership. A subtle form of discrimination is called the **glass ceiling effect**, an invisible barrier or "ceiling" that prevents women and minorities from rising above a certain level of organizational responsibility. Scholar Judith Rosener warns that the loss caused by any form of discriminatory practices is "undervalued and underutilized human capital."

Many voices call diversity a "business imperative," meaning that today's increasingly diverse and multicultural workforce should be an asset that, if tapped, creates opportunities for performance gains. A female vice president at Avon once posed the diversity challenge this way: "Consciously creating an environment where everyone has an equal shot at contributing, participating, and most of all advancing." But even with such awareness existing, consultant R. Roosevelt Thomas says that too many employers still address diversity with the goal of "making their numbers," rather than truly valuing and managing diversity.

Intellectual capital is the collective brainpower or shared knowledge of a workforce.

A knowledge worker is someone whose mind is a critical asset to employers.

Workforce diversity describes differences among workers in gender, race, age, ethnicity, religion, sexual orientation, and able-bodiedness.

Prejudice is the display of negative, irrational attitudes toward members of diverse populations.

Discrimination actively denies minority members the full benefits of organizational membership.

The **glass ceiling effect** is an invisible barrier limiting career advancement of women and minorities.

Diversity Facts

- Women are 47% of the U.S. workforce and hold 50.3% of managerial jobs.
- African-Americans are 13.8% of the workforce and hold 6.5% of managerial jobs.
- Hispanics are 11.1% of the workforce and hold 5% of managerial jobs.
- Women hold 14.7% of board seats at *Fortune 500* companies; women of color hold 3.4%.
- For each $1 earned by men, women earn 80 cents; African-American women earn 64 cents; Hispanic women earn 52 cents.

Globalization

Japanese management consultant Kenichi Ohmae suggests that the national boundaries of world business have largely disappeared. What is the likelihood that you will someday work domestically for a foreign employer? When you call a customer service help line, do you know which country the service agent is speaking from? Can you state with confidence where a pair of your favorite athletic shoes or the parts for your personal computer were manufactured? More and more products are designed in one country, whereas their components are sourced, and final assembly is contracted in others, and all are for sale in still others. We have reached the point where top managers at Starbucks, IBM, Sony, Toyota and other global corporations have little need for the word "overseas" in everyday business vocabulary. They operate as global businesses that are equidistant from customers and suppliers, wherever in the world they may be located.

These are all part of the forces of **globalization**, the worldwide interdependence of resource flows, product markets, and business competition that characterizes our new economy. It is described as a process in which "improvements in technology (especially in communications and transportation) combine with the deregulation of markets and open borders to bring about vastly expanded flows of people, money, goods, services, and information."

Globalization isn't an abstract concept. It is increasingly a part of the fabric of our everyday lives, and with particular consequences for work and careers. In our global world, countries and peoples are increasingly interconnected through the news, in travel and lifestyles, in labor markets and employment patterns, and in financial and business dealings. Government leaders now worry about the competitiveness of nations, just as corporate leaders worry about business competitiveness. Employees in a growing number of occupations must worry about being replaced by workers in other countries who are willing and able to perform their jobs through outsourcing and at lower cost to employers. Even new college graduates must worry about lower-priced competition for the same jobs from graduates in other parts of the world.

Thomas Friedman, author of *The World Is Flat*, summarizes the challenge of globalization through comments made to him by one of India's business entrepreneurs: "Any activity where we can digitize and decompose the value chain, and move the work around, will get moved around." At a time when more Americans find that their customer service call is answered in Ghana, their CAT scan read by a radiologist in India, and their tax return prepared by an accountant in the Philippines, the fact that globalization offers both opportunities and challenges is quite clear indeed.

Technology

In many ways the forces of globalization ride on the foundations of the Internet and a continuing explosion in communication technologies. For better or worse we live and work in a technology-driven world

---

Globalization is the worldwide interdependence of resource flows, product markets, and business competition.

increasingly dominated by bar codes, automatic tellers, e-mail, instant messaging, text messaging, Web blogs, online media, electronic commerce, social networks, and more. And for a glimpse at what the future might hold, consider how many major firms are now participating in the virtual world of Second Life. If you log in and roam as an Avatar, you can visit such major corporations as Toyota, IBM, and Sony to sample and learn about new products and services.

From Second Life to real life, from the small retail store to the large multinational firm, technology is an indispensable part of everyday business—whether one is checking inventory, making a sales transaction, ordering supplies, or analyzing customer preferences. Physical distance hardly matters anymore; in "virtual space," people hold meetings, access common databases, share information and files, make plans, and solve problems together—all without ever meeting face-to-face. The new technologies have also added great flexibility to work arrangements, allowing people to "telecommute," "work from home," and maintain "mobile offices" while working in non-traditional ways and free from the constraints of the normal "8–5" schedules.

As all this transpires, everyone has to rush to stay informed and build what we might call their "Tech IQ." For example, job searches now increasingly involve multimedia resumes, and electronic portfolios that display skills and job qualifications. More than 31% of employers responding to one survey report using social networking sites in recruitment efforts. Some 44% or more of employers say they are now checking the online profiles of their job applicants. And, although an electronic persona is fun, it pays to remember that the "brand" one conveys online can spill over to affect one's reputation as a job candidate.

Ethics

When Jeffrey Skilling was sentenced to 24+ years in jail for crimes committed during the sensational collapse of Enron Corporation, the message was crystal clear. There is no excuse for senior executives in any organization to act illegally and to tolerate management systems that enrich the few while damaging the many. The harm done at Enron affected company employees who lost retirement savings and stockholders who lost investment values, as well as customers and society at large who paid the price as the firm's business performance deteriorated.

The issue raised here is **ethics**—a code of moral principles that sets standards of what is "good" and "right" as opposed to "bad" and "wrong" in the conduct of a person or group. And even though ethical failures like those at Enron are well publicized and should be studied, there are a plethora of positive cases and ethical role models to be studied as well.

The former CEO of Dial Corporation, Herb Baum, is one of the positive ethics examples. In his book *The Transparent Leader*, Baum argues that integrity is a key to leadership success and that the responsibility to set the ethical tone of an organization begins at the top. Believing that most CEOs are overpaid, he once gave his annual bonus to the firm's lowest paid workers. Baum also tells the story of an ethical role model—a rival CEO, Reuben Mark, of Colgate Palmolive. Mark called him one day to say that a newly hired executive had brought with him to Colgate a disk containing Dial's new marketing campaign. Rather than read it, he returned the disk to Baum—an act Baum called "the clearest case of leading with honor and transparency I've witnessed in my career."

You will find in this book many people and organizations that are exemplars of ethical behavior and whose integrity is unquestioned. They meet the standards of a new ethical reawakening and expectations for ethical leadership at all levels in an organization. They also show respect for such things as sustainable development and protection of the natural environment, protection of consumers through product safety and fair practices, and protection of human rights in all aspects of society, including employment.

Ethics set moral standards of what is "good" and "right" in one's behavior.

Careers

Globalization, emerging technologies, and the demand for talent make very personal the importance of initiative and self-renewal when it comes to careers. For most college students an immediate challenge is getting the first full-time job. And when the economy is down and employment markets are tight, the task of finding a career entry point can be daunting. It always pays to remember the importance of online resumes and job searches, and the power of social networking with established professionals. It's also helpful to pursue "internships" as pathways to first job placements. An article in *The Wall Street Journal,* for example, reports that some 62% of college hires have held internships and that many employers consider them prerequisites for job offers.

Today's career challenge isn't just finding your first job; it's also about successful career planning. British scholar Charles Handy uses the analogy of the Irish shamrock to discuss career patterns characteristic of the new economy. In one leaf of Handy's shamrock are the core workers. These full-time employees pursue traditional career paths. With success and the maintenance of critical skills, they can advance within the organization and may remain employed for a long time. In the second leaf are contract workers. They perform specific tasks as needed by the organization and are compensated on a fee-for-services basis rather than by a continuing wage or salary. They sell a skill or service and contract with many different employers over time. In the third leaf are part-time workers hired only as needed and for as long as needed. Employers expand and reduce their part-time staffs as business needs rise and fall.

You should be prepared to prosper in any of the shamrock's three leaves. It's likely that you will be changing jobs and employers over time, so your skills must be portable and always of value. These skills aren't gained once and then forgotten; they must be carefully maintained and upgraded all the time. For Handy this means being a **portfolio worker,** someone who always has the skills needed to readily shift jobs and even careers. Another career consultant describes this career challenge with the analogy of a surfer: "You're always moving. You can expect to fall into the water any number of times, and you have to get back up to catch the next wave." Later in this chapter we'll be talking more about important career skills and competencies, and how the learning opportunities in this book and your course can help strengthen your personal portfolio of capabilities.

ORGANIZATIONS IN THE NEW WORKPLACE

In his article "The Company of the Future," Robert Reich says: "Everybody works for somebody or something—be it a board of directors, a pension fund, a venture capitalist, or a traditional boss. Sooner or later you're going to have to decide who you want to work for." In order to make good employment choices and perform well in a career, you need a fundamental understanding of the nature of organizations. Management Smarts 1.1 provides a first look at some of the critical survival skills that you should acquire to work well in the organizations of today . . . and tomorrow.

What Is An Organization?

An **organization** is a collection of people working together to achieve a common purpose. It is a unique social phenomenon that enables its members to perform tasks far beyond the reach of individual accomplishment. This description applies to organizations of all sizes and types, from large corporations to the small businesses that make up the life of any community, to nonprofit organizations such as schools, government agencies, and community hospitals.

A portfolio worker has up-to-date skills that allow for job and career mobility.

An **organization** is a collection of people working together to achieve a common purpose.

Management Smarts 1.1

Early career survival skills

- *Mastery:* You need to be good at something; you need to be able to contribute something of value to your employer.
- *Networking:* You need to know people; links with peers and others within and outside the organization are essential to get things done.
- *Entrepreneurship:* You must act as if you are running your own business, spotting ideas and opportunities and stepping out to embrace them.
- *Love of technology:* You have to embrace technology; you don't have to be a technician, but you must be willing and able to fully utilize information technology.
- *Marketing:* You need to be able to communicate your successes and progress, both yours personally and those of your work group.
- *Passion for renewal:* You need to be continuously learning and changing, always updating yourself to best meet future demands.

All organizations share a broad purpose—providing goods or services of value to customers and clients. A clear sense of purpose tied to "quality products and services" and "customer satisfaction" is an important source of organizational strength and performance advantage. At Skype (now owned by eBay), founders Niklas Zennstrom and Janus Friis began with a straightforward sense of purpose: they wanted the whole world to be able to talk by telephone for free. When you open Skype on your computer and notice that there are millions of users making calls, you'll see the appeal of what Zennstrom and Friis set out to accomplish.

Organizations As Systems

Organizations are **open systems** that interact with their environments in the continual process of obtaining resource inputs and then transforming them into outputs in the form of finished goods and services for their customers. As shown in Exhibit 1.1, the external environment is both the supplier of resources and the source of customers. Feedback from the environment indicates how well an organization is doing.

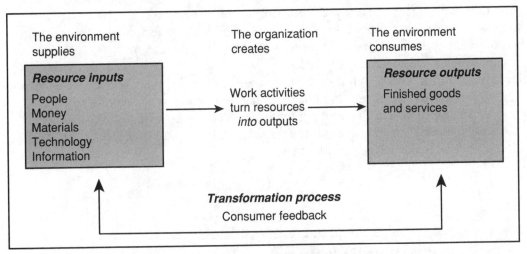

Exhibit 1.1   Organizations as open systems.

An **open system** is a system that interacts with its environment and transforms resource inputs and outputs.

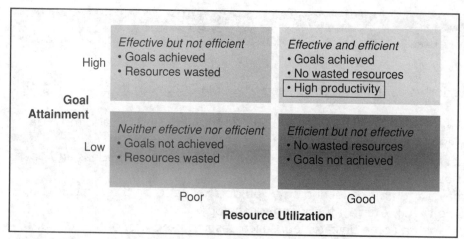

Exhibit 1.2   Productivity and the dimensions of organizational performance.

When customers stop buying a firm's products, it will be hard to stay in business for long unless something soon changes for the better. Anytime you hear or read about bankruptcies, for example, remember that they are stark testimonies to this fact of the marketplace: without loyal customers, a business can't survive.

Organizational Performance

If an organization is to perform well, its resources must be well utilized and its customers must be well served. This is a process of value creation through organizational performance. If operations add value to the original cost of resource inputs, then (1) a business organization can earn a profit—that is, sell a product for more than the cost of making it—or (2) a nonprofit organization can add wealth to society—that is, provide a public service that is worth more than its cost (e.g., fire protection in a community).

A common way to describe how well an organization is performing overall is **productivity.** It measures the quantity and quality of outputs relative to the cost of inputs. Productivity can be measured at the individual and group as well as organizational levels. And as Exhibit 1.2 shows, productivity involves two common performance measures: effectiveness and efficiency.

Performance effectiveness is an output measure of task or goal accomplishment. If you are working as a software engineer for a computer game developer, performance effectiveness may mean that you meet a daily production target in terms of the quantity and quality of lines of code written. This adds to productivity helping the company as a whole maintain its production schedule and meet customer demands for timely delivery and high-quality gaming products.

Performance efficiency is an input measure of the resource costs associated with goal accomplishment. Returning to the gaming example, the most efficient software production is accomplished at a minimum cost in materials and labor. If you are producing fewer lines of code in a day than you are capable of, this amounts to inefficiency; if you make a lot of mistakes that require extensive rewrites, this is also inefficient work. Such inefficiencies reduce productivity.

Productivity is the quantity and quality of work performance, with resource utilization considered.

Performance effectiveness is an output measure of task or goal accomplishment.

Performance efficiency is an input measure of resource cost associated with goal accomplishment.

Changing Nature of Organizations

Change is a continuing theme in society, and organizations are certainly undergoing dramatic changes today. Although not exhaustive, the following list of organizational trends and transitions is relevant to your study of management.

- *Renewed belief in human capital:* Demands of the new economy place premiums on high-involvement and participatory work settings that rally the knowledge, experience, and commitment of all members.
- *Demise of "command-and-control":* Traditional hierarchical structures with "do as I say" bosses are proving too slow, conservative, and costly to do well in today's competitive environments.
- *Emphasis on teamwork:* Today's organizations are less vertical and more horizontal in focus; they are increasingly driven by teamwork that pools talents for creative problem solving.
- *Preeminence of technology:* New opportunities appear with each development in computer and information technology; they continually change the way organizations operate and how people work.
- *Embrace of networking:* Organizations are networked for intense, real-time communication and coordination, internally among parts and externally with partners, contractors, suppliers, and customers.
- *New workforce expectations:* A new generation of workers brings to the workplace less tolerance for hierarchy, more informality, and more attention to performance merit than to status and seniority.
- *Concern for work-life balance:* As society increases in complexity, workers are forcing organizations to pay more attention to balance in the often-conflicting demands of work and personal affairs.
- *Focus on speed:* Everything moves fast today; in business those who get products to market first have an advantage, and in any organization work is expected to be done both well and in a timely manner.

MANAGERS IN THE NEW WORKPLACE

This chapter opened with an emphasis on people, along with their talents and intellectual capital, as key foundations of organizational success. In an article entitled "Putting People First for Organizational Success," Jeffrey Pfeffer and John F. Veiga argue forcefully that organizations perform better when they treat their members better. They note that "managers" in high-performing organizations act in ways that truly value people. They don't treat people as costs to be controlled; they treat them as valuable strategic assets to be carefully nurtured and developed. So, who are these "managers" and just what do they do?

What Is a Manager?

You find them in all organizations. They work with a wide variety of job titles—team leader, department head, supervisor, project manager, dean, president, administrator, and more. They always work directly with other persons who rely on them for critical support and assistance in their own jobs. Peter Drucker described their job as "to make work productive and workers effective." We call them **managers**, people in organizations who directly support, supervise, and help activate the work efforts and performance accomplishments of others.

For those serving as managers, the job is challenging and substantial. Any manager is responsible not just for her or his own work but for the overall performance accomplishments of a team, work group, department, or even organization as a whole. Whether they are called direct reports, team members,

A manager is a person who supports, activates, and is responsible for the work of others.

work associates, or subordinates, these "other people" are the essential human resources whose contributions represent the real work of the organization. And as pointed out by management theorist Henry Mintzberg, being a manager remains an important and socially responsible job:

No job is more vital to our society than that of the manager. It is the manager who determines whether our social institutions serve us well or whether they squander our talents and resources. It is time to strip away the folklore about managerial work, and time to study it realistically so that we can begin the difficult task of making significant improvement in its performance.

Levels of Managers

At the highest levels of organizations, as shown in Exhibit 1.3, common job titles are chief executive officer (CEO), president, and vice president. These **top managers** are responsible for the performance of an organization as a whole or for one of its larger parts. They are supposed to pay special attention to the external environment, be alert to potential long-run problems and opportunities, and develop appropriate ways of dealing with them. Top managers also create and communicate long-term vision, and ensure that strategies and objectives are consistent with the organization's purpose and mission.

Top managers should be future-oriented, strategic thinkers capable of making decisions under competitive and uncertain conditions. Before retiring as Medtronics' CEO, for example, Bill George repositioned the firm as a client-centered deliverer of medical services. The hours were long and the work demanding, but he loved his job, saying: "I always dreamed . . . of being head of a major corporation where the values of the company and my own values were congruent, where a company could become kind of a symbol for others, where the product that you represent is doing good for people."

Reporting to top managers are **middle managers** who are in charge of relatively large departments or divisions consisting of several smaller work units. Examples are clinic directors in hospitals; deans in universities; and division managers, plant managers, and regional sales managers in businesses. Middle managers work with top managers and coordinate with peers to develop and implement action plans to accomplish organizational objectives.

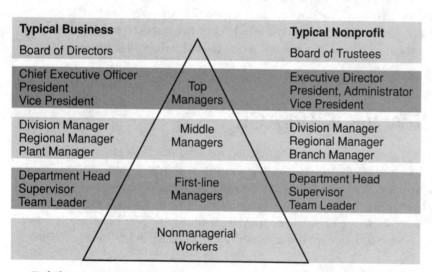

Exhibit 1.3   Management levels in typical businesses and nonprofit organizations.

Even though most people enter the workforce as technical specialists such as auditor, market researcher, or systems analyst, sooner or later they advance to positions of initial managerial responsibility. A first job in management typically involves serving as a **team leader** or supervisor—someone in charge of a small work group composed of nonmanagerial workers. Job titles for these first-line managers include such designations as department head, group leader, and unit manager. For example, the leader of an auditing team is considered a first-line manager, as is the head of an academic department in a university.

Top managers guide the performance of the organization as a whole or of one of its major parts.

Middle managers oversee the work of large departments or divisions.

Team leaders report to middle managers and supervise nonmanagerial workers.

Management Smarts 1.2

Nine responsibilities of team leaders

1. Plan meetings and work schedules.
2. Clarify goals and tasks, and gather ideas for improvement.
3. Appraise performance and counsel team members.
4. Recommend pay increases and new assignments.
5. Recruit, train, and develop team members.
6. Encourage high performance and teamwork.
7. Inform team members about organizational goals.
8. Inform higher levels of team needs and accomplishments.
9. Coordinate activities with other teams.

People serving in team leader positions create the building blocks for organizational performance. Bill George's goals at Medtronics could be met only with the contributions of people like Justine Fritz, who led a 12-member Medtronics team to launch a new life-altering medical product. She says, "I've just never worked on anything that so visibly, so dramatically changes the quality of someone's life," while noting that the demands are also great. "Some days you wake up, and if you think about all the work you have to do it's so overwhelming, you could be paralyzed." Management Smarts 1.2 offers advice for team leaders and other first-line managers.

Types of Managers

In addition to serving at different levels of authority, managers work in different capacities within organizations. **Line managers** are responsible for work that makes a direct contribution to the organization's outputs. For example, the president, retail manager, and department supervisors of a local department store all have line responsibilities. Their jobs in one way or another are directly related to the sales operations of the store. **Staff managers,** by contrast, use special technical expertise to advise and support the efforts of line workers. In a department store, again, the director of human resources and chief financial officer would have staff responsibilities.

In business, **functional managers** have responsibility for a single area of activity such as finance, marketing, production, human resources, accounting, or sales. **General managers** are responsible for activities covering many functional areas. An example is a plant manager who oversees purchasing, manufacturing, warehousing, sales, personnel, and accounting functions. In public or nonprofit organizations it is common for managers to be called **administrators.** Examples include hospital administrators, public administrators, and city administrators.

Line managers directly contribute to producing the organization's goods or services.

Staff managers use special technical expertise to advise and support line workers.

Functional managers are responsible for one area such as finance, marketing, production, personnel, accounting, or sales.

General managers are responsible for complex, multifunctional units.

An administrator is a manager in a public or nonprofit organization.

Managerial Performance

All managers help people, working individually and in groups, to perform. They do this while being held personally "accountable" for results achieved. **Accountability** is the requirement of one person to answer to a higher authority for performance results in his or her area of work responsibility. The team leader is accountable to a middle manager, the middle manager is accountable to a top manager, and even the top manager is accountable to a board of directors or board of trustees.

But what actually constitutes managerial performance: when is a manager "effective"? A good answer is that **effective managers** successfully help others achieve both high performance and satisfaction in their work. This dual concern for performance and satisfaction introduces the concept of **quality of work life.** It is an indicator of the overall quality of human experiences in the workplace. A "high-QWL" workplace offers such things as fair pay, safe working conditions, opportunities to learn and use new skills, room to grow and progress in a career, protection of individual rights, and pride in the work itself and in the organization. Would you agree that both performance and satisfaction are important management goals, and that productivity and quality of work life can and should go hand in hand?

Changing Nature of Managerial Work

Cindy Zollinger is president of Cornerstone Research and directly supervises 24 people. But she says: "I don't really manage them in a typical way; they largely run themselves. I help them in dealing with obstacles they face, or in making the most of opportunities they find." As Cindy's comments suggest, we are in a time when the best managers are known more for "helping" and "supporting" than for "directing" and "order giving." The words "coordinator," "coach," and "team leader" are heard as often as "supervisor" or "boss." The best managers are well informed regarding the needs of those reporting to or dependent on them. They can often be found providing advice and developing the support needed for others to perform to the best of their abilities.

The concept of the **upside-down pyramid** fits well with Cindy Zollinger's description of her job as a manager and in general reflects the changing nature of managerial work today. Shown in Exhibit 1.4, it offers an alternative and suggestive way of viewing organizations and the role played by managers within them. Notice that the operating workers are at the top of the upside-down pyramid, just below the customers and clients they serve. They are supported in their work efforts by managers below them. These managers clearly aren't just order-givers; they are there to mobilize and deliver the support others need to do their jobs best and serve customer needs. The upside-down pyramid view leaves no doubt that the whole organization is devoted to serving the customer, and that the job of managers is to support the workers.

THE MANAGEMENT PROCESS

If productivity in the form of high levels of performance effectiveness and efficiency is a measure of organizational success, managers are largely responsible for its achievement. The ultimate "bottom line" in every manager's job is to help an organization achieve high performance by best utilizing its human and material resources.

Accountability is the requirement to show performance results to a supervisor.

An **effective manager** helps others achieve high performance and satisfaction at work.

Quality of work life is the overall quality of human experiences in the workplace.

In the **upside-down pyramid** operating workers are at the top serving customers while managers are at the bottom supporting them.

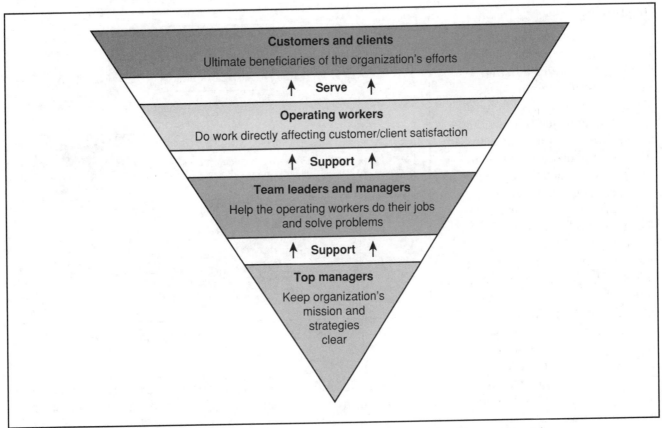

Exhibit 1.4   The organization viewed as an upside-down pyramid.

Functions of Management

The process of **management** involves planning, organizing, leading, and controlling the use of resources to accomplish performance goals. These four management functions and their interrelationships are shown in Exhibit 1.5. All managers, regardless of title, level, type, and organizational setting, are responsible for the four functions. However, they are not accomplished in a linear, step-by-step fashion. The reality is that these functions are continually engaged as a manager moves from task to task and opportunity to opportunity in his or her work.

Planning

In management, **planning** is the process of setting performance objectives and determining what actions should be taken to accomplish them. Through planning, a manager identifies desired results and ways to achieve them.

Take, for example, an Ernst & Young initiative that was developed to better meet the needs of the firm's female professionals. This initiative grew out of top management's concern about the firm's retention rates for women. The firm's chairman at the time, Philip A. Laskawy, launched a Diversity Task Force with the planning objective to reduce turnover rates for women. When the task force began its work, this turnover was running some 22% per year, and it cost the firm about 150% of a departing employee's annual salary to hire and train each replacement.

Management is the process of planning, organizing, leading, and controlling the use of resources to accomplish performance goals.

Planning is the process of setting objectives and determining how to accomplish them.

Organizing

Even the best plans will fail without strong implementation. This begins with **organizing**: the process of assigning tasks, allocating resources, and coordinating the activities of individuals and groups to implement plans. Through organizing, managers turn plans into actions by defining jobs, assigning personnel, and supporting them with technology and other resources.

At Ernst & Young, Laskawy organized to meet the planning objective by first creating a new Office of Retention and then hiring Deborah K. Holmes to head it. As retention problems were identified in various parts of the firm, Holmes also took initiative. She convened special task forces to tackle problems and recommend location-specific solutions. For example, a Woman's Access Program was started to give women access to senior executives for mentoring and career development.

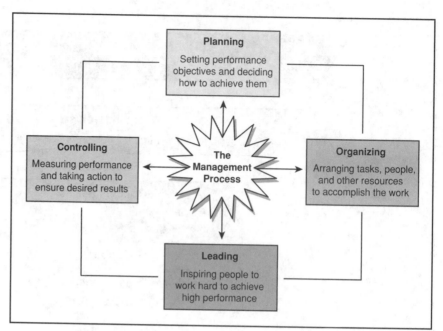

Exhibit 1.5   Four functions of management.

Leading

In management, **leading** is the process of arousing people's enthusiasm to work hard and inspiring their efforts to fulfill plans and accomplish objectives. By leading, managers build commitments to a common vision, encourage activities that support goals, and influence others to do their best work on the organization's behalf.

At Ernst & Young, Deborah Holmes identified a core problem: work at the firm was extremely intense, and women were often stressed because their spouses also worked. She became a champion for improved work-life balance and pursued it relentlessly. Although admitting that "there's no silver bullet" in the form of a universal solution, her office supported and encouraged better balance in a variety of ways. She started "call-free holidays," when professionals did not check voice mail or e-mail on weekends and holidays. She also started a "travel sanity" program that limited staffers' travel to four days a week so that they could get home for weekends.

Controlling

The management function of **controlling** is the process of measuring work performance, comparing results to objectives, and taking corrective action as needed. Through controlling, managers maintain active contact with people in the course of their work, gather and interpret reports on performance, and use this information to make constructive changes. In today's dynamic times, such control and adjustment are indispensable. Things don't always go as anticipated, and plans must be modified and redefined for future success.

Organizing is the process of assigning tasks, allocating resources, and coordinating work activities.

Leading is the process of arousing enthusiasm and inspiring efforts to achieve goals.

Controlling is the process of measuring performance and taking action to ensure desired results.

At Ernst & Young, Laskawy and Holmes had documented what the firm's retention rates for women were when they started the new program. With this baseline they were subsequently able to track progress to verify real improvements. Through measurement they were able to compare actual results with planning objectives, and identify changes in work-life balance and retention rates over time. As they reviewed the results, they continually adjusted their plans and activities to improve future performance.

Managerial Roles and Activities

Although the management process as just described may seem straightforward, planning, organizing, leading and controlling are more complicated than they appear at first glance. In his classic book *The Nature of Managerial Work*, for example, Henry Mintzberg describes the daily work of corporate chief executives as follows: "There was no break in the pace of activity during office hours. The mail . . . telephone calls . . . and meetings . . . accounted for almost every minute from the moment these executives entered their offices in the morning until they departed in the evenings." Today we would complicate things even further by adding ever-present e-mail, instant messages, text messages, and voice mail to Mintzberg's list of executive preoccupations.

Managerial Roles

In trying to better understand and describe the nature of managerial work, Mintzberg also identified a set of 10 roles that managers fulfill. The roles fall into three categories: informational, interpersonal, and decisional roles.

A manager's informational roles involve the giving, receiving, and analyzing of information. A manager fulfilling these roles will be a *monitor*, scanning for information; a *disseminator*, sharing information; and a *spokesperson*, acting as official communicator. The interpersonal roles involve interactions with people inside and outside the work unit. A manager fulfilling these roles will be a *figurehead*, modeling and setting forth key principles and policies; a *leader*, providing direction and instilling enthusiasm; and a *liaison*, coordinating with others. The decisional roles involve using information to make decisions to solve problems or address opportunities. A manager fulfilling these roles will be a *disturbance handler*, dealing with problems and conflicts; a *resource allocator*, handling budgets and distributing resources; a *negotiator*—making deals and forging agreements; and an *entrepreneur*—developing new initiatives. Exhibit 1.6 further describes all 10 roles.

Managerial Activities

Managers must not only understand and master their roles; they must also have the ability to implement them in an intense and complex work setting. The managers Mintzberg observed had little free time to themselves; unexpected problems and continuing requests for meetings consumed almost all the time

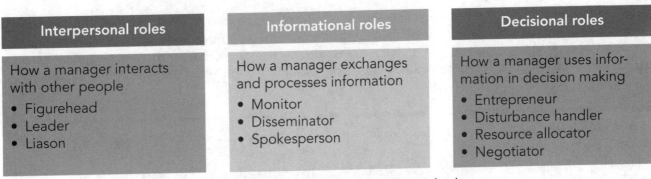

Exhibit 1.6   Mintzberg's 10 managerial roles.

that became available. Their workdays were hectic, and the pressure for continuously improving performance was all-encompassing. Mintzberg summarized his observations this way: "The manager can never be free to forget the job, and never has the pleasure of knowing, even temporarily, that there is nothing else to do. . . . Managers always carry the nagging suspicion that they might be able to contribute just a little bit more. Hence they assume an unrelenting pace in their work."

Without any doubt, managerial work is busy, demanding, and stressful for all levels of responsibility in any work setting. A summary of continuing research on the nature of managerial work offers this important reminder.

- Managers work long hours.
- Managers work at an intense pace.
- Managers work at fragmented and varied tasks.
- Managers work with many communication media.
- Managers accomplish their work largely through interpersonal relationships.

Managerial Agendas and Networks

On his way to a meeting, a GM bumped into a staff member who did not report to him. Using this opportunity, in a two-minute conversation he (a) asked two questions and received the information he needed; (b) reinforced their good relationship by sincerely complimenting the staff member on something he had recently done; and (c) got the staff member to agree to do something that the GM needed done.

This brief incident provides a glimpse of an effective general manager (GM) in action. It portrays two activities that management consultant and scholar John Kotter considers critical to a manager's success: agenda setting and networking. Through **agenda setting**, good managers develop action priorities that include goals and plans spanning long and short time frames. These agendas are usually incomplete and loosely connected in the beginning, but they become more specific as the manager utilizes information continually gleaned from many different sources. The agendas are always kept in mind and are "played out" whenever an opportunity arises, as in the preceding example.

Good managers implement their agendas by working with many people inside and outside the organization. This is made possible by **networking**, the process of building and maintaining positive relationships with people whose help may be needed to implement one's agendas. Such networking creates **social capital**—a capacity to attract support and help from others in order to get things done. In Kotter's example, the GM received help from a staff member who did not report directly to him. His networks and social capital would also include relationships with peers, a boss, higher-level executives, subordinates, and members of their work teams, as well as with external customers, suppliers, and community representatives.

LEARNING HOW TO MANAGE

Today's turbulent times present an ever-shifting array of problems, opportunities, and performance expectations for organizations, their managers, and their members. All of this, of course, means that your career success depends on a real commitment to **learning**—changing behavior through experience. In management the learning focus is on developing skills and competencies to deal with the complexities

---

Agenda setting develops action priorities for accomplishing goals and plans.

Networking is the process of creating positive relationships with people who can help advance agendas.

Social capital is a capacity to get things done with support and help of others.

Learning is in learning theory, any relatively permanent change in behavior resulting from experience.

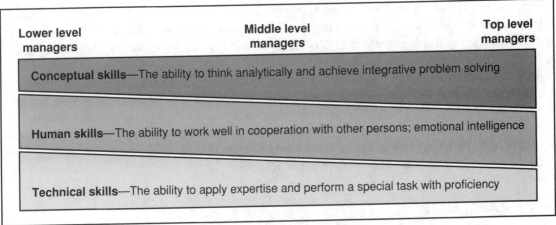

Exhibit 1.7   Katz's essential managerial skills.

of human behavior and problem solving in organizations. When you think about this goal, don't forget that it's not just formal learning in the classroom that counts. Indeed the long-term difference in career success may well rest with **lifelong learning**—the process of continuous learning from all of our daily experiences and opportunities.

Essential Managerial Skills

A **skill** is the ability to translate knowledge into action that results in desired performance. Harvard scholar Robert L. Katz has classified the essential, or baseline, skills of managers into three useful categories: technical, human, and conceptual. He suggests that their relative importance tends to vary by level of managerial responsibility, as shown in Exhibit 1.7.

Technical Skills

A **technical skill** is the ability to use a special proficiency or expertise to perform particular tasks. Accountants, engineers, market researchers, financial planners, and systems analysts, for example, possess technical skills. These skills are initially acquired through formal education and are further developed by training and job experience. Exhibit 1.7 shows that technical skills are very important at career entry levels. The critical question for you in preparation for any job interview comes down to this simple test: "What can I really do right from the start that offers value for an employer?"

Human and Interpersonal Skills

The ability to work well in cooperation with other persons is a **human skill** or an **interpersonal skill**. Given the highly interpersonal nature of managerial work, human skills are consistently important across all the managerial levels. They emerge in the workplace as the capacity to collaborate and network with others, to engage others with a spirit of trust, enthusiasm, and positive engagement. The next time you sign on to Facebook or Bebo or Linkedin, for example, think about how these social networking experiences can translate into workplace networking skills.

Lifelong learning is continuous learning from daily experiences.

A skill is the ability to translate knowledge into action that results in desired performance.

A technical skill is the ability to use expertise to perform a task with proficiency.

A human skill or **interpersonal skill** is the ability to work well in cooperation with other people.

A manager with good human skills will have a high degree of self-awareness and a capacity to understand or empathize with the feelings of others. This relates to **emotional intelligence**. Discussed also in later chapters for its leadership implications, "EI" is defined by scholar and consultant Daniel Goleman as the "ability to manage ourselves and our relationships effectively." Emotional intelligence is reflected in how well or poorly you recognize, understand and manage feelings while interacting and dealing with others. Someone high in emotional intelligence will know when her or his emotions are about to become disruptive, and act to control them. This same person will sense when another person's emotions are negatively influencing a relationship, and make attempts to understand and better deal with them. If you are willing to ask, a straightforward question can put your interpersonal skills and emotional intelligence to the test: "Just how well do I relate with and work with others?"

Conceptual and Analytical Skills

The ability to think critically and analytically is a **conceptual skill**. It involves the capacity to break problems into smaller parts, to see the relations between the parts, and to recognize the implications of any one problem for others. In the classroom we often call this "critical thinking." It is a diagnostic skill that facilitates effective decision making and problem solving. As people assume ever-higher responsibilities in organizations, they are called upon to deal with more ambiguous problems that have many complications and longer-term consequences. This is why Exhibit 1.7 shows that conceptual skills gain in relative importance for top managers. In respect to long-term career readiness, the question to ask is: "Am I developing the critical-thinking and problem-solving capabilities I will need for long-term career success?"

Developing Managerial Competencies

Katz's notion of essential managerial skills is taken further in ideas expressed by futurist Daniel Pink. In his book *A Whole New Mind*, Pink points out that our societal transition from information age into a new conceptual age is demanding a combination of conceptual and human skills that makes us good at both creating and empathizing. This "right brain" skills package is both *high concept*—the ability to see the big picture, identify patterns and combine ideas, and *high touch*—the ability to empathize and enjoy others in the pursuit of a purpose.

Management educators are devoted to helping students and practicing managers acquire and continually develop the skills needed for managerial success. To personalize the challenge, you might think of a **managerial competency** as a skill-based capability that contributes to high performance in a management job. A number of high concept and high touch competencies are listed here as a baseline checklist for you to consider.

- *Communication*—Ability to share ideas and findings clearly in written and oral expression—includes writing, oral presentation, giving/receiving feedback, technology utilization.
- *Teamwork*—Ability to work effectively as a team member and team leader—includes team contribution, team leadership, conflict management, negotiation, consensus building.
- *Self-management*—Ability to evaluate oneself, modify behavior, and meet performance obligations—includes ethical reasoning and behavior, personal flexibility, tolerance for ambiguity, performance responsibility.
- *Leadership*—Ability to influence and support others to perform complex and ambiguous tasks—includes diversity awareness, global understanding, project management, strategic action.

Emotional intelligence is the ability to manage ourselves and our relationships effectively.

A conceptual skill is the ability to think analytically to diagnose and solve complex problems.

A managerial competency is a skill-based capability for high performance in a management job.

- *Critical thinking*—Ability to gather and analyze information for creative problem solving—includes problem solving, judgment and decision making, information gathering and interpretation, creativity/innovation.
- *Professionalism*—Ability to sustain a positive impression, instill confidence, and maintain career advancement—includes personal presence, personal initiative, career management.

Management: Past to Present

From *John R. Schermerhorn, Jr. Management*, 10th Edition, 2009. Reprinted by permission of John Wiley & Sons, Inc.

In *The Evolution of Management Thought,* Daniel Wren traces management as far back as 5000 B.C., when ancient Sumerians used written records to assist in governmental and business activities. Management was important to the construction of the Egyptian pyramids, the rise of the Roman Empire, and the commercial success of 14th-century Venice. By the time of the Industrial Revolution in the 1700s, great social changes had helped prompt a major leap forward in the manufacturing of basic staples and consumer goods. Industrial development was accelerated by Adam Smith's ideas of efficient production through specialized tasks and the division of labor. At the turn of the 20th century, Henry Ford and others were making mass production a mainstay of the emerging economy. Since then, the science and practices of management have been on a rapid and continuing path of development.

One pathway in management is summarized in *Mary Parker Follett—Prophet of Management: A Celebration of Writings from the 1920s.* The book is a reminder of the wisdom of history. Although Follett wrote in a different day and age, her ideas are rich with foresight. She advocated cooperation and better horizontal relationships in organizations, taught respect for the experience and knowledge of workers, warned against the dangers of too much hierarchy, and called for visionary leadership. Today we pursue similar themes while using terms like "empowerment," "involvement," "flexibility," and "self-management."

There are many useful lessons in the history of management thought. Rather than naively believing that we are always reinventing management practice today, it is wise to remember the historical roots of many modern ideas and admit that we are still trying to perfect them.

CLASSICAL MANAGEMENT APPROACHES

Our study of management begins with the classical approaches: (1) scientific management, (2) administrative principles, and (3) bureaucratic organization. Exhibit 2.1 associates each with a prominent person in the history of management thought, and their names are still widely used in management conversations today. The exhibit also shows that the classical approaches share a common assumption: people at work act in a rational manner that is primarily driven by economic concerns. Workers are expected to rationally consider opportunities made available to them and to do whatever is necessary to achieve the greatest personal and monetary gain.

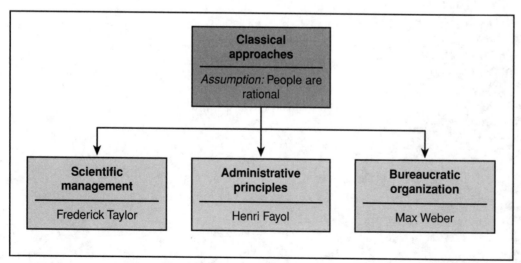

Exhibit 2.1   Major branches in the classical approach to management.

Scientific Management

In 1911, Frederick W. Taylor published *The Principles of Scientific Management,* in which he made the following statement: "The principal object of management should be to secure maximum prosperity for the employer, coupled with the maximum prosperity for the employee." Taylor, often called the "father of scientific management," noticed that many workers did their jobs their own ways and without clear and uniform specifications. He believed this caused them to lose efficiency and underperform. He also believed that this problem could be corrected if workers were taught and then helped by supervisors to always do their jobs in the right ways.

Taylor's goal was to improve the productivity of people at work. He used the concept of "time study" to analyze the motions and tasks required in any job and to develop the most efficient ways to perform them. He then linked these job requirements to both training for the worker and support from supervisors in the form of proper direction, work assistance, and monetary incentives. Taylor's approach is known as **scientific management** and includes four guiding action principles.

1. Develop for every job a "science" that includes rules of motion, standardized work implements, and proper working conditions.
2. Carefully select workers with the right abilities for the job.
3. Carefully train workers to do the job and give them the proper incentives to cooperate with the job "science."
4. Support workers by carefully planning their work and by smoothing the way as they go about their jobs.

Mentioned in Taylor's first principle, **motion study** is the science of reducing a job or task to its basic physical motions. Two of Taylor's contemporaries, Frank and Lillian Gilbreth, pioneered the use of motion studies as a management tool. In one famous case they reduced the number of motions used by bricklayers and tripled their productivity. The Gilbreths' work led to later advances in the areas of job simplification, work standards, and incentive wage plans—all techniques still used in the modern workplace. For example, speed was the focus in a recent study of workers editing computer documents and copying data among spreadsheets. It was found that persons using 24-inch monitors did tasks 52% faster than those using 18-inch monitors. Researchers estimated that use of the larger monitors could save up to 2.5 labor hours per day.

Administrative Principles

In 1916, after a career in French industry, Henri Fayol published *Administration Industrielle et Générale.* The book outlines his views on the proper management of organizations and of the people within them. It identifies the following five "rules" or "duties" of management, which closely resemble the four functions of management—planning, organizing, leading, and controlling—that we talk about today:

1. *Foresight*—to complete a plan of action for the future.
2. *Organization*—to provide and mobilize resources to implement the plan.
3. *Command*—to lead, select, and evaluate workers to get the best work toward the plan.
4. *Coordination*—to fit diverse efforts together and to ensure information is shared and problems solved.
5. *Control*—to make sure things happen according to plan and to take necessary corrective action.

Importantly, Fayol believed that management could be taught. He was very concerned about improving the quality of management and set forth a number of "principles" to guide managerial action.

Scientific management emphasizes careful selection and training of workers and supervisory support.

Motion study is the science of reducing a task to its basic physical motions.

A number of them are still part of the management vocabulary. They include Fayol's *scalar chain principle*—there should be a clear and unbroken line of communication from the top to the bottom in the organization; *the unity of command principle*—each person should receive orders from only one boss; and the *unity of direction principle*—one person should be in charge of all activities that have the same performance objective.

Bureaucratic Organization

Max Weber was a late-19th-century German intellectual whose insights have had a major impact on the field of management and the sociology of organizations. His ideas developed in reaction to his belief that the organizations of his day often failed to reach their performance potential. Among other things, Weber was concerned that people were in positions of authority not because of their job-related capabilities, but because of their social standing or "privileged" status in German society.

At the heart of Weber's thinking was a specific form of organization he believed could correct the problems just described—a **bureaucracy**. For him it was an ideal, intentionally rational, and very efficient form of organization founded on principles of logic, order, and legitimate authority. The defining characteristics of Weber's bureaucratic organization are as follows:

- *Clear division of labor:* Jobs are well defined, and workers become highly skilled at performing them.
- *Clear hierarchy of authority:* Authority and responsibility are well defined for each position, and each position reports to a higher-level one.
- *Formal rules and procedures:* Written guidelines direct behavior and decisions in jobs, and written files are kept for historical record.
- *Impersonality:* Rules and procedures are impartially and uniformly applied, with no one receiving preferential treatment.
- *Careers based on merit:* Workers are selected and promoted on ability, competency, and performance, and managers are career employees of the organization.

Weber believed that bureaucracies would have the advantages of efficiency in utilizing resources, and of fairness or equity in the treatment of employees and clients. In his words:

> The purely bureaucratic type of administrative organization . . . is, from a purely technical point of view, capable of attaining the highest degree of efficiency. . . . It is superior to any other form in precision, in stability, in the stringency of its discipline, and in its reliability. It thus makes possible a particularly high degree of calculability of results for the heads of the organization and for those acting in relation to it.

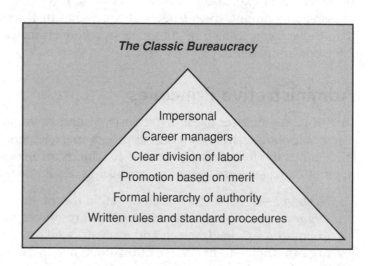

The Classic Bureaucracy

Impersonal
Career managers
Clear division of labor
Promotion based on merit
Formal hierarchy of authority
Written rules and standard procedures

This is the ideal side of bureaucracy. However, the terms "bureaucracy" and "bureaucrat" are now often used with negative connotations. The possible disadvantages of bureaucracy include excessive paperwork or "red tape," slowness in handling problems, rigidity in the face of shifting customer or client needs, resistance to change, and employee apathy. These disadvantages are most likely to cause problems for organizations that must be flexible and

A **bureaucracy** is an organizational structure that is characterized by an elaborate division of labor based on functional specialization, a hierarchy of authority assigned to different offices, a system of rules explaining how everyone is to perform, and impersonal relationships.

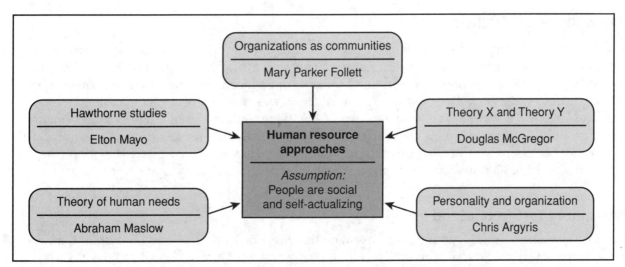

Exhibit 2.2   Foundations in the behavioral or human resource approaches to management.

quick in adapting to changing circumstances—a common situation today. Current trends in management include many innovations that seek the same goals as Weber but use different approaches to how organizations can be structured.

BEHAVIORAL MANAGEMENT APPROACHES

During the 1920s an emphasis on the human side of the workplace began to influence management thinking. Major branches in the behavioral or human resource approaches to management are shown in Exhibit 2.2. The behavioral approaches maintain that people are social and self-actualizing. People at work are assumed to seek satisfying social relationships, respond to group pressures, and search for personal fulfillment.

Follett's Organizations As Communities

The work of Mary Parker Follett, briefly mentioned earlier, was part of an important transition from classical thinking into behavioral management. She was eulogized upon her death in 1933 as "one of the most important women America has yet produced in the fields of civics and sociology."

In her writings, Follett views organizations as "communities" in which managers and workers should labor in harmony without one party dominating the other, and with the freedom to talk over and truly reconcile conflicts and differences. For her, groups were mechanisms through which diverse individuals could combine their talents for a greater good. And she believed it was the manager's job to help people in organizations cooperate with one another and achieve an integration of interests.

Follett's emphasis on groups and her commitment to human cooperation are still highly relevant themes today. Follett believed that making every employee an owner in a business would create feelings of collective responsibility. Today, we address the same issues under such labels as "employee ownership," "profit sharing," and "gain sharing plans." Follett believed that business problems involve a wide variety of factors that must be considered in relationship to one another. Today, we talk about "systems" and "contingency thinking." Follett also believed that businesses were service organizations and that private profits should always be considered vis-á-vis the public good. Today, we pursue the same issues under the labels "managerial ethics" and "corporate social responsibility."

The Hawthorne Studies

In 1924 the Western Electric Company commissioned a research program to study individual productivity at the Hawthorne Works of the firm's Chicago plant. The initial "Hawthorne studies" had a scientific management perspective and sought to determine how economic incentives and physical conditions of the workplace affected the output of workers. An initial focus was on the level of illumination in the manufacturing facilities; it seemed reasonable to expect that better lighting would improve performance. After failing to find this relationship, however, the researchers concluded that unforeseen "psychological factors" somehow interfered with their illumination experiments. This finding and later Hawthorne studies directed research attention toward better understanding human interactions in the workplace.

Relay Assembly Test-Room Studies

A team led by Harvard's Elton Mayo set out to examine the effect of worker fatigue on output. Care was taken to design a scientific test that would be free of the psychological effects thought to have confounded the earlier illumination studies. Six workers who assembled relays were isolated for intensive study in a special test room. They were given various rest pauses, as well as workdays and workweeks of various lengths, and production was regularly measured. Once again, researchers failed to find any direct relationship between changes in physical working conditions and output. Productivity increased regardless of the changes made.

Mayo and his colleagues concluded that the new "social setting" created for workers in the test room accounted for the increased productivity. Two factors were singled out as having special importance. One was the group atmosphere. The workers shared pleasant social relations with one another and wanted to do a good job. The other was more participative supervision. Test-room workers were made to feel important, were given a lot of information, and were frequently asked for their opinions. This was not the case in their regular jobs back in the plant.

Employee Attitudes, Interpersonal Relations, and Group Processes

Mayo's research continued until the worsening economic conditions of the Depression forced their termination in 1932. By then, interest in the human factor had broadened to include employee attitudes, interpersonal relations, and group dynamics. In one study, over 21,000 employees were interviewed to learn what they liked and disliked about their work environment. "Complex" and "baffling" results led the researchers to conclude that the same things (e.g., work conditions or wages) could be sources of satisfaction for some workers and of dissatisfaction for others.

The final Hawthorne study was conducted in the bank wiring room and centered on the role of the work group. A finding here was that people would restrict their output in order to avoid the displeasure of the group, even if it meant sacrificing pay that could otherwise be earned by increasing output. The researchers concluded that groups can have strong negative, as well as positive, influences on individual productivity.

Lessons of the Hawthorne Studies

As scholars now look back, the Hawthorne studies are criticized for poor research design, weak empirical support for the conclusions drawn, and the tendency of researchers to overgeneralize their findings. Yet their significance as turning points in the evolution of management thought remains intact. The studies helped shift the attention of managers and researchers away from the technical and structural concerns of the classical approach and toward social and human concerns as keys to productivity. They brought visibility to the notions that people's feelings, attitudes, and relationships with co-workers affected their work, and that groups were important influences on individuals. They also identified the **Hawthorne effect**—the tendency of people who are singled out for special attention to perform as anticipated because of expectations created by the situation.

The Hawthorne studies contributed to the emergence of the **human relations movement**, which influenced management thinking during the 1950s and 1960s. This movement was largely based on the viewpoint that managers who used good human relations in the workplace would achieve productivity. Importantly, this movement set the stage for what evolved into the field of **organizational behavior**, the study of individuals and groups in organizations.

McGregor's Theory X and Theory Y

Douglas McGregor was heavily influenced by both the Hawthorne studies and Maslow (discussed in Chapter 4). His classic book, *The Human Side of Enterprise*, advances the thesis that managers should give more attention to the social and self-actualizing needs of people at work. McGregor called upon managers to shift their view of human nature away from a set of assumptions he called "Theory X" and toward ones he called "Theory Y." You can check your managerial assumptions by completing the self-assessment at the end of the chapter.

According to McGregor, managers holding **Theory X** assumptions approach their jobs believing that those who work for them generally dislike work, lack ambition, are irresponsible, are resistant to change, and prefer to be led rather than to lead. McGregor considers such thinking inappropriate. He argues instead for **Theory Y** assumptions in which the manager believes people are willing to work, capable of self-control, willing to accept responsibility, imaginative and creative, and capable of self-direction.

An important aspect of McGregor's ideas is his belief that managers who hold either set of assumptions can create **self-fulfilling prophecies**—that is, through their behavior they create situations where others act in ways that confirm the original expectations. Managers with Theory X assumptions, for example, act in a very directive "command-and-control" fashion that gives people little personal say over their work. These supervisory behaviors create passive, dependent, and reluctant subordinates, who tend to do only what they are told to or required to do. This reinforces the original Theory X viewpoint.

In contrast to Theory X, managers with Theory Y assumptions tend to behave in "participative" ways that allow subordinates more job involvement, freedom, and responsibility. This creates opportunities to satisfy esteem and self-actualization needs; workers tend to perform as expected with initiative and high performance. The self-fulfilling prophecy thus becomes a positive one.

Theory Y thinking is consistent with developments in the new workplace and its emphasis on employee participation, involvement, empowerment, and self-management. When Betsy Holden became the president and CEO of Kraft Foods, Inc., for example, she had risen from division brand manager to CEO in just 16 years. She also showed a lot of Theory Y in her approach to leadership. Holden was praised for a "positive, upbeat, enthu-

© Najilah Feanny/CORBIS SABA

The **Hawthorne effect** is the tendency of persons singled out for special attention to perform as expected.

The **human relations movement** suggested that managers using good human relations will achieve productivity.

Organizational behavior is the study of individuals and groups in organizations.

Theory X assumes people dislike work, lack ambition, act irresponsibly, and prefer to be led.

Theory Y assumes people are willing to work, like responsibility, and are self-directed and creative.

A **self-fulfilling prophecy** occurs when a person acts in ways that confirm another's expectations.

siastic, collaborative, and team-oriented" management style, one that seems evident in the accompanying photo. She emphasized career development and focused on helping others with questions like these: "What skills do you need? What experiences do you need? What development do you need? How do we help you make that happen?"

Argyris's Theory of Adult Personality

Ideas set forth by the well-regarded scholar and consultant Chris Argyris also reflect the belief in human nature. In his book *Personality and Organization*, Argyris contrasts the management practices found in traditional and hierarchical organizations with the needs and capabilities of mature adults. He concludes that some practices, especially those influenced by the classical management approaches, are inconsistent with the mature adult personality.

Consider these examples. In scientific management, the principle of specialization assumes that people will work more efficiently as tasks become better defined. Argyris believes that this limits opportunities for self-actualization. In Weber's bureaucracy, people work in a clear hierarchy of authority, with higher levels directing and controlling lower levels. Argyris worries that this creates dependent, passive workers who feel they have little control over their work environments. In Fayol's administrative principles, the concept of unity of direction assumes that efficiency will increase when a person's work is planned and directed by a supervisor. Argyris suggests that this may create conditions for psychological failure; conversely, psychological success occurs when people define their own goals.

Like McGregor, Argyris believes that managers who treat people positively and as responsible adults will achieve the highest productivity. His advice is to expand job responsibilities, allow more task variety, and adjust supervisory styles to allow more participation and promote better human relations. He believes that the common problems of employee absenteeism, turnover, apathy, alienation, and low morale may be signs of a mismatch between management practices and mature adult personalities.

MODERN MANAGEMENT FOUNDATIONS

The concepts, models, and ideas discussed so far helped set the stage for continuing developments in management thought. The many themes reflected throughout this book build from them as well as from modern management foundations that include the use of quantitative analysis and tools, a systems view of organizations, contingency thinking, commitment to quality, the role of knowledge management learning organizations, and the importance of evidence-based management.

Quantitative Analysis and Tools

About the same time that some scholars were developing human resource approaches to management, others were investigating how quantitative analysis could improve managerial decision making. The foundation of these approaches is the notion that mathematical tools can be used for better problem solving. Today such applications in analytical decision sciences, often described by the terms **management science** and **operations research**, are increasingly supported by computer technology and software programs.

A typical quantitative approach to managerial problem solving proceeds as follows. A problem is encountered, it is systematically analyzed, appropriate mathematical models and computations are applied, and an optimum solution is identified. Consider these examples of real problems and how they can be addressed by using quantitative tools.

Management science and **operations research** use quantitative analysis and applied mathematics to solve problems.

Problem: An oil exploration company is worried about future petroleum reserves in various parts of the world. Quantitative approach—*Mathematical forecasting* helps make future projections for reserve sizes and depletion rates that are useful in the planning process.

Problem: A real estate developer wants to control costs and finish building a new apartment complex on time. Quantitative approach—*Network models* that break large tasks into smaller components. This allows project managers to better analyze, plan, and control timetables for completion of many different activities.

Problem: A "big box" retailer is trying to deal with pressures on profit margins by minimizing costs of inventories, but must avoid being "out of stock" for customers. Quantitative approach—*Inventory analysis*, on operations and services management, helps control inventories by mathematically determining how much to automatically order and when.

Problem: A grocery store is getting complaints from customers that waiting times are too long for check outs during certain times of the day. Quantitative approach—*Queuing theory* helps allocate service personnel and workstations based on alternative workload demands and in a way that minimizes both customer waiting times and costs of service workers.

Problem: A manufacturer wants to maximize profits for producing three different products on three different machines, each of which can be used for different periods of times and run at different costs. Quantitative approach—*Linear programming* is used to calculate how best to allocate production among different machines.

The field of **operations management** uses such quantitative approaches and applied mathematics to systematically examine how organizations can produce goods and services most efficiently and effectively.

Organizations as Systems

Operations management tries to understand an organization as a **system** of interrelated parts that function together to achieve a common purpose. This includes the roles of **subsystems**, or smaller components of a larger system.

An early management writer who used a systems perspective was Chester Barnard. His 1938 groundbreaking book, *Functions of the Executive*, was based on years of experience as a telephone company executive. Like Mary Parker Follett, Barnard described organizations as cooperative systems that achieve great things by integrating the contributions of many individuals to achieve a common purpose. He considered cooperation a "conscious, deliberate, and purposeful" feature of organizations. He also believed an executive's primary responsibility was to use communication to create cooperation.

In Chapter 1 organizations were described as **open systems** that interact with their environments in the continual process of transforming inputs from suppliers into outputs for customers. Exhibit 2.3 also shows that within the total system of the organization a number of critical subsystems make things happen. In the exhibit, the operations and service management subsystems center the transformation process while integrating with other subsystems such as purchasing, accounting, sales, and information. High performance by the organization occurs only when each subsystem both performs its tasks well and works well in cooperation with others.

Operations management is the study of how organizations produce goods and services.

A **system** is a collection of interrelated parts working together for a purpose.

A **subsystem** is a smaller component of a larger system.

An **open system** interacts with its environment and transforms resource inputs into outputs.

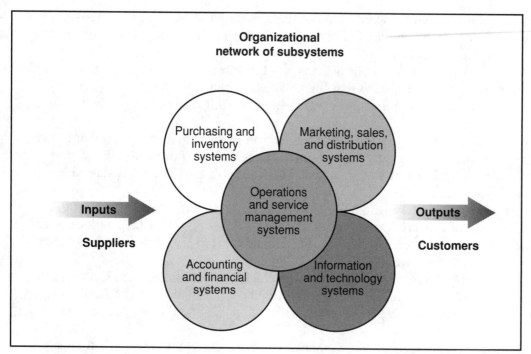

Exhibit 2.3   Organizations as complex networks of interacting subsystems.

Contingency Thinking

Modern management is situational in orientation; that is, it attempts to identify practices that are best fits with the demands of unique situations. This requires **contingency thinking** that tries to match managerial responses with the problems and opportunities specific to different settings, particularly those posed by individual and environmental differences. There is no expectation that one can or should find the "one best

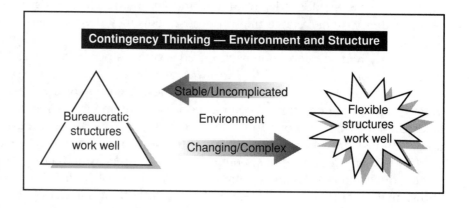

way" to manage in all circumstances. Rather, the contingency perspective tries to help managers understand situational differences and respond to them in ways appropriate to their unique characteristics.

Contingency thinking is an important theme in this book, and its implications extend to all of the management functions—from planning and controlling for diverse environmental conditions, to organizing for different strategies, to leading in different performance situations. Consider the concept of bureaucracy. Weber offered it as an ideal form of organization. But from a contingency perspective, the bureaucratic form is only one possible way of organizing things. What turns out to be the "best" structure in any given situation will depend on many factors, including environmental uncertainty, an organization's primary technology, and the strategy being pursued. As the exhibit suggests, a tight bureaucracy works best

Contingency thinking tries to match management practices with situational demands.

when the environment is relatively stable and operations are predictable and uncomplicated. In complex and changing situations more flexible structures are needed.

Quality Management

The work of W. Edwards Deming is a cornerstone of the quality movement in management. His story begins in 1951 when he was invited to Japan to explain quality control techniques that had been developed in the United States. The result was a lifelong relationship epitomized in the Deming Application Prize, which is still awarded annually in Japan for companies achieving extraordinary excellence in quality.

"When Deming spoke," we might say, "the Japanese listened." The principles he taught the Japanese were straightforward and they worked: tally defects, analyze and trace them to the source, make corrections, and keep a record of what happens afterward. Deming's approach to quality emphasizes constant innovation, use of statistical methods, and commitment to training in the fundamentals of quality assurance.

One outgrowth of Deming's work was the emergence of **total quality management**, or TQM. This is a process that makes quality principles part of the organization's strategic objectives, applying them to all aspects of operations and striving to meet customers' needs by doing things right the first time. Most TQM approaches begin with an insistence that the total quality commitment applies to everyone and everything in an organization—from resource acquisition and supply chain management, through production and into the distribution of finished goods and services, and ultimately to customer relationship management.

Joseph Juran was one of Deming's contemporaries in the quality movement and his long career also included consultations at major companies around the world. Juran is known for the slogan "There is always a better way" and for his three guiding principles—"plan, control, improve." This search for and commitment to quality is now tied to the emphasis modern management gives to **continuous improvement**—always looking for new ways to improve on current performance. The notion is that one can never be satisfied; something always can and should be improved upon.

An indicator of just how important quality objectives have become is the value given to **ISO certification** by the International Standards Organization in Geneva, Switzerland. It has been adopted by many countries of the world as a quality benchmark. Businesses that want to compete as "world-class companies" are increasingly expected to have ISO certification at various levels. To do so, they must refine and upgrade quality in all operations, and then undergo a rigorous assessment by outside auditors to determine whether they meet ISO requirements.

Knowledge Management and Organizational Learning

Our technology-driven world is both rich with information and demanding in the pace and uncertainty of change. And although this is a setting rich in possibilities, Peter Drucker has warned that "knowledge constantly makes itself obsolete." His message suggests that neither people nor organizations can afford to rest on past laurels; future success will be earned only by those who continually build and use knowledge to the fullest extent possible.

The term **knowledge management** describes the processes through which organizations use information technology to develop, organize, and share knowledge to achieve performance success. You can spot the significance of knowledge management with the presence of an executive job title—chief knowledge officer. The "CKO" is responsible for energizing learning processes and making sure that an

---

Total quality management is managing with an organization-wide commitment to continuous improvement, product quality, and customer needs.

Continuous improvement involves always searching for new ways to improve work quality and performance.

ISO certification indicates conformance with a rigorous set of international quality standards.

Knowledge management is the process of using intellectual capital for competitive advantage.

organization's portfolio of intellectual assets is well managed and continually enhanced. These assets include such things as patents, intellectual property rights, trade secrets, and special processes and methods, as well as the accumulated knowledge and understanding of the entire workforce.

Google can be considered a knowledge management company. It not only runs a business model based on information searches; it operates with an information-rich culture driven by creativity and knowledge. Google morphs and grows and excels, in part, because it continually taps the ever expanding knowledge of its members. Its information technologies and management philosophies help and encourage employees located around the world to share information and collaborate. The net result is a firm, that, so far at least, keeps competitors guessing what its next steps might be.

An emphasis on knowledge management is characteristic of what consultant Peter Senge calls a **learning organization**, popularized in his book *The Fifth Discipline*. A learning organization, he says, is one that "by virtue of people, values, and systems is able to continuously change and improve its performance based upon the lessons of experience." He describes

© James Brittain/VIEW/Corbis

learning organizations as encouraging and helping all members to learn continuously, while emphasizing information sharing, teamwork, empowerment, and participation.

Organizations can learn from many sources. They can learn from their own experience. They can learn from the experiences of their contractors, suppliers, partners, and customers. And they can learn from firms in unrelated businesses. All of this, of course, depends on creating an organizational culture in which people are enthusiastic about learning opportunities and in which information sharing is an expected and valued work behavior. Senge believes that those meeting his criteria for learning organizations tend to display the following characteristics:

1. Mental models—everyone sets aside old ways of thinking.
2. Personal mastery—everyone becomes self-aware and open to others.
3. Systems thinking—everyone learns how the whole organization works.
4. Shared vision—everyone understands and agrees to a plan of action.
5. Team learning—everyone works together to accomplish the plan.

When Google's CEO Eric Schmidt and his colleague Hal Varian describe their guiding management principles, they very much seem to fit the learning organization prototype. The Google principles of managing for knowledge development and organizational learning are:

- *Hire by committee*—let great people hire other great people.
- *Cater to every need*—make sure nothing gets in anyone's way.
- *Make coordination easy*—put people in close proximity to one another, physically and electronically.
- *Encourage creativity*—let people spend some time on projects they choose.

A **learning organization** continuously changes and improves, using the lessons of experience.

- *Seek consensus*—get inputs before decisions are made.
- *Use data*—make informed decisions based on solid quantitative analysis.
- *Don't be evil*—create a climate of respect, tolerance, and ethical behavior.

Research Brief

Great companies make the leap from doing good to doing great, while the others do not.
That's one of the messages in Jim Collins's best-selling book *Good to Great*. He opens the book with this sentence: "Good is the enemy of great." He goes on to describe an extensive study that compares companies that had moved to and then sustained "great" performance in cumulative stock returns over a 15-year period with those that hadn't. The study started by examining the records of 1,435 companies; only 11 made the final cut, joining the good-to-great set. The basic question addressed by Collins and his team of 21 researchers was "What did the good-to-great companies share in common that distinguishes them from the comparison companies?"

One of the major findings was that great companies demonstrate a unique form of leadership that Collins calls "Level 5." He says it is not leadership by celebrity, or leadership driven by compensation, or leadership based on a perfect strategy. Rather, Level 5 leadership is focused on people—getting the right people in, getting the wrong ones out; ambitious—wanting the best for the company and for the long term; resolute—showing a determination to succeed in creating a great firm; modest—not taking personal credit but recognizing the contributions of others. Collins summarizes it as a combination of personal will and humility, stating that Level 5 leaders want to build "something larger and more lasting than themselves." While the comparison leaders were seeking fame, fortune, and power, the great company leaders were trying to create and contribute.

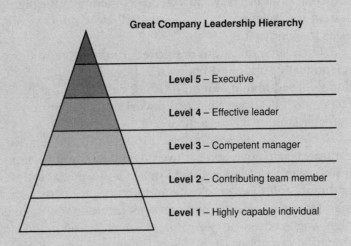

Great Company Leadership Hierarchy

Level 5 – Executive
Level 4 – Effective leader
Level 3 – Competent manager
Level 2 – Contributing team member
Level 1 – Highly capable individual

Reference: Jim Collins, *Good to Great: Why Some Companies Make the Leap. . . and Others Don't* (New York: Harper Business, 2001).

Evidence-Based Management

A book published by Tom Peters and Robert Waterman in 1982, *In Search of Excellence: Lessons from America's Best-Run Companies*, helped kindle interest in the attributes of organizations that achieve performance excellence. Peters and Waterman highlighted things like "closeness to customers," "bias toward action," "simple form and lean staff," and "productivity through people," all of which seemed to make good sense. Later findings, however, showed that many of the companies deemed to be "excellent" at the time encountered future problems.

Today's management scholars are trying to move beyond generalized impressions of excellence to understand more empirically the characteristics of **high-performance organizations**. You can think of

---

A **high-performance organization** consistently achieves excellence while creating a high-quality work environment.

these as ones that consistently achieve high-performance results while also creating high quality-of-work-life environments for their employees. A brief summary, for example, suggests that many high-performance organizations are:

- *People oriented*—they value people as human assets, respect diversity, empower members to fully use their talents, and are high in employee involvement.
- *Team oriented*—they achieve synergy through teamwork, emphasize collaboration and group decisions, and allow teams to be self-directing.
- *Information oriented*—they mobilize the latest information technologies to link people and information for creative problem-solving.
- *Achievement oriented*—they are focused on the needs of customers and stakeholders, and are committed to quality operations and continuous improvement.
- *Learning oriented*—they operate with an internal culture that respects and facilitates learning, innovation, and constructive change.

Even with the above broad points available, managers and management scholars are always searching for scientific answers to even more precise questions like these: What is the best way to do performance appraisals? How do you select members for high performance teams? How should a merit pay system be designed and implemented? How directive should a leader be? How do you structure organizations for innovation?

When such questions are posed, furthermore, the goal is to answer them with empirically sound and scientifically supported findings. A book by Jeffrey Pfeffer and Robert Sutton makes the case for **evidence-based management**, or *EBM*, defined as the process of making management decisions on "hard facts"—that is about what really works, rather than on "dangerous half-truths"—things that sound good but lack empirical substantiation.

In pursuing his own research in this area, Pfeffer, for example, has studied the ways in which organizations achieve competitive advantage through human resource management practices. Using data from a sample of some 1,000 firms, a colleague and he found that firms using a mix of selected practices had more sales per employee and higher profits per employee than those that didn't. The positive human resource management practices included employment security, selective hiring, self-managed teams, high wages based on performance merit, training and skill development, minimal status differences, and shared information. Examples of other principles of EBM include: challenging goals accepted by an employee are likely to result in high performance; unstructured employment interviews are unlikely to result in the best person being hired to fill a vacant position.

Basic Scientific Methods
- A research question or problem is identified
- One or more hypotheses, or possible explanations, are stated
- A research design is created to systematically test the hypotheses
- Data gathered through the research are analyzed and interpreted
- The hypotheses are accepted or rejected based upon the evidence

As scholars use scientific methods to advance knowledge in management, some carve out new and innovative territories while others build upon and extend knowledge that has come down through the history of management thought. The *Research Brief* feature, found earlier and in each chapter, introduces the types of studies that are being done and the types of evidence that are being accumulated. By staying abreast of such developments and findings, managers can have more confidence that they are approaching decisions from a solid foundation of evidence rather than on mere speculation or hearsay.

Evidence-based management involves making decisions based on hard facts about what really works.

Motivating Effectively

CHAPTER OUTLINE

WHAT IS MOTIVATION?

Motivation comes from the Latin *movere,* "to move." Motivation is about moving ourselves and others to some goal. Motivation requires arousal to initiate behavior toward a goal, direction to properly focus that behavior, and persistence to ultimately attain the goal. In the following sections we will examine a variety of approaches to motivation. Think of these as a toolkit. Depending on the situation you are facing, you will find that various theories will provide you with the guidance and insights you need to decide on an appropriate course of action to take to handle that situation.

Some of the approaches (called **content theories** or **need theories**) help us understand what people want and *why* they want it. Others—called **process theories**—focus on *how* a person becomes motivated as part of an overall process. The questions asked and the corresponding theories we will address are:

- How can valued outcomes be tied to behaviors in order to reinforce desired behaviors and eliminate undesired behaviors that are related to the achievement of an organization's objectives? This is the domain of **learning theory**.
- How can goals be set to properly motivate behavior and how is the process of attaining goals managed? This is the question addressed by **goal-setting theory**.
- What elements must be present in a situation if a person is to be motivated to pursue a desired outcome? **Expectancy theory** addresses this issue.
- What causes a person to see his or her work environment as fair or unfair, and how does this influence motivation? **Equity theory** and related theories of fairness examine this question.

WHY IS MOTIVATION IMPORTANT?

Motivation is a key determinant of individual performance. Maybe you know of a friend, family member, or acquaintance who achieved great things not because he or she was necessarily the smartest or most talented, but because of his or her perseverance, drive, and intense focus.

For you as managers, managing the motivation of your workers will be a challenging and ongoing process. It is important to remember that the motivation and performance of your workers will be viewed as a direct reflection of your competency as a manager by many people in your organization. Remember also that your work unit as a whole will be much more likely to achieve its business objectives if you effectively motivate your employees. As you will learn in this chapter, each of your workers will likely be motivated by different factors. Money may work as a reward for some people, but not for everyone. Clarifying goals for workers, monitoring their progress toward these goals, and providing support for the achievement of their goals will be a time-consuming process. It is also likely that you will have to deal with a poor performing worker or unmotivated worker at some point. In all, keeping your employees motivated will be a critical aspect of your job as a manager in a real-world organization.

UNDERSTANDING EMPLOYEE NEEDS

All people have needs. A **need** is something that people require. **Satisfaction** is the condition of need fulfillment, such as when a hungry person eats or when a person driven by the desire for success finally achieves that goal. Motivation is the attempt to satisfy a need. The need satisfaction process is shown in Exhibit 3.1. The practice of management is largely concerned with motivating employees to work harder, more efficiently, and more intelligently. We will look at five theories of motivation and at how each relates to motivating people in the workplace. We will see that these theories have some similar implications for rewarding employees.

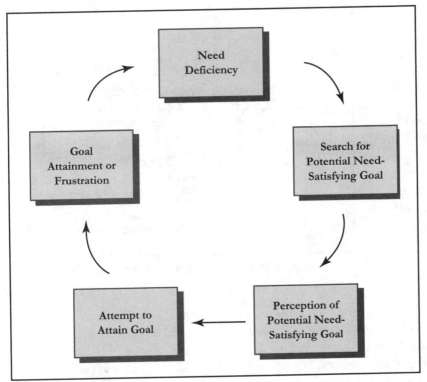

Exhibit 3.1 The Need Satisfaction Process

Maslow's Need Hierarchy

Psychologist Abraham Maslow did much of the classic work on motivation theory. He believed that the key to motivating people is in understanding that they are motivated by needs, which are arranged in a hierarchy of importance. This hierarchy is known as **Maslow's need hierarchy** (see Exhibit 3.2). Maslow theorized that people seek to satisfy needs at the lowest level of the hierarchy before trying to satisfy needs on the next-higher level. What needs motivate a person depends on where that person is on the hierarchy at that time. In particular, Maslow believed that motivation should be examined in terms of five sets of needs:

Psychologist Abraham Maslow is known for his studies on motivation theory.

1. **Physiological.** The need for food, sleep, water, air, and sex
2. **Security.** The need for safety, family stability, and economic security
3. **Social or affiliation.** The need to belong, to interact with others, to have friends, and to love and be loved
4. **Esteem.** The need for respect and recognition from others
5. **Self-actualization.** The need to realize one's potential, to grow, to be creative, and to accomplish

Maslow argued that as we satisfy any one of these five sets of needs, that set becomes less important to us and motivates us less. Eating, for example, satisfies the physiological need of hunger and leaves us less interested in food. In the same way, the need for affiliation and friendship is strongest for someone who feels excluded. Once this person makes friends, the need to "belong" becomes less important.

Climbing the Hierarchy

Maslow believed that these needs were arranged in a hierarchy from "lowest" to "highest," as shown in Exhibit 3.2. He suggested that we "climb" the hierarchy. That is, we first satisfy our basic physiological needs. Only when we have done so are we motivated by the needs at the next-higher level of the hierarchy: the need for safety and security. When this group of needs is met, we move on to the next level, and so on. This move up the hierarchy as needs are satisfied is called **satisfaction progression**.

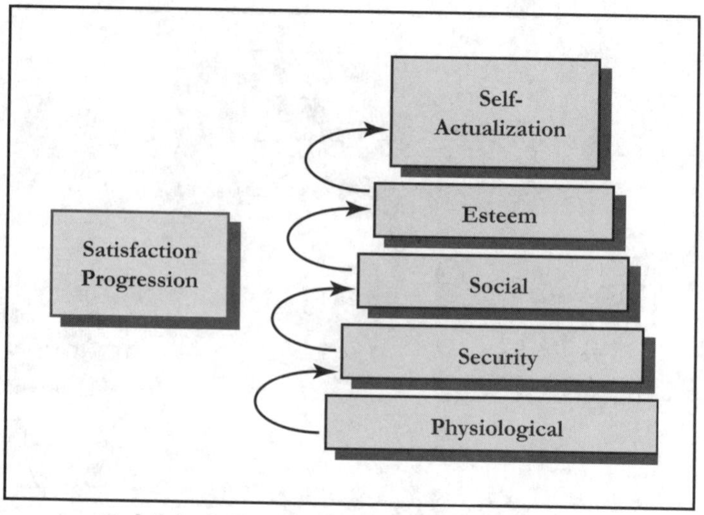

Exhibit 3.2   Maslow's Need Hierarchy

Lessons from Maslow's Hierarchy

Maslow's view of motivation shows that people have a variety of needs. People work for many reasons besides the paycheck that buys them food and shelter. We work so that we can be with others, gain respect, and realize our potential. Management must consider these needs when it designs reward systems for employees. Also, Maslow's hierarchy emphasizes that people differ in the needs that are currently most important to them. For example, a worker faced with heavy mortgage payments may focus primarily on security needs. Another, with the mortgage paid off, may be more concerned about social needs. While the former employee might be strongly motivated by money, the latter may be more motivated by being included in a group. Finally, the hierarchy also makes it clear that need importance and need satisfaction are very different things—need importance (which drives motivation) often flows from dissatisfaction.

Maslow's need hierarchy provides useful perspectives for understanding motivation, and it has been widely accepted. However, more recent research suggests that it is only partially correct. For instance, satisfying needs at the top of the hierarchy generally does not lead to a decrease in motivation. Instead, people who are able to self-actualize become *more* motivated to take on self-actualizing activities. Further, instead of five sets of needs, people's needs seem to cluster in just two or three sets, as discussed later. Also, the climb up the hierarchy is rather unpredictable; once we've satisfied needs at the lowest levels, needs at any of the other levels may become more important to us. Exhibit 3.3 presents a summary of Maslow's hierarchy of needs and the organizational factors that can be addressed by managers to motivate individuals who have "active" or unsatisfied needs for each level in the model.

Alderfer's ERG Theory

Maslow's need hierarchy provided an important starting point for an improved theory of human needs. Clayton Alderfer developed the **existence–relatedness–growth (ERG) theory**, which revised Maslow's theory to make it consistent with research findings concerning human needs.

There are three key differences between Alderfer's ERG theory and Maslow's need hierarchy. First, since studies have shown that people have two or three sets of needs rather than the five Maslow hypothesized, Alderfer collapsed his needs into three sets:

1. **Existence needs.** These include all forms of material and physical desires;
2. **Relatedness needs.** These include all needs that involve relationships with others; Relatedness needs include anger and hostility as well as friendship. For instance, we may feel the need to yell at one person and befriend another. Isolation from others would cause deprivation of relatedness needs in either case;
3. **Growth needs.** These include all needs involving creative efforts that people make toward themselves and their environment.

Need Level	Organizational Factors
Self-Actualization	• Challenging job • Opportunities for creativity • Advancement in the organization • Opportunities for achievement on the job
Esteem	• Important job title • Merit pay increase • Recognition from peers • Recognition from supervisors • The work itself • Responsibility
Social	• Quality of supervision • Compatible work group • Professional friendships
Security	• Safe working conditions • Fringe benefits • General salary increases • Job security
Physiological	• Heat and air conditioning • Base salary • Cafeteria • Physical working conditions

Exhibit 3.3 Maslow's Hierarchy of Needs: Summary of Organizational Factors for Satisfying Needs

Alderfer revised Maslow's theory in other ways as well. First, he argued that the three need sets form a hierarchy only in the sense of increasing abstractness, or decreasing concreteness. As we move from existence to relatedness to growth needs, the ways to satisfy the needs become less and less concrete.

Second, Alderfer recognized that, while satisfying our existence and relatedness needs may make them less important to us, such is not the case for growth needs. Instead, our growth needs become increasingly important as we satisfy them. As we are able to be creative and productive, we raise our growth goals and are again dissatisfied until we satisfy these new goals. Recall that this is consistent with the evidence we reviewed concerning Maslow's need hierarchy.

Finally, Alderfer reasoned that we are likely to focus first on needs that can be satisfied in concrete ways. We then attend to those with more abstract means of satisfaction. This is similar to Maslow's idea of satisfaction progression. However, Alderfer added the idea of frustration regression. **Frustration regression** occurs when our inability to satisfy needs at a particular level in the hierarchy causes us to regress and focus on more concrete needs. If we are unable to satisfy our growth needs, we will "drop back" and focus on relatedness needs. If we are unable to satisfy our relatedness needs, we will focus on existence needs. Alderfer's needs, as well as satisfaction progression and frustration regression, are illustrated in Exhibit 3.4. The combination of satisfaction progression and frustration regression can result in cycling as we focus on one need, then another, then back again.

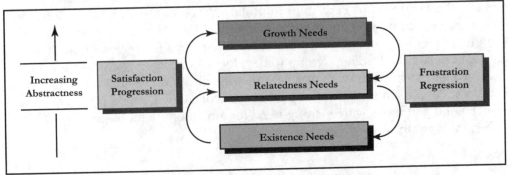

Exhibit 3.4 Alderfer's ERG Theory

McClelland's Manifest Needs

Management theorist David McClelland offered another way to look at motivation. Whereas Maslow argued that people were born with a particular set of needs, which become more or less important over time depending on their satisfaction, McClelland believed that needs were acquired through the interaction of the individual with his or her environment. Because these needs are not innate but rather become apparent (that is, manifest themselves) over time, they are called **manifest needs**. McClelland focused primarily on three manifest needs: the need for achievement, the need for affiliation, and the need for power over others.

1. **Need for achievement.** People with a strong **need for achievement** want to do well no matter what goal they pursue. They also desire personal responsibility and want quick feedback about how well they have done at a given task. Some jobs, such as those in sales, are best for people with a strong need for achievement because of the responsibility and feedback they provide. Strong need for achievement, however, is not necessary in all work situations. For example, McClelland tested a large number of scientists, including several Nobel Prize winners, and found them to be only about average in need for achievement. He reasoned that people with high need for achievement would not be drawn to such jobs, since research is conducted over many years and feedback may be very slow.

   Differences in need for achievement are evident even among children. When asked to play a game of ring toss and told they can stand as far from the peg as they want, children with low need for achievement tend to one of two extremes—they either stand directly over the peg and simply drop the ring or they stand far away, tossing with abandon and relying primarily on luck. Conversely, children with high need for achievement tend to stand at the peg, back away, and determine a tossing distance that is far enough away to provide a challenge but not so far that luck becomes more important than skill. Similarly, adults with high need for achievement tend to set moderately difficult goals.

   McClelland argued that the need for achievement can be developed in people by getting them to believe that they can change and by helping them to set personal goals. This process also includes learning to "speak the language of achievement." By this we mean that people can be taught to think, talk, and act as if they were achievement-oriented.

   In practice, McClelland was successful in developing the need for achievement. For example, after he conducted training sessions for 52 businesspersons in Kakinada, India, the achievement activity of the trainees nearly doubled while that of people who couldn't participate in the programs because of space constraints remained about the same. Achievement activity meant starting a new business or sharply increasing company profits. One trainee raised enough money to put up the tallest building in Mumbai—the Everest Apartments.

2. **Need for affiliation.** The **need for affiliation** is the desire to establish and maintain friendly and warm relations with other people, much like Maslow's social need. People with a strong need for affiliation welcome tasks requiring interaction with others, while those having less of this need may prefer to work alone.

3. **Need for power.** The **need for power** is the desire to control other people, to influence their behavior, and to be responsible for them. McClelland saw the need for achievement as most important for entrepreneurs and the need for power as most important for managers of large organizations. Those who have a strong need for power can try to dominate others for the sake of dominating, deriving satisfaction from conquering others. Or they can satisfy their need for power through means that help the organization, such as leading a group to develop and achieve goals. McClelland felt that the need for power, when exhibited in ways that help the organization, was the most important factor in managerial success. People who have a strong need for achievement might be overly concerned with personal achievement, and those with a strong need for affiliation might not take necessary actions if they could offend the group.

Lessons from McClelland's Perspective

McClelland's work gives us an expanded view of workers' needs. It also suggests that appropriate training might actually develop employees' needs in ways that could benefit both their careers and the organization. While Maslow essentially viewed needs as buckets to be filled, McClelland saw them as seeds to be grown. This is an important difference from Maslow's theory. Also, McClelland's perspective helps identify the characteristics of people who may be most suitable for particular kinds of jobs in organizations.

Practical Implications of Need Theories

Taken together, the three need theories we have considered have a number of important implications for managing effectively.

- **Different people have varying need structures as well as differing needs that may be salient at a given time.** Some people generally care more about a particular need or set of needs, such as relatedness needs, than others. In addition, people at a given point in time will vary in the level to which the needs they care about are satisfied.
- **While satisfaction occurs when needs are met, motivation flows from lack of need satisfaction.** We must be careful not to fall in the trap of equating satisfaction with motivation. Some things that are very satisfying may be *demotivating*. For example, an employee whose pay is so high that she can afford anything she wants may not be motivated to gain an incentive for reaching a particular performance goal.
- **A reward may satisfy multiple needs.** It is sometimes tempting to assume that a particular reward, such as pay, will satisfy only certain needs, such as lower-order needs. However, such a viewpoint is simplistic. For example, employees may use money to buy food, pay the mortgage, go on a **date**, purchase a prestigious automobile, or finance a hobby or self-improvement class.
- **Needs appear to form two clusters (lower-order and higher-order) or three (existence, relatedness, and growth).** It is useful to understand how needs cluster in order to find ways to satisfy needs in a particular set. For example, recognizing that employees tend to have a cluster of needs called growth needs permits us to explore ways to satisfy that cluster. Conversely, if employees had a very large set of clusters of needs—say, 10 or 20—we would need to look more narrowly at ways to satisfy each salient need set.
- **While most people focus first on existence needs when those needs are not satisfied, it is not possible to say which needs will next become most important.** Again, there is no lockstep climb up a fixed need hierarchy. We should not expect that we can easily predict which needs an employee will focus on next.
- **Both satisfaction progression and frustration regression are important.** Not only do employees move from a focus on one need to a focus on another, but they also somehow move back again. This is a continuous, dynamic process in which multiple needs are likely to be somehow salient at the same point in time.
- **The "top" cluster of needs, sometimes called growth needs, behaves differently from others.** While most needs become less motivating as they are satisfied, growth needs become more motivating. Thus, designing jobs or otherwise rewarding employees in ways that satisfy growth needs may cause people to place more emphasis on those needs rather than less. This is encouraging, since it suggests there is no "cap" on growth needs.
- **It may be possible to develop people's needs.** The structure of needs may not be fixed. For example, some employees who never placed much emphasis on growth needs may develop those needs when given the opportunity to satisfy them. Thus, employees may "grow into" jobs offering challenge and responsibility, giving greater importance to growth needs in the face of enriched job demands.

The following Bottom Line presents a process model showing how need theories can be applied to manage employee motivation.

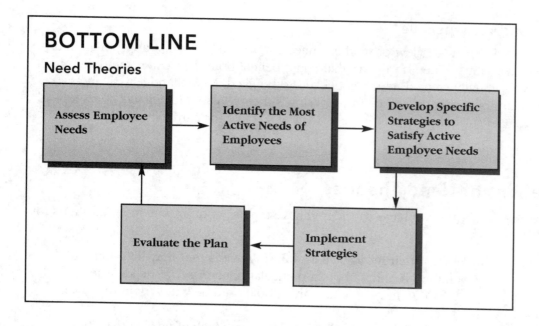

BOTTOM LINE

Need Theories

Assess Employee Needs → Identify the Most Active Needs of Employees → Develop Specific Strategies to Satisfy Active Employee Needs → Implement Strategies → Evaluate the Plan → (back to Assess Employee Needs)

APPLYING LEARNING THEORIES

According to learning theory, **learning** is any relatively permanent change in behavior produced by experience. Changing a person's behavior can be extremely difficult to do. Think about how hard it is for most people to change their behavior to achieve weight loss or smoking cessation. In a similar vein, much of what a manager needs to do "boils down to" the active management and changing of worker behaviors that are related to their jobs.

Changes in behavior due to physical variations, such as growth, deterioration, fatigue, and sleep, are not learning. Similarly, temporary changes are not true learning. Also, the changes may not be desirable; we have probably all learned some behaviors that have caused us to be less effective or less adaptive than before. Here, we will review three types of learning: classical conditioning, operant conditioning, and social learning. Together, these learning theories help explain how our behaviors are determined through our own experiences as well as the experiences of others. These theories will also enable you as managers to identify and implement more effective strategies for managing desirable and undesirable worker behaviors in real-world organizations.

Ivan Petrovich Pavlov (1849–1936) was a famous Russian physician.

Classical Conditioning

To many people, mention of learning theory brings to mind thoughts of Pavlov's dog. In his experiments, Ivan Pavlov taught a dog to salivate in response to any of a variety of stimuli, such as a touch on the paw or the sound of a bell. He did this by continually pairing the bell or other stimulus, which originally produced no increase in saliva, with food. Salivation was a normal physiological response to food in the mouth. The repeated pairing of the bell with the food caused the dog to salivate simply upon hearing the bell. Exhibit 3.5 shows this process.

The learning that took place in these experiments is called **classical** or **Pavlovian conditioning**. It occurs when, through pairing of stimuli, a new stimulus is responded to in the same way as the original stimulus. The thought of dangling rewards in front of salivating employees is a bit unseemly. Happily, this

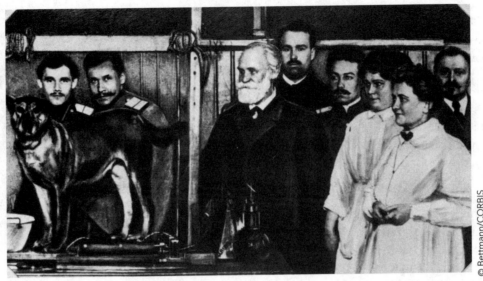

Ivan Pavlov and his staff demonstrating the conditioned reflex phenomenon with a dog.

is *not* the sort of learning that is most relevant in organizational settings. There are at least three reasons for this:

1. It is often difficult to use classical conditioning;
2. There are ethical concerns about its use;
3. It can't be used to teach a new behavior—it is useful only for transferring an existing behavior from one stimulus to another. Since the point of applying learning theory is often to teach and change the strength of current behaviors, other approaches are needed.

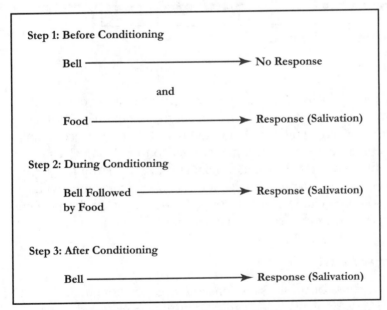

Step 1: Before Conditioning

    Bell ——————————————→ **No Response**

                and

    Food ——————————————→ **Response (Salivation)**

Step 2: During Conditioning

    Bell Followed ——————————→ **Response (Salivation)**
    by Food

Step 3: After Conditioning

    Bell ——————————————→ **Response (Salivation)**

Exhibit 3.5   Classical Conditioning

Operant Conditioning

Some of you may recall a feature on the David Letterman Show in which various people would demonstrate "Stupid Pet Tricks" much to the amusement of the live and TV audiences of the show. Virtually none of these animals knew how to demonstrate their "trick behaviors" when they were born. Most likely, these animals learned these behaviors based on the use of learning principles described on the following page. Although early research and application of learning principles focused on animals, these same principles have been implemented with excellent results involving human behavior in a variety of settings including business organizations.

The David Letterman Show featured a segment on "Stupid Pet Tricks." The animals most likely learned these "tricks" through operant conditioning.

Most learning in organizations relies on the law of effect. The **law of effect** states that behavior that is rewarded will tend to be repeated; behavior that is not rewarded will tend not to be repeated. So if we want someone to continue acting in a certain way, we should see that they are somehow rewarded for acting in that way. If we want them to stop particular undesirable behaviors, we should make sure we are not rewarding them for those behaviors. The sort of conditioning that relies on the law of effect is called **operant conditioning** or, after its best-known researcher and theorist, **Skinnerian conditioning**. Exhibit 3.6 illustrates operant conditioning.

Individuals enter organizations, and particular situations within organizations, with very different histories of reinforcement. That is, they have learned different things. Some have learned that working hard is the way to get ahead. Others have learned to be stubborn in the face of challenge. Still others have learned to avoid troublesome situations. Thus, many differences in behaviors among employees may be due to the different ways their behaviors have been rewarded or punished in the past.

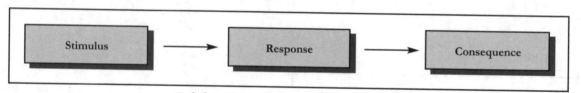

Exhibit 3.6   Operant Conditioning

Social Learning

Both classical conditioning and operant conditioning focus on learning as something that develops out of our own experiences. However, much of what we have learned comes from the experience of others. Because others have been burned by a hot stove or have failed in their attempts to start a new company or have found that certain leader behaviors are ineffective, we don't have to get "burned" ourselves to learn what they learned. Instead, we can benefit from social learning. **Social learning** is learning that occurs through any of a variety of social channels—newspapers, books, television, conversations with family members, friends, and coworkers, and so on. Social learning accounts for much of our knowledge. Coaching and mentoring are important organizational examples of social learning.

Using Contingencies of Reinforcement

We said earlier that operant conditioning uses rewards or unpleasant consequences to strengthen desired behaviors or to weaken undesired behaviors. The various ways we can tie consequences to behaviors are called **contingencies of reinforcement**. Exhibit 3.7 shows three contingencies of reinforcement—positive reinforcement, escape learning, negative reinforcement, and avoidance learning—that are used to strengthen desired behaviors.

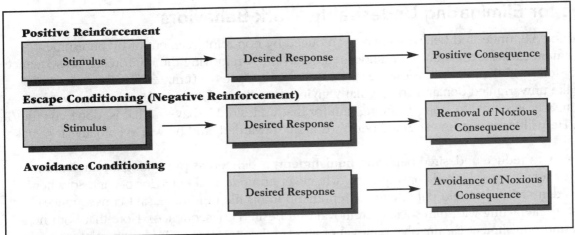

Exhibit 3.7 Arranging Contingencies to Increase Desired Behaviors

Strategies for Motivating Desired Behaviors

Positive reinforcement involves giving a reward when desired behavior occurs, in order to increase the likelihood that the behavior will be repeated. A bonus for a job well done or verbal recognition/praise for a good effort are examples. In many jobs, bonuses and other forms of merit-based compensation are very important, often exceeding base salaries. One common problem with the use of positive reinforcement by managers in real-world organizations is that they simply don't use it. One lesson here is that managers should be more aware of the degree to which they are using positive reinforcement to increase the likelihood that workers will continue to engage in desired work behaviors. Recognition, one form of positive reinforcement, can be a low-cost or a no-cost strategy and it can be as effective as other consequences in many cases.

Another way to increase the likelihood of desired behavior is to remove some unpleasant consequence when that behavior occurs. For example, suppose a rat is subjected to a loud, irritating noise until it presses a lever. Once it presses the lever, the noise stops. The rat would soon learn to press the lever to escape the grating noise. This is called **escape conditioning**. If pressing the lever would actually prevent the onset of the noise, this would be called **avoidance conditioning**. In some companies, there are certain jobs that employees feel are very good, and others that are clearly "the pits." If employees feel that they will be transferred from the bad jobs if they perform well, we have an example of escape conditioning. If employees in good jobs feel they can avoid being transferred to bad jobs if they continue to perform well, we have an example of avoidance conditioning. Another example of escape learning is customer service behaviors. An airline could train its employees on the types of behaviors for dealing with customers who might be frustrated or angry due to a flight delay/cancellation or problems with their reservations or baggage. Employees could learn the desired behaviors to engage in to respond effectively to customers' concerns in these situations, with the consequence being that the customer will hopefully have his/her concern resolved and walk away from the interaction feeling like a valued customer (i.e., the negative situation has been removed). An example of avoidance learning would be an event manager who organizes and coordinates events for large groups (e.g., weddings, corporate meetings) in a hotel. The event manager could emphasize to her staff that there are certain behaviors that they need to engage in when dealing with customers to prevent problems from occurring. This would be more of a preventive strategy. Good management focuses on preventive strategies whenever possible, as problems are typically easier to prevent rather than to fix after they have occurred.

Strategies for Eliminating Undesirable Work Behaviors

As seen in Exhibit 3.8, undesired behaviors may be reduced by non-reinforcement or by punishment. **Non-reinforcement** causes extinction of an undesired behavior by removing the reinforcing consequence that previously followed the behavior. Consider the case of Sam. We have (unintentionally) been teaching Sam to make unwarranted demands by regularly giving in to those demands. How can we get him to stop? One answer is simply to stop rewarding him for that undesired behavior. That is, don't give in to the demands. He will learn that unwarranted demands aren't rewarded, and he will eventually stop making them.

A second way to reduce undesired behavior, **punishment**, is defined as presenting an unpleasant consequence, or removing a desired consequence, whenever an undesired behavior occurs. So when Sam makes his demands, we could put a letter of reprimand in his file (an unpleasant consequence), or we could stop interacting with him socially (removal of a desired consequence). Note that both non-reinforcement and punishment can involve removal of a desired consequence. With non-reinforcement, the reward we would withhold (agreeing to demands) was the one previously tied to the behavior. With punishment, the reward withheld (social interaction) was not previously a reinforcer of that behavior.

It is often tempting to apply punishment, and there are certainly situations in which punishment can't be avoided. However, punishment should be used only as a last resort. Problems with punishment include the following:

- Managers don't like to punish others so they may avoid using it even when it should be used. This may send a message to others that you are a weak leader because you are not willing to deal with problem behaviors;
- Managers may feel constrained from using punishment because of company policy or threat of reprisal;
- Punishment may engender resentment from others, resulting in strained relationships with a manager's workers;

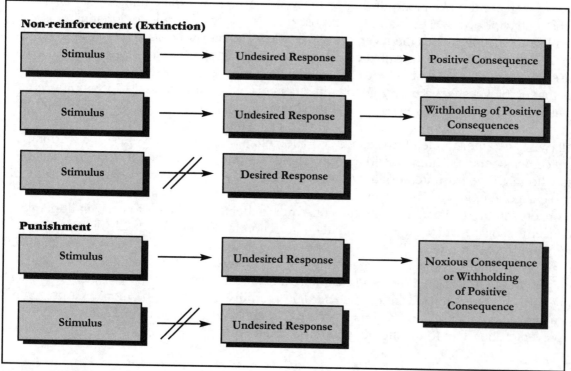

Exhibit 3.8   Arranging Contingencies to Reduce Undesired Behaviors

- Punishment may lead to revenge and retaliation from some employees. In extreme cases, this may include violent behaviors against a manager;
- Punishment leads to adherence only when the person administering the punishment is present or monitoring;
- Others may misinterpret the reasons for punishment;
- Punishment may reduce an undesired behavior, but it doesn't directly teach a desired behavior.

As an example of the application of punishment, Russia punished several senior military commanders for "gross negligence" that contributed to the crash of a military helicopter in Chechnya that killed 119 soldiers and civilians a little more than two weeks earlier. The commanders were said to have defied orders and violated basic safety rules. Former Russian President Vladimir Putin, who was strongly criticized for his halting response to the sinking of the nuclear-powered submarine Kurst two years earlier, was sharply disparaging of the commanders after the crash. Putin apparently felt that rapid punishment was needed to clearly demonstrate that such behavior would not be tolerated.

The Potential Cost of Not Using Punishment

While there are many reasons to be cautious about using punishment to eliminate undesired behaviors, it is important to consider the potential drawbacks of *not* using punishment when it is warranted in a given situation. First, the employee who is engaging in the undesired behavior may learn that it is acceptable for him/her to engage in that behavior. Second, it may inadvertently communicate the message to this employee that he/he can get away with other undesired behaviors because you won't do anything about it. Third, this could demoralize the other workers in your unit who see your unwillingness to deal with the problem behavior as a sign of weakness in your leadership of the unit. This could lower the motivation of your good employees and motivate some of them to consider other job opportunities.

Applying Reinforcement Schedules

One learning theory issue, which we've just addressed, is *how* outcomes should be tied to behaviors to motivate desired behaviors and minimize undesired behaviors. However, suppose we decide that we are going to use money to reward employees for high performance. How do we decide *when* we should give the money? Should we give it immediately after the desired behavior? After the desired behaviors have continued for a week? Every 10 times the desired behavior occurs? That is, what should be our **schedule of reinforcement**?

In choosing a schedule of reinforcement, there are several things we might seek:

- **Rapid learning.** Ideally, we would use a schedule of reinforcement that very quickly teaches desired behaviors;
- **High response rate.** We would like a high "bang for the buck." That is, we would like to choose a schedule of reinforcement that yields high levels of motivation at relatively little cost;
- **High response stability.** We would like to encourage employees to engage in desired behaviors on a regular basis. We wouldn't, for instance, want an employee to work hard only the day before he or she will be paid, or to take safety precautions only before a scheduled inspection;
- **Low extinction rate.** Once a desired behavior is learned, we would like it to be maintained even if we might have to stop rewarding it for a while.

There are many ways to arrange schedules of reinforcement, and we will see that they vary in terms of the degree to which they might satisfy the conditions we've just discussed. One basic distinction is whether or not behavior is reinforced every time it occurs (such as for every unit produced). **Continuous reinforcement** occurs if every behavior is reinforced. Continuous reinforcement leads to rapid learning. However, if for some reason it is necessary to stop reinforcing (for instance, if the supervisor must leave the room), rapid extinction occurs. Most of the time, it is simply impractical to reinforce on a continuous basis, so a partial-reinforcement schedule is used.

Partial-reinforcement schedules can be time-based or behavior-based. Also, they can be administered on a fixed, unchanging basis, or they can be varied around some mean. There are four basic partial-reinforcement schedules.

With a **fixed-interval schedule**, a reinforcer is given at fixed time intervals, such as once a week. Weekly paychecks and monthly inspections are common examples. Fixed-interval schedules, while easy to use, result in slow learning and a moderately fast extinction rate. They also have a low response rate (that is, frequency of response per reinforcement) and very low response stability (people speed up just before the time of reinforcement and then slow down).

A **variable-interval schedule** is also time-based. However, a reinforcer is administered randomly around some average interval. For instance, an instructor might announce that there will be four pop quizzes during the semester, but will not say when they will occur. Learning rate, extinction rate, response rate, and response stability are all better for the variable-interval than for the fixed-interval schedule. However, they are generally not as good as for ratio-based schedules.

Slot machines are programmed to reward game players on a variable-ratio schedule of reinforcement.

A **fixed-ratio schedule** provides a reinforcer after a given number of acceptable behaviors. Commissions given on the basis of sales levels (such as for every 10 sales) and bonuses given for every three meritorious behaviors are examples. Fixed-ratio schedules have very high response rates and response stability. They have high learning rates but, unfortunately, rapid extinction rates as well. Fixed-ratio schedules can be "stretched" to foster learning and increase response rate. For instance, we might want to teach a new behavior by first reinforcing every instance of that behavior (that is, by using a continuous-reinforcement schedule), then stretch the schedule so a reward is given for only two instances of the behavior (called a 2:1 schedule), then for three instances (a 3:1 schedule), and so on. By stretching schedules in this way, Skinner trained pigeons to peck at rates faster than machine-gun fire.

While a fixed-ratio schedule reinforces after every *n* responses, a **variable-ratio schedule** reinforces *on average* after every *n* responses. For instance, a "one-armed bandit" in a casino might have a payoff an average of once in every 10 pulls of the handle. However, precisely when the payoff will occur is unknown. Response rates and response stability are similar to those for fixed-ratio schedules, but learning is slower. However, extinction is very slow. Companies have made some very creative attempts to use variable-ratio schedules. For instance, in one firm, names of employees who didn't use their sick leave were placed in a lottery for a large prize. Sick-leave costs fell by 62 percent. Many companies use a computer program named Snowfly. Managers give employees electronic tokens for achieving certain goals. Employees use the tokens to wager on games such as a slot machine, horse race or fishing contest. Employees always win something—anywhere from the equivalent of $.02 to $50. Managers say the game has increased sales, reduced turnover, and improved morale.

It is clear in looking at Exhibit 3.9 that there are some trade-offs when using the various schedules of reinforcement. For example, a variable-ratio schedule is very powerful in most ways, but results in slow learning. So, it may be desirable to combine schedules. For example, as noted earlier, a behavior might be taught by initially using continuous reinforcement, followed by stretching of the schedule to yield a fixed-ratio schedule, and then adding a variable element.

Of course, there are other practical considerations in choosing schedules. For instance, employees need to pay their bills on a regular basis and may count on a weekly paycheck (a fixed-interval schedule). Also, it is easy to administer a fixed-interval schedule. Nevertheless, the relatively greater power of other schedules suggests that we should seek creative ways to employ other schedules of reinforcement whenever possible.

Measure	SCHEDULE OF REINFORCEMENT				
	Continuous	Fixed Ratio	Variable Ratio	Fixed Interval	Variable Interval
Learning Rate	Very Fast	Fast	Slow	Very Slow	Moderate
Response Rate	Very Low	Very High	Very High	Low	Moderate
Response Stability	Very High	High	High	Very Low	Low to Moderate
Extinction Rate	Very Fast	Fast	Very Slow	Moderately Fast	Slow

Exhibit 3.9   Comparing the Schedules of Reinforcement

Organizational Behavior Modification

Organizational behavior modification (OBM) is the use of the principles of learning theory to manage behavior in organizations. Organizational behavior modification practitioners and theorists typically use some combination of operant conditioning techniques and social learning to achieve their goals.

Here are eight guidelines for effectively using learning techniques in organizations.

1. **Don't give the same reward to all.** Reward those who exhibit desired behaviors (such as high performance) more than those who don't.
2. **Recognize that failure to respond to behavior has reinforcing consequences.** Managers must remember that inaction, as well as action, has reinforcing consequences. They should ask, "What behavior will I reinforce if I do nothing?"
3. **Tell a person what behavior gets reinforced.** Make the contingencies of reinforcement clear to employees. Don't make them guess which behaviors will be rewarded or punished.
4. **Tell a person what he or she is doing wrong.** If the manager does not make clear to an employee why, for instance, a reward is being withheld, the employee may attribute the action to a past desired behavior rather than the behavior the manager wants to extinguish.
5. **Don't punish in front of others.** When employees are punished in front of others, they "lose face" and are doubly punished. This can cause resentment and a variety of problems in managing these individuals in the future.
6. **Make the consequences equal to the behavior.** Over-rewarding desired behavior makes an employee feel guilty. Under-rewarding desired behavior or over-punishing undesired behavior causes anger. Under-punishing undesired behavior seems like a "slap on the wrist" and may have little impact.
7. **Reinforce behaviors as soon as possible.** As suggested in the nearby Focus on Management, immediate rewards can be very powerful.
8. **Make sure that the consequence that you are linking to the desired behavior is positively valued by the individual whose behavior is being reinforced.** This is harder than you may think as every individual is different in terms of what he/she positively values.

Note that some of the rules we've listed rely heavily on cognition. This recognizes that employees can learn through observation and advice as well as from their own experiences.

Think about some of the more complex types of behaviors that you have learned over the course of your life from driving a car, scoring well on the SAT exam, doing well on college exams, interviewing for a job, making a presentation, and writing reports. These are all examples of the type of behaviors that you as a manager (and your employees) will need to learn to be successful in your jobs in a real-world organization. Organizational behavior modification uses a technique called behavioral shaping that can be used to enable people to learn complex behaviors.

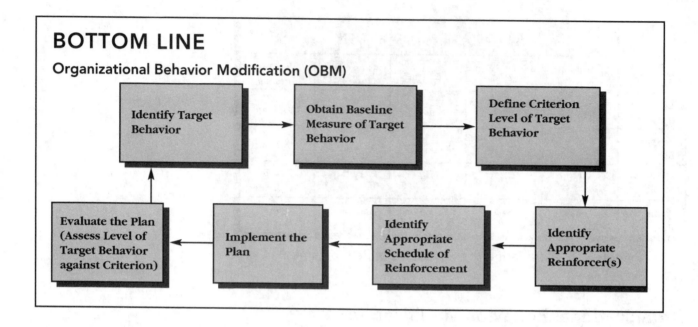

BOTTOM LINE

Organizational Behavior Modification (OBM)

Behavioral shaping is the learning of a complex behavior through successive approximations of the desired behavior. Initially, the employee gets a reward for any behavior that is in any way positively related to the desired behavior. Subsequently, responses are not reinforced unless they are more and more similar to the desired behavior. Responses are "shaped" until the desired complex behavior is achieved.

Properly applied, learning theory works very well. Many firms, including Emory Air Freight, General Electric, and Weyerhaeuser, have implemented very successful programs. In fact, some critics worry that learning theory works *too* well, possibly pushing the employee to exhaustion or to other undesirable outcomes. They see this as especially troublesome, since this behavior—particularly when noncognitive, operant conditioning is used—is to some extent outside the control of the employee, overriding free will. From this perspective, learning theory has Orwellian overtones.

We feel that, when used with intelligence and caution, learning theory can be extremely useful. After all, managers are reinforcing behavior all the time, even if by inaction; the trick is to do it right. Cognitive approaches, in which employees know why they are being rewarded or punished and are aware of the contingencies of reinforcement, overcome some of the concerns that employees are being ruthlessly manipulated. In addition, proponents of learning theory are essentially unanimous in advocating positive reinforcement (the carrot) over punishment (the stick). As such, proper application of learning theory helps guarantee that employees get the rewards they want while fostering desired organizational outcomes.

The Bottom Line above shows how organizational behavior modification can be systematically implemented to encourage the learning of desired behaviors, as well as the unlearning of undesired behaviors.

EFFECTIVE GOAL-SETTING

A goal is simply a desired end state, that is, something we want. Certainly, employee behavior often seems to be goal-directed. Employees may strive to reach quotas, to win contests, to make it through the workday, or to outperform their coworkers. Sometimes their goals are difficult, sometimes easy. Sometimes they are very specific and sometimes vague. As we will see, the nature of employee goals, and how they are set, can be very important. Goal-setting is also simple and inexpensive.

Functions of Goals

Goals serve a variety of important functions. For example:

- Goals let employees know what they are expected to do;
- Goals relieve boredom. Consider how boring most games would be if you didn't keep score and try to reach goals;
- Reaching goals and getting positive feedback leads to increased liking for the task and satisfaction with job performance;
- Attaining goals leads to recognition by peers, supervisors, and others;
- Attaining goals leads to feelings of increased self-confidence, pride in achievement, and willingness to accept future challenges.

Setting Effective Goals

Research on goal-setting has yielded some clear and useful findings. Here are some guidelines for effective goal-setting (see Exhibit 3.10).

- **Set specific goals.** Quite simply, specific goals lead to higher performance than just "do your best" goals. In fact, "do your best" goals have about the same effect as no goal at all. Imagine a runner circling a track, shouting to her coach, "How much farther do I have to go?" A reply from the coach of "Just do your best" won't help much. One famous example of a successful specific goal was President John F. Kennedy's 1961 goal of putting a man on the moon by the end of the decade.

    Specific goals are sometimes so powerful as to overwhelm other things. In one study, subjects were assigned to either a "low-motivation" or a "high-motivation" group based on performance, ability, and attitude ratings. The low-motivation group received specific task goals, while the high-motivation group was told to "do your best." Performance of the low-motivation group quickly caught up to that of the high-motivation group. Of course, goals must be appropriate. If some goals are specific and others are not, the nonspecific goals will not receive much emphasis. Also, there is a danger that

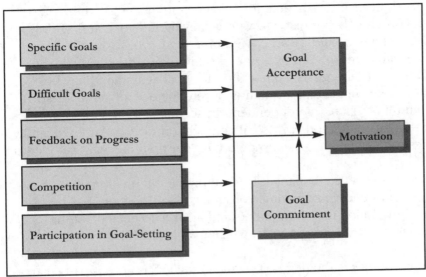

Exhibit 3.10   Important Goal Characteristics

Goal commitment The degree to which individuals are dedicated to reach the goals they have adopted.

Goal acceptance The degree to which individuals accept a specific goal as a realistic target.

a manager may really care about X but, because Y is easier to quantify, will set goals for Y instead. The Focus on Management on the following page provides an example.

Apollo 17 astronaut Gene Cernan touches an American flag on the surface of the moon. A gibbous Earth is in the sky above.

- **Set difficult goals.** There is a positive, linear relationship between goal difficulty and task performance. That is, the more difficult the goal, the better the task performance. This relationship holds for various kinds of tasks, time horizons, and ages of subjects. However, employees must believe the goal is attainable. If not, they will not accept it. Also, people pursue many goals at the same time. If they believe one is too difficult, they will focus on other, more attainable goals. Interestingly, when people face difficult goals, they engage in more problem analysis and creative behavior than when faced with simple goals. So they both work harder and work smarter. Managers need to keep in mind that goal difficulty also depends on the characteristics of the workers involved in the situation. For a very achievement-oriented worker, a manager may want to set "stretch goals" for him/her that provide a high level of challenge. However, for an employee with low levels of self-confidence or someone who does not have much job experience, a manager may need to be more conservative in setting "difficult goals" for these individuals as they may be more easily de-motivated if they feel that a goal is too challenging for them.

- **Give feedback on goal progress.** Feedback keeps behavior on track. Feedback may also stimulate greater effort (we will see later in this chapter that feedback from the job itself is a major determinant of the motivating potential of a job). A video game without a score would soon be abandoned. And when people get feedback concerning their performance, they tend to set personal improvement goals. The nature of the feedback makes a difference. As we will discuss later in the chapter, feedback from the job itself is generally better than that provided by others. Finally, feedback is clearly more important for some people than for others. We've seen elsewhere, for example, that people with a high need for achievement have especially strong desires for feedback. Managers need to remember that it is generally a good practice to schedule formal check-in meetings where the manager and the worker can discuss progress being made toward achieving the goal, and to provide a forum for giving feedback. These meetings should be scheduled on a regular basis.

- **Consider peer competition for goal attainment.** If employees are working toward individual goals, such as salespersons pursuing independent sales goals, competition for goal attainment may be useful. Its impact is especially great in zero-sum situations, that is, where there is a fixed "pie" to divide. However, competition can hurt if tasks are interdependent. In such a case, an employee's attempts to excel may harm the performance of another. Also, if competition focuses on the quantity of output, quality may suffer. In these situations, managers should consider the potential use of group or team-based goals.

- **Use participation in goal-setting.** Participation isn't a panacea. Some people simply don't like to participate, and in some situations (such as under severe time constraints), participation may be inappropriate. In general, however, participation increases understanding and acceptance of the goal. Participation often leads to setting of more difficult goals, which may in turn lead to higher performance.

- **Encourage goal acceptance. Goal acceptance** is the degree to which individuals accept particular goals as their own. If a goal is not accepted, the other goal attributes don't matter. Goal acceptance is likely to be lacking if the individual sees goals as unreachable or sees no benefit from reaching the goal. This is a critical issue, as it ultimately determines whether an individual feels a sense of ownership for a goal. Goal acceptance also means that a manager is in a stronger position to ensure that workers are accountable for achieving their goals.

- **Encourage goal commitment. Goal commitment** is the degree to which individuals are dedicated to trying to reach the goals they have adopted. Like goal acceptance, it is a necessary condition for goal-directed effort. Goal commitment is affected by the same factors as goal acceptance. Those factors influence goal acceptance before the goal is set and goal commitment once the individual is pursuing the goal.

Of course, most goal-setting involves changes in a number of goal attributes. As one example, consider a field experiment in the logging industry. Trucks carrying logs from the woods to the mill varied in the number of trees they hauled from one time to the next since the trees varied in size. As a result, considerable judgment entered into the decision of what was a full load. However, analyses showed that trucks were carrying an average of only about 60 percent of their legal net weight. Eventually the researchers, management, and the union decided that a goal of 94 percent of legal net weight was difficult but reachable. The drivers, who were responsible for loading the trucks, were assigned this 94 percent goal. After about a month, performance increased from the initial 60 percent to about 80 percent of capacity. It then dipped to 70 percent for another month before rising to 90 percent, where it remained for the next six months. Company accountants estimated the results translated into a savings to the company of a quarter of a million dollars worth of new trucks alone. Several goal attributes had been changed—goals were difficult, were more specific than in the past, and had apparently been accepted.

Management by Objectives

Management by Objectives (MBO) is a motivational technique in which the manager and employee work together to set employee goals. The employee's performance is later measured against these goals. Management by objectives combines many of the goal-setting principles we have just described. The MBO process begins by identifying general areas of responsibility that are important to the firm. Once this has been done, the employee and manager get together and agree on specific objectives that the employee will meet during some future period of time. For example, one key responsibility area in sales management might be sales volume, and the objective might be to increase sales by 35 percent over the next six months. Once the manager and the employee have agreed on specific objectives, they develop a strategy together for meeting these objectives. The manager and the employee then meet periodically to review how the employee has done relative to the agreed-upon objectives. If there is a problem, they discuss why objectives have not been met. The final step in the MBO process is either to set new goals for the next time period or to develop new strategies to meet the previously agreed-upon goals. The entire procedure then begins anew.

Management by Objectives was one of the most popular motivational tools in the 1960s and 1970s, and it is still widely used in various forms and under various names. However, MBO is not perfect. For example, it may be difficult and time consuming to implement. Sometimes the agreed-upon goals are not specific enough, resulting in employee frustration. Also, MBO has been faulted for encouraging people to focus only on goals that can be easily expressed in numbers (such as the number of units produced in a week or the average number of sales calls made per day), ignoring goals that are hard to measure (such as quality of products or creativity).

On the other hand, MBO does encourage planning and goal-setting, and it lets employees know how they are doing on the job. Also, it allows employees to participate in setting goals, which is good for morale and motivation. It helps spot deviations from performance goals before it is too late to do anything about them. Since MBO combines three elements that have been found to improve productivity—goal-setting, feedback, and participation—it might be expected that MBO would also be successful. In fact, one review found that 68 of 70 major studies on the issue showed MBO to result in productivity gains. These studies also demonstrate that top-management commitment to MBO is critical for success. When top-management commitment was high, MBO resulted in an average productivity gain of 56 percent. When top-management commitment was low, the average gain in productivity was only 6 percent.

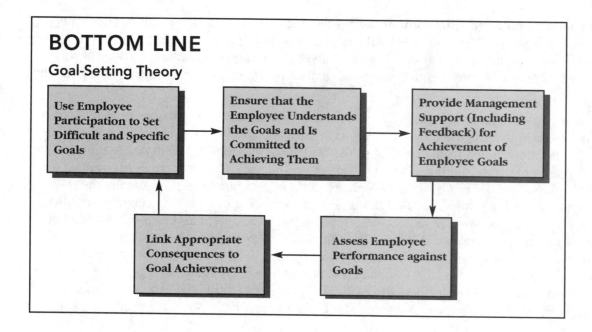

The process model presented in the preceding Bottom Line illustrates how goal-setting principles can be applied in order to enhance employees' motivation and job performance.

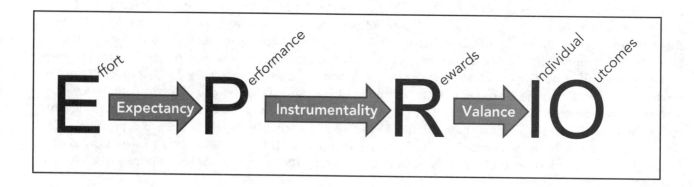

EXPECTANCY THEORY: A CHOICE THEORY OF MOTIVATION

You face many choices in your everyday life. Which courses do you take this term? Do you go to the big football game this weekend or go home and see your family? Which job offer do you accept after graduation? As a manager, you will need to make decisions about how hard to work, which projects to devote your attention to, and so on.

If someone is going to try to engage in some behavior, three conditions have to be satisfied. First, the person must believe that his or her efforts are somehow tied to the behavior. If not, why try? Second, the behavior must somehow be tied to outcomes. If not, why attempt the behavior? Third, those outcomes must be *valent* (that is, valued). If the outcomes aren't valued, why try to attain them? If any of these three conditions isn't satisfied, the individual has no reason to try. This simple idea is the essence of expectancy theory. **Expectancy theory** is an approach to the understanding of motivation that examines the links in the process from effort to ultimate rewards.

Expectancy Theory Concepts

The key elements of expectancy theory are as follows.

- **First-order outcome.** A **first-order outcome** is the direct result of effort. The first-order outcome may be performance, creativity, low absenteeism, low turnover, or any other desired behavior. There may be more than one first-order outcome.
- **Second-order outcome.** A **second-order outcome** is anything, good or bad, that may result from attainment of the first-order outcome. Typically, there are many second-order outcomes, such as pay, esteem of coworkers, and approval of the supervisor.
- **Expectancy. Expectancy** is the perceived linkage between effort and the first-order outcome. There is an expectancy for each first-order outcome. If a worker feels that trying harder won't improve his or her performance, the expectancy of effort for the attainment of performance would be low. If a worker feels that more effort will translate directly into higher performance, expectancy would be high. Expectancies are often expressed as probabilities. Exhibit 3.11 shows some of the things that may affect the actual linkage between effort and the firstorder outcome of performance. One of these, of course, is ability. If ability is completely lacking, effort won't help much. Another is the situation. In some situations, such as the assembly line, the employee is constrained. Greater effort simply won't speed up the line. A final factor is role perceptions. If employees don't know what their roles are (that is, what management expects of them), they will probably misdirect their efforts. Each of these factors is likely to influence expectancies.
- **Instrumentality. Instrumentality** is the perceived linkage between a first-order outcome and a second-order outcome. There is an instrumentality for each combination of first- and second-order outcomes. Like expectancy, instrumentalities are often expressed as probabilities. If an employee feels that higher performance will lead to pay increases, the instrumentality of performance for the attainment of pay increases would be high. If an employee feels that performance and pay are unrelated, that instrumentality would be zero.
- **Valence. Valence** is simply the value an individual attaches to an outcome. The valences of second-order outcomes are the values of such things as pay increases, supervisory approval, security, and esteem of coworkers. The valence of a first-order outcome, such as performance, depends upon the valences of second-order outcomes and on the instrumentalities of the first-order outcome for the attainment of those second-order outcomes. In particular, it is the sum of the products of the valence

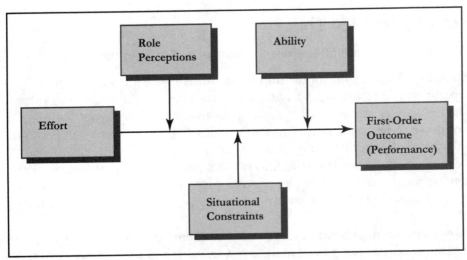

Exhibit 3.11   The Linkage of Effort to a First-Order Outcome

of the first-order outcomes and the instrumentality of the first-order outcome for the attainment of the second-order outcomes. That is:

One benefit of expectancy theory is that the theory suggests we should try to directly assess the value employees attach to outcomes. Often, managers assume they know what their subordinates want. As evidenced by the Focus on Management, that follows, employees may simply not value what are often assumed to be highly desirable outcomes.

- **Force to perform, or effort.** As Exhibit 3.12 shows, the degree to which an employee exerts **force to perform**, or **effort**, to attain a first-order outcome depends on both the expectancy that effort will lead to an increase in that first-order outcome and the valence of the first-order outcome. For instance, expectancy theory would predict that an employee would exert no effort to perform at a higher level if he or she either saw no possibility that effort would lead to higher performance or did not value higher performance. In more practical terms, expectancy theory simply says that an individual will be motivated to pursue the behavior that is most attractive in terms of his/her perceptions of expectancy, instrumentality, and valence. Specifically, a behavior that a person will be highly motivated to engage in will be one in which a person perceives the following:

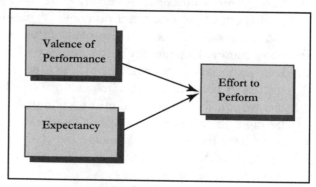

Exhibit 3.12   Determinants of Effort to Perform

- If I exert effort, I can successfully achieve the desired behavior (expectancy);
- My successful achievement of the desired behavior will be linked with specific outcomes or consequences (instrumentality);
- I positively value the outcomes or consequences linked with the desired behavior (valence).

Expectancy theory is at base, then, a theory that focuses on values and perceived (sometimes called subjective) probabilities. People may place different values on outcomes, and they may have very different perceptions about probabilities. Expectancy theory suggests that managers should not assume they know what employees want or think. Expectancies and instrumentalities are usually rated on scales of 0 (no chance the outcome will occur) to 1 (the outcome will definitely occur).

Practical Implications of Expectancy Theory

Expectancy theory provides a variety of important implications for managers. For example:

- **Recognize that three conditions are necessary for motivation to perform.** These are valued rewards, a perceived link of effort to performance (expectancy), and perceived links of performance to valent outcomes (instrumentalities). If *any* of those elements is missing, motivation will be low.
- **Assess perceptions of each of those three conditions.** This can provide extremely useful information. For example, you may find that employees don't really value some of the rewards you have been using or that they don't believe their efforts will translate into performance or their performance into rewards. Conversely, you may be surprised to find that employees place great value on rewards that could be easily and inexpensively provided or that employees have surprisingly strong expectancy or instrumentality perceptions.
- **Identify gaps between employee and management perceptions.** For example, a common response of management upon learning that employees don't believe their rewards are tied to their performance levels is "They're wrong! We tightly link pay and other rewards to performance." From an expectancy

theory perspective, whether or not the employees' perceptions are wrong is irrelevant; perceptions drive behavior. If rewards actually are tied to behaviors in ways that employees don't recognize, management's job is to convince employees of that fact.

- **As suggested earlier, and consistent with our discussion of need theories, make sure that you are giving employees rewards that they value.** One option is to employ **cafeteria-style benefit plans**. In these plans, employees can choose from a range of alternative benefits. For instance, employees of differing ages or marital status may desire different benefits. One employee may choose all salary with no other benefits; another may choose the total allowance for pension and insurance contributions. As an example, Du Pont's U.S. employees can choose from a menu of medical, dental, and life insurance options as well as financial planning.
- **Ask what factors may be weakening expectancy perceptions.** Do employees know what they are supposed to do? Have they been properly trained? Are there characteristics of the situation—resource constraints, poor tools, or whatever—that make it difficult for employees to perform well regardless of their efforts?
- **Ask what factors may be weakening instrumentality perceptions.** Is it true that rewards really aren't tied to performance? Is management simply not communicating well with employees about the nature of the reward system?
- **If employees appear to be poorly motivated, work backwards.** Try to determine which of the expectancy theory conditions may be lacking.

The process diagram in the Bottom Line that follows, shows how expectancy theory can be applied to effectively manage employee motivation and performance.

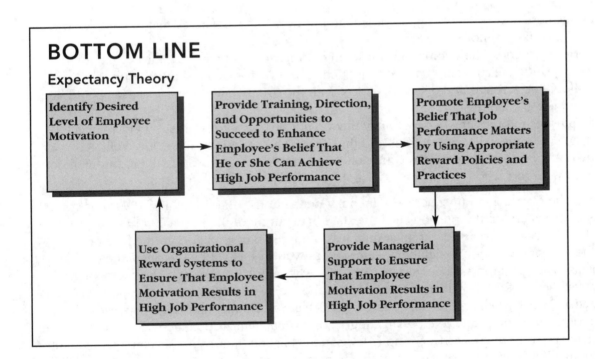

BOTTOM LINE

Expectancy Theory

Identify Desired Level of Employee Motivation → Provide Training, Direction, and Opportunities to Succeed to Enhance Employee's Belief That He or She Can Achieve High Job Performance → Promote Employee's Belief That Job Performance Matters by Using Appropriate Reward Policies and Practices → Provide Managerial Support to Ensure That Employee Motivation Results in High Job Performance → Use Organizational Reward Systems to Ensure That Employee Motivation Results in High Job Performance → (back to Identify Desired Level of Employee Motivation)

ASSURING FAIRNESS

It goes without saying that we should treat people fairly. What, though, do we mean by fair? Certainly, fairness has something to do with not cheating others or blatantly playing favorites. But fairness is more complex than that. There are at least two important types of fairness: distributive fairness and procedural fairness. These deal, in turn, with fairness in regard to the sorts of things we get and the processes used to allocate rewards.

Equity theory, which focuses on distributive fairness, is one of a family of theories based on the idea that people want to maintain balance. By focusing on the balance of the inputs, or contributions, people make to the outcomes they receive, equity theory helps us understand how employees determine whether they are being treated fairly. Employee perceptions of fairness influence their level of motivation and the specific behaviors that they are motivated to engage in.

Why Be Fair?

According to equity theorists, people want to maintain distributive fairness. **Distributive fairness** exists when someone thinks people are getting what they deserve—not less, certainly, but *not more either.* According to equity theory, people feel uncomfortable when they get less than they deserve (because they feel cheated) or more than they deserve (because they feel guilty). Research evidence supports this contention. Some people—called **equity sensitives**—are especially focused on equity considerations. There are several reasons why people want distributive fairness. For instance:

- When people experience a situation they feel is not fair, they experience an unpleasant state of tension. Restoration of distributive fairness reduces that tension;
- Some people try to be fair because they think others will reward them for being fair;
- Behaving fairly may bolster a person's self-esteem;
- Most people find it comforting to believe that life is fair. By giving others what we think they deserve, we strengthen that belief.

Employers may have other, more specific reasons for wanting to treat their employees fairly. They may, for example, want to do the following:

- **Conform to business norms.** For example, people in business generally agree that employees who do better work should get more rewards.
- **Attract superior workers to their company and weed out inferior workers.** If rewards are fairly tied to performance, a positive relationship between satisfaction and performance should result. Thus, high performers should be satisfied and disposed to stay with the firm, while low performers should be dissatisfied and leave the firm.
- **Motivate employees to produce.** As expectancy theory indicates, tying rewards to performance should enhance instrumentality perceptions and thus increase motivation to perform well.
- **Develop trust.** A trusting environment is extremely important to workers, especially in turbulent job environments. Managers who don't treat their employees fairly will not be trusted.

As an example of the resentment engendered by inequity perceptions, IBM in the mid 1990s confronted the worst crisis in its history. In the previous eight years, it had cut more than 180,000 of its 405,000 jobs, and by the end of the year it would report an annual loss of more than $8 billion. In the face of these cutbacks and the threat of further belt tightening, employees were dismayed by the perks the company maintained for managers and top salespeople—country clubs with golf courses and skeet-shooting; a large fleet of private jets; a Rose Bowl Parade float; and elaborate sales meetings featuring a five-act circus, Bob Newhart, Larry King, Liza Minelli, and others. Whatever the merits of such expenses, they created a sense of great inequity and led to many angry complaints. Similar outrage was evident when it was revealed that American International Group (AIG) spent $442,000 on a conference at a fancy California resort, including $23,000 for spa services, less than a week after the government bailed it out in late 2008 with $150 billion of taxpayers' funds.

Similarly, there has been a global debate over CEO pay, with the levels of CEO compensation skyrocketing relative to that of the average hourly worker—today's average CEO in large U.S.-based organizations makes about 370 times the pay of the average hourly worker, compared to 85 times in 1990 and 42 times in 1980. As one notable example, Richard Fuld, who continued to lead Lehman Brothers after its bankruptcy filing in September, 2008, received almost half a billion dollars in total compensation since 1993. In 2007 he earned $45 million—or about $17,000 an hour. Further, 90 percent of stock-option plans for Standard & Poor's 500 companies don't attach performance conditions to option grants. The growing compensation gap has led to charges of greed and concerns about the impact of perceived inequities. U.S. employees aren't the only ones complaining about inequities—CEO compensation packages are beginning to rise worldwide as foreign executives are eyeing the staggering sums received by their U.S. counterparts.

Determining Equity

How do people determine whether outcomes are equitable? J. Stacey Adams proposed the following equation for an equitable relationship. It is based on the writings of an earlier student of behavior, Aristotle:

$$\frac{O_p}{I_p} = \frac{O_o}{I_o}$$

Where:

O_p is the person's perception of the outcomes he or she is receiving.
I_p is the person's perception of his or her inputs.
O_o is the person's perception of the outcomes some comparison person (called a comparison other) is receiving.
I_o is the person's perception of the inputs of the comparison other.

This equation says that equity exists when a person feels the ratio of his or her outcomes to his or her inputs is *equal to* that ratio for some comparison other. Neither is seen as getting less or more than his or her inputs justify. Note that *each* of the elements in the equation is a perception. While actual conditions may (or may not) influence those perceptions, they do not directly enter the equity calculations.

The comparison other may be another individual (such as a coworker or friend), a group of other people (such as workers on another job), or some abstract combination of people. It may even be the perceiving person at an earlier point in time.

Inputs and Outcomes

At base, inputs are anything employees believe they are contributing to the job. Outcomes are anything they believe they are getting from the job. So inputs might include such things as seniority, time, performance, appearance, dedication to the organization, effort, intelligence, and provision of needed tools. Outcomes might include pay, promotional opportunities, job status, job interest, esteem of coworkers, monotony, praise, fatigue, and dangerous working conditions. Note that employees may view some outcomes of the job negatively, such as fatigue and dangerous working conditions. Obviously, different people care about different inputs and outcomes. An input for one person may even be an outcome for another. For instance, one worker may value increased responsibility, viewing it as an outcome. Another may see that same increased responsibility as a burdensome input.

Restoring Equity

If an individual perceives a situation to be inequitable, there are many ways to restore equity. For example, suppose that Frank feels underpaid relative to his coworker Karen. He could try to restore equity in each of the following ways.

- **He can raise his actual outcomes.** For instance, Frank might demand and get a raise;
- **He can lower his inputs.** Frank might slow down on the job, withhold important information, or stop doing unpaid overtime work;

- **He can perceptually distort his inputs and/or outcomes.** Frank could reason that he was actually getting things out of the job he hadn't been considering, or he could downgrade the values of his inputs;
- **He can perceptually distort Karen's inputs and/or outcomes.** Frank could devalue the nonpay outcomes Karen is receiving, or he could increase his estimates of Karen's inputs;
- **He can leave the situation.** With a big enough feeling of inequity, Frank might psychologically withdraw from the situation or might actually apply for a transfer or quit;
- **He can act to change Karen's inputs and/or outcomes.** Frank could try to convince Karen to raise her inputs, could talk to the boss about lowering Karen's pay, or could take steps to try to make Karen leave her job;
- **He can change his comparison other.** Frank could begin to compare his situation to that of Paul rather than to that of Karen.

People do use these mechanisms to restore equity. For instance, field studies and laboratory experiments have shown that individuals withdraw from tasks when they are inequitably treated—even, in some cases, when they are overpaid. There is also considerable evidence that people change their perceptions to restore equity. Underpaid workers often perceive that they have made relatively low inputs and begin to see themselves as less qualified than others. Some also exaggerate their outcomes, rating their jobs as far more interesting than do others in the same positions.

As an example of the ways employees may take action to restore equity, consider the case of a manufacturing plant that made small mechanical parts for the aerospace and automotive industries. When important contracts were canceled, the company announced a 15 percent pay cut for all employees in the plant. Compared to employees in another plant, whose pay was not cut, the affected employees reacted by doubling their normal theft rate of tools and supplies from the company, and turnover jumped to 23 percent (compared to a normal 5 percent). When the pay cut ended after 10 weeks, theft returned to normal levels. Apparently, employees in the plant experienced underpayment inequity, and some reacted by stealing. It seems that others decided simply to leave the inequitable situation.

While equity theory would permit any of a wide range of adjustments to restore equity, it would be useful to know specifically which change is most likely to occur. Adams has provided the following set of propositions concerning how people choose from among the alternatives available to reduce inequity.

- They will first try to maximize valued outcomes;
- They will be reluctant to increase inputs that are difficult or costly to change;
- They will resist actual or perceived changes in inputs or outcomes that are central to their self-concept and self-esteem;
- They will be more resistant to changing perceptions about their own inputs and outcomes than to changing perceptions about their comparison others' inputs and outcomes;
- They will leave the situation only when inequity is great and other means of reducing it are not available. Partial withdrawal, such as absenteeism, will occur more frequently and under lower conditions of inequity;
- They will be reluctant to change their comparison others.

The process model presented in the Bottom Line that follows, shows how equity theory can be systematically implemented to establish and maintain an employee's sense of perceived equity in his or her work situation.

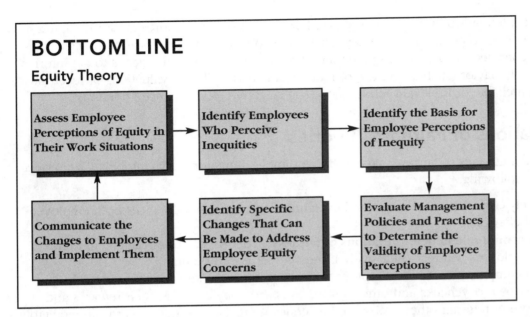

BOTTOM LINE

Equity Theory

| Assess Employee Perceptions of Equity in Their Work Situations | → | Identify Employees Who Perceive Inequities | → | Identify the Basis for Employee Perceptions of Inequity |

Communicate the Changes to Employees and Implement Them ← Identify Specific Changes That Can Be Made to Address Employee Equity Concerns ← Evaluate Management Policies and Practices to Determine the Validity of Employee Perceptions

Other Rules for Determining Distributive Fairness

Equity theory is based on the contributions rule. The **contributions rule** says that distributive fairness is determined by equating contributions (inputs) with outcomes. However, people may use other rules when determining distributive fairness. They may, for example, employ the **needs rule**, feeling it is fair to give people what they need rather than what they contribute. Or they may employ the **equality rule**, arguing that it is fair for everyone to get the same amount.

A variety of things determine the weights we give to these various rules, including the following:

- **Self-interest.** People tend to assign higher weights to rules that favor them. A high performer will likely favor the contributions rule, while a needy person will favor the needs rule;
- **Conformity.** People tend to conform to the beliefs and behaviors of others with whom they regularly interact. So if all of a manager's coworkers favor the equality rule, the manager may also apply that rule;
- **Availability of relevant information.** People are reluctant to use a rule for which they don't have sufficient information. For instance, if a manager doesn't know what subordinates need, the needs rule probably won't be applied.

In addition, some things affect the weights given to specific rules. For instance, if it is important that high performers maintain their output levels, the contributions rule will be weighted heavily. When someone feels responsible for the receivers' welfare, the needs rule is likely to be applied. And the equality rule is easy to apply. People may also turn to the equality rule when needs and contributions are hard to assess.

Procedural Fairness

Distributive fairness depends on whether receivers get what they deserve. People may also be concerned with procedural fairness. **Procedural fairness** is whether the process used to allocate outcomes is fair. If procedures seem unfair, people may also question the distribution of rewards. On the other hand, even if people don't get what they want, they may be satisfied as long as they believe the allocation process was fair. Procedural fairness seems to have important consequences. Research has shown, for instance, that survivors' reactions to a major reorganization depended on perceptions of procedural fairness, with procedural justice predicting organizational commitment, job satisfaction, intentions to stay with the firm, and trust in management. Similarly, job satisfaction and organizational commitment of untenured management professors subsequent to their tenure and promotion processes were found to be related to perceptions of both distributive and procedural fairness.

Not surprisingly, people tend to think procedures are fair when those procedures favor their interests. They also believe procedures to be fairer when they have some control over the allocation process. Further, they are likely to consider a procedure to be unfair when it uses questionable means to get information about the receivers' behavior (such as the use of hidden cameras) or if the evaluations of receivers seem to be based on unreliable or irrelevant information (such as faulty performance appraisals).

Practical Implications of Fairness Theories

Equity theory and related theories of fairness have important implications for managing behavior in organizations, including the following.

- **Fairness is absolutely critical to employees (and everyone else).** Fairness influences both employee attitudes and their behaviors.
- **Perceptions play a central role in determinations of fairness.** Whether or not management thinks something is fair, employees will react negatively if they perceive it to be unfair.
- **Fairness involves a comparison process.** Employees don't decide whether something is fair by looking only at their own paychecks and other rewards. Instead, they compare their rewards and contributions to those of relevant others. As such, it is critical to make sure that rewards are equitably distributed across employees.
- **Both distributive fairness and procedural fairness are important.** While employees obviously care about whether they're getting what they think they deserve, they also are very concerned about whether the process used to determine rewards was fair. Even if employees are pleased with what they received, they may have qualms if they think the allocation process was unfair. They may, for instance, feel guilt, or they may question whether the process will give them what they deserve next time. If employees get less than they feel they deserve, a clear explanation of exactly how rewards were determined may temper their reactions. This, of course, puts the onus appropriately on management to actually use a fair allocation process.
- **Both over-reward and under-reward may cause problems.** While underreward may cause anger, over-reward may cause guilt.
- **Employees may consider inputs and outcomes that are different from those we may expect.** Indeed, what some employees consider inputs, others may see as outcomes.
- **We need to find what people really value and what they think they are contributing.** We cannot assume that people value what we expect them to value or that they see their contributions as we do. Perhaps the best way to find what people see as inputs and outcomes is to ask them.
- **Employees may find many ways to reduce perceived inequity.** In the case of under-reward inequity, these might include producing less, producing lower-quality work, quitting, or even sabotage or theft.
- **While the exact means employees will use to reduce inequity may be difficult to predict, almost all are harmful to organizations and perhaps to the individuals themselves.** Not only may inequity lead to bad outcomes for the organization, it may also generate stress in employees and perhaps even cause them to question their self-worth.

DESIGNING MOTIVATING JOBS

Some jobs are naturally motivating to the people who perform. Consider the examples of a NASCAR racecar driver, a professional baseball player, or a professional musician. Unfortunately, a lot of other jobs are not quite so motivating in and of themselves. So, we as managers need to understand different ways in which a job can be designed or redesigned to make it as motivating as possible.

Jobs are central to the lives of most people. They consume a large part of our days and often our nights. To a great extent, many of us rate our success in life on the basis of the status, pay, and other characteristics of our jobs. And others often size us up by our response to "Tell me, what do you do?" Indeed, it is hard to imagine not working. Albert Camus has written, "Without work, all life goes rotten. But

Some intriniscally motivating jobs include a NASCAR driver, a professional baseball player, and a rock star.

when work is soulless, life stifles and dies." What is it about jobs that makes them important to people? What makes them exciting? Why are some soulless? What makes jobs "good" or "bad"? Does everyone want the same things from jobs? And what can management do to improve jobs and increase their motivating potential?

The Case for Specialization

There is a famous episode from a TV show called, "I Love Lucy" starring Lucille Ball in which Lucy and her friend Ethel get a job working at a candy factory. Their jobs consist of taking pieces of candy that are on an assembly line and wrapping them in paper. This was their one and only responsibility all day long. This is an example of what we call task specialization, which is part of a broader approach to job design called scientific management.

Frederick Taylor introduced scientific management in the early 1900s. According to scientific management, the "one best way" to perform a job should be found. That "one best way" usually results in job simplification, with each worker performing the same few activities over and over. Advantages cited for specialization include the following:

- The worker should be better able to perform the task and should find it to be easier;
- Time is not lost moving from one piece of machinery to another;
- The use of specialized machinery is encouraged;
- Replacement of employees who are absent or who leave the organization is easier, since the job is simpler and easier to learn;
- Especially where assembly lines are used, the worker will adjust to the required pace and be drawn along by "traction."

Scientific management was credited with some notable successes. For instance, application of its principles in one case increased the number of bricks laid per worker-hour from 120 to 350. Further, scientific management permitted the worker to maximize performance by focusing on a narrow range of activities. If the worker was paid on a piece-rate basis, this would result in higher pay. As a result, scientific management was widely adopted in the United States and elsewhere.

Taylor also adopted scientific management principles in his own life. For example, he studied tennis and determined that, rather than have both players stand at the back line as was the convention of the time, one player should stand at the net and the other back. Using that logic—and new, spoon-handled tennis rackets that he designed—Taylor and his brother-in-law won the first U.S. Men's Doubles Lawn Tennis Championship (now the U.S. Open). He also made major contributions

Lucy and Ethel performing their candy-wrapping skills on the assembly line.

A young Hong Kong woman wearing a dust mask sews rapidly in a garment sweat shop under poor conditions.

to golf club and golf course design, and employed a unique baseball pitching delivery that caused opposing players to regularly pop up.

However, Taylor is now often criticized for his emphasis on efficiency at the possible expense of employee satisfaction. He did consider the human element, but many of his views today seem inhumane. He wrote, for instance, that the kind of person who made a good pig-iron handler was "of the type of the ox." Whether or not criticisms of Taylor are correct, it does seem that the simplified, routine jobs he proposed may have some unforeseen results. For instance, they may lead to boredom, dissatisfaction, or other negative outcomes, as shown in Exhibit 3.13.

It is interesting to note that although scientific management is not as popular in the United States now as it was back in the early 1900s, you can see elements of this approach still being practiced in some developing countries (e.g., Indonesia, China, Malaysia) where simple, routine, repetitive tasks are still performed in jobs such as manufacturing garments and assembling electronics.

Job Size

If we believe "small" jobs are demeaning and dissatisfying for workers, a logical question to ask is how we can make jobs larger. There are at least two major dimensions to job size. They are job depth and job scope, or range.

Job depth refers to the degree to which employees can influence their work environments and carry out planning and control functions. **Job scope** is the number of different activities the worker performs, regardless of their content. Increases in job depth are usually called **job enrichment**, while increases in job scope are referred to as **job enlargement**. Most job changes are likely to influence both depth and scope, but these are separate dimensions and they can be independently changed.

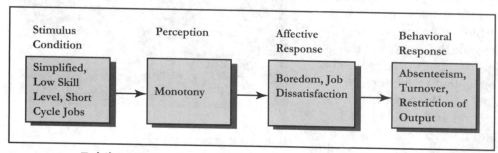

Stimulus Condition	Perception	Affective Response	Behavioral Response
Simplified, Low Skill Level, Short Cycle Jobs	→ Monotony	→ Boredom, Job Dissatisfaction	→ Absenteeism, Turnover, Restriction of Output

Exhibit 3.13 Potential Reactions to Specialized Jobs

The following are among the suggested advantages of increases in scope:

- There should be less fatigue of particular muscles, since a greater variety of muscles may be used;
- Since the employee will complete a larger part of the task, there may be more of a feeling of accomplishment;
- The employee may exercise a greater variety of skills;
- Large increases in scope may enhance managerial flexibility. For instance, if a company uses assembly teams rather than assembly lines, it can shut down a small number of the benches used by assembly teams rather than the entire line.

The presumed benefits for increased depth are primarily psychological. For instance, Chris Argyris has suggested that, since small, routine jobs are frustrating to the drives of "mature" individuals, they may result in use of a variety of defense mechanisms. Those **defense mechanisms** are ways in which the employee may try to reduce the tensions caused by frustration. They might involve physically leaving the source of frustration (such as through absenteeism or turnover), mentally leaving (through apathy or daydreaming), or striking back (perhaps by slowing down on the job or by making negative comments about the company). As shown in Exhibit 3.14, Argyris has argued that the typical firm's response to such defense mechanisms is to make jobs even more specialized, tighten up on rules, and emphasize authority relationships. These actions further frustrate maturity drives, and a self-reinforcing cycle occurs. Argyris reasons that to break out of that cycle, it is necessary to treat employees as mature individuals. Giving them more opportunity for planning and control is one step in that direction.

Others made similar arguments. For instance, M. Scott Myers said the assumption underlying work simplification is that there are two groups of employees. One group, responsible and highly motivated, is known as *managers*. The other, irresponsible and in need of close supervision, is called *workers*.

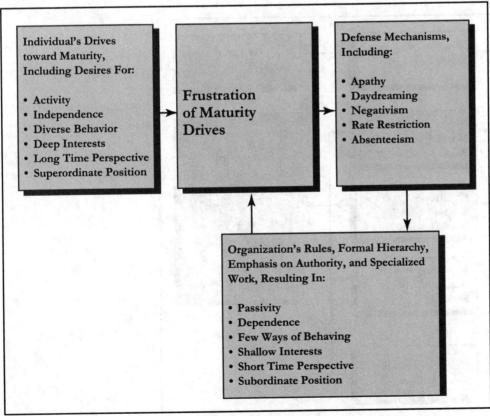

Exhibit 3.14   The Argyris Maturity Drive Frustration Cycle

Because of those assumed differences, companies call on managers to plan, direct, and control. They expect workers simply to carry out orders. Myers argued that companies must break down this artificial dichotomy and "make every employee a manager." This would involve turning many planning and control functions over to workers. That is, it would require enriching their jobs. Such job enrichment would be expected to enhance **intrinsic motivation**. Unlike things such as pay, which are forms of **extrinsic motivation**, intrinsic motivation comes from the job itself—just doing the job is motivating, independent of other rewards.

Companies in many industries are using job enrichment. In the hotel industry, for instance, front-desk clerks, housekeepers, bellhops, and other employees are being given more authority to make decisions on their own and to handle disputes with customers. At the Ritz-Carlton Hotel Company, for instance, front-desk clerks can now take off up to $2,000 from a guest's bill if the guest feels service was not up to par. At John Deere & Co., workers who assembled parts for machines are now, after six months of training, traveling around the Midwest speaking to groups of farmers as part of the Deere marketing team. Other hourly workers routinely give advice on cost cutting and improving product quality. Job enrichment is part of Deere's plan to use its workers as a source of competitive advantage.

The Job Characteristics Model

If we want to change jobs, we need to know which job dimensions are important to employees. In particular, before we can enrich jobs, we need to know what makes a job enriched. The examples we have just cited provide some clues. The jobs might, for instance, involve more responsibility, freedom, and challenge and a richer set of job duties. But are these necessary conditions for enrichment? Are there additional elements to enrichment?

The **job characteristics model**, shown in Exhibit 3.15, describes jobs as having five core task dimensions and two interpersonal dimensions.

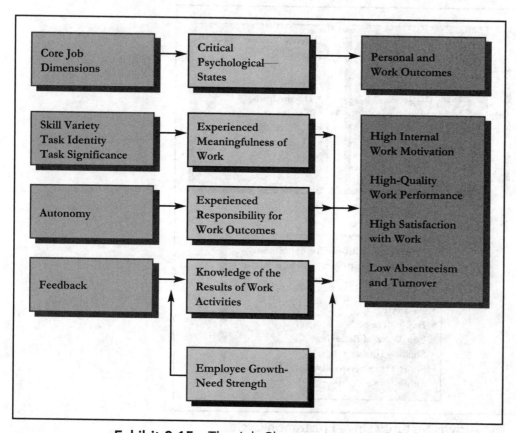

Exhibit 3.15 The Job Characteristics Model

Core Task Dimensions

The **core task dimensions** are characteristics of the job itself that are believed to be key influences on employee motivation. They include the following:

- **Skill variety.** The degree to which the job requires employees to perform a wide range of operations in their work and/or the degree to which employees must use a variety of equipment and procedures in their work;
- **Autonomy.** The extent to which employees have a major say in scheduling their work, selecting the equipment they will use, and deciding on procedures they will follow;
- **Task identity.** The extent to which employees do an entire piece of work and can clearly identify the result of their efforts;
- **Task significance.** The extent to which the job has a strong impact on the lives and work of other people;
- **Feedback.** The degree to which employees receive information while they are working that reveals how well they are performing on the job.

Interpersonal Dimensions

The **interpersonal dimensions** (not shown in the figure) are job characteristics that influence the degree to which employees engage in relationships with others on the job. They are:

- **Dealing with others.** The degree to which a job requires employees to deal with other people (inside or outside the firm) to complete their work
- **Friendship opportunities.** The degree to which a job allows employees to talk with one another on the job and to establish informal relationships with other employees at work

Sample items measuring each of the core task dimensions are shown in Exhibit 3.16. Can you match each item to the appropriate dimension?

According to the model, the core task dimensions have an impact on three **critical psychological states**: experienced meaningfulness of work, experienced responsibility for work outcomes, and knowledge of the actual results of work activities. Further, the model indicates that perceptions of the core task dimensions fit together to yield the **motivating potential score** of the job. This model implies that if any of the three components are very low, overall motivating potential of the task will be low. Further, as long as any of the three remain at very low levels, increases in the others will do little to improve overall motivating potential.

Evidence Regarding the Job Characteristics Model

The job characteristics approach has dominated recent job design efforts. Questions have been raised concerning whether all employees actually view their jobs on these specific dimensions. It does seem, however, that the dimensions may serve as useful guides for understanding reactions to jobs and for planning redesign strategies.

Studies show that perceptions of the core task dimensions are positively related to job satisfaction, job involvement, organizational commitment, and other favorable attitudes. However, those perceptions are usually not related in any consistent way to quantity of performance. Employees on enriched jobs typically get the benefits of enrichment simply by carrying out the task, regardless of their performance levels. So we would expect the core task dimension perceptions to translate into increased performance only when persistence on the task is important.

Research shows that the combinatory model proposed by the job characteristics model (in which a very low level on one dimension would neutralize the impact of changes in other dimensions) is prob-

Listed below are five statements that may (or may not) describe your job. You are to indicate the degree to which each statement is an accurate description of the job on which you work. Do this by writing the appropriate number in the left-hand margin, based on the following scale:

1	2	3	4	5	6	7
Very untrue of the job	Mostly untrue of the job	Slightly untrue of the job	Uncertain	Slightly true of the job	Moderately true of the job	Very true of the job

Please make your descriptions as objective and factually accurate as possible, without regard for whether you like or dislike jour job.

1. The job requires me to use a variety of complex or high-level skills.

2. The job gives me considerable opportunity for independence and freedom in how I do the work.

3. The job provides me with the chance to finish completely the pieces of work I begin.

4. Just doing the work required by the job provides many chances for me to figure out how well I'm doing.

5. The job is one where a lot of other people can be affected by how well the work gets done.

Source: Adapted from J. R. Hackman and G. Oldham, *Work Redesign.* Reading, MA: Addison, Wesley, 1980, pp. 300-301.

Exhibit 3.16   Measuring the Core Task Dimensions

ably not valid. That is, task dimension perceptions somehow seem to "add up" to influence reactions, rather than to represent a series of hurdles. This is a welcome finding, since it suggests that improvements on any of the dimensions may help.

The Focus on Perceptions

Remember that the job characteristics approach focuses on employee perceptions of task characteristics. This is appropriate since we act on the basis of our perceptions. However, many things may affect perceptions. For instance, in one study students were asked to perform a simple assembly task. The task was the same for all students, but the way they perceived the task depended on their ages and personalities. As an example, older students felt the task offered more skill variety and feedback but less task identity than did younger students. In general, we might expect that an employee with considerable experience and training on a task would see it very differently than would a "rookie."

This makes the task of job design more difficult. It is not enough to make objective changes in feedback, skill variety, or the other task dimensions. We must also discover how those objective changes translate into perceptions.

Implementing Job Enrichment

Implementing principles for job redesign are job changes that might influence the core task dimensions. Exhibit 3.17 presents those implementing principles. As our previous examples suggest, implementing principles include such actions as giving workers tasks to perform that require a larger variety of skills, letting workers do a larger part of the job in order to increase task identity and task significance, permit-

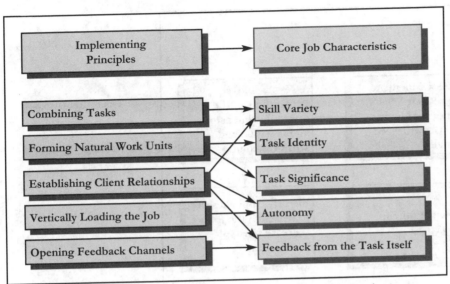

Exhibit 3.17   Implementing Principles for Job Redesign

ting employees to have increased contact with clients in order to increase skill variety, autonomy, and feedback, vertically loading the job (that is, giving more "management" responsibility) to enhance autonomy, and opening new feedback channels. Another, related, way to enhance the core task dimensions is through job rotation. With **job rotation**, employees systematically move from one job to another, getting a change of pace and duties, learning more about the company, and often developing a broad foundation for future advancement.

These principles may be useful in providing suggestions for how companies can change jobs to increase levels of the core task dimensions. However, their use must take place as part of a systematic assessment of the particular situation. For instance, if job enrichment is to be successful, it must fit with the organization's employees, practices, structure, and technology.

The Conditions for Successful Redesign

A family of jobs should be considered for redesign if:

- **The employees perceive their jobs to be deficient in the core task dimensions.** It is important to stress here that worker perceptions, not just the assumptions of management or consultants, are crucial;
- **Employees are fairly well satisfied with pay, fringe benefits, and working conditions.** If workers are unhappy with these factors, they are likely to resent and resist job redesign;
- **The current structure and technology of the unit where the jobs are housed are hospitable to enriched jobs.** If the overall organization has a mechanistic structure or technology such as assembly lines, redesign attempts may be expensive and hard to implement. They are also likely to ultimately fail;
- **Employees want the sorts of things—variety, autonomy, feedback, and so on—that enriched jobs provide.**

These conditions suggest that job redesign should be undertaken carefully and selectively. It may be appropriate only in a limited set of situations and, as we discuss in the next section, it must be carefully and systematically implemented.

Who Wants Job Enrichment?

You probably know some people who would like more challenge, variety, and responsibility from their jobs and others who might be indifferent to them. Still others might say, "If you're going to give me all the decision-making responsibility of my boss, give me my boss's pay." The most direct measure of the

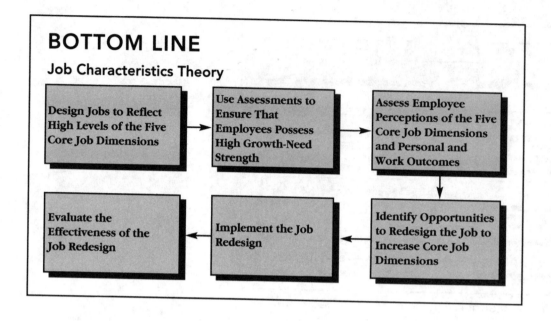

degree to which an employee wants an enriched job is called **growth-need strength (GNS)**. This is basically the degree to which an individual wants such things as challenge and responsibility. While most employees respond positively to high levels of the core task dimensions, those with strong GNS react most favorably. This suggests a simple and reasonable way to determine who wants job redesign: If we don't know whether employees are likely to react favorably to job enrichment, we can ask them.

The process model presented in the Bottom Line that follows, illustrates how job characteristics theory can be applied in order to enhance employees' intrinsic motivation and yield desirable personal and organizational outcomes.

TOP TEN LIST: KEY POINTS TO REMEMBER

How to Motivate Effectively

10. Assess employee needs and identify those that are most active (unsatisfied). Take specific actions to satisfy these needs through an employee's job and overall work experience in your organization.

9. Align the satisfaction of employee needs with the achievement of organizational goals through your managerial policies and practices.

8. Demonstrate to employees that good job performance "makes a difference" by linking positive outcomes or rewards to performance.

7. Demonstrate to employees that poor performance will not be tolerated by linking negative outcomes with poor performance or by eliminating positive outcomes that inadvertently led to the poor performance.

6. Develop and implement personal and job-related strategies for managing yourself more effectively.

5. Set specific and challenging goals and objectives for your employees, and ensure that the goals and objectives are aligned with the goals of the overall work unit. Monitor progress toward goal achievement and take appropriate corrective action as needed.

4. Develop and maintain employee motivation by ensuring that they feel that they have the ability to be successful on their job, that consequences are linked to performance, and that these consequences are appropriately valued by employees.

3. Provide managerial support for employee motivation so that it results in high levels of job performance.

2. Monitor employee perceptions of their treatment by you and the organization. Take action to ensure that employees feel that they are treated fairly.

1. Design jobs so that the characteristics of the job provide a good fit with the knowledge, skills, abilities, goals, and values of each employee.

Foundations of Behavior

CHAPTER OUTLINE

PERCEPTION

An understanding of perception is important because it has such an enormous impact on understanding individual behavior. No two people share the same reality; for each of us, the world is unique. We cannot understand behavior unless we understand why two people observing the same event can honestly see something entirely different. Furthermore, we need to understand that through our perceptions we are not simply passive observers of the drama of life, but active participants, helping to write the script and play the roles. The behavior of others is influenced by how you perceive them.

The Perceptual Process

Perception is the process of receiving and interpreting environmental stimuli. In a world filled with complex environmental stimuli, our perceptions help us categorize and organize the sensations we receive. We behave according to our interpretation of the reality we see. What we fail to appreciate is that the reality we see is almost never the same as the reality perceived by others. The perceptual process consists of three major components, as shown in Exhibit 4.1: sensation, attention, and perception. These three components are involved in perceiving both physical objects and social events.

Sensation

At any given moment we are surrounded by countless environmental stimuli. We are not aware of most of these stimuli, either because we have learned to ignore them, or because our sense organs—sight, smell, taste, touch, and hearing—are not capable of receiving them. Environmental stimuli can only produce sensations in the human body if the body has developed the sensing mechanism to receive them. Whether you are consciously aware of these sensations depends on the next step in the perception process—attention.

Attention

Although we are capable of sensing many environmental stimuli, we attend to only a very small portion of them and ignore the rest. Numerous factors influence the attention process.

1. *Size.* The larger the size of a physical object, the more likely it is to be perceived.

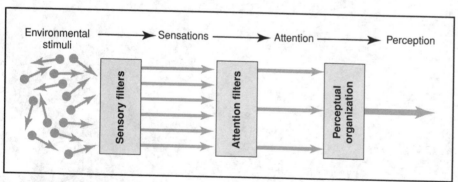

Exhibit 4.1   Perceptual Process

Sensations
Environmental stimuli that we are capable of receiving through one or more of the five sense mechanisms—sight, smell, taste, touch, and hearing.

Attention
Part of the perceptual process in which we acknowledge the reception of sensations from the environment. The major characteristics involved in attending to physical stimuli include size, intensity, frequency, contrast, motion, change, and novelty.

2. *Intensity.* The greater the intensity of a stimulus, the more likely it is to be noticed. A loud noise, such as shouting, is more likely to get attention than a quiet voice.

3. *Frequency.* The greater the frequency with which a stimulus is presented, the greater are the chances you will attend to it. This principle of repetition is used extensively in advertising to attract the attention of buyers.

4. *Contrast.* Stimuli that contrast with the surrounding environment are more likely to be selected for attention than stimuli that blend with the environment. The contrast can be created by color, size, or any other factor that distinguishes one stimulus from others, as shown in Exhibit 4.2.

5. *Motion.* Since movement tends to attract attention, a moving stimulus is more likely to be perceived than a stationary object. An animated sign, for example, attracts more attention than a fixed billboard. An object with blinking lights, such as a Christmas tree or sign, attracts more attention than one without blinking lights.

6. *Novelty.* A stimulus that is new and unique will often be perceived more readily than familiar stimuli. Advertisers use the impact of novelty by creating original packaging or advertising messages.

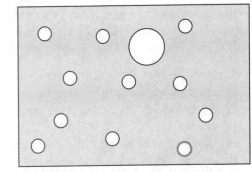

Exhibit 4.2   The Effects of Size, Intensity, and Contrast on Attention

Perception

The process of **perception** involves organizing and interpreting the sensations we attend to. Visual images, sounds, odors, and other sensations do not simply enter our consciousness as pure, unpolluted sensations. As we attend to them, we consciously try to organize or categorize the sensations into a meaningful perception that somehow makes sense to us.

Although we would like to think of ourselves as open-minded, unbiased, and nonjudgmental in our perceptions, the demands of the situation make it impossible; we are forced to draw quick inferences based on very sparse information. If you were a counselor in a college advisement center and a student came for assistance, you would be required to make rapid inferences based on only limited information. Your recommendations on course loads and elective classes would depend on your perception of the student's situation.

We tend to categorize people using limited pieces of information and then act on this information, even though most of our inferences have not been confirmed. This process is called making **perceptual inferences**, since we are required to diagnose our situation and make rapid inferences about it from scanty clues.

We cannot wait until we have complete information about each individual before we respond. If we waited until we were fully informed about each person's unique personality and problems, we would never respond. Instead, we develop a system of categories based on only a few pieces of information and use this system to organize our perceptions. For example, college students tend to categorize other college students according to sex, marital status, year in school, and major. If you started a casual conversation with another student, your conversation would likely be much different if you thought that student

---

Perception
The process of interpreting and organizing the sensations we attend to.

Perceptual inferences
The process of extrapolating from a small amount of information to form a complete perception about an object or event. Often we are required to act on only limited pieces of information from which we infer what more information might tell us.

was a married graduate student majoring in engineering rather than an unmarried freshman majoring in sociology.

The process of grouping environmental stimuli into recognizable patterns is called **perceptual organization**. Rather than just seeing the stimuli as random observations, we attempt to organize them into meaningful, recognizable patterns. Some of the principles we use to organize these sensations include these:

1. **Figure-ground.** People tend to perceive objects that stand against a background. In a committee meeting, for example, most people see the verbal conversation as *figure*, and fail to attend to the background of nonverbal messages that may be far more meaningful in understanding the group processes.

2. **Similarity.** Stimuli that have common physical traits are more likely to be grouped together than those that do not. Athletic teams wear uniforms to help players recognize their teammates. Some companies that have open floor plans color-code partitions and other furniture to visually define separate functions and responsibilities, such as General Mills, which uses different color schemes to separate the various departments at its headquarters. Because of the principle of similarity, the management style of top managers sets the stage for how the feedback and instructions of middle managers will be perceived by their subordinates.

3. **Proximity.** Stimuli that occur in the same proximity, either in space or in time, are often associated. For example, if you see two people together frequently, you will tend to attribute the characteristics you learn about one individual to the other, until your perceptions become more accurate. An illustration of proximity in time occurs when the boxes in the hall are removed on the same day that you complain about them. You may assume that your complaints led to their removal, without realizing that it would have occurred anyway.

4. **Closure.** Since most of the stimuli we perceive are incomplete, we naturally tend to extrapolate information and project additional information to form a complete picture. For example, a pole placed in front of a stop sign may prevent us from seeing the entire eight-sided figure. But since we have seen many stop signs before, the principle of closure causes us to "see" the complete sign. If we watch an employee work for fifteen minutes and complete the first half of a task, and return twenty minutes later to find the task completed, we attribute the entire task to the employee because of the principle of closure. However, we only saw this person perform half the task, and so our inference about the last half may be incorrect.

Perceiving social events and people is more difficult than perceiving physical objects. If two people disagree about the length of an object, they can measure it. But if they disagree about whether a supervisor is pleased with their work, they may have difficulty verifying which one is right, even if the supervisor's comments were filmed. Although the inferences we make about someone's personality should be based upon the behavior we observe, our perceptions are influenced by a variety of physical characteristics, such as appearance and speech.

The appearance of others influences how we perceive and respond to them, as has been amply demonstrated by the dress-for-success literature. Although many people, especially college students, feel somewhat repulsed by the implications of the research, the data nevertheless show that people who dress in conservative business attire are more likely to be hired, be promoted, make a sale, obtain service, and be treated as someone important[1] We generally assume that people who are dressed in business suits and uniforms are professional or technical employees performing their assigned functions. Therefore, we tend to respond to them with respect and deference, and willingly comply with their requests.

Perceptual organization
The process of organizing our perceptions into recognizable patterns. Four of the principles we use to assist in this effort include figure-ground separation, similarity, proximity, and closure.

On the other hand, we assume that people dressed in work clothes are lower-level employees, who possess little, if any, authority to tell us what to do. We are more likely to treat them in a discourteous manner.

How people speak also influences our perceptions of them. As we listen to people talk, we make rapid inferences about their personalities, backgrounds, and motives. We notice tone of voice to detect whether individuals are happy, sad, angry, or impatient. We notice the precision and clarity in the messages communicated to us, and we generally assume that a message spoken in a very emphatic and distinct manner is supposed to be carefully attended to. When individuals speak in a particular dialect or accent, we make inferences about their geographic and cultural background. The topics people choose to discuss not only reveal their educational training, but also their personal interests and ways of thinking. In a leaderless group discussion, a female student with a soft, nonassertive voice frequently has difficulty getting the other group members to listen to her ideas. On the other hand, individuals who speak with a distinct, authoritative tone of voice often receive greater credibility than their contributions deserve. A person speaking less than perfect English may be perceived as unintelligent although he or she may be fluent in many languages.

We also draw numerous inferences from nonverbal communications such as eye contact, hand motions, and posture. Sitting up straight, looking the other person in the eye, and nodding your head in agreement indicate to other people that you are interested, and they will perceive you as being friendly and concerned.

The way we organize and interpret environmental stimuli is also influenced by our own characteristics. How we feel about ourselves has an enormous effect on how we perceive others. When we understand ourselves and can accurately describe our own personal characteristics, we can more accurately perceive others. For example, secure people tend to see others as warm rather than cold, and our own sociability influences the importance we attach to the sociability of others. When we accept ourselves and have a positive self-image, we tend to see favorable characteristics in others. We are not as negative or critical about others if we accept ourselves as we are.

Our perceptions are also influenced by our cognitive complexity and our expectations. When we have complex thinking and reasoning structures, we are able to perceive small differences in what we see. **Cognitive complexity** allows us to differentiate people and events using multiple criteria, which increases the accuracy of our perceptions. Furthermore, we tend to see things that our past experience and personal values have taught us to see. If we are prepared and expecting to see something, we might see it even if it is not there.

Perceptual Errors

As we observe people and events, we make countless perceptual errors. This section analyzes six of the most frequent perceptual errors.

Halo Effect

The **halo effect** refers to the tendency to allow one personality trait to influence our perceptions of other traits. For example, if we see a person smiling and looking pleasant, we may conclude, as one study found, that the person is more honest than people who frown. However, there is no necessary connection between smiling and honesty. One potentially serious application of the halo effect is when it occurs in a performance evaluation. If one particular attribute, positive or negative, colors a supervisor's

Cognitive complexity
The degree to which individuals have developed complex categories for organizing information.

Halo effect
One of the perceptual errors in which individuals allow one characteristic about a person to influence their evaluations of other personality characteristics.

perception of other unrelated attributes, the performance evaluation process can be extremely unfair and misleading.

Selective Perception

The process of systematically screening out information we don't wish to hear is referred to as **selective perception**. This process is a learned response; we learn from past experience to ignore or overlook information that is uncomfortable and unpleasant. Occasionally we face stimuli that are so threatening or embarrassing that we refuse to perceive them, and this process is also called **perceptual defense**.

Implicit Personality Theories

Based on our interactions with many people, we create our own system of personality profiles and use them to categorize new acquaintances. To the extent that our personality profiles are accurate, they facilitate our ability to perceive more rapidly and accurately. Since each person is unique, however, our implicit personality theories can serve at best as only a rough approximation for categorizing people. If we continue to observe carefully, we may find that many of our expectations were not correct.

Projection

The tendency to attribute our own feelings and characteristics to others is called **projection**. As with other perceptual errors, projection is occasionally an efficient and reasonable perceptual strategy. If we don't like to be criticized, harassed, or threatened, it is reasonable to assume that others would not like it any better. However, projection usually refers to more than just attributing our thoughts and feelings to others. Instead it is used to describe the dysfunctional process of attributing to others the undesirable thoughts and traits we possess but are not willing to admit. In essence, we attribute or project onto others the negative characteristics or feelings we have about ourselves. Projection serves as a defense mechanism to protect our self-concept and makes us more capable of facing others, whom we see as imperfect.

First Impressions

When we meet people for the first time, we form impressions based on limited information that *should* be open for correction on subsequent encounters. Research evidence indicates, however, that first impressions are remarkably stable. In recruiting interviews, for example, it has been found that recruiters form a fairly stable impression of the applicant within the first three or four minutes. Negative first impressions seem to require abundant favorable information to change them, and some recruiters are so opinionated that they refuse to perceive contradictory information.

Allowing first impressions to have a disproportionate and lasting influence on later evaluations is known as the **primacy effect**. The primacy effect explains why the first few days on the job may have a

---

Selective perception
A source of perceptual errors caused by people choosing to perceive only the information that they find acceptable.

Implicit personality theories
The process of allowing our personal stereotypes and expectations regarding certain kinds of people to create a perceptual set that influences how we respond to other people.

Projection
A form of perceptual bias in which we project our own personal feelings and attitudes onto others as a means of helping us interpret their attitudes and feelings.

Primacy effect
The tendency for first impressions and early information to unduly influence our evaluations and judgment.

large impact on the attitudes and performance of new employees. Likewise, the opening comments in a committee meeting may have a lasting impact on the remainder of the group discussion because of the primacy effect.

Stereotyping

The process of **stereotyping** refers to categorizing individuals based on one or two traits, and attributing other characteristics to them based on their membership in that category. Stereotypes are frequently based on sex, race, age, religion, nationality, and occupation. Although stereotypes help us interpret information more rapidly, they also cause serious perceptual errors. When we create fixed categories based on variables such as sex, race, and age, and resist looking more carefully to confirm our expectations, we make serious perceptual errors that damage ourselves and others.

Since the passage of the Civil Rights Act (1964), significant progress has been made to reduce the use of stereotypes, particularly in hiring new employees. However, we continue to use stereotypes because they serve a useful purpose: they facilitate our rapid perception of others. Occasionally these stereotypes are very useful, especially age and sex stereotypes. For example, it is reasonable to guess that older workers are not as interested in new training programs and opportunities for promotion as younger workers are, because such differences have indeed been documented. Likewise, it may seem reasonable to think that female employees would be less interested in working overtime, since many women, especially those with small children in the home, find working overtime a particular burden. But, even if these assumptions are true in general, they are not necessarily true for a particular person. Some older workers may be very excited about a new training program, and some mothers may be very anxious to work overtime. Although it is impossible to confirm all our stereotypes, we should constantly question the accuracy of our perceptions, and maintain a flexible system of categories.

Discrimination and Prejudice

Illegal discrimination on the basis of race, religion, or sex typically occurs because of prejudice, which is defined as an unreasonable bias associated with suspicion, intolerance, or an irrational dislike for people of a particular race, religion, or sex. To understand the nature of prejudice, it is important to appreciate the psychological impact of individuality and uniqueness. The simple fact that one or two individuals differ significantly from other members of the group will cause them to be perceived and treated differently regardless of whether the differences are on the basis of race, religion, sex, or any other visible characteristic. This can best be illustrated by looking at the letters below.

X X x x x X x O x   X

If you studied this configuration briefly and then attempted to describe it, you would probably say that it consisted of some big and little *X*'s with an *O*. Unless you studied it carefully, you would probably not remember how many big *X*'s and little *x*'s there were or how they were arranged in the configuration, but you would probably remember the *O* and where it was located.

The same process occurs among a group of individuals when one or more individuals differ significantly from the others because of their unique sex or race. They are perceived differently, and they attract more attention, regardless of which race or sex constitutes the majority. This perceptual process occurs simply because the minority stands out from the majority. Three perceptual tendencies explain why minorities experience prejudice within the group: visibility, contrast, and assimilation.[3]

Stereotyping
The process of using a few attributes about an object to classify it and then responding to it as a member of a category rather than as a unique object.

Visibility

When a small percent of the group belong to a particular category, these individuals are more visible. Therefore, if a committee consisted of one female and several males, it is likely that everyone will remember where the woman sat in the committee meeting, what she wore, what she said, and how she voted. The minority tend to capture a larger share of the awareness within that group.

Contrast

When one or more individuals who are different are added to a group, their presence creates a self-consciousness among the dominant group about what makes them a separate class. Each group defines itself partly by knowing what it isn't. Consequently, a polarization and exaggeration of differences occurs, highlighting the differences between the minorities and majorities. Both groups become more aware of their commonalities and their differences, and group processes tend to accentuate the differences by creating stereotypes to separate the two groups.

Assimilation

The third perceptual tendency, assimilation, involves the application of stereotypes and familiar generalizations about a person's social category. Minority group members are not perceived as unique individuals but as representatives of a particular category. In essence, their behavior is assimilated into a stereotype of how members of their particular group are expected to behave. An illustration of assimilation is when a Japanese business executive who is meeting with a group of American executives is asked how other Japanese executives would react to a particular proposal. The question assumes that all Japanese executives respond alike, and that one person can represent them all.

Assimilation and contrast appear to be a function of how much effort people are willing to make to form accurate impressions. While some people challenge their assumptions and seek additional information, others label behavior and ignore uniqueness.

Prejudice and discrimination occur in a variety of settings and range in intensity from very innocent and unintended to very injurious and nasty. Some of the most obvious forms of racism and sexism include name-calling and slurs directed toward a specific individual. Such cruel behavior is considered entirely unacceptable in today's organizations; it is both immoral and illegal. Other forms of prejudice and discrimination, however, are much more subtle because the acts are not directed toward a specific individual and are often said in jest. Such behavior, however, is still considered inappropriate. Jokes and other comments that reflect negatively on another person's race or sex are both insulting and demeaning to everyone.

The Self-Fulfilling Prophecy

An interesting application of biased perceptions is the **self-fulfilling prophecy**, also called the **Pygmalion effect**.[4] We are not passive observers of our own social worlds, but active forces in shaping those worlds. To an important extent we create our own social reality by influencing the behavior we observe in others. The self-fulfilling prophecy explains how the expectations in the mind of one person about how others should behave are communicated in a variety of ways, until these individuals actually behave in the way expected. However, the self-fulfilling prophecy involves more than just one person having strong expectancies that influence the behavior of others. As illustrated in Exhibit 4.3, this process requires that:

Self-fulfilling prophecy
A phenomenon that occurs when a person acts in a way that confirms another's expectations.

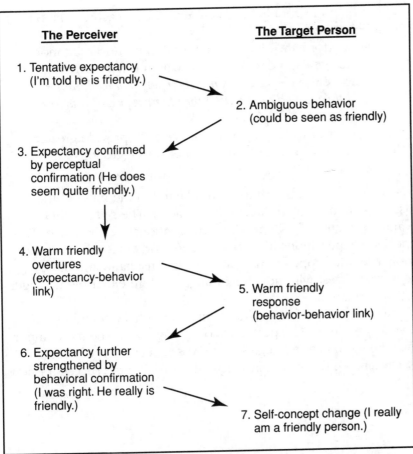

Exhibit 4.3   A Social Interaction Sequence in Which Both Perceptual and Behavioral Confirmation Create the Self-fulfilling Prophecy

Adapted from Edward E. Jones, "Interpreting Interpersonal Behavior: The Effects of Expectancies." *Science*, Vol. 234, (3 October 1986), p. 43.

- the expectation in the mind of the perceiver influences how the behavior of the target person is interpreted—the perceiver "sees" what he/she expects to see;
- thinking that the expectations are true, the perceiver then treats the target person differently;
- because of the differential treatment, the target person's behavior changes to confirm the perceiver's expectation;
- the perceiver views this behavior as unsolicited evidence that the expectancy was right all along.

Example—
A teacher was told that certain randomly selected students in her class were expected to make significant academic improvements that school year, based on the results of a fake test. At the end of the year, the performance of these randomly selected students was much greater than the other students, much to the surprise of the teacher when she was told about the experiment.

The self-fulfilling prophecy has been demonstrated in several experiments with both children and adults.[5] Four elements have been proposed to explain why the self-fulfilling prophecy occurs.

1. **Input.** Individuals who are expected to do well receive better ideas and suggestions than people who are expected to do poorly. As the quantity and quality of information increase, it helps them perform better, and communicates a sense of urgency and importance about the task.

2. **Output expected.** Specific comments about how much individuals are expected to achieve help them establish realistic levels of aspiration and higher performance goals.
3. **Reinforcement.** Individuals from whom high performance is expected tend to be rewarded more frequently when they achieve their performance goals. Individuals from whom low performance is expected usually perform poorly and are not reinforced. *But even if they perform well, they may not be rewarded, because their supervisors feel threatened or irritated that their expectations are disconfirmed.*
4. **Feedback.** Managers who communicate high performance expectations typically provide greater feedback. This feedback occurs more frequently, and usually contains specific suggestions for improvement.

The self-fulfilling prophecy normally starts when the expectations are planted in the mind of the leader. However, the expectations can also be communicated directly to the actor. The self-fulfilling prophecy has been recommended as a valuable strategy for improving organizational performance. The key is to start the sequence by creating positive expectations in managers and workers for themselves and the organization. Expectations can originate with upper management or a consultant, and must be both challenging and realistic. This strategy works best with new beginnings—before either the manager or workers have prior expectations about performance.

When new employees are introduced into an organization, the self-fulfilling prophecy contributes importantly to their career success. Some have argued that the expectations of managers may be more important than the skills and training of the new trainees in determining their success.[6] An analysis of management training programs suggests that the self-fulfilling prophecy is particularly crucial to the success of new managers.

PERSONALITY

Behavior has traditionally been explained as a combination of personality and environmental forces, as expressed by the formula: $B = fn\ (P,E)$. This formula suggests that our behavior at any given time is a combination of unique personality traits and the demands of the environment.

Personality traits refer to enduring characteristics that describe an individual's attitudes and behavior. Examples are friendliness, dominance, aggressiveness, and shyness. These traits are thought to be quite stable over time such that friendly people usually act friendly and welcome new associations. However, research has also shown that situational forces exert a much larger impact on behavior than personality factors. Indeed, several reviews of the research literature suggest that correlation coefficients are almost always less than .30 between any measured personality variable and actual behavior.[7] Most people find this quite surprising, because they believe the way we behave is a direct reflection of our personalities—friendly people are friendly, and aggressive people are aggressive. However, the evidence indicates that in a friendly environment everyone will be friendly, and in an aggressive environment even passive people will push back when they are pushed long enough. This tendency to overestimate the influence of personality in understanding human behavior is called the **fundamental attribution error**.

Although the impact of personality on behavior is usually rather small, it is not insignificant. Occasionally personality factors are sufficiently strong to overcome all environmental forces. Furthermore, over time people have an opportunity to create their own situations that match their personalities. **Attribution theory** examines how we assign responsibility to the person and the situation.

Personality
The attributes and predispositions associated with each individual that make that person unique and predict how that person will likely behave in many different situations.

Fundamental attribution error
The tendency to overestimate the influence of personality factors when interpreting the actions of people.

Attribution Theory

When we perceive social events, part of the perceptual process includes assigning responsibility for behavior. Are people responsible for their own behavior because of their personal characteristics, or were they forced to behave as they did because of the situation? The assignment of responsibility and the cognitive processes we use to understand why people act as they do are known as **attribution theory**.[8]

According to attribution theory, the assignment of responsibility stems from our observations of people over time. For example, if we observe a group of people attempting to use a word processor and find that many of them have difficulty getting the printer to function properly, we perceive the problem as being caused by the situation. But if only one person has difficulty with the printer, we attribute the cause of the problem to that individual's personal skills or abilities. Studies on attribution theory have generated the following conclusions:

1. When we observe someone else's behavior, we tend to overestimate the influence of personality traits and underestimate situational influences.
2. When we explain our own behavior, we tend to overestimate the importance of the situation and underestimate our own personality characteristics.

The explanation for these contrasting conclusions is that as actors we are more aware of the differing situations we face, and therefore we attribute our behavior to these differing situations. But since we are not as knowledgeable about the variety of situations others face, we overlook the situation and attribute their behavior to their personalities. This explanation has been confirmed by a study showing that when observers had empathy for another person, they were more likely to take the actor's perspective and were better able to notice situational causes for the actor's behavior. Conversely, distant observers tended to only notice personality characteristics.[9]

3. As we observe others in casual situations, we tend to attribute their successes to personality traits, such as effort and ability, and their failures to external factors, such as the difficulty of the task.

It is not clear why we attribute success to the person and failure to the situation in casual situations, but apparently this tendency does not extend to an organizational setting. In fact, studies of attribution in organizations suggest that the results are the opposite.

4. In evaluating the performance of employees, poor performance is generally attributed to internal personal factors, especially when the consequences are serious.

A study of nursing supervisors found that they were more likely to hold their employees accountable for poor performance as performance problems became more serious.[10] The behavior of subordinates reflects on their managers; therefore, when subordinates do well, managers are quick to accept partial credit for success; but when problems occur, they are quick to blame subordinates to exonerate themselves.

5. Employees tend to attribute their successes to internal factors and their failures to external causes.

Because of our need to maintain a positive self-image, we attribute our own successes to our personal skills and abilities. When we fail, however, we blame external causes.

Big Five Personality Model

Over the years, dozens of personality traits have been identified and numerous scales have been developed to measure them. Extensive research has attempted to associate the various personality dimensions

Attribution theory
A theory that explains how we assign responsibility for behavior either to personality characteristics or environmental circumstances.

with political behavior, leadership talent, interpersonal skills, and various pro-social behaviors. More recently, efforts have been made to consolidate these results and simplify our understanding of personality. The result has been the identification of five broad personality traits that seem to be conceptually different and empirically distinct. These five personality dimensions are called the **Big Five Model**:

1. **Conscientiousness** represents the degree to which an individual is dependable or inconsistent, can be counted on or is unreliable, follows through on commitments or reneges, and keeps promises or breaks them. Those who rate high on conscientiousness are generally perceived to be careful, thorough, organized, persistent, achievement oriented, hardworking, and persevering. Those who score lower on this dimension are more likely to be viewed as inattentive to detail, uncaring, disrespectful, not interested or motivated, unorganized, apt to give up easily, and lazy.

2. **Agreeableness** measures the degree to which people are friendly or reserved, cooperative or guarded, flexible or inflexible, trusting or cautious, good-natured or moody, soft-hearted or tough, and tolerant or judgmental. Those scoring high on the first element of these paired traits are viewed as agreeable and easy to work with, while those rating low are viewed as more disagreeable and difficult to work with. Being too agreeable could cause people to be too accommodating, however, and others may take advantage of this weakness.

3. **Emotional stability** (versus Neuroticism) characterizes the degree to which people are consistent or inconsistent in how they react to certain events, they react impulsively or weigh their options before acting, and they take things personally or look at the situation objectively. Those who rate high on emotional stability are viewed as generally poised, calm, able to manage their anger, secure, happy, and objective. Those who rate low are more likely to be anxious, depressed, angry, insecure, worried, and emotional.

4. **Openness to experience** characterizes the degree to which people are interested in broadening their horizons or limiting them, learning new things or sticking with what they already know, meeting new people or associating with current friends and co-workers, going to new places or restricting themselves to known places. Individuals who score high on this factor tend to be highly intellectual, broad-minded, curious, imaginative, and cultured. Those who rate lower tend to be more narrow-minded, less interested in the outside world, and uncomfortable in unfamiliar surroundings and situations. Professionals who are open to experience are more willing to contemplate on feedback for personal development.

5. **Extroversion** represents the degree to which people are outgoing, social, assertive, active, and talkative. The opposite is **introversion**, which refers to those who are shy, antisocial, passive, and quiet. Extroversion or introversion, in itself, is not necessarily bad, but extremes at both ends of the spectrum can be equally dysfunctional. A person who is too outgoing could be perceived as overbearing, and a person who is too reserved would lack the skills to relate to others.

These five personality dimensions are somewhat related to work-related behaviors and how well people perform on the job.[11] For example, jobs involving conflict situations, such as customer relations, are generally performed better by people who measure high in agreeableness. And, people with high emotional stability tend to work better in high stress situations than those who score high on neuroticism. However, these correlations are generally too small to be useful in employee selection and placement. The best trait for predicting job performance and organizational citizenship behaviors has been conscientiousness. This dimension appears to be a valuable personal attribute that is relevant to a broad range of jobs. Conscientious employees set higher personal goals for themselves, are more highly motivated, and have higher performance expectations than employees with low conscientiousness.

Other Personality Dimensions

Three additional personality traits that contribute to our understanding of individual differences in organizations are the locus of control, self-esteem, and self-efficacy.

Locus of Control

The **locus of control** refers to the degree to which individuals believe that their actions influence the rewards they receive in life. Individuals with an **internal locus of control** believe that the rewards they receive are internally controlled by their own actions, whereas individuals with an **external locus of control** believe external forces such as luck, chance, or fate control their lives and determine their rewards and punishments.[12] If an unexpected opportunity for advancement were presented to two people, the externally controlled individual would probably attribute it to luck or being in the right place at the right time. The internally controlled individual would be more inclined to attribute the opportunity to hard work, effort, and knowledge. As with other personality factors, however, people vary along a continuum and cannot be neatly placed into one category or the other.

Individuals behave differently depending on whether they believe their rewards are internally or externally controlled. In contrast to externals, internals believe that how hard they work will determine how well they perform and how well they will be rewarded. Consequently, internals generally perceive more order and predictability in their job-related outcomes, and usually report higher levels of job satisfaction.[13] Since managers are required to initiate goal-directed activity, it is not surprising that they tend to be internally controlled.

In times of upheaval and disruption, externals generally experience more frustration and anxiety than internals and are less able to cope with the situation. A study of how people responded to a flood following a hurricane found that externals were more concerned than internals about coping with their own tension and frustration. They tended to withdraw from the task of rebuilding and to express bitterness and aggression about the "rotten hand" they had been dealt. Internals, on the other hand, went immediately to the task of acquiring new loans, gathering new resources, and rebuilding their homes and businesses. Obviously, no one could have prevented the storm from happening, but the internals had faith that an active, problem-solving response could determine whether the flood would be a conclusive tragedy or only a temporary setback.[14]

The locus of control is determined largely by an individual's past experiences. Internals are the product of an environment where their behaviors largely decided their outcomes, while externals experienced futility in trying to set their own rewards. Child-rearing practices are thought to have an important influence on the development of locus of control: an internal locus of control is created by predictable and consistent discipline, by parental support and involvement, and by parental encouragement of autonomy and self-control. Some evidence also suggests that the locus of control can be influenced over a long period of time by the way employees are reinforced at work. At least one study has shown that the locus of control becomes more internal as a result of exposure to a work environment where important rewards are consistently associated with individual behavior.[15]

Self-Esteem

Our self-concept is presumed to be a particularly human manifestation, and refers to our own conscious awareness of who we are. We see ourselves relative to others, and form evaluative impressions about our skills, abilities, and behaviors. Our self-concept is a collection of the attitudes, values, and beliefs we have acquired about ourselves from our unique experiences. We form opinions about our behavior, ability, appearance, and overall worth as a person from our own observations and the feedback we receive from others.

Locus of control
A personality trait that is determined by whether individuals think the rewards they obtain are based on internal factors such as knowledge, effort, and skill, or external factors such as luck, chance, and fate.

Over time, our accumulated experiences establish our self-concept. This self-concept determines how we feel about ourselves, and influences how we respond to others. Individuals with high self-esteem are generally more creative, independent, and spontaneous in their interactions with others. Because of their positive feelings about themselves, they can concentrate on the issues at hand and focus on new and original ideas without being as concerned about how people feel about them. On the other hand, people with low self-esteem tend to feel overly concerned about the evaluations of others, which dilute their ability to concentrate on problems and to think creatively. Their low self-esteem often causes them to withdraw from the task or social situation.

Extensive research has shown that the behaviors of individuals are consistent with their self-concepts. Students, for example, who see themselves as competent academic achievers quite consistently perform better in school than students who don't. Individuals with high self-esteem are generally more accurate in their perceptions of social situations than those with low self-esteem.[16]

Problems of low self-esteem are often attributed to inadequate positive reinforcement from others. Although people with low self-esteem have usually experienced less praise than others, the solution is not to simply give them more praise and recognition. Our self-esteem is greatly influenced by how well we have actually performed. Although the comments of others help us interpret our performance, how well we have actually done has a greater impact on our self-esteem. Therefore, in raising an individual's self-esteem, praise and compliments may not be as effective as actually helping the individual perform better.

Self-Efficacy

Self-efficacy refers to one's belief in one's capability to perform a specific task. In many respects the concept of self-efficacy is similar to the concepts of self-esteem and locus of control. However, self-efficacy is task-specific rather than a generalized perception of overall competence.

Self-efficacy emerged from the research on social cognitive theory, and represents an important personality variable that explains variations in individual performance. Several studies suggest that self-efficacy is a better predictor of subsequent performance than past behavior is.[17] Although knowing how well people have performed in the past helps to predict their future performance, an even better predictor is knowing how capable they feel regarding a specific task.[18]

Self-efficacy has three dimensions: magnitude, strength, and generality. **Magnitude** refers to the level of task difficulty that a person believes he or she can attain, and is related to the concept of goal-setting. Some people think they can achieve very difficult goals. **Strength** refers to the amount of confidence one has in one's ability to perform, and it can be strong or weak. Some people have strong convictions that they will succeed even when they face difficult challenges. **Generality** indicates the degree to which one's expectations are generalized across many situations or restricted to an isolated instance. Some people believe they can succeed in a variety of situations.

Self-efficacy is a learned characteristic that is acquired by four kinds of information cues:

1. **Enactive mastery**: The most influential stimulus contributing to the development of self-efficacy is enactive mastery, which refers to the repeated performance or practicing of the task. For example, a nurse who has inserted many IV needles should have high self-efficacy in being able to do it again.
2. **Vicarious experience**: Observing the behavior of others (modeling) can be almost as effective as enactive mastery, especially when the person and the model are similar in terms of age, capability, and other characteristics, and when the model's behavior is clearly visible.
3. **Verbal persuasion**: In the development of self-efficacy, verbal persuasion is less effective than practicing or modeling; nevertheless, it can be an important source of efficacy information, especially if the source has high credibility and expertise, and if there are multiple sources who agree.

Self-efficacy
A belief in one's ability to perform a specific activity, determined primarily by how well the person has learned and practiced the task.

4. **Perceptions of one's physiological state**: Efficacy perceptions are influenced by momentary levels of arousal as illustrated by these statements of athletes: "We were ready for them," "They were really up for this game," "I was mentally prepared," and "He was really psyched for this match."

Efficacy perceptions appear to be self-reinforcing. Self-efficacy influences the kinds of activities and settings people choose to participate in, the skills they are willing to practice and learn, the amount of energy they are willing to exert, and the persistence of their coping efforts in the face of obstacles. People with high self-efficacy tend to engage more frequently in task-related activities and persist longer in coping efforts; this leads to more mastery experiences, which enhance their self-efficacy. People with low self-efficacy tend to engage in fewer coping efforts; they give up more easily under adversity and demonstrate less mastery, which in turn reinforces their low self-efficacy.[19]

Self-efficacy can predict performance in a variety of settings, as long as the efficacy measure is tailored to the specific tasks being performed. Consequently, efficacy perceptions are relevant in many organizational settings, such as employee selection, training and development, and vocational counseling. Employees with high self-efficacy would be expected to respond more favorably to most personnel programs, such as performance evaluation, financial incentives, and opportunities for promotion.[20]

ATTITUDES

Attitudes are involved in almost every aspect of organizational life. Employees have attitudes about hundreds of things, including their pay, their supervisors, top management, the work they do, and their co-workers. Outstanding employees are commended for their "good attitudes," while uncooperative workers are reprimanded for having "bad attitudes." Managers worry about how their decisions will influence employee attitudes, and whether the employees will resist change. Events that occur away from work influence the attitudes of employees, who carry these attitudes into the work setting. People can control their attitudes and how they react to them. When you are stuck in traffic you can choose to be angry and pound on the steering wheel or you can calmly accept the situation and listen to a radio program.

An attitude is a **hypothetical construct**; it is not a physical reality or something you can see, taste, or touch. Consequently, it is something that exists only because we can define it or infer it from the things people say or do. An attitude is defined as the positive or negative feelings we hold toward an object. Therefore, when we speak of positive job attitudes we refer to the pleasant feelings we have when we think about our jobs. It is possible to have positive feelings about some aspects of the job and negative feelings about other aspects. The early research on attitudes identified three attitude components: cognitive, affective, and behavioral tendency.

- The **cognitive component** consists of the beliefs and information a person possesses about the attitude object. This information includes descriptive data such as facts, figures, and other specific knowledge.
- The **affective component** consists of the person's feelings and emotions toward the attitude object. This component involves evaluation and reaction, and is often expressed as a liking or disliking for the attitude object.
- The **behavioral tendency component** refers to the way the person intends to behave toward the object, such as whether the person intends to follow, help, injure, abandon, or ignore the attitude object.

Hypothetical construct
An abstract concept regarding the relationships between people and events that exists because we can operationally define it even though it does not have a physical reality. Satisfaction, intelligence, commitment, and honesty are examples.

Emotions

The affective component of attitudes consists mostly of emotions and feelings. Our emotions are complex reactions that have both physiological and psychological implications. Emotions come from a different location in the brain than the location where cognitions are stored. In the formation of attitudes and perceptions, we often think that the cognitive component creates the affective component: that is, knowledge and beliefs come first, followed by feelings and emotions. According to neuroscience research, however, incoming information from our senses is routed to the emotional center as well as the cognitive (logical reasoning) center of our brain. Therefore, our emotions play an important role in determining how we process new information and anticipate responding to it.[21]

The process of attitude formation in influenced by the way emotions impact the perceptual interpretation process described earlier. When receiving incoming information, the emotional center quickly and *imprecisely* evaluates whether the new information supports or threatens our innate drives, and then attaches emotional markers to the information. These are not calculated feelings; they are automatic and unconscious emotional responses based on very transient sensory information. Positive emotions create positive attitudes.

Example—

An employee who hears about a possible merger with a competitor may strongly object to the planned merger due to a fear of being replaced. Another employee may feel excited about the merger and welcome the potential changes. While the merger represents a threat to the first person, the second person perceives it as an opportunity.

An understanding of emotions helps us interpret our own behavior and analyze the reactions of others. Some people are much better than others when it comes to interpreting emotions and knowing how to manage them appropriately. **Emotional intelligence (EI)** refers to the set of competencies that allow us to perceive, understand, and regulate emotions in ourselves and others. People with high levels of emotional intelligence have the ability to express and perceive emotions, assimilate emotions in their thoughts, understand and reason with emotion, and regulate emotions in themselves and others. Emotional intelligence is organized into four dimensions representing (a) the *recognition* of emotions in ourselves versus others and (b) the *regulation* of emotions in ourselves versus others:

- **Self awareness**: Self-awareness refers to understanding our own emotions as well as our strengths, weaknesses, values, and motives. Self-aware people are better able to describe their emotional responses to specific situations, and to use this awareness as conscious information.
- **Self-management**: Self-management represents how consistently we control our internal feelings, impulses, and reactions. It includes keeping disruptive impulses in check, acting with honesty and integrity, having flexibility in times of change, maintaining the drive to perform well and to seize opportunities, and remaining optimistic even after failure.
- **Social awareness**: Social awareness is mainly about empathy, which involves understanding another person's situation, experiencing the other person's emotions, and knowing that person's needs even though they are unstated. Empathy is a crucial skill in effective communication.
- **Relationship management**: This dimension refers to managing other people's emotions. It is linked to a wide variety of interpersonal skills that are discussed in other chapters, such as developing other's capabilities, supporting teamwork and collaboration, resolving conflict, influencing people's beliefs and attitudes, inspiring others, and managing change.

Emotional intelligence (EI)
The competencies that allow us to perceive, understand, and regulate emotions in ourselves and others.

The acquisition of these four competencies is mostly a sequential process that starts with acquiring self-awareness. Until you are aware of your own emotions and have some skill in recognizing them and talking about them, it is unlikely that you will be prepared to regulate your emotions or recognize the emotions of others. At the other extreme, relationship management cannot occur effectively until you have mastered the competencies of the other three dimensions; you cannot reasonably expect to manage other people's emotions unless you can recognize them and also know how to regulate your own emotions.

Although we still have much to learn about emotional intelligence, it appears to be an important attribute that contributes to a person's effectiveness on the job. People with higher levels of emotional intelligence are more skilled in interpersonal relations, they perform better in jobs requiring emotional understanding, and they are more successful in many aspects of job interviews. Teams with members who have high emotional intelligence initially perform better than teams with lower levels. Emotional intelligence appears to be a personality trait that is associated with conscientiousness; however, it can also be learned by training programs that describe and demonstrate various emotions.[22]

The Relationship between Attitudes and Behavior

We often assume that attitudes cause behavior; therefore, if you want to get people to change their behavior, you must first get them to change their attitudes. Unfortunately, the relationship is much more complex. The relationship between attitudes and behavior appears to be a reciprocal interaction in which each factor influences the other, as shown in Exhibit 4.4. Attitudes influence behavior by first influencing the behavioral intentions, whereas behavior influences attitudes by requiring individuals to justify their behavior.

Behavioral Intentions

Most of our attitudes do not have a direct impact on our behavior. We have an enormous number of attitudes about countless objects, and only a small percent of these attitudes ever get translated into behavior. An intervening process between attitudes and behavior is **behavioral intentions**, a term that refers to the extent to which we actually expect to perform a given act.

Intentions are similar to motives or desires; they can be very specific, such as to call a client or to take a patient's blood pressure, or they can also be very general, such as to increase sales or to provide quality patient care. According to the model, attitudes affect behavior only to the extent that they influence our intentions to act.

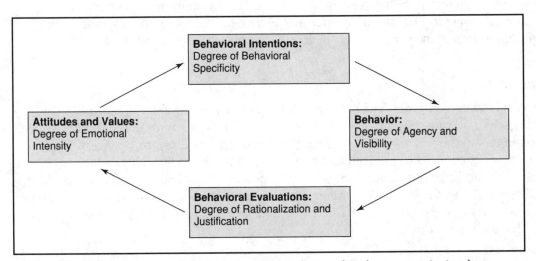

Exhibit 4.4   A Model Showing the Relationship between Attitudes and Behavior

How are behavioral intentions formed? The model indicates that behavioral intentions are influenced to some extent by attitudes, but they are also influenced by other situational forces that may be more important:

- Reinforcement contingencies providing specific rewards or punishments;
- Normative pressures from peer expectations and group norms;
- Random situational influences and alternative behaviors.

Specificity of Intentions

Goal setting and reward expectations have a sizable impact on our behavioral intentions and help us develop specific intentions to act. Specific intentions, once formed, are usually associated with specific behaviors. Four elements determine the degree of specificity:

1. How well the particular behavior has been visualized in clear detail;
2. Whether the target object toward which the behavior will be directed has been determined;
3. How clearly the situational context in which the behavior will be performed has been defined, including where and with whom;
4. Whether the time when the behavior should occur has been established.

Each of these elements helps to determine whether the behavior is specifically identified or only loosely contemplated. The most specific situation involves an intention to perform a clearly defined act toward a specific target in a defined place at a given time.

Example—

The behavioral intention to "learn something about computers as soon as it's convenient" is a very loosely defined behavioral intention that would not have as much impact on behavior as the behavioral intention to "meet Larry in the computer lab tomorrow at 10:00 A.M. to learn how to download a program." To the extent that distinct behaviors are specifically articulated, the intentions are more closely tied to actual behavior.

This model contains some key insights into attitudes and behavior. To change the behavior of people, it is much more productive to focus directly on changing their behavioral intentions than indirectly trying to change their attitudes. Specific behavioral intentions are much more likely to lead to behavior than general intentions are.

Example—

If employees have been negligent in accomplishing a task (e.g., accounting reports or safety inspections) it is more effective to help them set specific behavioral intentions to complete it than to lecture them about the importance of the task, which they probably already understand.

Behavioral Evaluations

The reciprocal interaction between attitudes and behaviors, as illustrated in Exhibit 4.4, illustrates the way our behavior changes our attitudes. The intervening process between behavior and attitudes, called **behavioral evaluations**, refers to the process of interpreting and making sense of our behavior. We do not view ourselves or others as capricious, random actors. We like to think of ourselves as rational beings whose behavior is conscious and planned. Therefore, we feel a need to explain and justify our behavior both to others and especially to ourselves. According to consistency theory and cognitive dissonance theory, our attitudes and behaviors need to be in harmony. When they are dissonant, the easiest way to create harmony is by changing our attitudes.

According to this model, the effects of behavior on attitudes depend on our felt need to justify our behavior. Therefore, the amount of attitude change increases as the need to justify behavior increases. This occurs when

- individuals are asked to explain their behavior;
- the explanation is a public declaration;
- there are alternative ways to behave;
- they are free to choose how to behave.

When people misbehave, they will probably rationalize and justify their misbehavior, which means their attitudes will change more than their behavior. Although people may have a negative emotional feeling the first time they misbehave, each succeeding time will be easier to justify. Employees who do things wrong (e.g., falsify an expense account or exceed the speed limit) may feel guilty the first time they do it. But, they will rationalize the mistake and feel less guilty in time as they continue doing it.

Example—
The first time a partner in a law firm added a few hours to the billing statement that his firm submitted to the government for consulting work he felt a little guilty. But as he continued to add even more hours, he rationalized that his firm deserved the added revenue since the government rates for consulting were less than the rates for private industry. Eventually he was convicted of fraud although he claimed he had done nothing really wrong.

Job Satisfaction

Job satisfaction consists of the attitudes employees hold regarding factors in their work environment, particularly pay and benefits, the characteristics of the job, supervision, fellow workers, and opportunities for advancement. Managers are concerned about the job satisfaction of their employees because high job satisfaction contributes to organizational commitment, job involvement, improved physical and mental health, and a greater quality of life both on and off the job. On the other hand, job dissatisfaction contributes to absenteeism, turnover, labor problems, labor grievances, attempts to organize a labor union, and a negative organizational climate.

Satisfaction and Performance

Our primary interest in job satisfaction stems from the common belief that satisfaction is directly tied to productivity—that happy workers will be productive workers. To stimulate higher levels of productivity, therefore, managers need to create better jobs and a better work environment. Unfortunately, the relationship between satisfaction and productivity is not this simple. Lazy workers may also be highly satisfied, perhaps because they are allowed to laugh and loiter on the job without any pressure to change. Hundreds of studies examining the relationship between satisfaction and productivity have produced both positive and negative correlations, but most correlations have only been slightly positive and not statistically significant.[23] Some have even suggested reversing the direction of the relationship claiming that productivity determines satisfaction—that happiness comes from succeeding on the job and being highly productive.[24]

Rather than causing each other, both satisfaction and productivity are determined by the reward structure in each respective situation. Employees generally express high levels of job satisfaction when they feel rewarded and recognized at work and when their expectations are met or exceeded. Productivity depends on the reinforcement. Employees tend to be highly productive when important rewards are directly tied to their job performance. This means that the correlations between satisfaction and productivity could be either positive or negative depending on how employees are rewarded. When employees are rewarded for their performance, the most productive employees will be the most satisfied because they receive the most rewards. When everyone is rewarded equally, however, the relationship may be zero or possibly negative because the most productive employees may be disappointed about not getting what they think they deserve.[25]

Attendance: Absenteeism and Tardiness

Absenteeism and tardiness are sometimes referred to as withdrawal or avoidance behaviors and they are consistently, although only moderately, related to job satisfaction. Individuals who are highly satisfied with their jobs are seldom absent from work, and faithfully see that their job is performed in spite of personal illnesses, family emergencies, or bad weather. Individuals who are unhappy or dissatisfied at work tend to miss work or come late more frequently than those who are satisfied.

Turnover

Turnover is caused mostly by job dissatisfaction and favorable economic conditions. The highest turnover levels are found in companies where employees report the greatest dissatisfaction. Employees also tend to leave their jobs when alternative jobs that better satisfy their needs become available. Consequently, turnover levels are generally high in companies with poor working conditions, undesirable jobs, wage inequities, poor communication, and limited opportunities for advancement.

Mental and Physical Health

Studies have found that job satisfaction contributes to better overall mental and physical health, while dissatisfaction caused by stress, conflict, and boredom at work contribute to higher incidences of death due to heart disease. The two most important job attributes for good mental and physical health seem to be (1) challenging work and (2) opportunities to use one's abilities and skills. Some research has even found that job satisfaction influences one's life expectancy. An analysis of numerous physical and attitudinal variables, including physical conditioning and tobacco use, revealed that the single best predictor of longevity was work satisfaction. Those who felt their work was meaningful and useful outlived their less satisfied co-workers.[26]

Job Involvement

Job involvement refers to the strength of the relationship between an individual's work and his or her self-concept. Individuals are said to be highly involved in their job if they actively participate in it, view it as a central life interest, and see their job and how well they perform it as a central part of their self-concept.[27]

People who are highly involved in their jobs tend to be ego-involved with their work. They spend long hours working at their jobs, and think about them when they are away from work. If a project they have completed fails, they may feel intense frustration and despair. When they perform poorly, they feel embarrassed and disappointed. Since they identify with their work, they want others to know them for their work and to know that they do it well. For them, work is the most important aspect of life.

Individuals tend to have greater job involvement if they are committed to the work ethic, and if they define their self-concepts according to their performance. Higher job involvement is also associated with how long they have performed their jobs and whether they have meaningful opportunities to make important decisions.

Individuals who are highly involved in their jobs tend to be more satisfied than those who are not as involved. They are also generally happier with the organization, more committed to it, and absent less frequently. This evidence suggests that job involvement is a desirable characteristic that managers ought to encourage.

Some individuals, however, become so highly involved in their job that they become workaholics. A **workaholic** is someone who is literally addicted to work, which by definition is an unhealthy condition.[28] This need to work incessantly can arise from many different sources. People may feel anxious or guilt

Workaholics
People so involved in their work that they are addicted to working and unable to pursue other meaningful activities without feeling nervous, anxious, or guilty.

ridden and turn to work as a means to salve their conscience; or they may suffer from feelings of insecurity and turn to work to obtain a sense of permanence, usefulness, and competence. Some people rely on their work to support their feelings of self-righteousness and self-worth.

Organizational Commitment

Organizational commitment refers to the relative strength of an individual's identification with and involvement in an organization. Three characteristics are associated with organizational commitment:[29]

- a strong belief in and acceptance of the organization's values and goals, called **normative commitment**;
- a strong emotional attachment to the organization and a willingness to exert considerable effort in behalf of it, called **affective commitment**;
- a strong desire to maintain membership in the organization, called **continuance commitment**.

These three characteristics suggest that organizational commitment involves more than mere passive loyalty to the organization. It involves an active relationship with the organization, in which employees are willing to give of themselves and make a personal contribution to help the organization succeed. Studies on organizational commitment have identified four primary factors that contribute to organizational commitment.[30]

1. *Personal factors.* Organizational commitment is generally higher among older and more tenured employees. Those who have greater intrinsic work values are more committed. As a group, female employees tend to be more committed to organizations than males, and employees who have less education also tend to display more commitment than highly educated employees.
2. *Role-related characteristics.* Organizational commitment tends to be stronger among employees in enriched jobs and jobs that involve low levels of role conflict and ambiguity.
3. *Structural characteristics.* Organizational commitment is stronger among employees in worker-owned cooperatives and among employees in decentralized organizations, who are more involved in making critical organizational decisions.
4. *Work experiences.* Organizational commitment tends to be stronger among employees who have had favorable experiences at work, such as positive group attitudes among one's peers, feelings that the organization has met the employee's expectations, feelings that the organization could be relied upon to fulfill its commitments to its personnel, and feelings that the individual is important to the organization. Employees manifest higher levels of commitment when firms have well-developed recruitment and orientation procedures, and well defined organizational value systems.

Employees who have high levels of either affective or continuance commitment generally have better attendance records and are more likely to stay with the company. Job performance, however, is generally only correlated with affective commitment. Individuals who have high levels of affective commitment tend to be more satisfied with their jobs, they feel better about their opportunities for career advancement, and they find greater fulfillment in life away from work.

NOTES

1. J. T. Malloy, *Dress for Success* (New York: Warner Books, 1975); M. Snyder, E. D. Tanke, E. Berscheid "Social perception and interpersonal behavior: on the self-fulfilling nature of social stereotypes" *Journal of Personality and Social Psychology*, vol. 35 (1977), p. 656–666.
2. Douglas McGregor, *The Human Side of Enterprise* (New York: McGraw-Hill, 1960).
3. Rosabeth Moss Kanter, *Men and Women of the Corporation* (New York: Basic Books, 1977), Chapter 8.
4. Robert Rosenthal and L. Jacobson, *Pygmalion in the Classroom* (New York: Holt, Reinhardt, and Winston, 1968).
5. Ibid. See also Jack Horn "Pygmalion vs. Golem in a high school gym." *Psychology Today*, vol. 18, (July 1984), pp. 9–10.

6. J. Sterling Livingston, "Pygmalion in Management," *Harvard Business Review*, (July-August 1969), pp. 81–89; L. Sandler, "Self-fulfilling prophecy: Better training by Mayle." *Training: The Magazine of Human Resource Development*, vol. 23, (Feb. 1986), p. 60–64.

7. Lee Ross and Richard E. Nisbett, *The Person and the Situation*. (New York: McGraw Hill, 1991).

8. F. Heider, *The Psychology of Interpersonal Behavior* (New York: Wiley, 1958); Steven E. Kaplan, "Improving Performance Evaluation", *CMA—The Management Accounting Magazine*, vol. 61, (May-June, 1987), p. 56–59.

9. Jean M. Bartunek, "Why Did You Do That? Attribution Theory in Organizations," *Business Horizons*, vol. 24, No. 5, (1981) pp. 66–71; Edward E. Jones and Richard E. Naisbett, *The Actor and the Observer, Divergent Perceptions of the Causes of Behavior* (Morristown, N.J.: General Learning Press, 1971); J. C. McElroy and C. B. Shrader, "Attribution theories of leadership and network analysis," *Journal of Management*, vol. 12, (Fall 1986), pp. 35.

10. Harold H. Kelley and John L. Michela, "Attribution Theory and Research," *Annual Review of Psychology* (1980), pp. 457–501.; Terence R. Mitchell and Robert E. Wood, "Supervisors' Responses to Subordinate Poor Performance: A Test of an Attributional Model," *Organizational Behavior and Human Performance* (1980), pp. 123–128.

11. A. Witt, L. A. Burke, and M. R. Barrick, "The Interactive Effects of Conscientiousness and Agreeableness on Job Performance," *Journal of Applied Psychology* 87 (2002) 164–169.

12. Julian B. Rotter, "Generalized Expectancies for Internal Versus External Control of Reinforcement," *Psychological Monographs*, vol. 80, 1966, pp. 1–28.

13. Virginia T. Geurin and Gary F. Kohut, "The Relationship of Locus of Control and Participative Decision Making Among Managers and Business Students," *Mid-Atlantic Journal of Business*, vol. 25, (February 1989), p. 57–66; Mia Lokman, "Participation in Budgetary Decision Making, Task Difficulty, Locus of Control, and Employee Behavior: An Empirical Study", *Decision Sciences*, vol. 18, (Fall 1987), pp. 547–561; Paul E. Spector, "Development of the Work Locus of Control Scale," *Journal of Occupational Psychology*, vol. 61, (December 1988), p. 335–340.

14. C. Anderson, Donald Hellriegel, and John Slocum, "Managerial Response to Environmentally Induced Stress," *Academy of Management Journal*, vol. 20, 1977, pp. 260–272; see also Phillip L. Storms and Paul E. Spector, "Relationships of Organizational Frustration with Reported Behaviorial Reactions: The Moderating Effect of Locus of Control," *Journal of Occupational Psychology*, vol. 60, (December 1987), pp. 227–234.

15. S. Eitzen, "Impact of Behavior Modification Techniques on Locus of Control of Delinquent Boys," *Psychological Reports*, vol. 35 (1974), pp. 1317–1318; Charles J. Cox and Gary L. Cooper, "The Making of the British CEO: Childhood, Work Experience, Personality, and Management Style," *Academy of Management Executive*, vol. 3, (August 1989), pp. 241–245.

16. R. H. Combs and V. Davies, "Self-conception and the relationship between high school and college scholastic achievement," *Sociology and Social Research*, vol. 50, (1966), pp. 460–471; B. Borislow, "Self-evaluation and academic achievement," *Journal of Counseling Psychology*, vol. 9, (1962), pp. 246–254; D. E. Hamachek, ed. *The Self in Growth, Teaching, and Learning*. (Englewood Cliffs, N.J.: Prentice-Hall, 1965).

17. Albert Bandura, "Self-Efficacy: Toward a Unifying Theory of Behaviorial Change," *Psychological Review*, vol. 84, (1977), p. 191–215; Albert Bandura, "Self-Efficacy Mechanism in Human Agency," *American Psychologist*, vol. 37, (1982), p. 122–147; Albert Bandura, N. E. Adams, A. B. Hardy, G. N. Howells, "Tests of the Generality of Self-Efficacy Theory," *Cognitive Therapy and Research*, vol. 4, (1980), p. 39–66.

18. John Lane and Peter Herriot, "Self-Ratings, Supervisor Ratings, Positions and Performance," *Journal of Occupational Psychology*, vol. 63, (March 1990), p. 77–88; Robert Wood, Albert Bandura, and Trevor Bailey, "Mechanisms Governing Organizational Performance in Complex Decision-Making Environments," *Organizational Behavior and Human Decision Processes*, vol. 46, (August 1990), p. 181–201.

19. Albert Bandura, D. H. Shunk, "Cultivating Confidence, Self-Efficacy, and Intrinsic Interest Through Proximal Self Motivation," *Journal of Personality and Social Psychology*, vol. 41, (1981), p. 586–598.

20. Marilyn E. Gist, "Self-Efficacy: Implications for Organizational Behavior and Human Resource Management," *Academy of Management Review*, vol. 12, (July 1987), p. 472–485.

21. R. H. Fazio, "On the Automatic Activation of Associated Evaluations: An Overview," *Cognition and Emotion* 15 (2001): 115–141.

22. P. N. Lopes et al., "Emotional Intelligence and Social Interaction," *Personality and Social Psychology Bulletin* 30, (2004): 1018–1034.

23. A. H. Brayfield and W. H. Crockett, "Employee Attitudes and Employee Performance," *Psychological Bulletin*, vol. 52 (1955), pp. 396–424; Dennis W. Organ, "A Restatement of the Satisfaction-Performance Hypothesis," *Journal of Management*, vol. 14 (December 1988), pp. 547–557.

24. Edward E. Lawler, III, and Lyman W. Porter, "The Effect of Performance on Job Satisfaction," *Industrial Relations, A Journal of Economy and Society*, vol. 7, no. 1 (October 1967), pp. 20–28.

25. David J. Cherrington, H. Joseph Reitz, and William E. Scott, Jr., "Effects of Contingent and Non-Contingent Reward on the Relationship between Satisfaction and Task Performance," *Journal of Applied Psychology*, vol. 55 (1971), pp. 531–537; Dennis W. Organ, "A Reappraisal and Reinterpretation of the Satisfaction-Causes-Performance Hypothesis," *Academy of Management Journal*, vol. 2, (no. 1, 1977), pp. 46–53.

26. E. Palmore, "Predicting Longevity: A Follow-Up Controlling for Age," *Gerontologist*, vol. 9 (1969), pp. 247–250.

27. S. D. Saleh and J. Hosek, "Job Involvement: Concepts and Measurements," *Academy of Management Journal*, vol. 19 (1976), pp. 213–224.

28. David J. Cherrington, *The Work Ethic: Working Values and Values That Work* (New York: AMACOM Publishing, 1980), Ch. 12.

29. Natalie J. Allen and John P. Meyer, "The Measurement and Antecedents of Affective, Continuance, and Normative Commitments to the Organization," *Journal of Occupational Psychology*, vol. 63 (1990), pp. 1–18.

30. Richard M. Steers, "Antecedents and Outcomes of Organizational Commitment," *Administrative Science Quarterly*, vol. 22 (1977), pp. 46–56.

Understanding Groups and Teams

GROUP FORMATION

Groups and work teams are a central part of our everyday lives, and at any given time we are members of many groups, such as work teams, student clubs, church groups, athletic teams, professional associations, dormitory groups, political parties, and our families. At any one time the average individual belongs to five or six groups. The study of group dynamics is important for two reasons:

1. Groups exert an enormous influence on the attitudes, values, and behaviors of individuals. Groups teach us how to behave and help us understand who we are. Unique behavior occurs within groups because of group roles and norms;
2. Groups have a powerful influence on other groups and organizations. Much of the work that gets done in organizations is done by teams within the larger organization, and the success of an organization is limited by the effectiveness of its teams.

The collective action of a team of individuals can be much greater than the sum of individuals acting alone. Therefore, we need to know how to build effective teams.

Group Development

A group consists of two or more people interacting interdependently to achieve a common goal or objective. The principal characteristics of this definition are people, face-to-face interaction, and at least one common goal. A collection of people who use the same copy machine is not a group, even though they have face-to-face contact, because they are not interacting dependently. Members of a group must think they belong together; they must see themselves as forming a single unit. This feeling of self-awareness usually happens because the group members share common beliefs and attitudes and accept certain group norms. A cohesive group that has a common objective is often called a team.

Why People Join Groups

Formal groups, such as work teams and committees, are typically created to satisfy a particular organizational objective or to solve a specific problem. However, informal groups, such as friendship groups and reference groups, are created for personal reasons, and these reasons explain why people maintain their membership in them.

When individuals join a group, they voluntarily surrender part of their personal freedom, since they must be willing to accept the standards of the group and behave in prescribed ways that are sometimes very restrictive. Musical groups and athletic teams, for example, place heavy demands on members regarding attendance at practices and performances, dressing in the proper attire, and behaving in prescribed ways even outside the group. Although the loss of freedom varies from group to group, every individual voluntarily relinquishes at least some personal freedom as a member of a group. Why then do individuals want to join a group and sacrifice part of their personal freedom? People form groups for four primary reasons:

1. **Goal Accomplishment.** People work together in groups because they need the help of others to achieve important goals. Many goals require the cooperative efforts of other people, such as building a high-rise tower, extinguishing a forest fire, and playing a basketball game. Some goals could be accomplished by individuals, but groups do them better, such as developing a new consumer product, restructuring the production process, and evaluating applications for college scholarships.
2. **Personal identity:** Membership in a group helps us know more about ourselves. Comments of peers generally have a great impact on our self-esteem because they come from people we respect; therefore, we have confidence in what they say. Their comments are also more credible because we assume they know us well and are concerned about our well-being.

3. **Affiliation.** People like to associate with other people, particularly if they have something in common. The mere presence of others provides friendship, social stimulation, and personal acceptance. College students and factory workers alike form informal peer groups simply to avoid the discomfort of being alone.

4. **Emotional Support.** To handle the pressures of daily living, and especially when situations are threatening or uncertain, people rely on others for emotional support. A person facing a stressful situation is comforted by the physical presence of another person facing the same stress.

Stages of Group Development

Most groups experience similar conflicts and challenges that need to be resolved as they strive to become effective. Groups do not immediately function as highly effective teams until they have gone through various stages of development and addressed the kinds of issues that separate effective from ineffective teams. Every work group, whether it is a surgical team, a quality control circle, or a production crew, has to resolve similar issues, and the way it resolves these issues determines the group's effectiveness.

Although the developmental process is not highly standardized, most effective groups go through four stages: **orientation**, **confrontation**, **differentiation**, and **collaboration**, as shown in Exhibit 5.1.[1] A useful mnemonic for remembering these developmental stages is forming, storming, norming, and performing. Groups may not necessarily advance through each of these four stages; indeed, some groups never advance to the later stages because of internal conflicts.

Orientation ("Forming")

The first stage for almost every group is an **orientation** stage when members learn about the purposes of the group and the roles of each member. This stage is marked by caution, confusion, courtesy, and commonality. Individual members must decide how the group will be structured and how much they are willing to commit themselves to the group. The formal leader, or the person who assumes the leadership role, typically exerts great influence in structuring the group and shaping member expectations. Members strive to discover the "rules of the game," and the biases and motives of other group members. During this stage, members should get acquainted with each other and share their expectations about the group's goals and objectives. Efforts to rush this process by expecting members to be fully open and express their real feelings can be very destructive, both to the individuals and the group. The trust and openness necessary for members to feel willing to share intimate details comes in later stages of development.

Confrontation ("Storming")

Although conflict is not a necessary phase of group development, the purposes of the group and the expectations of group members are eventually challenged in most groups. This stage contains conflict, confrontation, concern, and criticism. Struggles for individual power and influence are common. Challenging the group's goals can be a healthy process if the conflict results in greater cohesiveness and acceptance.[2] If the conflict becomes extremely intense and dysfunctional, the group may dissolve, or continue as an ineffective group that never advances to higher levels of group maturity.

Orientation
The first stage of group development when members are getting to know each other.

Confrontation
The second stage of group development when members resolve issues regarding conflicting roles and expectations.

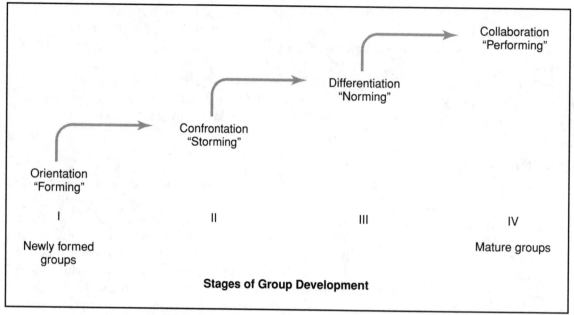

Exhibit 5.1   Stages of Group Development

Differentiation ("Norming")

The major issues at this stage of development are how the tasks and responsibilities will be divided among members and how members will evaluate each other's performance. Individual differences are recognized, and task assignments are based on skills and abilities. If a group can resolve its authority conflicts and create shared expectations regarding its goals and task assignments, it can become a cohesive group and achieve its goals. At this stage, the members often feel the group is successful as they pursue their group goals, and indeed their short-term effectiveness may look rather impressive. As unique situations arise that violate personal expectations, however, the long-term effectiveness of the group will require additional maturity in resolving conflicts and reestablishing shared expectations.

Collaboration ("Performing")

The highest level of group maturity is the stage of **collaboration**, where there is a feeling of cohesiveness and commitment to the group. Individual differences are accepted without being labeled good or bad. Conflict is neither eliminated nor squelched, but is identified and resolved through group discussion. Conflict concerns substantive issues relevant to the group task rather than emotional issues regarding group processes. Decisions are made through rational group discussion, and no attempts are made to force decisions or to present a false unanimity. The members of the group are aware of the group's processes and the extent of their own involvement in the group.

Separation ("Adjourning")

Some groups go through an "adjourning" stage by consciously deciding to disband, usually because the group has completed its tasks or because members choose to go their separate ways. This stage is typi-

---

Differentiation
The third stage of group development when members divide the work to be done and perform their assigned tasks.

Collaboration
The fourth stage of group development when group members form a cohesive relationship and are committed to the group's success.

cally characterized by feelings of closure and compromise as members prepare to leave, often with sentimental feelings.

Virtual Teams

A **virtual team** is a group that relies on technology to interact and accomplish its tasks. They may occasionally meet together in face-to-face interaction; but most of their interactions rely on various types of technology while their members are in different locations and possibly different time zones. The technologies they use can be either synchronous or asynchronous, depending on whether the interaction is in real time or delayed. Synchronous technologies allow team members to communicate with each other simultaneously in real time through teleconferencing, videoconferencing, instant messaging, and electronic meetings. Asynchronous technologies allow members to respond according to their own schedule, and include e-mail, electronic bulletin boards, and websites. The use of virtual teams in organizations has dramatically increased in recent years. Global teams are being used to collaborate with other countries, and technology has allowed for the increased use of global teams across a variety of industries.

> ### *Example—*
> International Business Machines Corp. programmer Rob Nicholson has never met most of the 50 colleagues with whom he collaborates on writing software; they are scattered across three continents. But Mr. Nicholson feels part of a team from the moment he logs on each morning in Hursley, England. When his colleagues in India learn that he is online, they begin asking questions. Mr. Nicholson checks notes on interactive bulletin boards, or wikis, that his team shares. One day, for example, he found notes from teammates in India suggesting changes to a proposed software design that he had posted the previous night; he revised the design that day.[3]

Characteristics of Effective Teams

Some teams are considerably more successful than others in accomplishing their goals and satisfying the needs of their members. Douglas McGregor identifies eleven dimensions of group functioning and argues that these dimensions make the difference between highly effective teams and ineffective teams.[4] Each dimension presents a continuum showing the differences between effective teams on the right and ineffective teams on the left.

1. **Atmosphere and relationships**: What kinds of relationships exist among team members?
   Formal and reserved ←————————→ Close and friendly

2. **Member participation**: Does everyone participate in the group activities and interactions?
   Some participate more ←————————→ There is equal
   than others   participation

3. **Goal understanding and acceptance**: How well do members accept the objectives of the team and commit themselves to them?
   No commitment ←————————→ Total commitment

4. **Listening and sharing information**: Are people willing to listen to each other or are they afraid of looking foolish for suggesting creative ideas?
   There is no listening ←————————→ People listen and
   or sharing   share

Virtual team
Groups that rely on electronic communication rather than
face-to-face interaction.

5. **Handling conflicts and disagreements**: Are conflict and disagreement tolerated and used to improve the group or are they avoided, brushed aside, or flamed into conflict?

If they are not ignored, ←————————→ Conflict is dealt with
they result in hostility   and resolved

6. **Decision making**: How are decisions made? How many members participate in making group decisions and have an opportunity to provide input?

Autocratically   ←————————→ By consensus

7. **Evaluation of member performance**: What kind of feedback do members receive about their performance?

Criticism and personal   Frank, frequent, and
attacks   ←————————→ objective feedback

8. **Expressing feelings**: Do members feel free to express their feelings openly on more than just task issues?

True feelings must   ←————————→ Open expression
remain hidden   is welcomed

9. **Division of labor**: Are task assignments clearly made and willingly accepted?

Poorly structured   ←————————→ Effective job
job assignments   specialization

10. **Leadership**: How are the leaders selected? Are the leadership functions shared?

Leadership is lacking   ←————————→ Leadership is shared
or dominated by one   and effective
person

11. **Attention to process**: Is the group conscious of its own operations? Can it monitor and improve its own processes?

Unaware of group   ←————————→ Aware of operations
operations   and monitors them

Effective teams share several important characteristics: the atmosphere is close and friendly; all members participate in the group; all members are committed to the team's goals; members listen to each other and share information; decisions are made by consensus; conflict is dealt with openly and resolved; members receive frank and objective feedback and feel free to express their feelings openly; there is a division of labor with shared leadership; and the team is aware of its own operations and able to monitor itself.

GROUP STRUCTURE

As a group develops, a structure emerges that influences what it does and how well it performs. Group structure is not an easy concept to explain because it does not refer to specific, observable objects. Group structure is the stable pattern of relationships among group members that maintain the group and help it achieve its goal. The major variables defining group structure are the group's roles and norms. **Group roles** are the task activities and responsibilities the group members perform; **group norms** are general expectations about how members ought to behave. Situational factors that alter the relationships among group members also influence group structure, and this section examines three of these situational factors: group size, social density, and nature of the task. Later sections examine group roles and group norms in greater detail.

Group Size

Perhaps the most visible factor influencing group structure is the size of the group. Groups vary enormously in size, from a dyad (two-person group) or a triad (three-person group) to as large as 400 to 500 members (such as the House of Representatives).

Size and Participation

Small groups provide opportunities for each member to be actively involved in the group. As the group gets larger, however, participation declines rather rapidly. A small graduate seminar with four students, for example, allows each student to participate freely in the discussion, while students in large classes have limited opportunities. Large, informal groups must develop a method that allows members to participate in an orderly manner so that everyone doesn't speak at once. When an informal group exceeds eight to twelve individuals, a significant part of the time, called **process time**, can be wasted simply trying to decide who should participate next.

Size and Satisfaction

As the size of a group increases, the satisfaction of the group members with the group and their involvement in it tend to increase—"the more the merrier"—but only up to a point. A five-person group provides twice as many opportunities for friendly interaction as a three-person group. Beyond a certain point, however (probably fewer than ten to fifteen members), increasing size results in reduced satisfaction. Members of an extremely large group cannot identify with the group's accomplishments nor experience the same degree of cohesiveness and participation as members of a smaller group.

Size and Performance

The relationship between group size and performance depends on whether the task is an additive task, conjunctive task, or disjunctive task.

On **additive tasks** the final group product is the sum of the individual contributions. Additive tasks are sometimes referred to as **pooled interdependence**, since the individual contribution of each member simply adds to the group product. On additive tasks, larger groups should produce more than smaller groups. However, as the size of the group increases, the average productivity of each member tends to decline due to social loafing, a concept that will be discussed later.

Example—
Interviewing customers leaving a store as part of a consumer survey is an additive task. Three interviewers working together will survey more customers than one interviewer working alone, but the three working together in one location will probably not conduct as many interviews as they would have if they had been working alone in separate locations.

Conjunctive tasks are those that can be divided into interdependent subtasks and then assigned to various group members through a "division of labor." The overall performance depends on the successful completion of each subtask. The group's maximum performance is limited by the capacities of the least capable member. A chain, for example, is only as strong as its weakest link.

Example—
The filming of an event by a television news team is a conjunctive task and each member's contribution is essential to the final product. A mistake by any member means failure for the whole group, whether it is a bad interview, a bad picture, or bad sound.

Additive tasks
An independent group task in which the contributions of all members are simply summed or pooled to form the group product.

Conjunctive tasks
A group task that is divided into interdependent subparts and the successful completion of each subpart is necessary for overall task accomplishment.

Disjunctive tasks are decision-making tasks that require the group to select the best solution. Disjunctive tasks include making simple dichotomous decisions (yes or no) as well as selecting the best solution from a list of alternatives.

Example—

An early study on the performance of individuals and groups in performing a disjunctive task, asked individuals working alone or groups working together to arrive at a solution to the following problem: "On one side of a river are three wives and three very jealous husbands. All of the men but none of the women can row. Get them all across the river in the smallest number of trips by means of a boat carrying no more than three people at one time. No man will allow his wife to be in the presence of another man unless he is also there."[5]

Disjunctive tasks require at least one individual with sufficient insight to solve the problem. As a group gets larger, there is a greater probability that the group will contain at least one person with superior insight. In the study just mentioned, correct solutions to the problem of the three couples were produced by 60 percent of the groups, but only 14 percent of the individuals who worked alone.

On disjunctive tasks, therefore, the potential performance of the group depends on the performance of its best member. The term **potential performance** is used here instead of **actual performance** because the actual performance is usually something less than the potential performance. Although the potential performance of a group performing a disjunctive task increases with group size, the actual performance is typically less because the group suffers from process losses. **Process losses** are the inefficiencies that arise from having to organize and coordinate larger groups. The use of appropriate technology, such as computer mediated communication networks, can facilitate the flow of information in large groups and reduce the process losses to some extent. Large groups tend to restrict communication, inhibit creative thought processes, and reduce the personal commitment of group members.[6] Therefore, actual performance equals potential performance minus process losses.

$$\text{Actual Performance} = (\text{Potential Performance} - \text{Process Losses})$$

Social Density

The interactions among group members are influenced by the physical or spatial locations of group members—whether they are physically separated or close together. Consequently, considerable interest has been expressed in the effects of modern architectural arrangements. Many modern offices use an open office plan with many desks in a large open room or small cubicles separated by partitions rather than separate rooms connected by long hallways. The concentration of people within an area is called **social density**, which is measured by square feet per person or the number of group members within a certain walking distance. Walking distance is used rather than straight-line distance since it is the distance someone must go to have face-to-face contact that is important.

Some organizational studies have found that greater social density improves performance because of greater accessibility. In a research-and-development organization, for example, reducing the distance between desks tended to improve performance by increasing the flow of technical information. In another technical organization, engineers reported less stress and tension when colleagues and other authority figures were located in close proximity. Likewise, the employees of a petroleum company reported greater feedback, friendship opportunities, and satisfaction with work when their social density was increased because of relocation.[7]

Disjunctive tasks
A group task involving some form of decision making or problem analysis that requires a yes or no decision.

Process losses
Inefficiencies that arise from having to coordinate the contributions and activities of group members.

Social density
The number of people physically located within a confined area.

Obviously, the performance of a group will not endlessly increase as social density increases. At some point, the conditions become too crowded and people get in each other's way. The optimal social density depends on the nature of the task, the amount of feedback members need from each other, and their needs for privacy. Most studies of open office plans have found that employees generally dislike open office plans because of a lack of privacy. A large number of studies have shown that high levels of social density in organizations produce feelings of crowdedness, intentions to quit, high levels of stress, and low levels of satisfaction and performance. Although high social density normally has only a small effect on performance, the effects appear to be larger among employees who have a high need for privacy and who are performing complex tasks that require intense concentration.[8]

Nature of the Task

The kinds of interactions among group members depend on the kinds of tasks they are performing. Three types of tasks have already been described: additive, conjunctive, and disjunctive tasks. The need for coordination among group members is much greater for conjunctive tasks than it is for additive or disjunctive tasks.

Example—

If five students decided to sell tickets by telephone, they could divide the student directory into five sections, and each one could call the students in one section. Since this is an additive task, the need for coordination is minimal, and the performance of the group would simply be the sum of each individual's sales. Deciding how to divide the student directory would be a disjunctive task that could be done by one individual or a brief discussion, and it, too, requires minimal coordination.

With a conjunctive task the need for coordination increases as the task becomes more complex.

Example—

Organizing and presenting a new product development conference is a conjunctive task that would require the coordinated efforts of many people from several departments, including research, sales, training, production, and finance. Playing basketball, another conjunctive task, is an even more complex activity that requires team members to constantly coordinate their efforts and even anticipate each other's moves.

The relationships among group structure, the nature of the task, and task difficulty help to determine the best organizational structure. There we will see that the structure of an organization needs to vary depending on the nature of the task and the need for coordination. Organizations that have highly specialized tasks require special structures to coordinate the activities of employees, especially when the activities change frequently. The same general conclusion applies here in the study of groups. Groups that perform complex conjunctive tasks require greater coordination among group members than groups performing simple additive or disjunctive tasks.

Example—

As a basketball team develops more complex offensive and defensive plays, team members are assigned to perform specialized activities, and the need for constant coordination among team members during the game increases.

GROUP ROLES

A *role* refers to the expected behaviors attached to a position or job. In organizations, roles are briefly described by position titles and more extensively described by job descriptions. In athletic teams, positions have designated titles, such as point guard, power forward, middle linebacker, and goalie. Informal groups usually do not have explicitly stated roles; one group member may perform several roles or several members may alternate performing the same role. In formal groups, however, roles are usually designated or assigned. These **assigned roles** are prescribed by the organization as a means of dividing the labor and assigning responsibility. **Emergent roles** develop naturally to meet the needs of group members or assist in achieving formal goals. The dynamics in many groups often result in emergent roles replacing assigned roles as people express their individuality and assertiveness.

Work Roles and Maintenance Roles

Group members may be expected to perform a variety of different behaviors. Exhibit 5.2 makes a distinction between three major kinds of group roles: work roles, maintenance roles, and blocking roles.[9]

Work roles are task-oriented activities involved in accomplishing the work and achieving the group objective. Work roles include such activities as clarifying the purpose of the group, developing a strategy for accomplishing the work, delegating job assignments, and evaluating progress.

Maintenance roles are the social-emotional activities of group members that maintain their involvement and personal commitment to the group. These roles include encouraging other members to participate, praising and rewarding others for their contributions, reconciling arguments and disagreements, and maintaining a friendly group atmosphere.

Blocking roles are activities that disrupt or destroy the group, such as dominating the discussion, attacking other group members, disagreeing unreasonably with other group members, and distracting the group with irrelevant issues or unnecessary humor. Deciding whether someone is performing a blocking role is sometimes difficult because the behavior may not be intentional. For example, a member may question a conclusion to force the group to think more carefully about an issue. Other group members may feel that this person is stubbornly resisting the emerging consensus, simply trying to disrupt its progress. Likewise, a good joke may help to relieve tension and keep the group working together, or it may disrupt the group discussion and prevent the group from returning to a crucial issue.

Both work roles and maintenance roles are necessary for effective group functioning, and they can be performed either by a designated leader or as emergent roles by someone else.

Role Episode

Role expectations are communicated to individuals during a **role episode**, which is the interaction between role senders and the person receiving the role.[10] A role episode is diagrammed in Exhibit 5.3. **A role**

Assigned roles
Group roles that are formally assigned to group members.

Emergent roles
Group roles that are voluntarily performed by group members without being formally assigned.

Work roles
The activities performed by one or more group members that help the group accomplish its task and pursue its goals; for example, structuring the tasks, delegating assignments, and initiating action.

Maintenance roles
The activities performed by one or more group members that are designed to maintain the members' willingness to participate in the group.

Blocking roles
Group roles that prevent the group from functioning effectively because they attack other group members or divert the group's attention.

Role episode
An encounter between a role sender and the focal person in which role expectations are sent, received, and evaluated.

Work Roles	Maintenance Roles	Blocking Roles
1. *Initiator:* Proposing tasks or actions; defining group problems; suggesting a procedure.	1. *Harmonizer:* Attempting to reconcile disagreements; reducing tension; getting people to explore differences.	1. *Aggressor:* Deflating another's status; attacking the group or its values; joking in a barbed or semi-concealed way.
2. *Informer:* Offering facts; giving expression of feeling; giving an opinion.	2. *Gatekeeper:* Helping to keep communication channels open; facilitating the participation of others; suggesting procedures that permit sharing remarks.	2. *Blocker:* Disagreeing and opposing beyond reason; resisting stubbornly the group's wish for personal reasons; using a hidden agenda to thwart the movement of a group.
3. *Clarifier:* Interpreting ideas or suggestions; defining terms; clarifying issues for the group.	3. *Consensus tester:* Asking if a group is nearing a decision; assessing whether there is agreement on a possible conclusion.	3. *Dominator:* Asserting authority or superiority to manipulate the group; interrupting contributions of others; controlling by means of flattery or patronizing behavior.
4. *Summarizer:* Pulling together related ideas; restating suggestions; offering a decision or conclusion for the group to consider.	4. *Encourager:* Being friendly, warm and responsive to others; indicating by facial expression or remark the acceptance of others' contributions.	4. *Comedian:* Making a comical display of others or one's lack of involvement; using sarcasm and humor to disrupt the group; seeking recognition in ways not relevant to the group task.
5. *Reality tester:* Making a critical assessment of the situation and problem; testing an idea against data to see if it would work.	5. *Compromiser:* Offering a compromise that yields status; admitting error; modifying the group's policies or objectives.	5. *Avoidance behavior:* Pursuing special interests not related to task; staying off the subject to avoid commitment; preventing group from facing controversy.

Source: Kenneth D. Benne and Paul Sheats, "Functional Roles of Group Members," *Journal of Social Issues,* 2 (1948), pp. 42–47.

Exhibit 5.2   Group Roles

sender may be anyone attempting to change the behavior of another individual, called the **focal person**. In formal groups, the most legitimate role senders are generally supervisors, project directors, and other organizational leaders responsible for delegating assignments. In reality, however, every group member participates as a role sender to other group members. Even subordinates tend to communicate how they expect their supervisors to behave.

Role senders typically communicate only a small percentage of their role expectations. Some expectations are so self-evident that they do not need to be communicated (such as answering your telephone

Focal person
The person in a role episode to whom the role expectations are communicated.

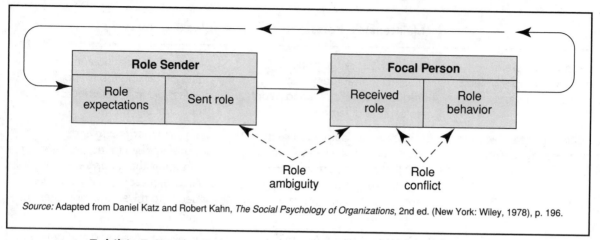

Exhibit 5.3   The Role Episode: Role Ambiguity and Role Conflict

when you hear it ring), while others are not communicated because of uncertainty on the part of the role sender (such as whether the supervisor should say anything to group members involved in horseplay).

The focal person may or may not respond to the role sender. Communication problems may create a discrepancy between the sent role and the received role. But even if the expectations are accurately received, the focal person may not respond because of a lack of motivation or inadequate ability. The feedback loop, going from the focal person back to the role sender, illustrates the ongoing nature of a role episode. A role episode is a continuous process of evaluating each other's behavior and communicating expectations, both overtly and covertly.

An important factor influencing how well the focal person will respond to a sent role is the focal person's state of role readiness. **Role readiness** concerns the focal person's ability and willingness to accept the responsibility associated with a new role.

Example—

A new employee who has had a broad background of relevant experience and is prepared to immediately perform a new job would have a high degree of role readiness. A lack of role readiness occurs when union stewards resist promotions to supervisory positions because they have difficulty changing their thinking from hourly wages, seniority, and job security to salary, merit pay, and raising productivity.

Role Ambiguity

Role ambiguity occurs when there is a discrepancy between the sent role and the received role, as shown in Exhibit 5.3. Ambiguity often comes from confusion when delegating job responsibilities. Many jobs do not have written job descriptions and when employees are told what to do, their instructions are often unclear. Supervisors may contribute to the ambiguity because they may not understand how the job should be done, what the standards of acceptable performance are, how performance will be evaluated, or the limits of the employees' authority and responsibility. Even when supervisors know this information, the instructions usually overwhelm new employees.

Role readiness
An individual's preparation to perform a group role by possessing the appropriate motivation and/or ability.

The consequences of role ambiguity are frustration and other signs of stress. Moderate levels of ambiguity may be tolerable and even desirable, since some employees like to structure their own environment. However, extreme role ambiguity creates an unhealthy condition that contributes to dissatisfaction and turnover.

Role Conflict

Role conflict comes from inconsistency between the received role and role behavior, as shown in Exhibit 5.3, but role conflict is not the same as role ambiguity. The conditions that create role conflict and the amount of discomfort it creates seem to be unique to each person. The same situation may cause more stress for one person than for another. There are four major types of role conflict.[11]

Intrasender role conflict occurs when a single role sender communicates incompatible role expectations to the focal person. For example, a manager could tell the staff members that they are each expected to perform the role of critical evaluator and challenge every decision, but they are also expected to work together cooperatively and be team players.

Intersender role conflict occurs when two or more role senders communicate incompatible expectations to the focal person. The first-line supervisors in most organizations typically experience rather intense intersender role conflict. Upper management expects them to tighten the controls to increase productivity, reduce errors, and eliminate wasted time. In contrast, their subordinates send messages that the supervisors need to loosen the controls and be less interested in productivity, quality, and wasted time. Boundary role occupants, those who straddle the boundary between the organization and its clients and customers, are also prone to experience intersender role conflict. For example, salespeople, schoolteachers, and purchasing agents often receive incompatible instructions from people within the organization and external clients or customers.

Person-role conflict occurs when people are asked to behave in ways that are inconsistent with their personal values. An administrative aide, for example, may be told that a report must be completed before going home, even if it means several hours of overtime. But working overtime would mean missing the school play, and the aide's daughter is the star of the play. Employees experience person-role conflict when they are asked to do something illegal or unethical, such as falsifying reports or lying to customers.

Role overload is caused by the conflicting demands of too many roles (also called inter-role conflict). People fill a variety of roles, both within the organization and in their personal lives. We cannot be in two places at one time, and conflicting time schedules often create severe role overload, forcing us to reassess which role should take precedence. A human resource manager, for example, may experience role overload because of the inconsistent demands accompanying numerous roles, such as affirmative action officer, safety director, facilitator of a quality control circle, career development counselor, and manager of the Human Resource planning system. In addition to the roles she fills in the organization are her roles outside the organization as a wife, mother, and fundraiser for the United Way campaign. These multiple roles contain conflicts of time, interests, and loyalty, because they cannot all be filled simultaneously.

Intersender role conflict
Role conflict created by incompatible demands and expectations of two or more role senders.

Person-role conflict
Role conflict created by asking people to behave in ways that violate their personal values.

Role overload
Role conflict caused by too many demands on a person.

GROUP NORMS

Group norms are the commonly held beliefs of group members about appropriate conduct. As such, they represent general expectations or codes of conduct that imply a duty or obligation. Group norms identify the standards against which the behavior of group members will be evaluated and help group members know what they should or should not do. Group norms typically develop around the eleven issues presented earlier regarding group effectiveness. Every group creates its own norms and standards for evaluating the appropriateness of individual behavior.

Example—

The members of a fraternity created a group norm that it wasn't "cool" to act like dedicated students—a little studying was OK, but it should not interfere with social activities. To get good grades, several fraternity members had to lie about how they spent their time and not admit that their dates and weekend trips were actually to the library.

Example—

The norm in an engineering firm was that no one should leave before the supervisor leaves. None of the engineers actually accomplished very much after the regular working hours; but even though they quit working, they did not leave.

Group norms are essential to group effectiveness. Although norms limit individuality and restrict the creativity of individuals, they create greater predictability within the group by structuring its activities.

Example—

In a typical classroom most students adhere to the norm of raising their hands when they want to comment. This hand-raising norm prevents some class members from making insightful comments, but it also provides for an orderly class discussion.

Development of Norms

Over time, groups develop a variety of norms regarding many aspects of behavior. The most crucial group norms are those regarding issues of central concern to the group. In general, groups tolerate less deviation from norms regarding important group concerns.

Example—

A highly enforced norm for the offensive unit of a football team is that no one talks in the huddle but the quarterback. Accuracy in listening to the quarterback's instructions is vital to the success of the team. Wearing wristbands or putting stickers on helmets, however, are not closely enforced norms because they are not as important to the team's success.

Group norms are typically created and enforced for four reasons:

- they identify the "rules of the game" which helps the group survive;
- they teach group members how to behave and make their behavior more predictable;
- they help the group avoid embarrassing situations;
- they express the central values of the group and clarify what is distinctive about its identity.

Group norms
General expectations of a demand nature regarding acceptable group behavior.

Example—

The norms governing the use of elevators call for people leaving the elevator to exit before other passengers enter. This unwritten procedure may be slightly slower than when everyone moves at once, but it is more orderly.

Example—

After weeks of confusion and conflict, the members of a department established a norm of going around the circle and allowing each member to make a report. This process allowed for a much more orderly flow of conversation than when the members competed to present their ideas first.

Two almost opposite theories explain how group norms are developed. In one explanation, norms are viewed as the product of the shared attitudes and beliefs that group members bring to the group. These are called **injunctive norms** since they result from the influence attempts of group members and are enforced through peer pressure.[12] The norms emerge from the group consensus after the group discusses the issue or from a dominant group member who simply voices an opinion. If no one expresses a dissenting view, the group may adopt the dominant member's viewpoint.

Example—

A norm of no smoking during the weekly planning meetings was created when one of the division managers took the ashtray off the table, put it on the shelf behind her, and said, "There's no need to get lung cancer." Her action went uncontested and no one said anything; thereafter, a no-smoking norm existed.

Another explanation for how group norms are created is that they are post-hoc (after the fact) justifications. These are called **descriptive norms**, since they emerge from watching how others behave and then adopting the same patterns. After the group has been functioning for a while, we observe certain patterns of behavior and explain them as being a group norm. Many performance norms are simply justifications for what has happened in the past.

Example—

At Quigley Refractory all of the machines are stopped twenty minutes early so workers can wash up, and 38 pallets are considered a full day's work. These standards have never been part of the labor agreement; they are simply norms that have evolved over time.

Generally Accepted Norms

Our day-to-day behavior is influenced by so many general social norms that we often fail to recognize them. Most people are members of numerous groups, and these multiple memberships generate a lengthy list of norms, lending regularity and predictability to our behavior.

Social Conduct

Social conduct norms are designed to create a pleasant social atmosphere, such as smiling when you pass a friend in a hallway, answering the phone when it rings by saying hello, and saying goodbye before you hang up. When we are introduced, we shake hands and say, "I'm pleased to meet you," whether it's true or not. If someone asks, "How are you?" the norm is to say "Fine!" not to give a full medical report. Walking away while someone is talking to you is considered a norm violation, and leaving in the middle of a lecture or public address is generally considered impolite.

Dress Codes

Some organizations, such as the military, police, hospitals, restaurants, and hotels, have formal dress standards for their members. The dress codes in other organizations may be more informal and unwritten, but just as powerful. Many organizations, especially financial institutions and law firms, expect employees to wear conservative dresses, shirts, ties, and suits.

Performance Norms

How fast group members are expected to work and how much they should produce are important issues to most groups. Therefore, performance norms are created to guide individual efforts. Supervisors can become very frustrated with a group's performance norms when they are unreasonably low or inconsistent with the organization's goals. Sometimes they appear to be very irrational because they are not in the worker's best interests either. In many work groups, productivity is determined more by the group's performance norms than by the ability and skill of the employees.

Example—
In the bank-wiring experiment of the famous Hawthorne Studies, a group of men maintained an arbitrarily low production norm that restricted productivity, even though the workers were paid according to how much work they did, and this study was conducted during the Great Depression when the workers needed additional income.

Reward Allocation Norms

Groups develop norms governing how rewards should be distributed to the group members. The most commonly studied reward allocation norms are equality, equity, and social responsibility.

- The norm of **equality** suggests that everyone should be treated the same. We all share equally in our status as group members; therefore, the rewards that come to the group should be distributed equally to everyone.
- The norm of **equity** suggests that the rewards should be allocated on the basis of merit according to each person's contribution to the group. Those who have made the largest contribution to the group's product, either through effort, skill, or ability, should receive a larger share of the rewards.
- The norm of **social responsibility** suggests that the rewards should be allocated on the basis of need. People who have special needs, especially those who are disadvantaged or disabled, should receive special consideration and a larger share of the rewards, regardless of their contribution.

Norm of Reciprocity

The **norm of reciprocity** suggests that when people make an effort to help you, you should feel an obligation to help them at a later time. Among some people, this norm is a very firmly held expectation, and they keep track of favors and who owes whom. Although some people feel that service should be rendered specifically to those who have helped them, others have a much broader interpretation of whom they should help. For example, a mentor may be very happy to help a new employee, not because the mentor expects help from the new employee in the future, but because of the help that the mentor received as a new employee from someone else in the past.

Norm of reciprocity
A widely accepted social norm that insists that if person A helps person B, then person B has an obligation to help others, especially person A.

Norm Violation

Although group norms are a group product, they may not match the private beliefs of all members. Norms are accepted in various degrees by the group members. Some norms may be completely accepted by all group members, while other norms are only partially accepted. Norms vary according to their inclusivity, or the number of people to whom they apply. Some norms are nearly universal in nature while others apply only to specific group members.

> *Example—*
> The prohibition against theft is so widely shared that it applies to all members of society, regardless of status or position. Production norms, however, may not equally apply to everyone, especially a lead worker who is expected to spend part of the time training other employees.

For a norm to be maintained there must be a shared awareness that the group supports it and thinks it is appropriate. Although some members may violate the norm, it will continue to survive as long as the majority uphold and accept it. If adherence to the norm continues to erode, it will eventually collapse and no longer serve as a standard for evaluating behavior.

> *Example—*
> Most students have witnessed the disintegration of student conduct norms. One or two students may violate the norm of raising their hands without the norm being destroyed, but when three or four more students begin to violate the norm, the class dissolves into a shouting match where all the students are speaking at once rather than raising their hands and waiting to be acknowledged.

Conformity to the essential group norms is a requirement for sustained group membership. Group members who do not conform to important norms are excluded, ignored, or ridiculed by the group as punishment. The ultimate punishment is to be expelled from the group.

Because of their status, group leaders are in a better position to violate the norms than are other group members. Indeed, leaders sometimes deviate slightly from accepted group norms as a means of asserting their uniqueness or superiority over other group members.

> *Example—*
> Group members must not come late to work and tardiness is often enforced by peer pressure. But, managers think they can come when they want as a privilege of being a manager and escape the censure of the group.

Group norms are difficult to change. Since they were created by the group, they must be changed by the group. Organizational leaders are sometimes successful in helping groups change norms by communicating new expectations of behavior. They are successful to the extent that they can get the group to accept what they say as the new standard of behavior.

CONFORMITY

Group norms provide regularity and predictability to the behavior of group members, but only if members conform to them; norms do not exist without conformity. Unless the members create pressure to enforce the group norms, they will disappear and be replaced by other norms. Conformity means yielding to group influence by doing or saying something you might otherwise choose not to do. To say you have conformed means you have succumbed to social influence and behaved differently from how you would have behaved in the absence of the influence.

Why do people conform? Organizations have been criticized for needless pressures that force people to conform in their thinking, dress, and living habits. Although conformity does reduce variability in the ways people behave, it also increases individual freedom by providing greater predictability and regularity of behavior. Group norms help groups achieve their goals, and as conformity increases, the likelihood of success also increases. Therefore, conformity reduces individuality and personal autonomy, but it also contributes to greater success for both the group and its members.

Pressures to Conform

Groups use two major social influence processes to obtain conformity: **reward dependence** and **information dependence**.[13]

Reward Dependence

Groups have the capacity to reward or punish their members. Leaders of formal groups can use organizational rewards and punishments to induce conformity, such as promotions, pay increases, performance evaluations, and job assignments. Informal groups have powerful rewards for inducing conformity among group members, such as praise, recognition, and social approval for good behavior, or criticism, ridicule, and harassment for deviant behavior.

Information Dependence

Individuals also conform to group pressure because they depend on others for information about the appropriateness of their thoughts, feelings, and behavior. We are particularly dependent on others in novel situations. We rely heavily on others to know how to behave, to interpret our feelings, and to help us understand our emotions.

Levels of Conformity

People conform to social pressure at three very different levels depending on their motives. Walking on the right side of a sidewalk illustrates a very different level of conformity from refusing to accept a bribe from a client because it violates company policy. When you conform to these accepted norms, what are your motives? Conforming to group norms occurs for three significantly different motives: **compliance**, **identification**, and **internalization**.[14]

Compliance

At the lowest level of conformity, people comply with social pressure either to obtain rewards or to avoid punishment. Peer pressure and fear of harassment or criticism induce group members to comply. Compliance, however, is usually quite temporary and is limited to the specific situation. If a police officer is parked at an intersection, the fear of being ticketed will probably induce compliance to stop for the stop sign. If the fines for overdue library books are exorbitantly high, students will probably return them on time. If supervisors receive a $50 bonus for a good safety rating, they will probably conduct periodic safety inspections simply to obtain the reward.

> *Example—*
> The members of a university's privacy committee decided that they did not understand the Family Educational Rights and Privacy Act (FERPA) adequately to properly monitor its implementation

---

Reward dependence
When group members feel induced to conform to group pressure because there are positive or negative consequences attached to doing so.

Information dependence
When group members feel induced to conform to group pressure because they depend on the group to provide important information to help them know what to do.

Compliance
The first level of conformity, in which the individual's motive is to obtain rewards or avoid punishment.

on campus. The committee members agreed that each member should read a training booklet explaining the act before the next meeting. To motivate them, the chair said that she would construct a short exam to test their knowledge at the next meeting. Not wanting to fail this exam was the primary motivation for several committee members to study the material.

Identification

The second level of conformity is called identification because the motive is the desire to be accepted by others who are perceived as important. Identification is the process of behaving like "significant others" and adopting their characteristics and personal attributes. Not only do we want to be like them and acquire their attributes, we also want them to think well of us and to approve of our attitudes and actions. Through imitative learning, we tend to model their behavior and accept what they say and how they behave. People who identify with a significant other will stop at stop signs, return library books, and work independently on take-home exams if that is the way they think the significant other expects them to behave.

Example—
Some members of the FERPA Committee were motivated to study the act before the next meeting because they respected the committee chair and she asked them to do it. They knew that privacy violations at the university would reflect negatively on her because she had a legal responsibility to monitor compliance and they wanted to help her.

Internalization

At the highest level of conformity, the standards of behavior are internalized and become part of the person's basic character. At the internalization level of conformity norms are followed because the person accepts the beliefs, attitudes, and values supporting the norms. Conformity does not occur because it achieves rewards, avoids punishment, or pleases others; it occurs because the behavior is perceived as morally right and proper. At this level you stop for stop signs, return library books, and avoid cheating on exams not to avoid punishment nor to receive the praise of others, but because you personally believe it is right and you are committed to abide by your own personal standards of right and wrong, which coincide with the group norms.

Example—
A couple of FERPA Committee members were motivated to study the act and participate actively in the committee discussions because they strongly believed in the right of privacy and their obligation to help the university operate effectively and lawfully. Their desires were to ensure that the correct policies were established, that all faculty and administrators understood the policies, and that they were fairly administered.

Factors Influencing Conformity

Some situations exert greater pressures on group members to conform than others. As a general rule, the pressures to conform are greater in the following situations:

- Larger groups tend to exert greater pressure than smaller groups;

Identification
The second level of conformity, in which the motive to conform is to please or be like others.

Internalization
The highest level of conformity, in which the motive to conform is based on the group member's acceptance of the prescribed behavior as a basic principle of right and wrong.

- Group members who are perceived as experts or as highly qualified or experienced persons exert greater pressures to conform than members who are not considered highly skilled;
- A united group exerts much greater pressure to conform than a group divided by dissension. In some cases, the presence of a single dissenter is enough to destroy the influence of the group;
- Conformity increases as the situation becomes more ambiguous. When people do not know what is expected of them, they become increasingly dependent on the influence of others;
- People who are insecure and lack self-confidence are more likely to conform than people who are confident in their judgments. When insecure people discover that their opinions do not agree with the majority opinion, they tend to question their own judgments and perceptions. People who are high in self-confidence, however, discredit the group when their opinions differ from the groups' opinions;
- The pressure to adhere to a social norm increases when conformity is essential to the group's success. As a group gets closer to achieving its goal, the anticipation of success increases the pressure to conform and makes nonconformity less acceptable. Deviation from the group norm becomes absolutely unacceptable at crucial times.

Example—

During the playoff games at the end of a season, team members experience particularly strong pressures to abide by the group norms. As the probability of a strike increases, unions demand greater conformity among union members as a show of strength to management.

EFFECTS OF THE GROUP ON INDIVIDUAL BEHAVIOR

How does the presence of a group influence an individual's performance? Suppose you were laying bricks with four other bricklayers. Would more bricks get laid if the five of you worked together as a group along one side of a wall, or would it be better to assign each of you to different walls on the construction site? Two contrasting processes have been identified to explain the effects of the group on individual performance: social facilitation and social loafing. Another concept, called **deindividuation**, also explains the effects of a group on individual behavior.

Social Facilitation

Early studies in social psychology noted that people performed better as members of a group than they did when performing alone. It was observed, for example, that cyclists rode faster if they raced in head-to-head competition than when they raced alone to beat the clock. Subsequent research showed that the presence of an audience or crowd or simply the presence of other coworkers facilitated the performance of well-learned responses, such as crossing out letters and words, doing multiplication problems, and other simple tasks. This process, called the **social facilitation effect,** is caused by the mere presence of others rather than direct competition between individuals, since a number of studies found that subjects performed better even in front of a passive audience. The social facilitation effect has been observed not only on people, both adults and children, but also on an unusual assortment of other animals including, ants, fish, chickens, rats, and cockroaches.

One explanation for the social facilitation effect is called **evaluation apprehension.** According to this explanation, the presence of others creates a higher level of arousal and motivation because we expect others to evaluate our performance, and their opinions matter to us. When others are watching we want to look good, sometimes for no other reason than that we want others to think well of us.

Social facilitation effect
The tendency for the presence of other people to increase motivation and arousal, which tends to help the individual perform better.

Evaluation apprehension
The concern that people experience when they know they are being observed and evaluated by others.

Although the presence of others may improve performance, it can also inhibit performance on some tasks. This process, called **social inhibition effect,** has been observed on complex learning tasks such as learning a maze or a list of nonsense syllables. Since the social inhibition effect is the opposite of the social facilitation effect, it is important to know when the presence of others will inhibit and when it will facilitate an individual's performance.

Perhaps the best explanation of the contradictory results relies on an important distinction between learning a new task and performing a well-learned task. The presence of others increases our level of arousal and motivation, which helps us perform well-learned responses.[15] Therefore, the presence of others tends to improve our performance on well-learned responses such as walking, running, bicycling, or playing the piano (for a highly skilled pianist). However, if the response has not been well learned, which is the case with all new learning situations, then the presence of others produces higher levels of arousal which inhibits performance. Therefore, according to social facilitation the learning of complex new tasks is best accomplished in isolation, but the performance of well-learned tasks will be facilitated by an audience.

Example—
Larry Bird (Indiana State 1977–1979; Boston Celtics 1979–1992) was an extremely talented basketball player who was such an excellent shooter that he excelled under pressure. During his 13-year career, his field goal percentage averaged .496 and his free throw percentage averaged .896. One season he made 71 consecutive free throws and he won three consecutive NBA Long Distance Shootout titles. Larger crowds and more intense competition motivated him to shoot better.[16]

Social Loafing

Social loafing occurs when the members of a group exert less effort while working as a group than when working as individuals. Social loafing is the opposite of social facilitation, but it is different than social inhibition. The social inhibition effect occurs when the presence of others leads to such high levels of arousal that it disrupts the person's limited abilities. Social loafing, in contrast, is not attributed to a decline in ability but to a decline in motivation.

Example—
One of the earliest studies in social loafing examined how much effort individuals exerted in pulling on a rope, either individually or in a group. The average pressure exerted by each individual was 63 kilograms, which was more than double the average pressure exerted by a group of eight people pulling together (248 kilograms per group, or 31 kilograms per person).[17]

Social loafing occurs primarily because the presence of other group members reduces each individual's identifiability. When individuals cannot be identified, there is no relationship between their efforts and their outcomes; therefore, they cannot be individually recognized for good effort or punished for poor performance. The social loafing effect becomes increasingly apparent in larger groups because of reduced personal identifiability. Social loafing also occurs in decision-making groups with cognitive tasks: people in groups exert less effort and less concentration, and they also use less complex judgment strategies than do single judges or judges working in pairs.

Deindividuation

The issue of identifiability is related to another process of group dynamics: **deindividuation**. Individuals often become lost in crowds and perform acts they would not perform if they were alone. Unruly

---

Social inhibition effect
The tendency for the presence of other people to disrupt performance and cause them to perform poorly.

Social loafing
The tendency to exert less effort when working as a member of a group than when working alone.

Deindividuation
The loss of individuality that occurs by being a member of a large crowd.

crowds at rock concerts have produced hysterical screaming and uncontrolled emotions, angry fans at athletic contests have thrown objects at athletes and assaulted referees, and groups of union picketers have destroyed property and committed acts of violence. Stories of lynch mobs illustrate how individuals in a group get carried away and do things they would not have done without the presence of the group. Crowds have the capacity to create a mental homogeneity, called a **collective mind**, that is frequently irrational and often functions at lower moral and intellectual levels than isolated individuals.

Three mechanisms have been proposed to explain the process of deindividuation in groups. First, people are anonymous because they lose their sense of individual identification. Second, the contagion of the group causes people to act differently by reducing their inhibitions and allowing them to behave like other group members. Third, people become more suggestible in groups where they feel greater pressures to conform.

The loss of individuality has often been associated with rather undesirable social consequences. In a study of the warfare patterns of many cultures, for example, it was found that in cultures where warriors deindividuate themselves by wearing masks and paint, there is a greater tendency to torture captives than in cultures whose warriors are not deindividuated. Another study of trick-or-treaters on Halloween found that they were more likely to steal when they wore masks and remained anonymous than when they were clearly identifiable.[18]

Perhaps the most shocking study of deindividuation was the Stanford Prison study, conducted by Phillip Zimbardo.[19] In this study, twenty-four male students who were described as mature, emotionally stable, normal, intelligent people were randomly assigned to play the roles of guards or prisoners. Both the prisoners and the guards were given appropriate uniforms, and the prisoners were placed in three-man cells for the duration of the experiment, which was to be two weeks. The guards were instructed to run the prison, and the experimenter served only as a warden. The guards wore silver reflector sunglasses, which increased the level of deindividuation. The prisoners made only meager attempts to escape, and their behavior was described as that of servile, dehumanized robots. The behavior of the guards became tyrannical and brutal, and the situation became so ugly and repressive that the experiment had to be terminated after only six days instead of the two weeks originally planned.

Deindividuation does not necessarily create undesirable social behavior; it can also be positive. Although they don't attract as much attention, many groups have noble purposes and worthwhile social goals that sweep people along in productive activities. Schools, charitable foundations, religious groups, and even business organizations frequently create groups where individuals lose a sense of their own personal identity and are carried along as part of the group in activities that contribute to their own growth and development and to the betterment of society. Therefore, although groups can be destructive and abusive, they don't necessarily need to be that way. Those who have enjoyed the exhilaration of wildly cheering for their favorite athletic teams know how much fun being "lost in the crowd" can be.

NOTES

1. B. W. Tuckman, "Developmental Sequences in Small Groups," *Psychological Bulletin*, vol. 63 (1965), pp. 384–399; Toby Berman-Rossi, "My Love Affair with Stages of Group Development," *Social Work with Groups*, vol. 25 (no. 1/2, 2002), pp. 151–158; Diane L. Miller, "The Stages of Group Development: A Retrospective Study of Dynamic Team Processes," *Canadian Journal of Administrative Sciences*, vol. 20 (2003), pp. 121–134.

2. Karen A. Jehn and Elizabeth A. Mannix, "The Dynamic Nature of Conflict: A Longitudinal Study of Intragroup Conflict and Group Performance," *Academy of Management Journal*, vol. 44 (2001), pp. 238–251.

3. Phred Dvorak, "How Teams Can Work Well Together From Far Apart," *The Wall Street Journal*, 17 September 2007, B4.

4. Douglas McGregor, *The Human Side of Enterprise* (New York: McGraw-Hill, 1960), pp. 232–240; see also Anthony T. Pescosolido, "Group Efficacy and Group Effectiveness: The Effects of Group Efficacy

Over Time on Group Performance and Development," *Small Group Research*, vol. 34 (2003), pp. 20–42.

5. Marjorie Shaw, "A Comparison of Individuals and Small Groups in the Rational Solution of Complex Problems," *American Journal of Psychology*, vol. 44 (1932), pp. 491–504.

6. Paul Benjamin Lowry, Tom L. Roberts, Nicholas C. Romano, Jr., Paul D. Cheney and Ross T. Hightower, "The Impact of Group Size and Social Presence on Small-Group Communication: Does Computer-Mediated Communication Make a Difference?" *Small Group Research*, vol. 37 (2006), pp. 631–661.

7. T. J. Allen and D. I. Cohen, "Information Flow in R&D Laboratories," *Administrative Science Quarterly*, vol. 14 (1969), pp. 12–25; Robert H. Miles, "Roles Set Configuration as a Predictor of Role Conflict and Ambiguity in Complex Organizations," *Sociometry*, vol. 40 (1977), pp. 21–34; Andrew D. Szilagyi and W. E. Holland, "Changes in Social Density: Relationships with Perceptions of Job Characteristics, Role Stress, and Work Satisfaction," *Journal of Applied Psychology*, vol. 65 (1980), pp. 28–33.

8. Greg R. Oldham, "Effects of Changes in Workspace Partitions and Spatial Density on Employee Reactions: A Quasi-Experiment," *Journal of Applied Psychology*, vol. 73 (1988), pp. 253–258; Eric Sundstrom, *Work Places* (Cambridge, England: Cambridge University Press), 1986; Eric Sundstrom, Robert E. Burt, and Douglas Kamp, "Privacy at Work: Architectural Correlates of Job Satisfaction and Job Performance," *Academy of Management Journal*, vol. 23 (1980), pp. 101–107.

9. Kenneth D. Benne and P. Sheats, "Functional Roles of Group Members," Journal of Social Issues, vol. 2 (1948), pp. 42–47; Hal B. Gregersen, "Group Observer Instructions," in J. B. Ritchie and Paul Thompson, *Organizations and People*, 3rd ed. (St. Paul, Minn.: West, 1984), pp. 231–234.

10. Daniel Katz and Robert L. Kahn, *The Social Psychology of Organizations*, 2nd ed. (New York: Wiley, 1978), chap. 7.

11. Robert L. Kahn, D. M. Wolfe, R. P. Quinn, J. D. Snoek, and R. A. Rosenthal, *Organizational Stress: Studies in Role Conflict and Ambiguity* (New York: Wiley, 1964).

12. Mark G. Ehrhart and Stefanie E. Naumann, "Organizational Citizenship Behavior in Work Groups: A Group Norms Approach," *Journal of Applied Psychology*, vol. 89 (2004), pp. 960–974; M. Deutsch and H. B. Gerard, "A Study of Normative and Informational Social Influences Upon Individual Judgment," *Journal of Abnormal and Social Psychology*, vol. 51 (1955), pp. 629–636.

13. Edward E. Jones and Harold B. Gerard, *Foundations of Social Psychology* (New York: Wiley, 1967), Chaps. 3 and 4; Rod Bond, "Group Size and Conformity," *Group Processes & Intergroup Relations*, vol. 8 (2005), pp. 331–354.

14. H. C. Kelman, "Compliance, Identification, and Internalization: Three Processes of Opinion Change," *Journal of Conflict Resolution*, vol. 2 (1958), pp. 51–60.

15. Robert Zajonc, "Social Facilitation," *Science*, vol. 149 (1965), pp. 269–274.

16. *http://www.nba.com/history/players/bird_bio.html* as of 28 September 2007.

17. This early study by Ringelmann is reported by J. F. Dashiel, "Experimental Studies of the Influence of Social Situations on the Behavior of Individual Human Adults," in Carl Murchison (ed.), *The Handbook of Social Psychology* (Worcester, Mass.: Clark University Press, 1935).

18. R. I. Watson, "Investigation into Deindividuation Using a Cross Cultural Survey Technique," *Journal of Personality and Social Psychology*, vol. 25 (1973), pp. 342–345; E. Diener, S. Fraser, A. Beaman, and Z. Kellem, "Effects of Deindividuation Variables on Stealing Among Halloween Trick-or-Treaters," *Journal of Personality and Social Psychology*, vol. 33 (1976), pp. 178–183.

19. Phillip Zimbardo, *The Psychological Power and Pathology of Imprisonment*, statement prepared for the U.S. House of Representatives Committee on the Judiciary, (Subcommittee No. 3, Robert Kastemeyer, Chairman, Hearings on Prison Reform). Unpublished paper, Stanford University, 1971; http://www.prisonexp.org/ as of 28 September 2007.

Leadership

LEADERSHIP

Leadership is an extremely popular topic in organizational behavior because of the role we assume it plays in group and organizational effectiveness. We assume that the success of a group depends primarily on the quality of leadership. A winning season requires a good coach, a military victory requires a great commander, and a productive work group requires a competent supervisor. Whether they deserve it or not, leaders are usually credited for the group's success and blamed for its failure. When a team has a losing season, the coach is fired, not the team.

The most useful definition of leadership is to view it as the **incremental influence** one individual exerts on another beyond mechanical compliance with routine directives. Leadership occurs when one individual influences others to do something voluntarily rather than because they were required to do it or they feared the consequences of noncompliance. It is this voluntary aspect of leadership that distinguishes it from other types of influence, such as power and authority. Although leaders may use force or coercion to influence the behavior of followers, they must also have the ability to induce voluntary compliance. By this definition, anyone in the organization can be a leader, whether or not that individual is formally identified as such. Indeed, informal leaders are extremely important to the effectiveness of most organizations.

Managers versus Leaders

Although leadership is similar to **management**, some writers make a clear difference between these topics to highlight the importance and distinctive nature of **leadership**.

Managing Things versus Leading People

One contrast between management and leadership focuses on what is influenced: managers manage *things,* while leaders lead *people.*[1] Managers focus their efforts on inanimate objects, such as budgets, financial statements, organization charts, sales projections, and productivity reports. Leaders focus their efforts on people as they encourage, inspire, train, empathize, evaluate, and reward. Leaders build organizations, create organizational cultures, and shape society. Managers focus on internal organizational issues as they maintain bureaucratic procedures and keep organizations running smoothly by solving problems.

It has also been said that *managers are people who do things right, and leaders are people who do the right thing.* This statement suggests that leaders and managers focus on different issues. To manage means to direct, to bring about, to accomplish, and to have responsibility for. The functions of management are planning, organizing, directing, and controlling. The successful manager is viewed as someone who achieves results by following the prescribed activities and maintaining behaviors and products within prescribed limits.

To lead, however, is to inspire, to influence, and to motivate. Effective leaders inspire others to pursue excellence, to extend themselves, and to go beyond their perfunctory job requirements by generating creative ideas. This distinction is somewhat overstated, because effective leaders do a lot of managing, and effective managers need to lead. But it serves to emphasize an important organizational outcome: we desperately need leaders who can create an energetic and highly committed work force that is success-

---

Incremental influence
The influence one individual exerts on others above and beyond their normal role requirements.

Management
The process of planning, organizing, leading, and controlling the use of resources to accomplish performance goals.

Leadership
Doing the right things; creating essential change by communicating a vision that inspires others.

fully adapting to the demands of a changing environment and competently producing viable products and services.

Controlling Complexity versus Producing Change

Another contrast between management and leadership focuses on maintaining stability versus creating change.[2]

- Management focuses on *controlling complexity*—creating order in the organization, solving problems, and ensuring consistency.
- Leadership focuses on *creating change*—recognizing the dynamic environment, sensing opportunities for growth, and communicating a vision that inspires others.

Both management and leadership involve influencing others through four common roles: planning, organizing, directing, and controlling. As they perform each of these roles, managers and leaders behave very differently because they focus on different outcomes, as summarized in Exhibit 6.1.

Planning—Deciding What Needs to be Done

Managers decide what to do by planning and budgeting—setting targets and goals for the future, establishing detailed steps for achieving them, and allocating resources to accomplish those plans. Planning and budgeting are the processes managers use to control complexity and produce orderly results; they are not used to create change.

Leadership involves helping an organization achieve constructive change, which requires setting a direction—developing a vision of the future and strategies for producing the changes needed to accomplish the vision.

Organizing—Creating Networks and Relationships to Get Work Done

Managers perform a variety of organizing and staffing activities to create a structure for getting work done. These activities include dividing the work into distinct jobs, staffing the jobs with qualified work-

Focus	Leadership Producing useful change	Management Controlling complexity
Role 1. Deciding what needs to be done	Setting direction Creating a vision and strategy	Planning and budgeting
Role 2. Creating a structure of networks and relationships to get work done	Aligning people with a shared vision Communicating with all relevant people	Organizing and staffing Structuring jobs Establishing reporting relationships Providing training Delegating authority
Role 3. Directing productive work	Empowering people	Solving problems Negotiating compromises
Role 4. Ensuring performance	Motivating and inspiring people	Implementing control systems

Exhibit 6.1   Comparison between Leadership and Management

ers, structuring jobs in defined units, establishing reporting relationships, and delegating authority for following the assigned procedures. By organizing and staffing, managers control a complex environment and create a stable structure for getting work done.

The corresponding leadership activity involves aligning people behind a shared vision of how the organization needs to change. Aligning people involves communicating a new direction to the relevant people who can work "unitedly" and form coalitions with a common vision and sense of direction. Change is not an orderly process, and it will be staggered and chaotic unless many people coalesce and move together in the same direction.

Directing Productive Work

Managers are problem solvers. They tend to view work as an enabling process, involving people with multiple talents and interests that may not coincide with each other or with the interests of the organization. They strive to create an acceptable employment exchange by negotiating agreements that satisfy the expectations of workers and the demands of the organization. Bargaining and compromise are used to establish an agreement, and rewards and punishment are used to maintain it.

Leaders rely on empowering people and letting them work autonomously according to their shared vision. Free to exercise individual initiative and motivated by a sense of ownership, people throughout the organization respond quickly and effectively to new opportunities and problems.

Controlling—Ensuring Performance

Managers ensure performance by implementing control systems—establishing measurable standards, collecting performance data, identifying deviations, and taking corrective action.

Leaders ensure performance by motivating and inspiring people to go above and beyond the formal job expectations. Motivation and inspiration energize people, not by monitoring their behavior as control mechanisms do, but by satisfying basic human needs for fulfillment: accomplishment, recognition, self-esteem, a feeling of control over one's life, and the ability to achieve one's ideals. These feelings touch people deeply and elicit a powerful response.

Control systems are supposed to ensure that normal people perform their work in normal ways, day after day. Managing routine performance is not glamorous, but it is necessary. Leadership that inspires excellence and helps organizations thrive in an uncertain world is glamorous, but it may not be any more necessary than management.

In this theory of leadership, leadership is not necessarily better than management, nor is it a replacement for it. Both functions are necessary in organizations, and some believe that the skills for both functions can be acquired by everyone. Others believe that managers and leaders require very different skills and personalities because they focus on almost opposite behaviors that must therefore be performed by different individuals. This issue is not resolved, and there are data supporting both views.

Transformational Leadership

Another contrast used to highlight a particular kind of leadership is transactional versus transformational leadership.[3] **Transactional leaders** manage the transactions between the organization and its members; they get things done by giving contingent rewards, such as recognition, pay increases, and advancement for employees who perform well. Employees who do not perform well are penalized. Transactional lead-

---

Transactional leadership
A style of leadership that focuses on accomplishing work by relying on contingent rewards, task instructions, and corrective actions.

Transactional Leadership
• Establishes goals and objectives
• Designs work flow and delegates task assignments
• Negotiates exchange of rewards for effort
• Rewards performance and recognizes accomplishments
• Searches for deviations from standards and takes corrective action

Transformational Leadership
• *Charismatic:* Provides vision and sense of mission, gains respect and trust, instills pride
• *Individualized consideration:* Gives personal attention, treats each person individually, coaches and encourages followers
• *Intellectually stimulating:* Promotes learning, shares ideas and insights, encourages rationality, uses careful problem solving
• *Inspirational:* Communicates high performance expectations, uses symbols to focus efforts, distills essential purposes, encourages moral behavior

Exhibit 6.2 Characteristics of Transactional and Transformational Leadership

ers frequently use the management-by-exception principle to monitor the performance of employees and take corrective actions when performance deviates from the standard.

Example—

Some political observers describe President Gerald Ford as an example of a great transactional leader who did an excellent job of working with Congress and managing the affairs of the United States. During the short time he served as president (1974–1977) he replaced all but two cabinet members and did much to stabilize the operations of many federal agencies, such as the Departments of Labor and Commerce. His justification for pardoning Richard Nixon was to end the political turmoil caused by the impeachment proceedings, so the government could move forward.

Transformational leadership focuses on changing the attitudes and assumptions of employees and building commitment for the organization's mission, objectives, and strategies. Transformational leaders are described as charismatic, inspirational, and intellectually stimulating, and they show individual consideration for each member. This form of leadership occurs when leaders broaden and elevate the interests of their employees, when they generate awareness and acceptance of the purposes and mission of the group, and when they stir their employees to look beyond their own self-interest for the good of the group. The major differences between transactional and transformational leaders are shown in Exhibit 6.2.

A result that is attributed to transformational leadership is the empowerment of followers, who are capable of taking charge and acting on their own initiative. **Empowerment** involves providing the conditions that stimulate followers to act in a committed, concerned, and involved way. The kinds of conditions that contribute to empowerment include providing relevant factual information; providing resources such as time, space, and money; and providing support such as backing, endorsement, and legitimacy.

Transformational leadership
A style of leadership that focuses on communicating an organizational vision, building commitment, stimulating acceptance, and empowering followers.

Empowerment
A condition created by leaders that stimulates followers to act on their own initiative and perform in a highly committed, intelligent, and ethical way.

Empowered followers make things happen without waiting for detailed instructions or administrative approvals.

Charismatic leadership is a special kind of influence that is attributed to outstanding and gifted individuals. Followers not only trust and respect charismatic leaders, they also idolize them as great heroes or spiritual figures. Charismatic leadership is evidenced by the amount of trust followers have in the correctness of the leader's beliefs, their unquestioning acceptance of the leader, their willing obedience, and their affection for the leader.

Charismatic leaders are described as people who have a high need for social power, high self-confidence, and strong convictions about the morality of their cause. They establish their influence most importantly by the example they model in their own behavior for followers. They maintain their status by managing their charismatic perception (impression management) to preserve the followers' confidence, by articulating an appealing vision of the group's goals in ideological terms, communicating high expectations for followers, and expressing confidence in their followers.

Example—

President Bill Clinton was recognized as a charismatic leader who had the capacity to capture the imagination of his listeners. Even when he was fighting threats of impeachment, he delivered an address before the United Nations that received a standing ovation.[4]

Transformational leaders seek to raise the consciousness of followers by appealing to higher ideals and values such as liberty, justice, equality, peace, and humanitarianism, rather than baser emotions such as fear, greed, jealousy, or hatred. This kind of leadership should be viewed as a priceless national treasure that is sorely needed to rejuvenate society and reform institutions. Many writers have suggested that many social and economic problems, including unemployment and the decline in international competitiveness, stem from insufficient transformational leaders who dream inspired visions and are able to motivate followers to pursue them.

Example—

President Franklin D. Roosevelt is often described as a great transformational leader because of the vision and wisdom he shared with Americans during his weekly radio broadcasts that helped the United States overcome a major depression and World War II. President Ronald Regan is another transformational leader because of his charismatic personality, his vision of economic changes, and his boldness in attacking communism.

Empirical support for the importance of transformational leadership comes from research that measured transformational and transactional leadership behaviors.[5] Transformational leadership is superior to transactional leadership in encouraging followers to exert extra effort.[6] Leaders who are rated high on transformational leadership factors have a much larger percentage of employees who say they exert extra effort, than do leaders who are rated low. For example, a study of 186 Navy officers on active duty found that transformational leaders obtained more extra efforts from their subordinates and higher satisfaction than did transactional or laissez-faire leaders.[7] Other research studies have likewise found that transformational leadership is associated with greater leader effectiveness and employee satisfaction.[8]

Studies indicate that transformational leadership can be learned and that it is greatly influenced by the kind of leadership modeled in an organization. Leaders at all levels can be trained to be more charismatic, to be more intellectually stimulating, and to show more individual consideration. Successful train-

---

Charismatic leadership
A type of leadership attributed to outstanding and highly esteemed leaders who gain the confidence and trust of followers.

ing programs have been conducted for a variety of groups, such as first-level supervisors in high-tech computer firms, senior executives of insurance firms, and officers in the Israeli military.[9]

Studies that have examined the relationship between personality and leadership quite consistently find that the Big Five personality traits are only modestly correlated with both transformational and transactional leadership. The best correlations suggest that transformational leaders tend to be a little higher than average on extraversion and emotional stability. But, meta-analyses of hundreds of studies find that even these correlations are, on average, low (.21 and .18 respectively).[10] These low correlations reinforce the idea that transformational and transactional leadership skills are not innate personality attributes but something that can be learned by training and experience.

LEADERSHIP TRAITS

Leadership has been studied at three different levels—the individual, the group, and the organization.

- At the individual level of analysis, leadership studies have focused on the traits of successful leaders.
- At the group level, leadership studies have focused on leadership behaviors of both formal and informal leaders.
- The organizational level of analysis has examined how organizational effectiveness is determined by the interaction between the leader, the follower, and the situation.

The traits of successful leaders have been studied for more than a century. World War I highlighted the need for selecting and training effective leaders, and for the quarter century between World War I and World War II, numerous studies investigated the characteristics of good leaders. These studies are generally referred to as **trait studies**, because their primary goal was to identify the personal traits of effective leaders.

In general, the trait studies were quite disappointing. Although several traits were frequently associated with effective leaders, the research was weak and sometimes contradictory because of methodological problems associated with identifying good leaders, measuring leader traits, and measuring group effectiveness. Because of weak results, the focus of leadership research shifted from trait studies to contingency studies, which examined more than just the traits of the leader.

The research on leadership traits should not be dismissed too quickly, however. Although the trait studies were disappointing, they were not worthless; when considered as a whole these studies help us understand more about how leaders influence others. Several traits produced a significant difference in leadership effectiveness, but they did not act alone. Four major reviews have surveyed the trait studies, and the results can be summarized in three categories: physical traits, intelligence, and personality traits.[11]

Physical Traits

Trait studies examined such physical factors as height, weight, physique, energy, health, and appearance. To the extent that anything can be concluded regarding the relationship among these factors and leadership, it appears that leaders tend to be slightly taller and heavier, have better health, a superior physique, a higher rate of energy output, and a more attractive appearance.

To illustrate, one early study on the effects of height found that executives in insurance companies were taller than policyholders, that bishops were taller than clergymen, that university presidents were taller than college presidents, that sales managers were taller than sales representatives, and that railway presidents were taller than station agents.[12] Results of this sort, however, have not always been consistent. While one literature review found nine studies showing that leaders tend to be taller, it reported two studies showing that leaders tended to be shorter. Attractiveness and a pleasant appearance were found

---

Trait studies
A stream of research that tried to identify the essential personality traits that contributed to effective leadership.

to be highly correlated with leaders among Boy Scouts; but among groups of delinquent youth, leaders were rated as more slovenly and unkempt than other members.[13]

In summary, studies of personal characteristics are not particularly interesting or useful. The results are generally too weak and inconsistent to use in selecting leaders, nor are they useful for training purposes, because very little can be done to change most of these physical traits. The results seem to say more about cultural stereotypes than they do about leadership. Thus, in unstructured situations we can understand why people who are larger, more attractive, better dressed, and more energetic generally succeed in exerting greater influence than others.

Intelligence

Many studies have investigated the relationship between leadership and intelligence, and they generally agree that leaders are more intelligent than nonleaders. The relationship between intelligence and leadership probably stems from the fact that so many leadership functions depend on careful problem solving, and this is a useful insight into effective leadership. One review of leadership studies reported twenty-three experiments showing that leaders were brighter and had greater levels of intelligence than did their followers. Only five studies reported that intelligence made no difference. In general, it appears safe to conclude that leaders are more intelligent than nonleaders, but again the correlations are small. Obviously, many variables other than intelligence influence leadership effectiveness.[14]

An interesting conclusion from these studies is the suggestion that leaders should be more intelligent than the group, but not by too wide a margin. Members who are significantly brighter than other group members are seldom selected as leaders. Because of their superior intellect, it appears that other group members tend to reject them; they are too different from the rest of the group. People with high IQs tend to have different vocabularies, interests, and goals from those of other group members; these differences create communication and interpersonal relations problems.

Leadership effectiveness also appears to be related to scholarship and knowledge. Leaders generally excel scholastically and receive better-than-average grades. General information, practical knowledge, and simply knowing how to get things done appears to be important for effective leadership and several studies have shown a positive relationship between general knowledge and leadership ability. These results contribute to our understanding of leadership and are potentially useful for both selecting and training leaders.

Personality Traits

Other personality traits appear to be related to leadership, although most of the relationships are not especially strong. A list of the personality traits most frequently associated with leadership is shown in Exhibit 6.3. This list is based on the 1948 review of 124 studies of leadership traits by Ralph Stogdill. This list suggests that the average leader is more social, displays greater initiative, is more persistent, knows how to get things done, is more self-confident, displays greater cooperativeness and adaptability, and

Capacity	Achievement	Responsibility	Participation	Status
Intelligence	Scholarship	Honesty	Activity	Socioeconomic
Alertness	Knowledge	Dependability	Sociability	Position
Verbal facility	Athletic accomplishment	Initiative	Cooperation	Popularity
Originality	Personality adjustment	Persistence	Adaptability	
Judgment		Aggressiveness	Humor	
		Self-confidence		
		Desire to excel		

Exhibit 6.3   Personality Factors Most Frequently Associated
with Effective Leadership

possesses greater verbal skills than the average person does. These results also help us understand more about leaders and what they need to do to succeed.

Studies examining emotional adjustment quite consistently found that leaders are more emotionally mature than nonleaders. Rather consistent support was also found for the relationship between leadership and self-confidence or self-esteem. Indeed, the relationship between self-confidence and leadership generally produced some of the highest correlations of any of the personality traits tested. Honesty or integrity is another characteristic attributed to good leaders. Several studies of the characteristics people admire most in leaders report that honesty and fairness are the most important traits.[15] Unless leaders are honest, no one seems to care much about their visions and goals.

Consequently, it is not correct to conclude that personal characteristics are unrelated to leadership; some characteristics are important, but their relationships are rather complex. Four major reviews have concluded that effective leadership does not depend solely on personality traits. Situational variables are also important and the situation often determines whether a personality characteristic will be positively or negatively associated with effective leadership. Each review concluded that leadership must be examined as an interaction of three variables: characteristics of the leader, characteristics of the subordinates, and the nature of the task.

More recently, research at the individual level has focused on leadership competencies, which refer to specific skills that leaders must be capable of performing at the right times and in the right ways. Three general leadership competencies that have been examined are leadership self-efficacy (being confident in one's ability to lead), leadership flexibility (being open to different perspectives and able to work with diverse people), and goal orientation (maintaining a focus on goal accomplishment).[16] Most leadership competencies, however, are unique to specific professions, such as HR competencies for human resource managers or clinical administrator leadership competencies for nursing.[17]

LEADER BEHAVIORS

A second line of leadership research examined leader behaviors in the context of the group and attempted to describe what leaders actually do. These studies examined whether certain ways of behaving were more effective than others: how do effective leaders behave differently from other group members? Most of these studies started in the 1940s and have continued since then.

Authoritarian, Democratic, and Laissez-faire Leadership

The contrasting political systems in the United States and Germany preceding World War II inspired one of the early classic studies of leadership that compared the effects of three leadership styles: authoritarian, democratic, and laissez-faire. Ten-year-old boys who were organized into groups of five boys participated in after-school activities under the leadership of a graduate student trained to provide democratic, autocratic, or laissez-faire leadership. Every six weeks the leaders were rotated among groups so that each group experienced each type of leadership. Under the **democratic leaders**, group decisions were made by majority vote in which equal participation was encouraged and criticism and punishment were minimal. Under the **autocratic leader**, all decisions were made by the leader and the boys were required to follow prescribed procedures under strict discipline. Under the **laissez-faire leader**, the actual leadership was minimized and the boys were allowed to work and play essentially without supervision.[18]

During the 18 weeks of this study, the performance of the boys was observed in order to assess the effects of the three leadership styles. Laissez-faire leadership produced the lowest levels of satisfaction and productivity, while autocratic leadership produced the highest levels of aggressive acts. Democratic leadership seemed to produce the most satisfied groups, who also functioned in the most orderly and positive manner, which is what the researchers hoped to find. However, the effects of the leadership styles on productivity were somewhat mixed, although actual measures of productivity were not obtained. Under autocratic leadership, the groups spent more time in productive work activity and had more work-related conversations, but appeared to be more productive only when the leader was present. When the leader left the room, the amount of work-related activity dropped drastically.

The results of this study were somewhat surprising to the researchers, who had expected the highest satisfaction and productivity under democratic leadership. This study was conducted under the direction of Kurt Lewin, a behavioral scientist who came to America from Germany just prior to World War II. Lewin believed that the repressive, autocratic political climate he had left in Germany was not as satisfying, productive, or desirable as a democratic society. He expected the results of the experiment to confirm his hypothesis. Although the boys preferred a democratic leader, they appeared to be more productive under autocratic leadership.

Other studies have also shown that democratic leadership styles are not always the most productive. In fact, some studies have found that both the satisfaction and the productivity of group members are higher under directive leaders than democratic leaders. For example, a study of 488 managers in a consumer loan company found that employees who had high authoritarianism scores (high acceptance of strong authority relationships) were more satisfied and productive when they worked for supervisors who had little tolerance for freedom.[19] Greater satisfaction with an authoritarian leader was also found in another study of over one thousand workers. This study found that employees who worked independently but were required to have frequent interaction with their superior preferred and were more satisfied with an autocratic leader. Some examples of such employees are fire fighters, police officers, and administrative aides.[20]

Conversely, laissez-faire leadership is not a zero type of leadership, but a destructive type of leadership that is often associated with workplace stressors, bullying at work, and psychological distress. When laissez-faire leaders abdicate the responsibilities and duties assigned to them, they fail to meet the legitimate expectations of others. Not only does their job not get done, but they also prevent others from doing it for them. At least one study has found that leaders who abdicate their responsibility to lead create situations that are characterized by high stress, role conflict, role ambiguity, and conflicts with coworkers.[21]

Production-centered and Employee-centered Leader Behaviors

Following World War II, a group of researchers at the University of Michigan began a series of leadership studies that identified two kinds of leadership behaviors that they called production-centered and employee-centered behaviors. Their research method involved nondirective interviews of supervisors and employees in matched units that performed similar work but differed in their performance levels. The high performing units had **employee-centered** supervisors who developed a supportive personal relationship with subordinates, avoided punitive behavior, and encouraged two-way communication with subordinates. The low performing units had **production-centered** supervisors who focused on establishing goals, giving instructions, checking on performance, and structuring the work of the group.[22] These two leader behaviors, which were viewed as opposite ends of a continuum, served as the foundation for the traditional human relations approach to leadership that called for more attention to the needs and interests of employees.

Subsequent research on the relationship between production-centered and employee-centered behaviors found them to be independent dimensions of leadership rather than opposite ends of one leadership continuum. A review of twenty-four studies dispelled a popular myth suggesting that supervisors focus on either production or people, and to the extent that they focus on one, they ignore the other. These studies indicated instead that supervisors can be interested in both production and employees. Therefore, a leader who has a strong production orientation is not necessarily uninterested in the employees, as illustrated in Exhibit 6.4.[23]

Employee-centered leadership
Behaviors that focus on helping group members feel satisfied and willing to contribute to the group.

Production-centered leadership
Behaviors that focus on performing the group's goals.

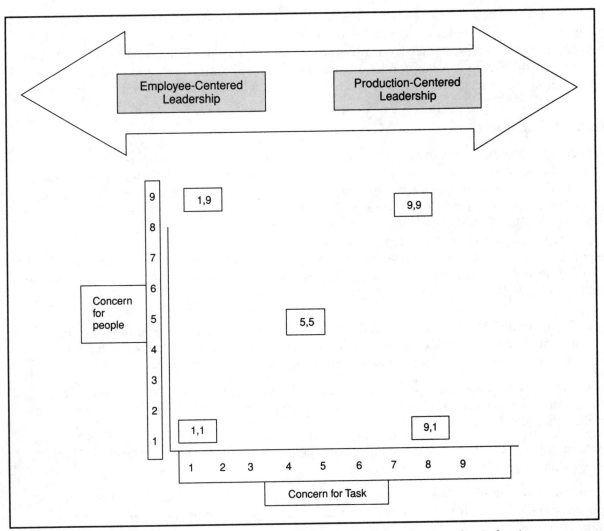

Exhibit 6.4   One-Dimensional versus Two-Dimensional Leader Behavior

Initiating Structure and Consideration

About the same time that the University of Michigan researchers were discovering the production-centered and employee-centered dimensions of leadership, a similar research program at The Ohio State University identified two similar dimensions of leader behavior which they called **initiating structure** and **consideration**.[24] These two dimensions were identified from questionnaires similar to the exercise at the end of this chapter that they developed and administered to thousands of employees and supervisors. **Initiating structure** consisted of leader behaviors associated with organizing and defining the work, the work relationships, and the goals. A leader who initiated structure was described as one who assigned people to particular tasks, expected workers to follow standard routines, and emphasized meeting deadlines. The factor of **consideration** involved leader behaviors that showed friendship, mutual trust, warmth, and concern for subordinates.

Survey data confirmed that initiating structure and consideration are independent dimensions of leadership behavior. Therefore, a leader could be high on both dimensions, low on both dimensions, or

Initiating structure
Leader behavior that focuses on clarifying and defining the roles and task responsibilities for subordinates.

Consideration
Leader behavior that focuses on the comfort, well-being, satisfaction, and need fulfillment of subordinates.

high on one and low on the other. Since both factors are important leader behaviors, the early studies assumed that effective leaders would be high on both dimensions; however, subsequent research failed to support this expectation. The most effective leaders are usually high on both dimensions, but not always. Occasionally other combinations have produced the highest levels of satisfaction and performance, including being high on one scale and low on the other or being at moderate levels on both dimensions.[25]

The Leadership Grid®

Another theory that combines concern for task accomplishment and a concern for people was created by Robert Blake and Jane Mouton using a 9x9 matrix called the **Leadership Grid**. The concern for production dimension is measured on a nine-point scale and represented along the horizontal dimension, while the vertical dimension measures an individual's concern for people, again using a nine-point scale, as illustrated in Exhibit 6.4. Blake and Mouton assume that the most effective leadership style is a 9,9 style, demonstrating both concern for production and concern for people.[26]

By responding to a questionnaire, individuals place themselves in one of the eighty-one cells on the Leadership Grid. Five different grid positions at the four corners and in the middle are typically used to illustrate different leadership styles:

1,9 Style—Country Club Management: a maximum concern for people with minimum concern for production. This individual is not concerned whether the group actually produces anything, but is highly concerned about the members' personal needs, interests, and interpersonal relationships.

9,1 Style—Authority-Compliance Management: primarily concerned with production and task accomplishment and unconcerned about people. This person wants to get the job done and wants to follow the schedule at all costs.

1,1 Style—Impoverished Management: minimal concern for both production and people. This person essentially abdicates the leadership role.

5,5 Style—Middle-of-the-road Management: a moderate concern for both people and production. This person organizes production to accomplish the necessary work while maintaining satisfactory morale.

9,9 Style—Team Management: a maximum concern for both production and people. This leader wants to meet schedules and get the job done, but at the same time is highly concerned about the feelings and interests of the group members.

The Leadership Grid is popular among managers, and it has been used extensively in management training to help managers move toward a 9,9 style. In spite of its popularity, however, the usefulness of the Leadership Grid has not been consistently supported by research. Most of the available research consists of case analyses that have been loosely interpreted to support it. Empirical research has failed to show that a 9,9 leadership style is universally superior. The demands of the situation, the expectations of other group members, and the nature of the work being performed interact in complex ways that call for a variety of leadership styles. Consequently, the 9,9 leadership style is not always the most effective.

Leader Behaviors as Leadership Roles

Research on leader behaviors helps us understand that both task-oriented and people-oriented leader behaviors are required for effective groups and someone in each group needs to perform these func-

---

Leadership Grid®
A matrix that combines two factors: concern for people and concern for production. Each factor is measured with a nine-point scale.

tions effectively. Rather than thinking of leadership strictly in terms of how a formal leader behaves, it is helpful to think of leadership as essential roles performed within a group. This line of thinking implies that leadership consists of essential leader behaviors that can be performed by any group member. The leadership roles of initiating structure and consideration are similar to the work roles and maintenance roles in groups. These two roles are necessary for a group to be effective and can be performed either by the formally appointed leader or by other group members.

If a task is already highly structured, or if other group members adequately structure the task themselves, then efforts by the leader to add additional structure are unnecessary and ineffective. Likewise, the maintenance roles of showing consideration and concern for group members may be performed by other group members, thereby eliminating the need for the formal leader to perform this role. Conversely, when the formally appointed leader fails to perform either of these vital leader behaviors, it is not unusual for an informal leader to emerge and perform them to help the group succeed.

SITUATIONAL LEADERSHIP

Research on both leader traits and leader behaviors failed to find one style of leadership that was universally superior. Extensive reviews concluded that effective leadership depended on more than the leader alone; what works well in one situation does not necessarily work well in other situations. These studies concluded that effective leadership depends on a combination of leadership styles, follower characteristics, and environmental factors. This approach to leadership is referred to as **situational leadership theory** or **contingency theories of leadership**.

Five situational leadership theories have received primary attention: (a) Paul Hersey and Ken Blanchard's life cycle theory of leadership, (b) Fred Fiedler's contingency theory of leadership, (c) Robert House's path-goal leadership theory, (d) Victor Vroom and Philip Yetton's decision-making model of leadership, and (e) Robert Tannenbaum and Warren Schmidt's model for choosing a leadership pattern.[27] All of these theories have contributed to our understanding of leadership and their conclusions provide valuable insights for leaders in specific settings. Rather than describing the development and results of each of these theories, they are combined into an integrated model of leadership effectiveness, and only the summary conclusions and applications are presented here. These theories all suggest that leader effectiveness depends on a combination of leader behavior styles, follower characteristics, and environmental factors, as illustrated in Exhibit 6.5.

Leader Behavior Styles

Leaders can select from among many different styles of leadership and these styles can involve varying levels of interpersonal sensitivity, affiliation, appreciation, and even humor. The most important variable influencing a person's leadership style is the degree to which the leader is willing to allow subordinates to participate in making decisions and directing their own actions. At one extreme is autocratic leadership where all decisions and influence come from the leader, and at the other end of the continuum is democratic leadership where the leader delegates authority to decide and act to the members of a group. This decision is influenced by the leader's value system, especially the value the leader places on participation and involvement by subordinates. The amount of confidence that leaders have in their subordinates, and the leader's ability to handle uncertainty, are also relevant considerations in selecting a leadership style.

When selecting a leadership style, a leader could choose any one of the following patterns that illustrate increasing levels of participation:

Contingency theories of leadership
Leadership theories that recognize the influence of situational variables in determining the ideal styles of leadership.

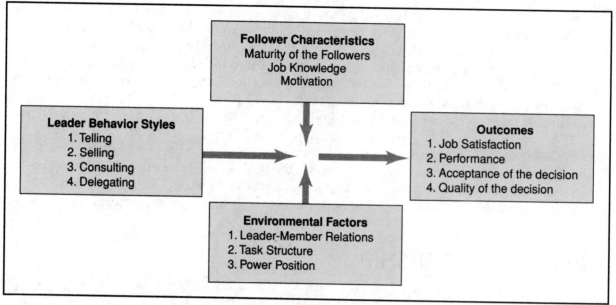

Exhibit 6.5   Situational Leadership Model

1. **Telling**: the leader makes all decisions; he or she simply announces them and tells subordinates what to do. This leadership style is the most autocratic and generally the least preferred by most subordinates. However, it may be appropriate when time is limited and an immediate decision is necessary.

2. **Selling**: the leader presents a tentative decision subject to change and attempts to sell the decision to subordinates. The leader may present ideas and invite questions so that subordinates feel that their ideas are heard. Most subordinates want their feelings and ideas to be considered: they like having an opportunity to ask questions.

3. **Consulting**: the leader presents the problem to the group and obtains their suggestions and preferences before making the decision. Group participation often yields higher quality ideas than when the leader acts alone. It also reduces resistance when implementing the decision.

4. **Delegating**: the leader may delegate the decision and its implementation to the group and let them handle it on their own, or the leader may join the group and participate as any other member in making and implementing the decision. This style requires great confidence in the ability and motivation of the group and usually requires much more time to make a decision. However, the acceptance of the decision is usually much faster and the implementation is much smoother when the entire group participates.

Involving subordinates in leadership decisions is often a good idea, but not always. To decide which is the most appropriate level of participation, a leader may want to consider the following questions:[28]

- As long as it is accepted, does it make any difference which decision is selected? Are some decisions qualitatively superior to others?
- Do I have enough information to make a high-quality decision, or do subordinates have additional information that ought to be considered?
- Is acceptance of the decision by subordinates crucial to effective implementation? If I make the decision by myself, will they accept it?
- Can I trust subordinates to base their decisions on the best interests of the organization?
- Will subordinates agree on the preferred solution or will there be conflict?
- How much time do we have to make this decision and what are the costs of delaying a decision to involve others?

Follower Characteristics

When selecting a leadership style, the leader should consider such follower characteristics as whether followers have high needs for independence, whether they are ready to assume responsibility for decision making, whether they are interested in the problems, and whether they have enough experience to deal with them. As subordinates gain greater skill and competence in managing themselves, leaders ought to give them more autonomy.[29]

The appropriate leadership style depends primarily on the maturity of the followers. Maturity is defined as the ability and willingness of people to take responsibility for directing their own behavior as it relates to the specific task being performed. An individual or group may demonstrate maturity on some tasks and immaturity on others. Maturity is determined by two components: job maturity (ability) and psychological maturity (willingness). Job maturity is the ability to successfully perform a task and is a function of the follower's job knowledge, training, experience, and skills. Psychological maturity refers to the willingness or motivation to perform the job and is a function of the follower's commitment and confidence.

Telling is an appropriate leadership style for subordinates who have low maturity and are both unable and unwilling to perform the job. Selling is appropriate for followers who are able but unwilling, while consulting is well suited for followers who are willing but unable to do the job. Delegation requires followers who are both able and willing.

Environmental Factors

Many environmental forces influence the appropriate leadership style, including the culture of the organization and its history of allowing subordinates to exercise autonomy, cohesiveness of the group and the degree to which the members work together as a unit, the nature of the problem itself and whether subordinates have the knowledge and experience needed to solve it, and the pressures of time, since group decision making is time-consuming and ineffective in a crisis situation.

Extensive research by Fred Fiedler found that some situations are much more favorable than others for leaders and his results showed that different situations call for different leader behaviors. The environmental factors that have the biggest impact on creating a favorable or unfavorable situation for a leader are:

1. **Leader-member relations**: whether the natural relationships in the situation are friendly and pleasant or unfriendly and unpleasant. A situation that naturally produces friendly relationships with group members is more favorable for a leader.
2. **Task structure**: whether the task is relatively structured and followers know what to do without being told, or unstructured so that the leader must clarify the goals, identify how the task is to be accomplished, and defend the selected solution. Having structured tasks where people know what to do is a more favorable situation for a leader than having to organize a chaotic situation.
3. **Power position**: whether the leader has a strong power position because of official recognition and the ability to administer rewards and punishments, or the leader has a weak power position that is not recognized or accepted. Leaders are in a more favorable position when their status as the leader is recognized and secure than when they have to negotiate or fight for it.

The combination of these three environmental factors determines whether the leader's situation is favorable or unfavorable. The most favorable position for a leader is to have positive leader-member relations, a structured task, and a strong power position. Conversely, the leader is in a very unfavorable situation when the leader-member relations are unpleasant, the task is unstructured, and the leader's power position is insecure. Between these two extremes, of course, are situations of moderate favorableness, which are very important in Fiedler's contingency theory because they call for a very different style of leadership from those of extremely favorable or unfavorable situations.

Fiedler conducted extensive research studies that examined the most effective leadership style in various situations. His research demonstrated that in extremely favorable situations, task-oriented leaders achieve the best results because they focus on getting the work done without worrying too much about their relationships with followers. In these situations, the personal needs of followers are apparently already satisfied and interpersonal sensitivity is unnecessary because there is already a friendly and comfortable situation.

Example—

The best leadership style in a professional association, such as the local Society for Human Resource Management, is a task-oriented leader because the situation is very favorable: the members usually like the leaders since they voluntarily chose to join, the leaders are formally elected, and the monthly luncheons are rather structured events. Task-oriented leaders succeed because they simply have to plan the events, advertise them, and keep the members united.

When the situation is extremely unfavorable, the same task-oriented style of leadership again achieves the best results because the job must get done and efforts to act friendly and concerned about followers will not make any difference. A task-oriented leader who simply focuses on getting the work done is more effective than a relationship-oriented leader who spends time fruitlessly trying to build good relationships in an impossible situation.

Example—

The best leadership style for substitute school teachers is a task-oriented style when they face a very unfavorable situation, such as when they are despised by the students, they cannot discipline students effectively, and they have to create their own lesson plans. To succeed in these situations, the substitute teachers must be firm, authoritative, and confident.

At intermediate levels of favorableness, however, a much different style of leadership is superior. Here, the ideal style is one that is sensitive to the feelings and interests of followers. Interpersonal sensitivity and involvement are important at intermediate levels, since followers need to feel included and relevant. Concern for the group members is apparently a necessary prerequisite for motivating them to perform well.

Example—

In a friendship group of co-workers who eat lunch together every Friday, the leader needs to be sensitive to the interests of group members. This situation is moderately favorable to the leader because, even though there are positive leader-member relations, the task is unstructured and the leader's position is vague. Therefore, the best leader style is one that invites suggestions about where the group wants to go and shows genuine concern for the feelings of each member.

DETERMINANTS OF LEADERSHIP EFFECTIVENESS

Strategies for Improving Leadership

Since the quality of leadership contributes so greatly to the effectiveness of an organization, knowing how to increase leader effectiveness is a serious issue. Improved leader behavior is not a panacea for all organizational problems, but quality leadership is so important that improving the quality of leadership should be an ongoing effort in every organization. Four of the most popular methods of increasing leadership effectiveness include organizational redesign, leadership training, managerial selection and placement, and rewarding leader behavior.

Organizational Engineering

The fastest and sometimes the most effective way to improve leadership is to change the situation so the leaders' skills and orientations match the demands of the situation. When people are placed in situations that are inconsistent with their leadership style, they are generally unsuccessful and they feel very frustrated until they are reassigned. Fiedler's research suggested that the basic leader orientations of most people are rather stable and not easily changed. Therefore, he recommends that organizations engineer the job to fit the manager.[30] This approach is particularly useful when a specific individual is necessary to the organization, yet that person does not possess a compatible leadership style. The job can be changed most easily by changing the degree of task structure or the power position of the leader.

Leadership Training

Although training can help leaders acquire better leadership skills, it is doubtful that such training will change a leader's basic leadership orientation or personality structure. Nevertheless, leadership involves important interpersonal skills that can be acquired through instruction and practice. Leaders can benefit from training in interpersonal skills and management functions—planning, organizing, directing, and controlling. Leaders need to know the differences between transactional and transformational leadership and have an opportunity to practice the skills involved in each kind of leadership. Leadership skills can be acquired through vicarious learning by watching effective leaders and observing how they solve problems and influence people. People who want to learn and who are willing to accept and respond to feedback can improve their leadership skills.

Managerial Selection and Placement

Since basic leadership orientations are not easily changed, companies should select leaders who have leadership styles that fit the situation. Biographical information examining a person's previous leadership experiences can help to predict future leadership effectiveness. Having an organization that is staffed with effective leaders depends far more on good selection than on training.

Rewarding Leader Behavior

Leaders can acquire new leadership skills and learn different leader behaviors if they are sufficiently motivated to experiment and learn. A variety of incentives can reward leaders for learning and developing. Pay increases and promotions are popular incentives that encourage leaders to improve. However, the most powerful incentive is probably the intrinsic satisfaction that comes from greater self-confidence and improved interpersonal relationships between leaders and members.

Reciprocal Influence of Leader and Follower

With thousands of books and articles written about leadership, it is surprising that so little has been written about "followership." We seem to assume that leadership is a one-way process in which leaders influence followers; we overlook the influence in the opposite direction. Only meager efforts have attempted to describe the influence of the group on the leader.

The discussion to this point has assumed that leaders influence followers—that the satisfaction and performance of the followers is caused by the leader's behavior. There are good reasons to reverse this statement, however, and argue that the behavior of the leaders is caused by the performance and satisfaction of the followers. When we acknowledge the leader's capacity to reward the behavior of followers, we should not overlook the capacity of the followers to reward the leader by the ways they perform. For example, organizations reward managers according to the performance of their group. Consequently, the managers of high-performing groups are highly rewarded because of their group's success.

One study has demonstrated the reciprocal nature of influence between leaders and subordinates. In this study, data were collected from first-line managers and two of the supervisors who reported to them. Leaders who were more considerate created greater satisfaction among their subordinates; at the same time, the performance of the subordinates caused changes in the behavior of the leaders. Employees who performed well caused their supervisors to reward them and treat them with greater consideration.

Although research on the reciprocal influence between leaders and followers is still rather limited, it is important to remember that leadership may be significantly constrained by the followers.[31]

Some observers contend that the leadership crisis in society is not really caused by bad leaders, but by incompetent or uncooperative followers who fail to complete their work in an active, intelligent, and ethical way. Effective followers are characterized as having (1) personal integrity that demands loyalty to the organization and a willingness to follow their own beliefs, (2) an understanding of the organization and their assigned roles, (3) versatility, and (4) personal responsibility.

Constraints on Leader Behavior

Leaders do not have unlimited opportunities to influence others. Leadership effectiveness is constrained by a variety of factors, such as the extent to which managerial decisions are preprogrammed because of precedent, structure, technological specifications, laws, and the absence of available alternatives. Leadership can also be constrained by a variety of organizational factors limiting the leader's ability either to communicate with or reinforce the behavior of subordinates. The constraints imposed on leaders include external factors, organizational policies, group factors, and individual skills and abilities.

1. **External factors.** Leaders are constrained in what they can do because of economic realities and a host of state and federal laws. For example, leaders are required to pay at least the minimum wage and they are required to enforce safety standards. Leaders who have unskilled followers will have difficulty leading regardless of their leadership style, and the availability of skilled followers is influenced by the external labor market. Some locations have a better supply of skilled employees than others.
2. **Organizational policies.** The organization may constrain a leader's effectiveness by limiting the amount of interaction between leaders and followers or by restricting the leader's ability to reward or punish followers. The history and culture of an organization may limit what a leader is allowed to do and what is considered acceptable.
3. **Group factors.** Group norms are created by the dynamics of the group. If the group is highly cohesive and very determined, it can limit the leader's ability to influence the group. Leaders depend on the cooperation of their groups; a united group has the capacity to blunt or even destroy the influence of a leader.
4. **Individual skills and abilities.** The leader's own skills and abilities may act as constraints, since leaders can only possess so much expertise, energy, and power. Some situations may simply require greater skills and abilities than the leader may possibly hope to possess.

Substitutes for Leadership

While some situations constrain leaders, other situations make leadership unnecessary. These variables are referred to as **leader substitutes** because they substitute for leadership, either by making the leader's behavior unnecessary or neutralizing the leader's ability to influence subordinates. An example of a variable that tends to substitute for leadership is training. Subordinates who have extensive experience, ability, and training tend to eliminate the need for instrumental leadership. Task instructions are simply unnecessary when subordinates already know what to do.

Substitutes for leadership
Subordinate, task, or organizational factors that decrease the importance of a leader's influence; forces within the environment that supplant or replace the influence of the leader.

Example—
When an ambulance arrives at the emergency room of a hospital, the ER employees do not wait for instructions from a leader before taking action. These employees are highly-trained professionals who have worked in similar situations, even if it has been with different co-workers, and they know what to do because of their training and experience.

Realizing that there are constraints on a leader's behavior and that other factors may serve to neutralize or substitute for the influence of a leader helps explain why the research on leadership has produced such inconsistent results. The inconsistency does not mean that leadership is unimportant; rather, it illustrates the complexity of the world in which leaders are required to function. The complexity of the situation, however, may prevent us from knowing in advance which leadership behaviors will be the most effective.

Leadership is an extremely important function that has an enormous influence on the effectiveness of groups and organizations. Our advice is that you take advantage of leadership opportunities and do your best to learn from them. Don't hesitate or be afraid to be a leader. Leadership skills improve in time with practice and feedback. Even great transformational leaders had to develop their interpersonal skills through successive experiences in which they often failed.

NOTES

1. Warren Bennis, *On Becoming a Leader* (Reading, Mass.: Addison-Wesley, 1989); Warren Bennis, "Why Leaders Can't Lead," *Training and Development Journal*, vol. 43 (April 1989), pp. 35–39; James Kotterman, "Leadership Versus Management: What's the Difference?" *The Journal for Quality and Participation*, vol. 29 (no. 2, 2006), pp. 13–17.

2. John P. Kotter, "What Leaders Really Do," *Harvard Business Review*, vol. 68 (May-June, 1990), pp. 103–111; Abraham Zaleznik, "Managers and Leaders: Are They Different?" *Harvard Business Review*, vol. 70 (March-April 1992), pp. 126–135; A. Zaleznik, "Managers and Leaders: Are They Different?" *Harvard Business Review on Leadership*, Harvard Business School Press, 1988.

3. Bernard M. Bass, "From Transactional to Transformational Leadership: Learning to Share the Vision," *Organizational Dynamics*, vol. 18 (Winter 1990), pp. 19–31; James M. Burns, *Leadership*, (New York: Harper & Row, 1978); Bruce J. Avolio, David A. Waldman, and Francis J. Yammarino, "Leading in the 1990s: The Four I's of Transformational Leadership," *Journal of European Industrial Training*, vol. 15, (no. 4, 1991), pp. 9–16.

4. Paul D. Cherulnik, Kristina A. Donley, Tay Sha R. Wiewel, and Susan R. Miller, "Charisma Is Contagious: The Effect of Leaders' Charisma on Observers' Affect," *Journal of Applied Social Psychology*, vol. 31 (2001), pp. 2149–2159.

5. Bernard M. Bass, *Leadership and Performance Beyond Expectations* (New York: Free Press, 1985); John J. Hater and Bernard M. Bass, "Superiors' Evaluations and Subordinates' Perceptions of Transformational and Transactional Leadership," *Journal of Applied Psychology*, vol. 73 (November 1988), pp. 695–702.

6. Bernard M. Bass, "From Transactional to Transformational Leadership: Learning to Share the Vision," *Organizational Dynamics*, vol. 18 (Winter 1990), pp. 19–31.

7. Francis J. Yammarino and Bernard M. Bass, "Transformational Leadership and Multiple Levels of Analysis," *Human Relations*, vol. 43 (October 1990), pp. 975–995.

8. Ronald J. Deluga, "Relationship of Transformational and Transactional Leadership with Employee Influencing Strategies," *Group and Organization Studies*, vol.13 (December 1988), pp. 456–467; Joseph Seltzer and Bernard M. Bass, "Transformational Leadership: Beyond Initiation and Consideration," *Journal of Management*, vol. 16 (December 1990), pp. 693–703; William D.

Spangler and Lewis R. Braiotta, "Leadership and Corporate Audit Committee Effectiveness," *Group and Organization Studies*, vol.15 (June 1990), pp. 134–157; David A. Waldman, Bernard M. Bass, and Francis J. Yammarino, "Adding to Contingent-Reward Behavior: The Augmenting Effect of Charismatic Leadership," *Group and Organization Studies*, vol. 15 (December 1990), pp. 381–394; Francis J. Yammarino and Bernard M. Bass, "Transformational Leadership and Multiple Levels of Analysis," *Human Relations*, vol. 43 (October 1990), pp. 975–995.

9. Bernard M. Bass and Bruce J. Avolio, "Developing Transformational Leadership: 1992 and Beyond," *Journal of European Industrial Training*, vol. 14, (no. 5, 1990), pp. 21–27; Micha Popper, Ori Landau, and Ury M. Gluskines, "The Israeli Defense Forces: An Example of Transformational Leadership," *Leadership and Organization Development Journal*, vol. 13, (no. 1, 1992), pp. 3–8; Francis J. Yammarino and Bernard Bass, Transformational Leadership and Multiple Levels of Analysis," *Human Relations*, vol. 43 (October 1990), pp. 975-995.

10. Joyce E. Bono and Timothy A. Judge, "Personality and Transformational and Transactional Leadership: A Meta-Analysis," *Journal of Applied Psychology*, vol. 89 (2004), pp. 901–910.

11. Bernard M. Bass, *Leadership, Psychology, and Organizational Behavior* (New York: Harper & Row, 1960); Cecil A. Gibb, "Leadership," in G. Lindzey and E. Aronson (Eds.), *The Handbook of Social Psychology*, 2nd ed., vol. 4 (Reading, Mass.: Addison-Wesley, 1969); R. D. Mann, "A Review of the Relationships Between Personality and Performance in Small Groups," *Psychological Bulletin*, vol. 56 (1959), pp. 241–270; Ralph M. Stogdill, "Personal Factors Associated with Leadership: A Survey of the Literature," *Journal of Psychology*, vol. 25 (1948), pp. 35–71; G. Yukl, A. Gordon, and T. Taber, "A Hierarchical Taxonomy of Leadership Behavior: Integrating a Half Century of Behavior Research," *Journal of Leadership and Organizational Studies*, vol. 9 (2002), pp. 15–32; S. J. Zaccaro, (2007). "Trait-based leadership." *American Psychologist, 62*, 6–16.

12. E. B. Gowin, *The Executive and His Control of Men* (New York: Macmillan, 1915).

13. Stogdill, op. cit.

14. Stogdill, op. cit.

15. Shelley A. Kirkpatrick and Edwin A. Locke, "Leadership: Do Traits Matter?" *Academy of Management Executive*, vol. 5 (May 1991), pp. 49–60; J. M. Kouzes and B. Z. Posner, *The Leadership Challenge: How to Keep Getting Extraordinary Things Done in Organizations* (San Francisco: Jossey-Bass Publishers, 1995).

16. David W. Chan, "Leadership and Intelligence," *Roeper Review*, vol. 29 (Spring, 2007), pp. 183–189.

17. *Leadership Competencies for Clinical Managers, The Renaissance of Transformational Leadership.* Edited by Anne M. Baker, Dori Taylor Sullivan, and Michael J. Emery. (Jones and Bartlett Publishers, 2006).

18. Kurt Lewin, R. Lippitt, and R. K. White, "Patterns of Aggressive Behavior in Experimentally-Created Social Climates," *Journal of Social Psychology*, vol. 10 (1939), pp. 271–301.

19. Henry Tosi, "Effect of the Interaction of Leader Behavior and Subordinate Authoritarianism," *Proceedings of the Annual Convention of the American Psychological Association*, vol. 6 part 1 (1971), pp. 473–474.

20. Victor H. Vroom and Floyd C. Mann, "Leader Authoritarianism and Employee Attitudes," *Personnel Psychology*, vol. 13 (1960), pp. 125–140.

21. Anders Skogstad, Stale Einarsen, Torbjorn Torsheim, Merethe Schanke Aasland, and Hilde Hetland, "The Destructiveness of Laissez-Faire Leadership Behavior," *Journal of Occupational Health Psychology*, vol. 12 (2007), pp. 80–92.

22. Daniel Katz, N. Maccoby, and N. C. Morse, *Productivity, Supervision, and Morale in an Office Situation* (Ann Arbor: University of Michigan Survey Research Center, 1950).

23. Peter Weissenberg and M. H. Kavanagh, "The Independence of Initiating Structure and Consideration: A Review of the Evidence," *Personnel Psychology*, vol. 25 (Spring 1972), pp. 119–130.

24. John K. Hemphill, *Leader Behavior Description* (Ohio State Leadership Studies Staff Report, 1950); Ralph M. Stogdill, *Handbook of Leadership* (New York: The Free Press, 1974), Chaps. 11 and 12.

25. E. A. Fleishman, "Twenty Years of Consideration and Structure," in E. A. Fleishman and J. G. Hunt (Eds.), *Current Developments in the Study of Leadership* (Carbondale: Southern Illinois University Press, 1973), pp. 1–40; E. A. Fleishman and E. F. Harris, "Patterns of Leadership Behavior Related to Employee Grievances and Turnover," *Personnel Psychology*, vol. 15 (1962), pp. 43–56.

26. Robert R. Blake and Anne Adams McCanse, *Leadership Dilemmas – Grid Solutions* (Houston: Gulf Publishing, 1991).

27. Paul Hersey, Ken Blanchard, and Dewey E. Johnson, *Management of Organizational Behavior*, 9th ed. (Upper Saddle River, N. J.: Prentice-Hall, 2008); Fred E. Fiedler and Martin M. Chemers, *Leadership and Effective Management* (Glenview, Ill.: Scott, Foresman, 1974); Robert J. House and Terrence R. Mitchell, "Path-Goal Theory of Leadership," *Journal of Contemporary Business* (Autumn 1974), pp. 81–98; Victor H. Vroom and Philip W. Yetton, *Leadership and Decision-Making* (Pittsburgh: University of Pittsburgh Press, 1973); Robert Tannenbaum and Warren H. Schmidt, "How to Choose a Leadership Pattern," *Harvard Business Review*, vol. 51 (May-June, 1973).

28. V. H. Vroom, "Leadership and the Decision-Making Process." *Organizational Dynamics*, vol. 28 (2000), pp. 82–94; Victor H. Vroom and Arthur G. Jago, "The Role of the Situation in Leadership," *American Psychologist*, vol. 62 (2007), pp. 17–24.

29. Seokhwa Yun, Jonathan Cox, and Henry P. Sims, "The Forgotten Follower: A Contingency Model of Leadership and Follower Self-Leadership," *Journal of Managerial Psychology*," vol. 21 (2006), pp. 374–388

30. Fred E. Fiedler, "Change the Job to Fit the Manager," *Harvard Business Review*, vol. 43 (1965), pp. 115–122; F. E. Fiedler, "Research on Leadership Selection and Training: One View of the Future," *Administrative Science Quarterly*, vol. 41, (1996), pp. 241–250.

31. Charles N. Green, "The Reciprocal Nature of Influence Between Leader and Subordinate," *Journal of Applied Psychology*, vol. 59 (April 1975), pp. 187–193; Ifechukude B. Mmobousi, "Followership Behavior: A Neglected Aspect of Leadership Studies," *Leadership and Organizational Development Journal*, vol. 12, no. 7 (1991), pp. 11–16.

Organizational Culture

DEFINING ORGANIZATIONAL CULTURE

Organizational culture consists of socially acquired rules of conduct that are shared by members of the organization. Some researchers believe that some aspects of an organization's culture are so intangible and pervasive that even the members of the organization cannot be expected to describe them accurately. Nevertheless, an understanding of organizational culture is essential to building effective organizations. Like the powerful undercurrents of ocean tides and rivers that move mighty ships, or the hidden icebergs that can destroy these ships, an organization's culture affects the entire organization.

Culture defines the basic organizational values and communicates to new members the correct ways to think and act and the ways things ought to be done. Culture enhances the stability of the organization and helps members interpret organizational activities and events. The focus of culture is to provide members with a sense of identity and to generate within them a commitment to the beliefs and values of the organization. In this chapter, we define culture and explain how it develops, how it is maintained, how it affects organizational events, and how it can be changed.

Organizational Climate

Each organization has its own unique constellation of characteristics and properties. **Organizational climate** and **organizational culture** are two terms that have been used to describe organizations and their subunits. Although these two terms are used interchangeably and refer to similar phenomena, a subtle distinction is often made regarding their permanence: **culture** generally refers to organizational rules and beliefs that are relatively enduring and resistant to change, whereas **climate** is used to describe characteristics that are temporary and capable of being changed. Climate typically refers to people's attitudes and how they feel about the organization. For example, we might characterize an organization's climate as "supportive," "trusting," or perhaps "fearful" or "hostile." These attitudes and feelings are often a function of the organization's culture. The weather has been used as a popular analogy to explain the differences between culture and climate. Like daily weather patterns, organizational climate (employee attitudes) can fluctuate from time to time because of organizational changes. Culture, however, is like the seasons of the year, which change slowly over time. The seasons are associated with stable and enduring weather characteristics that transcend daily variations.[1]

Organizational Culture

The people who study culture have tried to make a clear distinction between culture and climate. **Culture** refers to something that is more stable and enduring than climate, and it is more difficult to define and evaluate. While climate can be measured quantitatively by asking employees to complete a climate survey, culture is usually measured qualitatively using the ethnographic research methods from anthropology.[2]

Levels of Organizational Culture

Organizational culture is difficult to understand because it includes virtually every aspect of the organization, and the most important elements of culture are not visible. Culture can be studied from four very different levels of analysis: artifacts, norms, values, and underlying assumptions.

Organizational climate
The characteristics describing an organization that are relatively visible and stable, but amenable to change.

Organizational culture
The shared beliefs and expectations among the members of an organization that are relatively enduring and resistant to change.

Cultural Artifacts

The most superficial and visible level of organizational culture consists of artifacts and symbols. **Cultural artifacts** are tangible aspects of culture—the behaviors, language, and physical symbols—that we can perceive with our senses and that reflect the rules and core beliefs of the organization's culture. Many of these symbols are readily apparent to anyone who visits an organization and observes its surroundings.

Example—
The furnishings in the buildings and the appearance of the people at a police station are very different from those of the people at a corporate headquarters, a factory, or a university. The uniforms, badges, and other symbols of authority at a police station are intended to convey a much different message than the comfortable chairs and lavish surroundings of a corporate headquarters.

Ceremonies and rituals are also illustrations of cultural artifacts that reflect the rules governing behavior in the organization.

Example—
NuSkin Enterprises holds regular conventions for the people who distribute its products. These conventions are important cultural events because large numbers of members who normally have little contact with others gather to recognize and reward those distributors who have been successful. These recognition ceremonies reinforce the company's core values, and much of the convention is devoted to articulating the "rules" for getting ahead as distributors of the company's products.

Shared Norms

The next level of culture consists of **shared norms** of the organization. These norms, or situation-specific rules, are often not directly visible but can be inferred from the organization's artifacts. Key norms can often be determined by the degree of consistency in how group members act. For example, if students raise their hands and wait to be recognized before commenting in class, we can infer that there is a norm of hand raising. If the majority of team members report to committee meetings five or ten minutes late, we can infer that being on time is not an important norm. Some norms are explicitly spelled out, either verbally or in writing, often with penalties for not complying with the norms. Thus we can also look to formal documents such as employee manuals to glean some information regarding norms.

Example—
During the preschool orientation, the director of the MBA program told the students, "Don't show up unprepared to your team meetings." As a result of this comment, almost every field study team in the MBA program had an informal norm of coming prepared to team meetings, even though this was never discussed. Members would delegate assignments at each meeting and before the next meeting they would complete their assignment and e-mail a progress report to other team members.

Cultural artifacts
The visible symbols and objects that are unique to an organization and that suggest the kinds of shared beliefs and expectations of members.

Shared norms
The common expectations that guide the behavior of organizational members.

Cultural Values

The next level of culture, **cultural values**, represent the collective beliefs, ideals, and feelings of members about the things that are good, proper, valuable, rational, and right. Unlike the situation-specific nature of norms, values are broader rules that are applied across situations. Values are often identified in statements of corporate values or management philosophy.

Example—

The United States Air Force has the following core values that each member is expected to memorize and live: "Integrity first, service before self, and excellence in all we do." These values set the standards of conduct for every member and influence the culture throughout this branch of the military.

Example—

On its home page, General Mills advertises four values: (1) champion brands—building leading brands that our consumers trust around the world—making lives easier, healthier and more fun; (2) champion people—diverse, talented, committed people—constantly learning and growing and contributing to our communities; (3) championship innovation—developing and implementing innovative ideas to build our brands and drive our business; and (4) championship performance—delivering outstanding performance for our investors, our customers, our consumers, and ourselves.

Example—

The most well-known list of values is probably the Scout Laws of the Boy Scouts of America: "A scout is trustworthy, loyal, helpful, friendly, courteous, kind, obedient, cheerful, thrifty, brave, clean, and reverent." These values are expected to guide the behavior of scouts in a variety of situations, and scout leaders are expected to instill these values in the members of their troops.

Companies have multiple values and four criteria have been proposed for examining their usefulness to a company: values should be viable (feasible in the current business environment), balanced (relative to the importance of each other), aligned (consistent with each other), and authentic (sincerely and genuinely espoused).[3] If a value, such as "respond immediately to every patient request" is not feasible, then it is not viable. If undue emphasis is placed on it while other values are suppressed, it is not balanced. If it is inconsistent with other values, it is not aligned. And, if no one really believes in it, it is not authentic. In most organizations there is usually a discrepancy between the "ideal values" and the "real values;" not all members behave in ways consistent with the values. Thus, when studying an organization's values, we must be careful to articulate what people say they believe and what they actually do. In some organizations, the discrepancy between stated ideals and actual behavior is so great that it causes people to become disillusioned with the organization and has a negative impact on morale. For example, if a company publicly states that it values "serving the customer," but fails to provide employees with the necessary training or resources to serve customers well, then there will likely be significant cynicism and low morale in the workforce.

Cultural values
The social values that are shared among the members of an organization and tend to regulate their individual behaviors and induce collective conformity.

Shared Assumptions

The deepest level of culture consists of **shared assumptions** that provide a foundation for how people think about what happens in organizations. These assumptions represent beliefs about reality and human nature that are taken for granted and deeply embedded in the way we understand and interpret daily life. Consequently, shared assumptions are the most difficult to study.

Core Shared Assumptions

Although the shared assumptions in an organization are extremely difficult to identify and describe, these assumptions are the most interesting aspect of culture to study because of their pervasive impact on how people behave and their implications for improving organizational effectiveness. Efforts to understand organizational cultures have identified some of the most significant categories of shared assumptions:[4]

1. **Human Nature.** Are people basically good, basically evil, or neither good nor evil? Can people be trusted? What is the value of a human life and do people care for one another?
2. **The Nature of Relationships.** Are relationships between people primarily hierarchical, equivalent, or individualistic in nature? Is there a caste system, and do some people "matter" more than others because of their status in society or their position in an organizational hierarchy?
3. **The Nature of Truth.** Is truth revealed by external authority figures, or is the accuracy of information determined by a process of personal investigation or scientific testing?
4. **Our Fit with the Environment.** What is our relationship with the environment? Do members believe they have the capacity to master the environment? Are they supposed to live in harmony with it? Do they think they are controlled by it?
5. **Time Orientation.** Are members of the organization primarily oriented to the past, the present, or the future? How long is our history and how much does it constrain the present and the future?
6. **Assumptions about Activity.** Assumptions about the nature of human activity can be divided into three approaches: (a) a "doing" orientation where people are basically active and evaluated according to what they produce, (b) a "being" orientation where people are passive and tolerant of existing circumstances, and (c) a "becoming" orientation where people are continually developing and becoming an integrated whole.
7. **Universalism/Particularism.** Do we treat all members of the organization the same regardless of their background (**universalism**), or do we treat people differently based on certain criteria such as race, age, religion, family affiliation, and so on (**particularism**)?

These assumptions, while often unspoken, form the foundation of the culture and are reflected in the artifacts, norms, and values. For example, suppose a manager decided to organize his department around the assumption that his employees were lazy and couldn't be trusted to do their work. We might find a variety of control mechanisms—time sheets, spot checks, harsh punishment for mistakes—to be key artifacts of such a culture. These artifacts would reflect norms and values of distrust and high control on the part of the manager. The culture of the department would likely be quite different, however, if it were based on the assumption that all employees could be trusted to work hard and make significant contributions to the organization. Uncovering these tacit assumptions is an important part of cultural analysis.

Shared assumptions
The foundation beliefs that impact how people think about and respond to organizational events, but which are mostly subconscious.

DEVELOPMENT OF ORGANIZATIONAL CULTURE

Since culture refers to the complex configuration of shared artifacts, norms, values, and assumptions, it cannot simply be dictated by top management. Indeed, many researchers argue that the pronouncements and speeches of top management do very little to create the fundamental beliefs and values that are both created by and reflected in the ceremonies, stories, symbols, and slogans within the organization.[5] An organization's culture is not created by any single person or event, but by a complex combination of forces that include the visions of the founders, the expectations of leaders, the contributions of organizational members, and the way the organization has historically responded to problems of internal integration and external adaptation.

Founder Expectations

Founders have a large influence on the culture of an organization, especially in the beginning. Their expectations, their decisions, how they treat people, how they spend their time, and what they value have a major impact on what employees value and how outsiders perceive the organization. Unless the founder's influence becomes institutionalized, however, the impact of a founder diminishes as the organization grows. The impact of a founder is recognized by the kinds of questions that are typically included in a culture audit:[6]

1. Why was the organization started? What was the founder trying to achieve?
2. What problems did the founder encounter in managing the business? How were they solved?
3. What are the founder's values and assumptions concerning how the organization should be managed?

Later in the life of the organization, its culture will reflect a complex mixture of the assumptions and values of the founder as well as other early leaders. Current leaders can also have a significant impact on creating or changing an organization's culture, especially by the example they set. Because leaders are so visible, their actions and comments are observed by people both in and out of the organization. The leadership style of a CEO is often imitated by other managers and supervisors throughout an organization. Great transformational leaders have the capacity to create a new vision and inspire members to change how they think about the organization.[7]

Member Contributions

The members of an organization bring with them their own personal cultures which come from their families, their communities, their religions, any professional associations to which they belong, and their nationalities. The members of the organization have been raised in a particular society and thus bring the dominant values of the society into the firm. For example, the culture of the United States is much different from the culture in Egypt. In the United States, individuals learn to place a high value on freedom of speech, respect for individual privacy, and acceptance of new technology, for example. Egyptians place a high value on fundamental Islamic teachings and perpetuating traditional practices both at home and at work. Therefore, the culture of a company with mostly Americans would likely be very different from the culture of a company with mostly Egyptians.

The actions of members contribute to the culture of an organization, which means that its culture is constantly changing in small ways as people come and go. Some individuals are cantankerous, unhappy souls who can find endless opportunities to complain and criticize. These people create an unpleasant work environment that may be very destructive and difficult to change as long as they are there. Other individuals are unselfish and altruistic and find genuine satisfaction in performing random acts of kindness. These people create a happy and satisfying work environment that is contagious and spreads to other coworkers.

Example—
Steve Harrison, chairman of Lee Hecht Harrison, encourages people to perform regular acts of what he calls **business decencies**. Some examples of the kinds of deliberate decencies he tries to perform include: write one thank-you note on paper or via e-mail each day; give praise in public, criticism in private; take time to talk to receptionists, administrative assistants and maintenance people; acknowledge the family, friends, and outside interests of people who work for you; convey bad news in person; and make yourself easily accessible by having regular open office hours.[8]

Historical Accommodations

Every organization has to confront two major challenges that impact the development of its culture: (a) external adaptation and (b) internal integration.[9] **External adaptation** and survival refer to the way an organization secures its place in industry and the way it copes with a constantly changing external environment. As members of an organization attempt to solve various problems posed by the organization's environment, they develop "solutions" to these problems (e.g. how to find and treat customers, what products do customers want, how do we deal with downturns in the economy, etc.), which then form the rules that members of the organization will follow in the future. External adaptation requires the organization to face the following issues associated with its mission and strategy:

1. What major crises has the organization confronted? How did it deal with these crises?
2. What major changes have been made in its strategy, structure, technology, size, and leadership? How and why were the changes made? How did these changes affect the organization?
3. What are the specific goals the organization is striving to achieve? What problem has the organization solved that has allowed it to achieve its mission and goals?

Internal integration is concerned with establishing and maintaining effective working relationships among the members of an organization. Internally, organizational culture helps to define the criteria for the allocation of power and status. Every organization establishes a pecking order and rules for how members acquire, maintain, and lose power. These rules help members manage their expectations and feelings of aggression. The criteria for allocating rewards and punishments are also defined by the organizational culture. The legends and myths let members know which behaviors are heroic or sinful—what gets rewarded with status and power and what gets punished through withdrawal of rewards or excommunication. Internal integration is concerned with the following kinds of issues:

1. How does the organization reward and control its members?
2. Are decisions made participatively or autocratically?
3. Are the relationships between employees close and friendly or distant and individualistic?
4. What criteria are used for finding new recruits for the organization? How are these new recruits socialized and trained?
5. What does an employee need to know or do to become an accepted member of the organizativon and be successful?

An organization's culture emerges when members and leaders share ideas, values, aspirations, and assumptions as they discover ways to cope with issues of external adaptation and internal integration. The creation of a culture appears to be a complex combination of forces that involve members and leaders striving to adjust to internal and external demands.

External adaptation
How the organization responds to the external environment and the changes that occur in it.

Internal integration
How the organization coordinates its internal systems and processes.

MAINTAINING ORGANIZATIONAL CULTURE

Organizational cultures are maintained by a combination of many forces, especially (a) the selection and retention of employees, (b) the allocation of rewards and status, (c) the reactions of leaders, (d) the rites and ceremonies, (e) the stories and symbols, and (f) the reactions to crises.

Employee Selection

Organizations tend to hire people who match their culture. They want employees who will fit in and adapt to the organization's culture. The recruitment and selection procedures in a company are designed to identify not just the specific skills and talents of job applicants, but also their personalities and interests. The organization then maintains its culture by disciplining or even terminating employees who consistently deviate from accepted norms and practices. Thus, discipline procedures also become an important instrument for maintaining cultural values.

Other human resource practices also help to reinforce the organization's culture. For example, the assumptions, values, and beliefs of a company can be controlled and reinforced by those who establish the criteria for evaluating employees, decide which managers get promoted, set the standards that determine how pay increases are granted, and develop and present the orientation training. These practices become known throughout the organization and serve to maintain or change an existing culture.

Reward Allocations

An organization's reward system can either maintain or change its culture. The rewards and punishments attached to various behaviors convey to employees the priorities and values of both individual managers and the organization. A dramatic change in an organization's reward system can make a significant change in its culture almost overnight.

> ***Example—***
> The culture of a company in the agricultural industry changed quite dramatically after it implemented a profit sharing plan. Within a period of just two or three months, the culture changed from one of distrust and disregard for employees to a culture of caring and fairness. Rather than having all year-end bonuses distributed by managers to the assistant managers based on personal relationships, a fixed percent of the profit was distributed to all employees according to a formula that combined base pay and years of service. The plan was greeted with suspicion when it was first announced, but after the first profit share was distributed, a new culture quickly emerged that had a dramatic impact on the degree of cooperation, interpersonal relationships, patterns of communication, involvement in decision making, styles of leadership, distribution of power, and feelings of respect for all members.

Leader Behaviors

Although it is rather subtle, what managers pay attention to is one of the more powerful methods of maintaining organizational culture. Administrators perform a variety of symbolic activities that influence the power relationships in organizations. The following is a list of symbolic actions that explain what leaders can do to increase their personal power and exert greater influence in an organization.

1. **Spend time on activities that are important**. The amount of time an administrator spends on an activity communicates a message regarding the importance of that goal or function.
2. **Change or enhance the setting**. A new setting conveys the feeling that something new is happening. An enhanced setting with more elaborate furnishings generally means that the activity is more consequential and important. Changing the meeting from the lunchroom to the boardroom communicates a message of significance to the attendees.

3. **Review and interpret history**. Events have meaning only through our interpretations of them. The most important interpretations are those derived from a historical analysis that demonstrates a consistent line of meaning and direction. If current events appear to be consistent with historic trends, it is easier to obtain a consensus on a chosen course of action. For example, wage cuts and extra hours are more acceptable if it can be shown that the employees have always responded with loyalty and sacrifice during hard times.
4. **Establish a dominant value expressed in a simple phrase**. A simple phrase, one that reflects a dominant value and is easily remembered, can influence the behavior of organizational members by creating a consensus about appropriate behavior. For example, a simple slogan such as "Pride in performance brings excellence in service" can mobilize support for greater organizational commitment and dedication to work.

Rites and Ceremonies

Ceremonies are planned events that have special significance for the members and are conducted for their benefit. Ceremonies serve the same purpose for organizations that ordinations and initiations do for religious groups and social clubs. Ceremonies are special occasions when managers can reinforce specific values and beliefs. These occasions provide an opportunity to recognize heroes and induct them into the organization's hall of fame. For example, McDonald's Corporation conducts a nationwide contest to determine the best hamburger-cooking team in the country. Competition occurs among local teams and gradually progresses until the best teams from the company compete at the national level. The teams are judged on subtle details that determine whether the hamburger is cooked to perfection. This ceremony communicates to all McDonald's employees the value of hamburger quality. It also requires store managers to become very familiar with the 700-page policy and procedures book.

Rites and ceremonies provide opportunities to reward and recognize employees whose behavior is congruent with the values of the company. Six kinds of rites in organizations have been identified:[10]

1. **Rites of passage** show that an individual's status has changed, such as a promotion or a retirement.
2. **Rites of enhancement** reinforce the achievement and accomplishments of individuals, such as recognition awards and graduation ceremonies.
3. **Rites of renewal** emphasize changes and improvements in the organization, such as opening a new store or launching a new product.
4. **Rites of integration** unite diverse groups or teams within the organization and renew commitment to the larger organization, such as annual picnics and company newsletters.
5. **Rites of conflict reduction** focus on resolving conflicts or disagreements that arise in organizations, such as grievance hearings or union contract negotiations.
6. **Rites of degradation** are used by organizations to publicly punish or demean persons who fail to adhere to the accepted norms and values, such as a demotion or dissemination of a public apology.

Stories and Symbols

Organizational stories have a profound impact on culture regardless of whether they are true or false. Most stories are narratives based on true events that are shared among employees and told to new members to inform them about the organization. Some stories are considered legends because the events are historic, but may have been embellished with fictional details. Other stories may be **organizational myths**: not supported by facts, but directionally consistent with the values and beliefs of the organization.

Rites and ceremonies
The special events in organizations that recognize individuals and the ways they are treated.

Organizational myths
Significant stories that are told about an organization's earlier years that impact the way members think about its history even if they are not true.

Stories are important because they preserve the primary values of the organization and promote a shared understanding among all employees.

Example—

Hewlett-Packard Corporation effectively uses stories about its "H-P way" to preserve important aspects of its organizational culture. The H-P way consists of a constellation of attitudes and values, among which is an insistence on product quality, the recognition of achievement, and respect for individual employees. New employees are viewed with suspicion until they have demonstrated that they understand and follow the H-P way. Questions about sloppy work or careless performance are resolved immediately because sloppy work is inconsistent with the H-P way. A classic story that serves to symbolize and preserve the H-P way at Hewlett-Packard involves one of the founders, David Packard. One evening, as Packard was wandering around the Palo Alto lab after work hours, he discovered a prototype constructed of inferior materials. Packard destroyed the model and left a note saying, "That's not the H-P way. Dave."

A symbol is something that represents something else. In one sense, ceremonies, rites, and stories are symbols because they represent the deeper values and assumptions of the organization. Physical symbols are often used in organizations to represent and support organizational culture because they focus attention on a specific item and because they are so powerful. The value of physical symbols is that they communicate important cultural values. If the physical symbols are consistent with the ceremonies and stories, they are a powerful facilitator of culture.

Many organizations give ten- and twenty-year service pins as a form of recognition to employees who stay with the organization. Although these service pins are attractive pieces of jewelry, their significance to the employees far exceeds their economic value. Part of their value comes from the elaborate awards banquets at which they are presented. Such elaborate ceremonies and rites often contribute to the significance of physical symbols.

Almost every organization develops its own jargon and abbreviations, and these communication devices contribute to a unique organizational culture. Some companies use a specific slogan, metaphor, or saying to convey special meaning to employees. Metaphors are often rich with meaning and convey an entire sermon in only a short sentence.[11] Slogans can be readily picked up and repeated by employees as well as customers of the company. "IBM means service," Hallmark's "When you care enough to send the very best," and "Everybody at Northrup is in marketing" are examples of slogans that symbolize what the company stands for to both employees and the external public.

Reactions to Problems

The way managers and employees respond to a crisis reveals much about an organization's culture. When problems arise and employees do not have standard operating procedures telling them what to do or an opportunity to consult upper management to seek direction, they are forced to rely on their understanding of the organization's culture to do what they think is best.

Example—

When cyanide was found in some Tylenol capsules, the employees of Johnson & Johnson acted quickly to preserve public confidence in the company. Without waiting for direction from upper management or an order from the FDA, these employees removed all potentially harmful bottles from the shelves. Their actions were dictated by the company's credo and a culture that left no uncertainty about how they should act.

The way managers and employees respond to a crisis also has the potential to create or change an organization's culture. The way in which a crisis is handled can either reinforce the existing culture or generate new values and norms that change the culture in some way. For example, a company facing a dramatic reduction in demand for its products might react by laying off or firing employees. This reaction would communicate an important message that people are not very highly valued, regardless of how reasonable the terminations were or how well they were explained. Or the company might reduce employee hours or pay and ask employees to sacrifice temporarily while the company experienced an economic correction.

Example—

During the recessions of the 1980s, Lincoln Electric faced a situation of declining demand. It responded by reducing the hours of its employees in the arc welding and electric motor departments to 30 hours per week. Terminations were avoided and year-end bonuses were paid. However, some employees were reassigned and the overall workforce was reduced through normal retirement and attrition.

EFFECTS OF CULTURE

Worker Attitudes and Behavior

Scholars who study culture claim that the way people behave in an organization is determined more by its culture than by directives from senior management, and that culture has a greater impact on a company's success than anything else management can do. Moreover, most organizations find it impossible to implement any strategy—marketing, financial, or human resource—that is inconsistent with its culture.[12] A study that examined the cultures and financial performance of 200 companies over an eleven-year period found that companies that had "strong" cultures outperformed companies with "weak" cultures. Organizational cultures are strong when they are clearly defined, broadly understood, and extensively followed by all employees. Employees who embrace their company's cultures are also less likely to leave their company because top management believes that their employees have the ability to grow and learn.[13]

A classic illustration of the effects of organizational culture on worker attitudes and behavior is the culture of "family, fun, and LUV" at Southwest Airlines. The walls of the corporate headquarters are covered with pictures of people at parties. These people are the Southwest family and they have frequent employee parties. Although Southwest employees believe work is important and that they must perform their jobs with excellence, they also believe that work can be fun. Humor is used throughout the company to help anxious travelers remain calm and make work fun for the Southwest family. When you fly on Southwest Airlines, you may hear the traditional instructions to passengers sung to the tune of "Under the Boardwalk" or "I Heard It Through the Grapevine." An in-flight contest may be held to see which passenger has the biggest holes in his socks or bald spot on his head. When leaving the gate area, pilots have been heard to ask passengers next to the aisles to hold in their elbows so they can see to back up. When approaching the gate, the pilots have said over the intercom "Whoa big fella, whoa!"

Southwest's culture is reinforced by its CEO, Herb Kelleher, who has been seen at parties dressed as a chicken or Elvis. He frequently hugs and kisses his employees, and his commitment to affection is demonstrated by Southwest's ticker symbol of LUV on Wall Street. His commitment to efficiency is manifested by his willingness to help load luggage and serve peanuts and drinks to passengers. Herb also arm-wrestled a potential litigant to forestall a possible lawsuit.

Southwest's corporate culture is highly visible and it translates into unsurpassed customer service and efficiency. Through effective teamwork, Southwest succeeds in turning around most of its 2300 daily fights within twenty minutes at the gate. It has also created an extremely desirable place to work—Southwest has been ranked number one on the list of America's 100 Best Companies to work for.[14]

Culture and Ethical Behavior

Every organization faces the challenge of creating ethical norms that are understood and accepted. Employee theft, cheating, and embezzlement are common temptations in every company and seem to grow unchecked unless the organization has a vigorous program to counter them and tries to create a culture of honesty.

A culture that endorses ethical behavior has a profound influence on the honesty of employees and the profitability of the company. A moral culture exists when the group norms and social expectations in a company endorse the importance of honesty. In organizations where such a culture exists, employees feel a personal responsibility to behave honestly and expect others to do likewise. Saying things that are knowingly untrue, taking things that belong to others, giving false impressions, withholding relevant information, and mistreating others are widely recognized as unacceptable behaviors. When there is a culture of honesty, the suggestion to hide a defective part in the middle of a batch would be perceived as a joke—everyone knows that such an act would be unacceptable, and no one would seriously consider doing it. In a culture of dishonesty, however, the same suggestion would be perceived as an expedient way to dispose of a defective part.[15]

Whether a company's culture endorses honesty or dishonesty has a significant impact on the attitudes and behaviors of its members. A survey of 22 retail stores demonstrated that the norms regarding honesty within each store were positively related to the personal honesty of employees and negatively related to inventory shrinkage rates.[16]

A culture of honesty depends on establishing general standards of acceptable behavior and a clear perception that everyone accepts them. The following strategies have been suggested for creating a culture that endorses ethical behavior:

1. As a rule, visible moral acts speak louder than company communications. When executives are forced to make tough moral choices and they decide to act ethically in spite of the consequences, these decisions communicate a powerful message throughout the company about the importance of ethical behavior. For example, one CEO described how his company refused to pay an illegal bribe and walked away from a lucrative foreign contract, even though the state departments of both countries encouraged them to negotiate the deal and one government agency even offered to pay the bribe for them.[17] This moral decision became widely known throughout the company and served as a pattern for negotiating other contracts. This company found that its reputation for being open and honest contributed to its financial success; however, executives must be willing to make moral decisions that are right even if they do not seem expedient.

2. What employees do off the job influences how they are perceived at work. The degree to which employees are perceived as having firm commitments to honor and fidelity in their personal lives is an indication of the integrity that can be expected from them at work. The culture of honesty is enhanced when a significant number of employees, and especially top managers, are perceived as individuals who are devoutly religious or committed to a similar high moral code.

3. Develop and publish a code of ethics. Some companies have effectively solicited extensive input from employees as they developed their codes of ethics. Having employees participate in the development appears to increase their commitment to it and compliance afterwards. To ensure that the employees know the code and agree to abide by it, some organizations require employees to sign a statement saying that they understand the code, they agree to abide by it, and any deviations in their past have been discussed with management. Although a written code does not appear to have much impact on creating a culture of honesty, it has considerable impact when it is endorsed by management decisions and practices.

4. Company communications can contribute to a culture of ethical behavior by discussing the importance of integrity. The most frequently used information is statistical data showing how current levels of theft threaten the economic health of the company. Other helpful information includes reports of ethical conduct and statements endorsing integrity. The media may include company newsletters, posters on walls, bulletin boards, TV monitors, comments added to payroll check stubs, public address announcements, and even paid advertisements in the public media.

5. Encourage employees who observe unethical behaviors to report them, and then protect them from retribution. People who report corporate misdeeds are called whistle blowers, and the most difficult problem they face is being fired or mistreated for blowing the whistle. Employees should be encouraged to report unethical behaviors internally first and seek outside help only if internal efforts

have been unsuccessful. To encourage whistle blowing within the federal government, Congress passed the Whistle Blowers Protection Act to protect employees from being fired and to reward them financially.

International Cultural Differences

While we have discussed the characteristics of organizational culture, we must also remember that national cultures have an impact on organizational effectiveness. Cultural differences influence the psychological contracts between workers and their companies and these differences have occasionally created significant challenges for international companies as they have tried to spread into other countries.

Example—

When Euro-Disney built its Euro-Disney Fantasyland in Marne-la-Valee, France, it learned that employees from different cultures can have very different ideas about the promises their employers have made and their obligations in return. A 22-year-old French medical student who was hired to work in the Fantasyland shop described the new employee orientation as brainwashing. By the next weekend he left after a dispute with his supervisor over the timing of his lunch break, and took the entire shop personnel with him.[18]

Hofstede has studied cross-cultural comparisons among different nationalities and the way these differences affect business operations in an attitude survey of IBM employees from 50 countries.[19] He identified four cultural values that he used to explain differing reactions to problems in organizational life: power distance, uncertainty avoidance, individualism versus collectivism, and masculinity versus femininity. He found that these work-related values are related to societal norms that are embedded within countries and influence the functioning of families, education systems, and business organizations.

1. **Power distance** refers to the acceptability of power differentials within a society. In every society there are those who are powerful and those who are powerless, such as rich versus poor or leaders versus followers. Societies differ with respect to whether this power difference is considered acceptable or unacceptable. In low power distance countries, large power differentials are considered undesirable and illegitimate, such as Scandinavian and European countries. Inequality exists, but it is perceived as something that should be minimized. In high power distance countries, such as the Philippines, Mexico, India, and Singapore, power differences are perceived as neither legitimate nor illegitimate. In these countries powerful individuals are entitled to privileges, inequality is a fact of life, and the way to gain power is to overthrow those who have it.
2. **Uncertainty avoidance** refers to the degree of tolerance people have for ambiguity and whether they feel threatened by uncertain situations. People use various coping styles dictated by their culture to respond to the uncertainties of life. On a societal level this coping may be accomplished through the use of technology, laws, and religion. Countries and cultures strong on uncertainty avoidance, such as Greece, Japan, and Peru, attempt to structure risky situations in order to avoid risk and promote security. Other cultures see risk as unavoidable and have a greater tolerance for ambiguity, such as Singapore, Denmark, and Sweden.
3. **Individualism versus collectivism** refers to the relationship between the individual and the larger society. People in individualistic cultures, such as the United States and Canada, prefer to act as individuals; they believe in self reliance and do not build strong ties to other people. People in collectivistic cultures, such as Asian and South American countries, assume they are automatically

---

Power distance
The acceptability of status differentials between members of a society.

Uncertainty avoidance
The degree of ambiguity and uncertainty people are willing to tolerate.

Individualism versus collectivism
The degree to which people are willing to act individually as a unique person versus as a uniform member of a group.

members of a cohesive in-group to which they have belonged since birth. Loyalty to that group is not to be questioned. Someone outside the in-group will remain outside unless included by unusual circumstances. Individualistic countries have a tradition of more individualistic thinking and action, power is more evenly distributed, and there is greater occupational and economic mobility. Collectivistic societies tend to focus more on strong ties among individuals within their in-group, and differentiate between themselves and out-group members.

4. **Masculinity versus femininity** addresses how a society perceives role differences between men and women and how these differences should impact their roles and activities. Low masculinity countries, such as the Scandinavian countries, minimize this distinction, so that there is a blurring or overlap of social roles; high masculinity countries, such as Japan, Austria, and Italy, assume that social gender roles are clearly distinct and that there should be specific occupations for males and females. In high masculinity societies, "tough" values such as assertiveness, accomplishment, success, and competition prevail over more "tender" values such as empathy, supportiveness, and maintaining relationships.

While Hofstede's dimensions are just one approach to comparing cultures, his research emphasizes the importance of understanding cultural differences in today's global economy. Managers must be aware of and sensitive to these cultural differences. There are many examples of organizations failing because they violated some cultural value in a foreign country with the result being disgruntled employees, upset customers, or alienated suppliers.

CHANGING ORGANIZATIONAL CULTURE

Most cultural interventions are actually attempts to clarify the culture of the organization. These interventions are typically conducted with top-level managers in the organization in a series of group discussions that focus on such questions as "What is our unique mission?" "What do we want to be known for?" and "What are the ten commandments of this organization?"

Changing an organization's culture is considerably more dramatic and difficult than modifying other parts of a system. Acquiring new artifacts and symbols may not be too difficult; it may even be possible to change some group norms and patterns of behavior. But at the deepest level, a culture change requires alteration of the basic assumptions of the organization in its essential character. The following steps have been suggested for changing an organization's culture.[20]

1. **Conduct a Culture Audit**. The first step in the change process involves diagnosing the culture and subcultures within the organization. What are the assumptions, values, behaviors, and artifacts currently in the organization, and are there discrepancies between espoused beliefs and actual behavior? The goal of the diagnosis is to develop an accurate "map" of the culture, which generally requires extensive interviewing rather than written surveys.

2. **Assess the Need for Change**. Cultural change is needed if the current culture is not solving problems of integration or adaptation, or if it is producing negative consequences for individuals in the organization. As organizations grow and evolve, their cultures may become incompatible with the changing circumstances. Values and beliefs that may have been appropriate for a smaller company may be dysfunctional in a larger company.

3. **Unfreeze the Current Culture**. Change efforts are much more successful when there is a perceived need for change that compels people to be open to influence and willing to consider something new. Thus, an organization's culture will be more receptive to change if the current assumptions, values, and beliefs have been called into question, producing a high degree of tension. Most instances of

---

Masculinity versus femininity
The degree to which gender role differences are emphasized in terms of valuing assertive and aggressive male roles over more tender feminine attributes.

significant cultural change are not planned; they accompany sudden and cataclysmic events, such as the death or retirement of the founder, a decision to merge or sell the business, dramatic changes in growth or profitability, major technological changes, or fundamental changes in the strategy or structure. These events tend to "unfreeze" or destabilize the entire cultural system and prepare it to consider a major restructuring of the assumptions, values, and beliefs. Sharing data about the impact of the organization's culture—both positive and negative—can also create the impetus for change.

4. **Elicit Support from the Cultural Elite**. Top management and other opinion leaders compose the "cultural elite" in an organization; they are the ones who interpret events for members and establish the rules of conduct. Because successful change may be impossible without their assistance, a strategy for locating them and enlisting their support is essential. Another option is to hire a completely new leadership team that holds beliefs consistent with the organization's new direction.

5. **Implement an Intervention Strategy**. A variety of interventions are possible for changing the organization's culture, such as conducting team-building meetings, revising the training and development activities, installing new reward systems, changing the organizational structure, rewriting the mission statement, creating new group norms, developing a new language and metaphors, and negotiating new roles.[21] The replacement of key individuals who hold the "old" beliefs may also be necessary.

6. **Monitor and Evaluate**. Cultural change is incremental and rarely occurs quickly. A system for monitoring and evaluating the transition to a new set of values and beliefs can provide an ongoing process of transitional change.

Leadership succession has a major impact on an organization's culture. A new leader with different assumptions and values has great potential to alter the prevailing pattern of culture. Business history is replete with stories of cultures formed by remarkable organizational founders such as Henry Ford, John D. Rockefeller, Thomas Watson, Andrew Carnegie, Hewlett and Packard, James Cash Penney, and Willard Marriott. In his early examination of bureaucracies, Max Weber discusses the challenges of organizational change and suggests that a charismatic leader, whom others perceive as having extraordinary powers, could change the culture of an organization. From a position of power that is derived from respect and admiration, a new leader can articulate new patterns and values that are voluntarily accepted by members throughout the organization.

Example—

As the new CEO of Merrill Lynch Corporation, Stan O'Neal relied primarily on replacing top managers to reshape the company's culture into a performance-driven organization that puts greater emphasis on higher risk bets and relies less on just selling stocks. However, his higher tolerance for risk was accompanied with a low tolerance for mistakes. Within the first six months he ousted two top executives, including the man who helped engineer his ascent to the position of CEO. Several other top executives were also replaced as the company faced large losses from the mortgage industry. Although these replacements facilitated the cultural change, they also contributed to a loss of institutional memory and experience that some felt made Merrill less equipped to deal with the ups and downs of the market.[22]

Cultural interventions that focus on changing shared values should explain the need for the change, identify the new value, and generate enthusiasm for its acceptance.

Example—

A department store sought to create a culture that was centered on a commitment to excellence. This intervention involved a series of meetings attended by all employees in which the top administrators presented talks on the theme "What it means to me to have a commitment to excellence." People in the organization were asked to identify everyday common practices that did not reflect a commitment to excellence. Department supervisors and division heads were asked to analyze careless and sloppy practices that failed to conform to the commitment to excellence and eliminate them. Posters and plaques containing the theme, Commitment to Excellence, were given to employees to remind them of the discussions.

An important element in creating a new culture is creating cultural artifacts that support the new culture, such as the language, metaphors, stories, labels, and other supporting systems. For example, British Rail conducted a three-year development project designed to change its bureaucratic culture and relied greatly on being able to eliminate dysfunctional modes of thinking by negatively labeling them ("isms").[23] Similarly, General Mills used a label, "Company of Champions," to describe the new culture it wanted to create and used three words to define it: innovation, speed, and commitment. To implement and reinforce its new culture, General Mills made corresponding changes in its reward systems, its recognition program, and its education and training programs.[24] The words used by General Electric to support its new culture were **simplicity**, **self-confidence**, and **speed**.[25]

Metaphors can play an important role in cultural change. New ways of thinking require a departure from an *old world* view to a new set of ideas, values, and beliefs that are reflected in a new language. Metaphors can refocus familiar images in a new light and provide a shared vision that guides future actions and gives its members meaning and purpose. Metaphors from war, religion, and sports are common in business (and some of these metaphors have been criticized because they are associated with a predominantly male language that women feel uncomfortable using).[26] An important part of Jack Welch's success in changing the culture of General Electric to a leaner and more adaptable company was his frequent criticism of bureaucratic inefficiencies. Like fat on a bloated bureaucracy, these inefficiencies had to be eliminated in what were called "Work-Out" sessions. A six-inch stack of manuals was replaced with a one-page statement. The metaphor of an exercise program helped overcome resistance to removing layers of management and departmental boundaries. The metaphor also made employees think the company would ultimately be in better shape, which ultimately provided an acceptable foundation for building trust and cooperation. Metaphors are an essential medium through which reality is constructed, and they help to encourage and control change.[27]

NOTES

1. Eli Sopow, "The impact of culture and climate on change," *Strategic HR Review*, vol. 6 (Jan/Feb 2007), pp. 20–23.

2. Robert A. Cooke and Denise M. Rousseau, "Behavioral Norms and Expectations: A Quantitative Approach to the Assessment of Organizational Culture," *Group and Organization Studies*, vol. 13 (September 1988), pp. 245–273; W. Gibb Dyer, Jr., and Alan L. Wilkins, "Better Stories, Not Better Constructs, to Generate Better Theory: A Rejoinder to Eisenhardt," *Academy of Management Review*, vol. 16 (1991), pp. 613–619; Kathleen M. Eisenhardt, "Better Stories and Better Constructs: The Case for Rigor and Comparative Logic," *Academy of Management Review*, vol. 16 (1991), pp. 620–627.

3. Ken Hultman, "Evaluating Organizational Values," *Organization Development Journal*, vol. 23 (no. 4, 2005), pp. 32–44.

4. Edgar H. Schein, *Organizational Culture and Leadership*, (San Francisco: Josey-Bass, 1985).

5. Terrence E. Deal and Allan A. Kennedy, *Corporate Cultures* (Reading, Mass.: Addison Wesley, 1982); Harrison M. Trice and Janice M. Beyer, "Studying Organizational Cultures Through Rites and Ceremonials," *Academy of Management Review*, vol. 9 (1984), pp. 653–669.

6. The questions in this section come from W. Gibb Dyer, Jr. "Organizational Culture: Analysis and Change." In William G. Dyer, *Strategies for Managing Change*, (Reading, MA: Addison-Wesley, 1984), Ch. 20.

7. Mike Schraeder, Rachel S. Tears, and Mark H. Jordan, "Organizational Culture in Public Sector Organizations: Promoting Change through Training and Leading by Example," *Leadership & Organization Development Journal*, vol. 26 (2005), pp. 492–502; Val Kinjerski and Berna J. Skrypnek, "Creating Organizational Conditions that Foster Employee Spirit at Work," *Leadership & Organization Development Journal*, vol. 27 (2006), pp. 280–295.

8. Steve Harrison, *The Manager's Book of Decencies: How Small Gestures Build Great Companies* (McGraw-Hill, 2007).

9. Edgar H. Schein, "Coming to a New Awareness of Organizational Culture," *Sloan Management Review*, vol. 25 (Winter 1984), pp. 3–16.

10. H. M. Trice and J. M. Beyer, "Studying Organizational Cultures through Rites and Ceremonials," *Academy of Management Review*, vol. 9 (1984), pp 653–669.

11. Michael A. Gass and Simon Priest, "The Effectiveness of Metaphoric Facilitation Styles in Corporate Adventure Training (CAT) Programs," *The Journal of Experiential Education*, vol. 29 (no. 1, 2006), pp. 78–94.

12. Chip Jarnagin and John W. Slocum Jr., "Creating Corporate Cultures Through Mythopoetic Leadership," *Organizational Dynamics*, vol. 36 (2007), pp. 288–302.

13. John Kotter and James Heskett, *Corporate Culture and Performance*, (The Free Press, 1992).

14. John Stancavage, "Southwest has Fun, Profit," *Knight Ridder Tribune Business News*, 2 July 2006, p. 1.

15. D. Christopher Kayes, David Stirling, and Tjai M. Nielsen, "Building Organizational Integrity," *Business Horizons*, vol. 50 (2007), pp. 61–70.

16. David J. Cherrington and J. Owen Cherrington. "The Climate of Honesty in Retail Stores," in William Terris (ed.) *Employee Theft: Research, Theory, and Applications.* (Park Ridge, IL: London House Press, 1985), pp. 3–16.

17. Coleman Raphael, "The Ethical Dimensions of America's Corporate Practices: A Reexamination," in the Donald S. MacNaughton Symposium Proceedings, 1986, pp. 31–42.

18. David C. Thomas, Kevin Au, and Elizabeth C. Ravlin, "Cultural Variation and the Psychological Contract," *Journal of Organizational Behavior*, vol. 24 (no. 5, 2003), pp. 451–471.

19. Geert Hofstede, *Culture's Consequences: International Differences in Work-related Values.* (Beverly Hills, CA: Sage Publications, 1980); see also David G Sirmon and Peter J Lane, "A Model of Cultural Differences and International Alliance Performance," *Journal of International Business Studies*, vol. 35 (no. 4, 2004) pp. 306–319.

20. W. Gibb Dyer, Jr. "Organizational Culture: Analysis and Change." In William G. Dyer, *Strategies for Managing Change* (Reading MA: Addison-Wesley, 1984), Ch. 20.

21. Barry Mike and John W. Slocum, Jr., "Changing Culture at Pizza Hut and YUM! Brands, Inc.," *Organizational Dynamics*, vol. 32 (2003), pp. 319–330

22. Randall Smith, "CEO Transforms Merrill, but Shift Comes at a Cost," *The Wall Street Journal*, 8 October 2007, A1.

23. Paul Bate, "Using the Culture Concept in an Organization Development Setting," *Journal of Applied Behavioral Science*, vol. 26 (1990), pp. 83–106.

24. Stephanie Overman, "A Company of Champions," *HR Magazine*, vol. 35 (Oct 1990), pp. 58–60.

25. John F. Welch, Jr., "Working Out of a Tough Year," *Executive Excellence*, vol. 9 (Apr 1992), pp. 14–16.

26. Catherine Cleary, Thomas Packard, Achilles Armenakis, Arthur Bedeian, Laurie Larwood, and W. Warner Burke, "The Use of Metaphors in Organizational Assessment and Change: The Role of Metaphors in Organizational Change," *Group and Organization Management*, vol. 17 (Sept 1992), pp. 229–259; Fiona Wilson, "Language, Technology, Gender and Power," *Human Relations*, vol. 45 (Sept 1992) pp. 883-904.

27. Stratford P. Sherman and Cynthia Hutton, "Inside the Mind of Jack Welch," *Fortune*, 27 Mar 1989, pp. 39–49.

Ethics and Social Responsibility

HITT MICHAEL, BLACK, STEWART; PORTER LYMAN W., *Management,* 1st edition,© 2005,
pp. 149–181. Reprinted by permission of Pearson Education, Inc., Upper Saddle River, NJ.

NICOLO PIGNATELLI AND GULF ITALIA

Nicolo Pignatelli, president of Gulf Italia (a subsidiary of Gulf Oil), stared at the notice from the Italian government. "How could this be possible?" he thought. The government had given Pignatelli permission to build an oil refinery with a capacity of almost 6 million tons. He had just completed it at a cost of well over $100 million. Now the Italian government was telling him that he could only operate at slightly more than 50 percent capacity (3.9 million tons). On top of that, it was also telling him that not only would he need to get a "production permission" to go from 3.9 to 6.0 million tons in actual production, but then he would need a *separate* "implementation permission" to put into effect the "production permission." Pignatelli didn't know whether to be intimidated or infuriated. Every day that the plant was shut down would cost money. However, even if the refinery were allowed to operate, it needed to operate at or near capacity. If it did not, it would also lose millions because of the high fixed costs.

Pignatelli was understandably upset—he had spent seven long years implementing a strategy to take the company from being one of the small fries in the Italian oil and gasoline industry to one of the major players. When Pignatelli took over, Gulf had crude oil in the Middle East and in southern Italy and gas stations in northern Italy. To this Pignatelli added a retail presence in central and southern Italy by purchasing the 700 gasoline stations from Marathon Oil. This gave Gulf gas stations throughout Italy crude oil to bring into the country. What Gulf lacked was the middle part of the chain—a refinery. Without it, Pignatelli was dependent on competitors for both a refined gasoline supply and wholesale prices. Pignatelli felt that Gulf needed its own refinery to complete the chain from the wellhead to the gas pump.

Building a refinery in Italy proved to be a long and expensive task. Even after receiving permission to build the refinery in northern Italy, local community opposition resulted in five location changes for the company. These changes cost Gulf an additional $16 million. To ensure that the smoke and fumes would not contribute to the city smog, Pignatelli spent extra money on a 450-foot smokestack (twice as tall as normal). Pignatelli also installed a special combustion chamber so that flare towers (used to burn off waste gas) and the loud noise and noxious fumes associated with them weren't necessary. He also added a state-of-the-art water purification system. In fact, Pignatelli demonstrated the quality of the system by personally drinking the waste water. These environmental additions added over $1 million to the project.

To ensure that the refinery was profitable, Pignatelli arranged a joint venture with Mobil Oil. Mobil had many service stations in northern Italy where Gulf's refinery was located, but no refinery of its own. The money Mobil was to invest for its equity share would reduce Gulf's financial burden in building the refinery and cut the shipping costs for Mobil because its stations would be located near the new refinery. However, Mobil had the option of pulling out of the deal if Gulf's refinery could not operate at capacity, because in that case the refined gas would be too expensive for Mobil to buy.

It had taken seven years for the refinery to be approved and built. Over $100 million was on the line. Trying to obtain approval to operate at capacity and a separate authorization to implement that approval might take many more months, if not years. Pignatelli wondered if he was being purposely set up by government officials.

Four options occurred to Pignatelli: (1) play it straight and try to gain government authorization, (2) ask his more influential partners to put pressure on government officials, (3) pay a large sum of money ($1 million deposited to a Swiss bank account) to a "consultant" who had "debottlenecked" problems like this before and who promised Pignatelli that he could fix the situation quickly, or (4) pay money "under the table" directly to government officials to obtain the permissions needed to run the refinery economically.

Pignatelli considered each option. Playing it straight would likely take several months and possibly years before government authorization could be obtained. In the meantime, the refinery would not operate or would operate at such a low capacity that it would lose millions of dollars. Pignatelli was not certain that pressure from his partners would influence government officials. He wondered about the effect of going to the media. Given the current cost of the project, the thousands of jobs that depended on

Source: Personal conversations with Mr. Pignatelli, 1989, 1993.

an operating refinery, and time pressures, $1 million seemed like a small price to pay to a consultant to get things debottlenecked. He might be able to gain approval for even less money if he went directly to government officials.

The discussions above coupled with the opening case help to highlight the two key issues of this chapter: managerial ethics and corporate social responsibility. **Managerial ethics** is essentially the study of morality and standards of business conduct. **Corporate social responsibility** is concerned with the obligations that corporations owe to their constituencies such as shareholders, employees, customers, and citizens at large.

Strategic Overview

As the case of Pignatelli illustrates, managers face perplexing ethical and social responsibility issues. Pignatelli seems to be leaning in the direction of hiring a consultant, who might use part of the money for bribes. If Pignatelli does not pay the bribes directly, does this absolve him of responsibility? Bribes are illegal in Italy. Even if bribes are common practice there, does this justify paying them? Does Pignatelli have a responsibility to Italian citizens to build an environmentally friendly refinery above and beyond what is required by law? Is it appropriate for Gulf to spend this extra money and essentially take it away from shareholders? How would you feel if you were a lower-level employee in the company and learned that Pignatelli intended to pay bribes to get things "debottlenecked"? What would your ethical obligations be? Should you ignore the situation or confront Pignatelli? Should you inform your direct boss or go to the media?

Managers in large companies usually act as agents of the owners (as we explain later in this chapter). As such, top executives have an implied obligation to take strategic actions that are in the best interests of the owners or shareholders. If they take actions that help themselves, such as rejecting a takeover offer to keep their jobs, but that may be to the detriment of shareholders, are they acting in an ethical manner? In recent years, numerous executives of top corporations have acted opportunistically, making headlines in the process. Some acted not only unethically but illegally. They harmed both the shareholders and many employees, who lost their jobs when their bosses' misdeeds came to light and the companies went bankrupt.

Both managerial ethics and strategy begin at the top of the organization. For ethical decisions and practices to permeate the firm, top executives must build a culture based on those values. This includes establishing codes of ethics, implementing ethics training for employees, and rewarding ethical behaviors (as discussed later in this chapter). Moreover, it includes behaving in an ethical manner themselves.

An ethical organization is especially important when it comes to implementing the strategies developed by top managers. Managers at the top and throughout the organization along with other employees are likely to face many ethical dilemmas throughout the course of doing business. Although the ethical decisions facing Pignatelli seem extreme, most organizations face similar dilemmas on a regular basis.

Managers must also grapple with decisions about how to operate their firms efficiently, yet in a socially responsible manner. To do so, top executives may need to establish standards that exceed the requirements of the law. They must also consider the strategic and ethical impact of their decisions on the organization's stakeholders and employees. And their decisions must be perceived to be fair. (We will discuss the various approaches managers can take to organizational "justice" later in this chapter.)

Managerial ethics the study of morality and standards of business conduct

Corporate social responsibility the obligations that corporations owe to their constituencies such as shareholders, employees, customers, and citizens at large

RELEVANCE TO YOU

You may be wondering, "Why should I care about ethics and social responsibility? Aren't these the types of issues philosophers worry about?" To answer this question, you need only pick up recent newspapers or business magazines. Everything from Wall Street trading scandals to accounting frauds at Enron, World-Com, Tyco, and Global Crossing to environmental pollution cover-ups seems to be in the press daily. For example, Priceline.com lost billions in market value, even before the general market meltdown in 2000, when it was established that the firm had been reporting as revenue the total dollar value of transactions when only a small percentage actually came to Priceline.com as revenue for the service it performed. Thus, while a consumer might bid $500 for a flight to Europe and an airline accepted the bid, Priceline. com recorded the full value as sales when only a small fraction was sent to it for brokering the deal in cyberspace. Even its famous spokesperson, William Shatner (Captain James T. Kirk on the series *Star Trek*), said he was surprised by the practice.

Clearly, poor managerial ethics and corporate social responsibility can generate negative publicity, hurt a company's stock price and destroy shareholder value, or make it difficult for the firm to recruit high-quality employees. In contrast, well-managed ethical behavior and corporate social responsibility can have significant, positive consequences for employees, customers, shareholders, and communities. Exhibit 8.1 provides a listing of companies honored for "Excellence in Ethics" by *Business Ethics* magazine. As you read these examples, ask yourself whether you would be more or less likely to work for one of these firms because of its reputation. As a customer, would you be willing to pay a premium price for the product because of the company's reputation?

THE DEVELOPMENT OF INDIVIDUAL ETHICS

At this point in your life, do you think you have a fairly well-established set of ethical beliefs and values? If you do, how did you come by them? What role did family, friends, peers, teachers, religion, job experiences, and life experiences have on the development of your ethical beliefs? To explore this issue, think about a situation in which someone made a different ethical judgment from your own. What if you had been born in a different country, raised by a different family; had attended a different school system, experienced different religious influences; had different friends, and held different jobs? Would you hold the same ethical values you do now? Would you reach identical ethical judgments to those you reach now?

There is little debate that family, friends, peers, teachers, religion, job experiences, and life experiences play a significant role in the development of individual ethical values and judgments. What is debated is which factors play the strongest role because their influence varies from person to person. This debate is unlikely to be resolved soon. Nor is its resolution necessary for our purposes. The primary reason for raising the issue is to realize that in order to understand how others make decisions, you need to understand something about their backgrounds.

Simply labeling ethical judgments that are different from your own as wrong is likely to foster feelings of mistrust (in both directions) and hurt working relationships. The greater the diversity in the workforce, or more specifically among your set of colleagues and subordinates, the greater the need for tolerance and understanding. However, as a manager, tolerance does not mean simply allowing subordinates to come to whatever ethical decisions they individually deem right. Because individual decisions can have consequences for the organization, managers often need to shape and influence the ethical thinking, judgment, and decision making of subordinates.

Consider the following real case that was conveyed to us in a recent conversation. (We have disguised the names at the manager's request.) Imagine you are the marketing manager in a publishing company. Your assistant manager has just recruited a new sales representative, Martha, from a key competitor. Martha worked for your competitor, Dresden, for 11 months after graduating from college. Dresden pays employees a bonus based on performance after the first year of employment. Martha was expecting a $10,000 bonus from Dresden. In discussions with your assistant manager, Martha negotiated

2000 Winners

The Bureau of National Affairs, Inc.
For over a half-century of dedication to employee ownership, despite pressures to sell the company.

Iceland, Inc.
For a precedent-setting move in the United Kingdom toward the sale of all-organic store-brand food, at nonorganic prices.

Whole Foods Market
For a broad-based commitment to customer, stockholder, employee, community, and environmental service.

1999 Winners

St. Luke's (Award for Employee Ownership)
For creating a visionary model of employee ownership, out of the crisis of an unwanted merger.

Equal Exchange (Award for Stakeholder Relations)
For its path-breaking approach to fair trade, defining supplier welfare as part of business success.

Fetzer Vineyards (Award for Environmental Excellence)
For a broad-based approach to environmental sustainability, combined with financial excellence.

1998 Winners

SmithKline Beecham
For its $1 billion commitment to disease eradication.

Wainwright Bank
For dedication to social justice, internally and externally.

S.C. Johnson
For its focus on sustainable community development.

Source: www.business-ethics.com, accessed October 27, 2001.

Exhibit 8.1 Excellence in Business Ethics Award Winners

for a $10,000 signing bonus if Dresden failed to pay her the performance bonus. Part of the reason your assistant manager agreed to do this is because Martha had been exposed to a number of strategic operations and marketing plans in her first year of employment at Dresden. Given her somewhat junior position in the company, she had not been asked to sign, nor had she signed, a "noncompete" clause that would have prevented her from taking a job with a competitor for a specific time period or disclosing or using the knowledge gained during her time at Dresden. Legally, she was free to take the job with you.

Your assistant manager comes to you and asks if it is okay to try to get Martha to disclose as much as she knows about Dresden's marketing plans. What is your response? Do you think Dresden has an ethical obligation to pay Martha the $10,000 bonus even though she plans to leave only a few days short of completing 12 months of employment? If you were Martha, would you have any ethical misgivings about taking the new job and then relating all you knew about your previous employer's strategic plans? Would Dresden's paying you the end-of-year bonus have any bearing on what you would or would not reveal to your new employer?

UNDERSTANDING BASIC APPROACHES TO ETHICS

So how should you make decisions like these? Are there ethical approaches you can look to for guidance? The answer is that there are some basic approaches. The basic approaches have been around for a long time. This is in part because the challenge of ethical decision making is not a modern one. **Ethical dilemmas**, or the choice between two competing but arguably valid options, are not new and have confronted people throughout history.

In the next section we will describe these basic approaches for two reasons, hopefully without getting mired in the boring details. First, they can be helpful in trying to understand how others approach ethical dilemmas. Second, quite often the lack of a clear approach for making ethical decisions causes **ethical lapses** or decisions that are contrary to an individual's stated beliefs and policies of the company.

In thinking about the first reason, it is important to keep in mind the increasingly diverse workforce and global business environment. Now more than ever before, you are likely to encounter people who use widely different approaches and reach different conclusions about ethical conduct. This is illustrated in a recent study that examined the extent to which salespeople from the United States, Japan, and Korea viewed a set of actions as posing an ethical issue or not. The study found significant difference among these three nationalities. For example, Korean salespeople did not think that seeking information from a customer on the price quotation offered by a competitor in order to resubmit a more competitive bid was much of an ethical issue. American and Japanese salespeople saw this as largely unethical behavior. As a concrete example of this view, in most places in the United States a real estate broker cannot tell you how much someone else offered on a house you also want to buy. What do you think? Do you think asking a customer for information on the price submitted by your competitors is ethical or not?

Interestingly, from this same international study, researchers found that Korean salespeople did not think that giving free gifts was as much of an ethical issue, while American salespeople did. General Motors shares this general view and has a policy that restricts the giving of gifts. For example, in a conversation the president of GM's Asia Pacific region mentioned that he could not pay for the golf game of the president of the Philippines when they were discussing a potential new factory in the country. Do you think GM's policy is appropriate or has it gone too far?

Without understanding how or why others come to different conclusions, it is easy to label people holding the "wrong" beliefs as inferior. For example, in a recent study, Chinese and Australian auditors working for the same multinational accounting firms reached different decisions about proper ethical conduct because of different cultural assumptions. Chinese auditors looked to peers while Australian auditors looked to themselves in making ethical decisions. This reference point reflects the cultural group orientation of the Chinese and the individual orientation of Australians. If either set of auditors has simply judged the other to be wrong without a sensitivity to how culture might influence ethical decisions, imagine how difficult it might be for them to work together on a global audit team. In fact, research has shown that ethnocentricity, or the view that your perspective is correct and others are inferior, tends to hurt managerial effectiveness, especially in culturally diverse or international contexts. So, it is important for new managers to be able to examine the basic approaches to ethical decision making and recognize that individuals' backgrounds, including cultural values, influence ethical decisions and behavior.

As we stated, the second reason for examining basic approaches to ethical decision making is to avoid ethical lapses. Ethical lapses are more common than you might think. The pressures emanating from both the external environment and internal company environment often can be overwhelming. This is especially true if managers lack a systematized and explicit framework for thinking through dilemmas. For example, you may believe that because paying bribes is illegal in Italy it is wrong. However, if you were in Pignatelli's situation, the pressures from the external and internal environment would be staggering. You have invested $100 million of your company's money and the company has a strong perfor-

---

Ethical dilemmas having to make a choice between two competing but arguably valid options

Ethical lapses decisions that are contrary to an individual's stated beliefs and policies of the company

mance culture. In other words, if you don't perform, you don't have a career. You have invested millions more in buying service stations that won't be profitable if you can't refine your own gasoline because you will have to buy gasoline from other refiners. Not only would an enormous investment be lost but employee layoffs would be huge. The refinery offers many high-skilled and high-paying jobs benefiting individuals and the community. When you put the dilemma in these terms, $1 million in consulting fees seems like a small price to pay. Under pressures like these, can you imagine how it might be possible to make a decision contrary to your stated beliefs?

BASIC APPROACHES TO ETHICAL DECISION MAKING

Several frameworks, or approaches, to ethical decision making exist. We examine four of the most common: the utilitarian, moral rights, universalism, and justice approaches. An understanding of basic approaches to ethical decision making will help you as a manager to examine your own personal ethics and work more effectively with employees whose ethical perspectives are different.

Utilitarian Approach

The utilitarian approach focuses on consequences of an action. Simplified, using a **utilitarian approach**, results "in the greatest good." Assume you are trying to sell grain to a developing nation and a customs agent demands an extra fee before he will clear your shipment. From a utilitarian perspective, you would try to determine the consequences of the options available to you. For example, you could (1) pay the money, (2) not pay the money and let the grain sit there, or (3) seek intervention from a third party. Which action would result in the greatest good? If there are starving people waiting for the grain, would you argue that the "good" of saving lives outweighs the "bad" of paying an illegal bribe?

Keep in mind when talking about whether an outcome is good or bad that people may see the same outcome differently. In other words, the "goodness" or "badness" of an outcome is often subjective. Factors such as culture, economic circumstances, and religion can all affect those subjective judgments. For example, if you were in Pignatelli's shoes, would you argue that the good of saving 2,000 jobs justified paying off government officials? What if unemployment were high in the region? Would that affect your thinking?

But many situations are not as clear-cut as to whether they constitute an ethical dilemma or just a business decision. How would you handle a situation in which some members of your staff see an impending decision as strictly business with no ethical implications, while others see it as an ethical dilemma?

Even if you frame the Johannson situation as an ethical dilemma, using the utilitarian approach, what action results in the greatest good and over what time frame? In the short run, continuing to work with Creative Applications will likely hurt your customers as your products do not arrive as fast as you would like. If this persists, it may enable your competitors to move past you and take market share away to the point that you have to reduce your size and lay off some employees. On the other hand, demonstrating that you are serious about your promise to work with chosen suppliers could lead to additional commitment from Creative Applications and other suppliers and result in enhanced performance and product deliveries.

Moral Rights Approach

The **moral rights approach** to ethical decisions focuses on an examination of the moral standing of actions independent of their consequences. According to this approach, some things are just "right" or

---

Utilitarian approach focuses on the consequences of an action

Moral rights approach focuses on examination of the moral standing of actions independent of their consequences

"wrong," independent of consequences. When two courses of action both have moral standing, then the positive and negative consequences of each should determine which course is more ethical. Using this approach, you should choose the action that is in conformance with moral principles and provides positive consequences. From a moral rights approach, if not honoring unwritten commitments to suppliers is simply wrong (i.e., doesn't have moral standing), then cutting off the supplier to make more money is not justified. The managerial challenge here is that the moral standing of most issues is debatable. For example, you might want to say that it is wrong to lie. But is it wrong to make your competitors think you are about to enter one market when you are really about to enter another, in order to give your company the element of surprise? Is it just wrong to say you are not working on a particular new technology when you actually are, in order to influence your competitors not to invest in the new technology and thereby have an advantage when you finally perfect it? How would you handle the situation if one employee believes that honoring unwritten, implicit commitments is just right (i.e., has moral standing) and another employee does not? In many companies both explicit policies as well as corporate values often serve a vital role in defining what is right or wrong when there is no universally accepted determination.

Universal Approach

Immanuel Kant, perhaps one of the most famous moral philosophers, articulated the best-known ethical imperative, or **universal approach**. Simplified, Kant's moral imperative was "do unto others as you would have them do unto everyone, including yourself." If you follow this approach, you should choose a course of action that you believe can apply to all people under all situations and that you would want applied to yourself. At the heart of universalism is the issue of rights. For Kant, the basis of all rights stems from freedom and autonomy. Actions that limit the freedom and autonomy of individuals generally lack moral justification. If you were in Pignatelli's situation and took a universal approach to the decision of what to do, it might be difficult to justify paying bribes to government officials either directly or indirectly. To meet the "do unto others as you would have them do unto everyone" criterion, you would have to be willing to let everyone use bribes as a means of getting the ends they desired.

Justice Approach

The **justice approach** focuses on how equitably the costs and benefits of actions are distributed as the principal means of judging ethical behavior. In general, costs and benefits should be equitably distributed, rules should be impartially applied, and those damaged because of inequity or discrimination should be compensated.

Distributive Justice Managers ascribing to **distributive justice** distribute rewards and punishments equitably, based on performance. This does not mean that everyone gets the same or equal rewards or punishments; rather, they receive equitable rewards and punishments as a function of how much they contribute to or detract from the organization's goals. A manager cannot distribute bonuses, promotions, or benefits based on arbitrary characteristics such as age, gender, religion, or race. This is the basic rationale behind the U.S. Civil Rights Act of 1964. Under this law, even if a manager has no intention of discriminating against a particular minority group, if a minority group can demonstrate inequitable results (called *disparate impact*), legal action can be brought against the firm. For example, if 50 percent of a firm's applicants for promotion were women, but 75 percent of those receiving promotions were men, these data could be used to file a claim of discrimination based on the underlying notion of distributive justice.

Universal approach choosing a course of action that you believe can apply to all people under all situations

Justice approach focuses on how equitably the costs and benefits of actions are distributed

Distributive justice the equitable distribution of rewards and punishment, based on performance

Procedural Justice Managers ascribing to **procedural justice** make sure that people affected by managerial decisions consent to the decision-making process and that the process is administered impartially. Consent means that people are informed about the process and have the freedom to exit the system if they choose. As with distributive justice, the decision-making process cannot systematically discriminate against people because of arbitrary characteristics such as age, gender, religion, or race. Recent research involving employees across multiple countries consistently suggests that perceived justice is positively related to desired outcomes such as job performance, trust, job satisfaction, and organizational commitment, and is negatively related to outcomes such as turnover and other counterproductive work behavior. Procedural justice is generally studied and interpreted within the context of the organization. However, the findings of a recent study show that factors external to the firm may also have strong effects on counterproductive workplace behavior. In a study contrasting community violence and an organization's procedural justice, violent crime rates in the community where a plant resided predicted workplace aggression in that plant, whereas the plant's procedural justice climate did not.

Compensatory Justice The main thesis of **compensatory justice** is that if distributive justice and procedural justice fail or are not followed as they should be, then those hurt by the inequitable distribution of rewards should be compensated. This compensation often takes the form of money, but it can take other forms. For example, compensatory justice is at the heart of affirmative action plans. Typically, affirmative action plans ensure that groups that may have been systematically disadvantaged in the past, such as women or minorities, are given every opportunity in the future. For example, special training programs could be instituted for women who were passed over for promotions in the past because they were denied access to certain experiences required for promotion.

MORAL INTENSITY IN ETHICAL DECISION MAKING

As we have pointed out thus far in this chapter, one of the challenges of ethical decision making for a manager is that for many issues and consequences, people do not have identical perspectives. They differ in whether they see a situation as involving ethics and in how they would determine their course of action. So the practical question is whether managers can help people come to more common views on the moral intensity of issues. **Moral intensity** is the degree to which people see an issue as an ethical one. This is largely a function of the content of the issue. As a manager you can use this framework both to anticipate the moral intensity of an issue and to diagnose the reasons for differing views about the moral intensity of an issue among people. Moral intensity has six components, as illustrated in Exhibit 8.2: (1) magnitude of the consequences, (2) social consensus, (3) probability of effect, (4) temporal immediacy, (5) proximity, and (6) concentration of effect. In other words, the overall moral intensity of a situation is the result of adding each of these components together.

The **magnitude of the consequences** associated with the outcome of a given action is the level of impact anticipated. This impact is independent of whether the consequences are positive or negative. For example, laying off 100 employees because of a downturn in the economy has less of an impact than if 1,000 employees join the ranks of the unemployed. Many people would judge a 20 percent increase in the price of lawn fertilizer to be of a lower magnitude than 500 people killed or seriously injured because of an explosion in the fertilizer plant caused by poor safety procedures.

Procedural justice ensuring that those affected by managerial decisions consent to the decision-making process and that the process is administered impartially

Compensatory justice if distributive and procedural justice fail, those hurt by the inequitable distribution of rewards are compensated

Moral intensity the degree to which people see an issue as an ethical one

Magnitude of the consequences the anticipated level of impact of the outcome of a given action

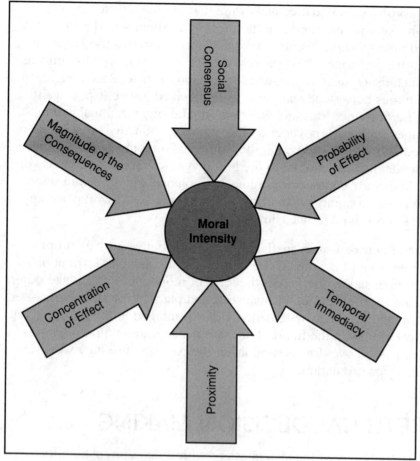

Exhibit 8.2   Factors of Moral Intensity

Social consensus involves the extent to which members of a society agree that an act is either good or bad. For example, in the United States, there is greater social consensus concerning the wrongness of driving drunk than speeding on the highway.

The third component of moral intensity is **probability of effect.** Even if a particular action could have severe consequences and people agree about the positive or negative nature of the impact, the intensity of the issue rises and falls depending on how likely people think the consequences are. For example, one of the reasons that the advertising of cigarettes has been restricted in many states is because of the increasing evidence of a link between smoking and health problems, including serious ones such as lung cancer. However, cigarette ads and smoking itself have not been completely outlawed in part because the probability of effect is not 100 percent. The higher the probability of the consequence, the more intense the sense of ethical obligation. Because people are highly likely to be injured if they are in a car accident, the intensity regarding the moral obligation of auto manufacturers to make safer cars is increasing. Options such as side-impact air bags are now available in cars. However, because there is no certainty that you will be in an automobile accident, many of the safety features are not required by law.

Social consensus the extent to which members of a society agree that an act is either good or bad

Probability of effect the moral intensity of an issue rises and falls depending on how likely people think the consequences are

Temporal immediacy is the fourth component of moral intensity and is a function of the interval between the time the action occurs and the onset of its consequences. The greater the time interval between the action and its consequences, the less intensity people typically feel toward the issue. For example, even if industrial pollution were certain to lead to global warming and result in catastrophic changes to weather patterns, because the consequences are likely to happen 50 years from now, the moral intensity of industrial pollution is much less than if the effects were to happen next year.

The fifth component is **proximity.** All other factors being equal, the closer the decision maker feels to those affected by the decision, the more the decision maker will consider the consequences of the action and feel it has ethical implications. Proximity does not just mean physical closeness. Proximity also involves psychological and emotional closeness and identification. Consequently, an affinity between the decision maker and those affected could be a function of many factors, including nationality, cultural background, ethnic similarity, organizational identification, or socioeconomic similarity. For example, if you feel a psychological and emotional affinity for young people in Africa, then decisions about laying off workers by seniority (meaning younger workers will get laid off first) will have greater moral intensity for you even if you live thousands of miles away. Likewise, a decision to close down a poorly performing but slightly profitable factory that could put your parents and neighbors out of work will also likely have greater moral intensity for you than a factory closure in which the affected workers are unknown to you.

The last component is the **concentration of effect,** or the extent to which consequences are focused on a few individuals or dispersed across many. For example, even though laying off 100 people has a lower magnitude of effect than laying off 1,000 people, laying off 100 people in a town of 5,000 has a greater concentration of effect than laying off 1,000 people in city of 10 million such as Los Angeles.

The importance of these six facets of moral intensity is twofold. First, as a manager, you can use these facets to anticipate issues that are likely to be seen as significant ethical dilemmas in the workplace. If you can better anticipate issues that are likely to become ethical debates, you have more time to prepare for and may be more effective at handling ethical dilemmas. Second, if you are working with a group that is using the same basic ethical approach and still can't agree on the ethical course of action, you can use these facets to determine the source of the disagreement. The disagreement may stem from different perceptions of the situation on one or more of the moral intensity components. For example, your group may be arguing over the ethics of terminating a relationship with a longtime supplier. In examining the source of the disagreement, you may discover a difference in perception as to the concentration of effect. For example, once it is clear that you represent 60 percent of the supplier's business, others who were discounting this factor may change their opinions. This alone may make it easier to reach a decision.

MAKING ETHICAL DECISIONS

The Manager

Part of the reason for exploring various approaches to ethical decision making is to help you refine your own approach so that when pressures arise, you can make decisions consistent with your ethical framework. To this end, there is perhaps no substitute for taking personal responsibility for ethical decisions.

Even after you have become more comfortable and explicit about how you would resolve ethical dilemmas, the question still remains as to how much you should change your approach to fit in with others or try to change their approach. Although it is probably impossible to argue that one of the approaches presented in this chapter is best, applied consistently, each approach does allow a consistent

---

Temporal immediacy a function of the interval between the time the action occurs and the onset of its consequences

Proximity the physical, psychological, and emotional closeness the decision maker feels to those affected by the decision

Concentration of effect the extent to which consequences are focused on a few individuals or dispersed across many

pattern of ethical decision making. This consistency may matter more to those with whom you interact than whether your decisions are always in agreement with theirs. This is in part because your consistency allows others to better understand your approach and trust you than if they perceive your decision making as random and inconsistent.

The Organization

Just as managers try to foster ethical decisions, organizations have a significant impact on ethical decision making. The overall culture of the company can play a significant role. For example, the emphasis on keeping customers happy and income flowing seemed to contribute to a number of rather lax audits by the accounting firm Arthur Andersen (which subsequently went out of business) for companies like Enron and WorldCom. In contrast, firms can also have a positive impact on ethical decision making and behavior. In many firms senior managers take explicit and concrete steps to encourage ethical behavior among their managers. Although there are a variety of ways organizations might accomplish this objective, codes of ethics and whistle-blowing systems are perhaps two of the more visible efforts.

Codes of Ethics Given the ethical dilemmas that managers face and the different approaches for evaluating ethical behavior, many firms have adopted codes of ethics to guide their managers' decision making. A **code of ethical conduct** is typically a formal statement of one to three pages that primarily outlines types of behavior that are and are not acceptable.

An examination of 84 codes of ethics in U.S. firms found three specific clusters of issues addressed in these statements. The first cluster included items that focused on being a good "organization citizen" and was divided into nine subcategories. The second cluster included items that guided employee behavior away from unlawful or improper acts that would harm the organization and was divided into 12 subcategories. The third cluster included items that addressed directives to be good to customers and was divided into three subcategories. Exhibit 8.3 provides a list and description of the clusters and specific categories of issues addressed in these written codes. Most firms did have items in each of the three clusters, though not in all 30 subcategories.

A study of codes of ethics for firms in the United Kingdom, France, and Germany found that a higher percentage of German firms had codes of ethics than British or French firms (see Exhibit 8.4). The greater cultural emphasis on explicit communication in Germany may partially explain this finding. Although only about one-third of the European firms in this study had codes of ethics, approximately 85 percent of U.S. firms have formal codes.

In a separate study, researchers found important differences among firms from what are generally considered more similar than different cultures: U.S., Canadian, and Australian firms. For example, the codes of ethics differed substantially in terms of explicitly commenting on ethics conduct regarding behavior concerning domestic government officials (87 percent of U.S. firms, 59 percent of Canadian, and 24 percent of Australian).

Exhibit 8.5 provides information about the content of the codes of ethics for the firms that in fact had formal codes. Interestingly, while 100 percent of the European firms covered issues of acceptable and unacceptable employee behavior in their codes, only 55 percent of U.S. firms covered these issues. By contrast, only 15 percent of the European firms covered issues of political interests (i.e., business/government relations) and 96 percent of U.S. firms covered these issues in their codes.

Research on codes of ethics indicates that organizations believe codes of ethics to be the most effective means of encouraging ethical behavior in their employees. Indeed, if a given firm had a code that covered all 30 categories listed in Exhibit 8.4, employees would have a comprehensive guide for behavior. Unfortunately, the research does not support a strong link between codes of ethics and actual employee behavior. Firms without formal codes seem to have no higher or lower incidents of unethical

---

Code of ethical conduct a formal settlement that outlines types of behavior that are and are not acceptable

Cluster 1
"Be a dependable organization citizen."

1. Demonstrate courtesy, respect, honesty, and fairness in relationships with customers, suppliers, competitors, and other employees.
2. Comply with safety, health, and security regulations.
3. Do not use abusive language or actions.
4. Dress in businesslike attire.
5. Possession of firearms on company premises is prohibited.
6. Follow directives from supervisors.
7. Be reliable in attendance and punctuality.
8. Manage personal finances in a manner consistent with employment by a fiduciary institution.

Unclustered Items

1. Exhibit standards of personal integrity and professional conduct.
2. Racial, ethnic, religious, or sexual harassment is prohibited.
3. Report questionable, unethical, or illegal activities to your manager.
4. Seek opportunities to participate in community services and political activities.
5. Conserve resources and protect the quality of the environment in areas where the company operates.
6. Members of the corporation are not to recommend attorneys, accountants, insurance agents, stockbrokers, real estate agents, or similar individuals to customers.

Cluster 2
"Don't do anything unlawful or improper that will harm the organization."

1. Maintain confidentiality of customer, employee, and corporate records and information.
2. Avoid outside activities that conflict with or impair the performance of duties.
3. Make decisions objectively without regard to friendship or personal gain.
4. The acceptance of any form of bribe is prohibited.
5. Payment to any person, business, political organization, or public official for unlawful or unauthorized purposes is prohibited.
6. Conduct personal and business dealings in compliance with all relevant laws, regulations, and policies.
7. Comply fully with antitrust laws and trade regulations.
8. Comply fully with accepted accounting rules and controls.
9. Do not provide false or misleading information to the corporation, its auditors, or a government agency.
10. Do not use company property or resources for personal benefit or any other improper purpose.
11. Each employee is personally accountable for company funds over which he or she has control.
12. Staff members should not have any interest in any competitor or supplier of the company unless such interest has been fully disclosed to the company.

Cluster 3
"Be good to our customers."

1. Strive to provide products and services of the highest quality.
2. Perform assigned duties to the best of your ability and in the best interest of the corporation, its shareholders, and its customers.
3. Convey true claims for products.

Source: Donald Robin, Michael Giallourakis, Fred R. David, and Thomas E. Moritz, "A Different Look at Codes of Ethics." Reprinted from *Business Horizons* (January—February 1989), Table 1, p. 68. Copyright 1989 by Indiana University Kelley School of Business. Used with permission.

Exhibit 8.3 Categories Found in Corporate Codes of Ethics

behavior than those with formal codes. This may be because simply having a formal statement written down is not sufficient. For example, although nearly all of the *Fortune* 500 U.S. firms have codes of ethics, only about one-third have training programs and ethics officers, and only half have distributed formal codes to all their employees.

Successfully Implementing Codes of Ethics

Establishing a formal, written code of ethical conduct is an important first step. However, actions speak much louder than words, and employees are unlikely to conform to the formal code unless other actions taken by the organization reinforce the code and communicate that the company is serious about compliance. In some companies positions of ethics officer or ombudsman are being instituted. These individuals are charged with ensuring that the flow of information is rich in both directions. In other words, they have the responsibility of helping information and policies get out to the employees and also to ensure that employees' concerns, observations of misconduct, and the like can flow up and into senior management levels where action to correct things can be taken.

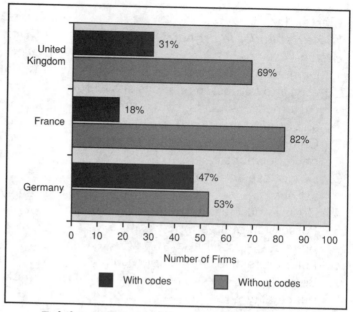

Exhibit 8.4   Adoption of Codes of Ethics

Communication The first step in effectively implementing a code of ethics is communicating it to all employees. For maximum impact, this communication needs to take a variety of forms and be repeated. It is not enough to simply send out a one-time memo. Rather, the code will need to be communicated

Subjects	United Kingdom n = 33 Number of Firms	%	France n = 15 Number of Firms	%	Germany n = 30 Number of Firms	%	Total European Countries Number of Firms	%	United States n = 118 Number of Firms	%	Significance Europe vs. U.S.
Employee conduct	33	100	15	100	30	100	78	100	47	55	SIG
Community and environment	21	64	11	73	19	63	51	85	50	42	NS
Customers	18	39	14	93	20	67	52	87	96	81	SIG
Shareholders	13	39	11	73	18	60	42	64	NA	NA	NA
Suppliers and contractors	7	21	2	13	6	20	15	19	101	86	SIG
Political interests	4	12	3	20	5	17	12	15	113	96	SIG
Innovation and technology	2	6	3	20	18	60	26	33	18	15	SIG

NS = Not significant
NA = No comparable data available
SIG = Significantly different

Exhibit 8.5   Subjects Addressed in Corporate Codes of Ethics

in memos, company newsletters, videos, and speeches by senior executives repeatedly, over a period of time, if people are to take the content of the message seriously.

Training For the code of ethical conduct to be effective, people will likely need training. For maximum impact, the training needs to be engaging. For example, Motorola developed approximately 80 different short cases. Each case presents a situation requiring a manager to make a decision. Individual participants in the training program were asked to collectively decide what they would do and discuss the ethical aspects of the decision. They then compared their decisions to those of senior executives, including the CEO, and what these executives believe is in keeping with the firm's code of ethics.

Lockheed Martin also takes an engaging approach to ethics training with an interesting, innovative twist. In the late 1990s, the company developed a board game based on Scott Adams' "Dilbert" character. The game consisted of 50 ethical dilemmas for which players have to decide among four possible responses. Participants rated this approach much higher in satisfaction than traditional ethics training and seemed to recall the learning points more effectively. Later, when the Dilbert craze wore off, Lockheed Martin used real business ethics problems as a basis for discussion. The company also has an ethics hotline employees can call if they are experiencing a business dilemma.

Although officials at organizations often think that ethics training programs are effective, current research is less conclusive. What we can say based on research is that the greater the psychological and emotional involvement of participants in the training, the greater their retention of the learning points. This may explain why Lockheed Martin's experience with ethics training has been positive.

Reward and Recognition In addition to communicating the code to employees and training them, it is critical to make sure that those who comply are recognized and rewarded. Otherwise, employees will simply view the written code as the "formal rhetoric but not the real deal."

ExxonMobil is a company that recognizes the importance of this principle. It regularly celebrates the story of an individual who has honored the company's code of conduct even when doing so might have cost the company money. For example, one of its drilling teams was setting up to drill for oil in the jungles of a developing country when a government official came by and stated that before they started the drill they needed to pay for an operating permit. However, the official wanted the payment (approximately $10,000) paid to him personally in cash. This was against the firm's code, so the team manager refused to pay. The drilling team and their expensive equipment sat idle for more than a week at a cost of over $1 million. Finally, the government official admitted that all the paperwork and permits were in order and the team was allowed to proceed. ExxonMobil celebrated this incident in its newsletter to reinforce to its employees that the company takes its code of ethical conduct seriously and rewards people who honor it, even if it costs the company money.

Whistle-Blowing A **whistle-blower** is an employee who discloses illegal or unethical conduct on the part of others in the organization. While some firms have implemented programs to encourage whistle-blowing, most have not. As a group, whistle-blowers tend *not* to be disgruntled employees but instead are conscientious, high-performing employees who report illegal or unethical incidents. In general, they report these incidents not for notoriety but because they believe the wrongdoings are so grave that they must be exposed. For example, Randy Robarge, a nuclear power plant supervisor, never intended to be a whistle-blower. To Robarge, raising concerns about the improper storage of radioactive material at ComEd's Zion power plant on Lake Michigan was just part of doing a good job. Research suggests that the more employees know about the internal channels through which they can blow the whistle and the stronger the protection of past whistle-blowers, the more likely they are to initially use those internal rather than external channels such as the media. IBM receives up to 18,000 letters a year from employees making confidential complaints through IBM's "Speak Up" program. Firms such as Hughes Tool Co.,

---

Whistle-blower an employee who discloses illegal or unethical conduct on the part of others in the organization

Companies frequently portray whistle-blowers as disgruntled employees, but more often they are conscientious, high-performing employees unable to accept wrong-doing around them. In 2002, *Time* magazine featured three whistle-blowers as its "Persons of the Year." They are (from left to right): Cynthia Cooper, a WorldCom staff auditor, who called attention to a multi-billion-dollar bookkeeping scandal; FBI agent Coleen Rowley, who revealed a 9/11-related scandal; and Sherron Watkins of Enron.

General Motors, and Bloomingdale's offer financial rewards to employees who report valid claims. In general, research suggests that the following steps can be effective in encouraging valid whistle-blowing.

- Clearly communicate whistle-blowing procedures to all employees.
- Allow for reporting channels in addition to the chain of command or reporting incidents to one's boss.
- Thoroughly investigate all claims based on a consistent procedure.
- Protect whistle-blowers who make valid claims.
- Provide moderate financial incentives or rewards for valid claims.
- Publicly celebrate employees who make valid claims.

Top Management Example The impact of setting an example is probably no more evident than it is in the case of ethical conduct. Top management both in terms of how they behave personally and how they reward, punish, or ignore the actions of others can severely damage the best intentions and designs of an implementation plan (e.g., communication, training, whistle-blowing, etc.). When it comes to skirting the law or making decisions that when open to public scrutiny fall short, the example of top management is often correlated with the behavior of middle managers. Managers are rarely persuaded by top executives to "do as I say, not as I do." Standard accounting rules were ignored so that higher revenues and profits could be recorded immediately. Once one rule, law, or policy is ignored by senior officers, who is to say that others shouldn't be? This pattern of illegal and unethical conduct was not confined to Enron but was complemented by the behavior of senior partners in the accounting firm that was supposed to monitor and certify Enron's accounting practices—Arthur Andersen. In an effort to retain Enron's auditing business and its more lucrative consulting engagements, leaders at Arthur Andersen ignored Enron's accounting irregularities despite its legal and ethical obligation to report them. In the end, leaders even instructed subordinates to destroy and shred documents (against company policy and legal statutes) in an effort to hide wrongdoing on both sides.

But by following the steps outlined earlier, managers can catch problems before they become national media events and seriously damage the firm's reputation. In addition, new laws in the United States both protect and reward whistle-blowers. Employers cannot discharge, threaten, or otherwise

© Ramin Talaie/Corbis

"The fish rots from the top of the head." The saying relates to the fact that people in an organization take their cues from the person leading it. Convicted of lying to federal officials about a stock trade, in 2004, homemaking maven Martha Stewart was sentenced to prison. The price of stock in her own company, Martha Stewart Living Omnimedia, plummeted as a result of the scandal: Having once traded for as much as $40 a share, it dropped to under $10 per share, taking a considerable toll on the company and Stewart's net worth.

discriminate against employees because they report a suspected violation of the law. Employees who blow the whistle on companies with federal government contracts can actually receive a small portion of the judgment if the company is found guilty. For example, Jane Akre was one of the first to receive such a reward. She was given $425,000 when she blew the whistle on her employer, a TV station that was deliberately distorting the news. However, an award of $52 million to three men who blew the whistle on SmithKline Beecham, a large drug company, really grabbed people's attention.

The Government

The governments of the United States and many other countries have also tried to foster ethical behavior. For example, the U.S. government has enacted a number of laws and regulations designed to achieve this objective. Perhaps the most discussed, given today's global environment, is the Foreign Corrupt Practices Act.

U.S. Foreign Corrupt Practices Act Few issues of ethical behavior have received more attention than questionable payments or bribes. For American managers this issue is at the heart of the **Foreign Corrupt Practices Act (FCPA).** This act was passed in 1977 primarily in response to the disclosure that U.S. firms were making payments to foreign government officials to win government contracts and receive preferential treatment.

One of the key incidents that sparked the FCPA was the revelation that Lockheed Corporation had made over $12 million in payments to Japanese business executives and government officials in order to

Foreign Corrupt Practices Act (FCPA) a law prohibiting employees of U.S. firms from corrupting the actions of foreign officials, politicians, or candidates for office

sell commercial aircraft in that country. Subsequent discoveries showed that nearly 500 U.S. companies had made similar payments around the world, totaling over $300 million.

Lockheed chairman at the time, Carl Kotchian, argued that the payments represented less than 3 percent of the revenue gained from the sale of aircraft to Japan. Further, these sales had a positive effect on the salaries and job security of Lockheed workers, with beneficial spillover effects for their dependents, the communities, and the shareholders. Mr. Kotchian said that he was "between a rock and a hard spot"; if he made the payments, people might criticize his actions as unethical, and if he did not make the payments, a competitor would. Consequently, the competition would get the contracts, and some Lockheed workers might lose their jobs. Whether you agree with Mr. Kotchian or not, it is instructive to assess which ethical approach he seems to be using. Is it a moral right approach, justice approach, or utilitarian approach?

Until the passage of the FCPA, these dilemmas were purely ethical ones. Upon its passage, many of these ethical decisions became legal decisions because the FCPA made it illegal for employees of U.S. firms to corrupt the actions of foreign officials, politicians, or candidates for office. The act also prohibits employees from making payments to *any* person when they have "reason to know" that the payments might be used to corrupt the behavior of officials. The act also requires that firms take steps to provide "reasonable assurance" that transactions are in compliance with the law and to keep detailed records of them. If Mr. Pignatelli were a U.S. citizen, it would be illegal for him to pay money to a consultant if he had reason to know that some of it might be used for bribes. He could not just claim he had no knowledge of the consultant's actions as a defense. Pignatelli would be bound by law to provide reasonable assurance that no bribes would be paid if the consultant were hired.

The FCPA does not cover payments made to business executives. For American managers, payments made to executives are ethical decisions, not legal ones. The FCPA also does not prohibit payments to low-level government employees to perform in a more timely manner the duties they normally would have performed. These types of payments are typically called *facilitating payments*. For example, a payment of $100 to a customs inspector not to delay the inspection of an imported product would not violate the FCPA because the payment simply facilitates something that the customs inspector would do anyway. However, the payment of $100 to pass a product *without* inspecting it would be a violation of the FCPA because the payment would entice the customs agent to do something he or she is not supposed to do.

Penalties for violation of the FCPA range up to $1 million in fines for the company and $10,000 in fines and up to five years' imprisonment for the responsible individuals. Clearly, a $1 million fine is not a deterrent when deals can be worth $100 million. Rather, the prison terms for individuals are the real teeth in the law.

Clearly, making ethical decisions is not easy. It takes an understanding of various frameworks at the individual level and intervention at the organization and government levels if compliance with particular points of view is to be achieved. While this section has focused on making ethical decisions from the individual point of view, the next section examines the general issues of ethics focusing on the organization. Typically, the issues we cover next are discussed under the general banner of corporate social responsibility.

SOCIAL RESPONSIBILITY

Corporate social responsibility is concerned with the constituencies to which corporations are obligated and the nature and extent of those obligations. As media coverage has increased and organizations such as Greenpeace, the Sierra Club, and the Ralph Nader Group have put more pressure on organizations, they have increasingly come to terms with the amount of resources they should devote to being socially responsible. Consider the following questions that confront managers daily:

- Should a firm implement environmental standards greater than those required by law?
- Should a firm insist on the same high level of safety standards in all its worldwide operations even if the laws of other countries accept lower standards?

- Do all employees, regardless of nationality or employment location, have the same rights?
- Should managerial actions that are illegal or morally unacceptable in one country be allowed in another country in which they are legal or morally acceptable?
- Should managers consider the interests of employees, customers, or general citizens over those of shareholders?

Questions such as these form the substance of social responsibility debates. Both social responsibility and managerial ethics focus on the "oughts" of conducting business. Although several approaches to corporate social responsibility exist, an examination of two fundamental perspectives will help you reflect on how you personally view the issue and how you might effectively interact with others holding differing perspectives.

The Efficiency Perspective

Perhaps no contemporary person presents the **efficiency perspective** of social resonponsibility more clearly than the Nobel Prize-winning economist Milton Friedman. Quite simply, according to Friedman, the business of business is business. In other words, a manager's responsibility is to maximize profits for the owners of the business. Adam Smith is perhaps the earliest advocate of this approach. Smith concluded over 200 years ago that the best way to advance the well-being of society is to place resources in the hands of individuals and allow market forces to allocate scarce resources to satisfy society's demands.

Managers as Owners When a manager of a business is also the owner, the self-interests of the owner are best achieved by serving the needs of society. If society demands that a product be made within certain environmental and safety standards, then it is in the best interests of the owner to produce the product to meet those standards. Otherwise, customers will likely purchase the product from competitors. Customers are more likely to purchase from firms that comply with widely shared and deeply held social values, so it makes sense for businesses to incorporate those values into their operations and products. To the extent that the cost of incorporating society's values is less than the price customers are willing to pay, the owner makes a profit.

Critics of the efficiency perspective, however, argue that quite often customers and society in general come to demand safety, environmental protection, and so on only after firms have caused significant visible damage. For example, society might hold strong values about not polluting the water and causing health problems. However, if the consequences of polluting a river are not visible and people are not immediately hurt, social pressure might not emerge to cause the owner to align his actions with societal values until years after the fact.

Managers as Agents In most large organizations today, the manager is not the owner. The corporate form of organization is characterized by the separation of ownership (shareholders) and control (managers). Managers serve as the agents of the organization's owners. Within this context, Friedman argues that managers should "conduct business in accordance with [owners'] desires, which will generally be to make as much money as possible while conforming to the basic rules of society, both those embodied in law and those embodied in ethical custom." From Friedman's perspective, managers have no obligation to act on behalf of society if doing so does not maximize value for the shareholders. For example, packaging products in recycled paper should be undertaken only if doing so maximizes shareholder wealth. Whether such an action satisfies or benefits a small group of activists is irrelevant. Managers have no responsibility to carry out such programs; in fact, they have a responsibility *not* to undertake such action if it is more costly because it does not maximize shareholder wealth. Similarly, charitable donations are

Efficiency perspective the concept that a manager's responsibility is to maximize profits for the owners of the business

not the responsibility of corporations. Instead, managers should maximize the return to shareholders and then shareholders can decide if and to which charities they want to make contributions. Simply put, the profits are not the managers' money, and therefore, they have no right to decide how or if it should be distributed to charitable causes.

From the efficiency perspective, it is impossible for managers to maximize shareholders' wealth and simultaneously attempt to fulfill all of society's needs. It is the responsibility of government to impose taxes and determine expenditures to meet society's needs. If managers pursue actions that benefit society but do not benefit shareholders, then they are exercising political power, not managerial authority.

Concerns with the Efficiency Perspective The efficiency perspective assumes that markets are competitive and that competitive forces move firms toward fulfilling societal needs as expressed by consumer demand. Firms that do not respond to consumer demands in terms of products, price, delivery, safety, environmental impact, or any other dimension important to consumers will, through competition, be forced to change or be put out of business. Unfortunately, however, corrective action often occurs after people are injured.

Arnold Dworkin, the owner of Kaufman's Bagel and Delicatessen in Skokie, Illinois, learned to pay attention to public safety the hard way. On a Wednesday, calls trickled in to the restaurant from customers complaining of vomiting, nausea, and stomach pains, and by Friday the restaurant had to be closed. Customers were suffering from salmonella bacteria, which was traced to corned beef being cooked at only 90 degrees rather than the 140 degrees required by local health regulations. Although corrective measures were taken, three weeks later another customer was hospitalized with salmonella poisoning. This time the cause was traced to a leaky floorboard above a basement meat-drying table. Kaufman's lost approximately $250,000 in sales and $10,000 in food, and its insurance company paid out more than $750,000 for individual and class-action suits and hospital claims. Interestingly, because Dworkin dealt with the situation in a straightforward manner by disclosing all the information he had to customers and the media, quickly making every repair, and following all the recommended actions suggested by the safety and health board regardless of cost, his business returned to 90 to 95 percent of its original level within two years.

The other major concern with the efficiency perspective is that corporations can impose indirect consequences that may not be completely understood or anticipated. In economic terms, these unintended consequences are called **externalities.** For example, the government of the United Kingdom enticed Nissan with tax and other incentives to build a new automobile plant there. However, the trucks going in and out of the plant created traffic congestion and wear on public roads that were not completely accounted for in the government's proposal. The government had to use tax revenue collected from citizens to repair the roads damaged by Nissan, to which it had given tax incentives (tax breaks). These poor road conditions slowed deliveries to the factory and also created inconveniences for the citizens. However, even when externalities can be anticipated, consumers often cannot correctly factor in or be willing to pay for the costs. For example, the consequences of poor safety controls at a grass fertilizer plant (explosion, fire, toxic fumes, injury, and death) are understood. As a consumer can you correctly assess the costs of a chemical disaster and the increased price you should pay to cover the needed safety expenditures? If the answer is "No," this may cause the plant manager to skip necessary safety practices in order to keep costs low and make a profit. It is not until inadequate safety policies and practices result in a chemical disaster and people are killed or injured that the impact of the externality (i.e., the chemical disaster) is fully appreciated by consumers and therefore appropriately priced in the market.

Externalities indirect or unintended consequences imposed on society that may not be understood or anticipated

Social Responsibility Perspective

The social responsibility perspective argues that society grants existence to firms; therefore, firms have responsibilities and obligations to society as a whole, not just shareholders. Thus, while the efficiency perspective states that it is *socially responsible* to maximize the return to the shareholder, the social responsibility perspective states that it is *socially irresponsible* to maximize only shareholder wealth because shareholders are not the only ones responsible for the firm's existence. For instance, creditors of a corporation cannot go beyond the assets of the corporation and seek repayment from the assets of the owners. This protection is termed *limited liability*. This privilege is granted to the corporation by society, not by shareholders. Thus, the existence of the firm is not solely a function of shareholders, and, therefore, the responsibilities of the firm cannot be restricted just to shareholders.

Stakeholders In the social responsibility perspective, managers must consider the legitimate concerns of other stakeholders beyond the shareholders. **Stakeholders** are individuals or groups who have an interest in and are affected by the actions of an organization. They include customers, employees, financiers, suppliers, communities, society at large, and shareholders. Customers have a special place within this set of constituencies because they pay the bills with the revenue they provide. Shareholders are also given special status, but in the stakeholder approach, shareholders are viewed as providers of "risk capital" rather than as sole owners. Consequently, shareholders are entitled to *reasonable* return on the capital they put at risk, but they are not entitled to a *maximum* return because they are not solely responsible for the existence of the firm. To maximize the return to shareholders would take away returns owed to the other stakeholders. Thus, managers must make decisions and take actions that provide a reasonable return to shareholders, balanced against the legitimate concerns of customers, employees, financiers, communities, and society at large. While the evidence is not definitive, there is research to suggest that there is a positive relationship between a stakeholder approach and firm performance.

Concerns with the Social Responsibility Perspective One of the key concerns with the social responsibility perspective is that important terms such as "reasonable returns" and "legitimate concerns" cannot be defined adequately. Given that reasonable returns to shareholders and legitimate concerns of other stakeholders could come into conflict, not knowing exactly what is reasonable or legitimate reduces managers' ability to find the appropriate balance and act in socially responsible ways. This is why from a practical standpoint, even if you believe in the stakeholder framework of corporate social responsibility, making decisions that balance the interests of the different stakeholders is a significant challenge for which there is no magic solution. It is not only possible but quite likely that customers, employees, financiers, communities, and society at large will have conflicting and competing concerns. Consider the case of a manager in a factory that makes corrugated boxes. His customers want sturdy boxes that can be stacked several levels high. Society increasingly seems to want a higher use of recycled paper. However, boxes made of recycled paper either have higher costs for the same strength or lower strength at the same cost compared to boxes made of nonrecycled paper. Shareholders want competitive returns. In such a case, how would you determine the most socially responsible action? If customers tell you that boxes must meet a certain strength requirement regardless of whether they use recycled paper or not, does this outweigh the desires of the other stakeholders? Should you devote more money to researching and developing stronger recycled boxes even though it takes money away from shareholders by increasing costs and reducing profits?

Comparing the Efficiency and Stakeholder Perspectives

The efficiency and social responsibility perspectives differ mainly in terms of the constituencies to whom organizations have responsibilities. The two perspectives differ little in their evaluations of actions that

---

Stakeholders individuals or groups who have an interest in and are affected by the actions of an organization

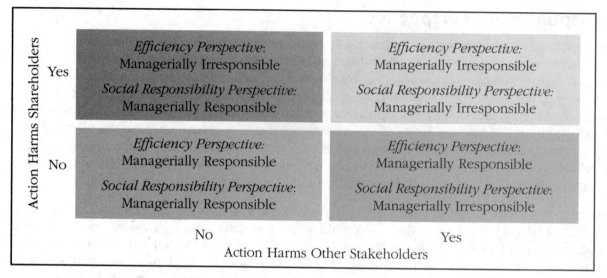

Exhibit 8.6   Comparing Efficiency and Social Responsibility Perspectives

either harm or benefit both shareholders and society (see Exhibit 8.6). Their evaluations differ most markedly when actions help one group and harm the other. Actions that benefit shareholders but harm the other legitimate stakeholders would be viewed as managerially responsible from the efficiency perspective, but socially irresponsible from the social responsibility perspective. Actions that harm shareholders but benefit the other legitimate stakeholders would be viewed as managerially irresponsible from the efficiency perspective, but socially responsible from the social responsibility perspective.

The following quotes illustrate how differently CEOs view the issue of corporate social responsibility.

Many factors go into establishing ExxonMobil's credentials as the world's premier petroleum and petrochemical company. One of the most important is operating with meticulous attention to the safety and health of our employees and the communities where we operate, as well as a conscientious regard for the environmental impact of our activities and products.

—Lee Raymond, CEO and Chairman, ExxonMobil

Profits are like breathing. If you can't breathe, you can forget everything else that you're doing because you're not going to be around much longer.

—Robert E. Mercer, CEO, Goodyear Tire & Rubber, 1983–1988

I work for the shareholders. I work for the employees. I work for the customers. If I don't make a good profit, I'm not doing a very good job for the owners and for the employees. If I make too much profit, my customers worry. And it's a constant balancing act.

—Richard E. Heckert, CEO, Du Pont, 1986–1989

The only way for a corporation to exist and capitalism to survive is to be part of the whole society. Companies have to be concerned with the owners, the shareholders, the employees, and the customers.

—David T. Kearns, CEO, Xerox, 1982–1990

Corporate Responses

As the previous quotes illustrate, how corporations react to the various pressures and constituencies connected to the topic of social responsibility varies widely. These reactions can be simplified and laid out on a continuum that ranges from defensive to proactive, as illustrated in Exhibit 8.7. Although we might imagine that firms adopting the efficiency perspective are more likely to be Defenders, Accommodaters,

	Defenders	**Accomodaters**	**Reactors**	**Anticipators**
Belief:	We must fight against efforts to restrict or regulate our activities and profit-making potential.	We will change when legally compelled to do so.	We should respond to significant pressure even if we are not legally required to.	We owe it to society to anticipate and avoid actions with potentially harmful consequences, even if we are not pressured or legally required to do so.
Focus:	Maximize profits. Find legal loopholes. Fight new restrictions and regulations.	Maximize profits. Abide by the letter of the law. Change when legally compelled to do so.	Protect profits. Abide by the law. React to pressure that could affect business results.	Obtain profits. Abide by the law. Anticipate harmful consequences independent of pressures and laws.

Exhibit 8.7 Corporate Responses

and Reactors, while firms adopting the stakeholder perspective are more likely to be Anticipators, we know of no research that has examined this specific association.

Defenders Companies that might be classified as defenders tend to fight efforts that they see as resulting in greater restriction and regulation of their ability to maximize profits. These firms often operate at the edge of the law and actively seek legal loopholes in conducting their business. Typically, they change only when legally compelled to do so.

Accommodaters These companies are less aggressive in fighting restrictions and regulations but they change only when legally compelled to do so. This type of firm tends to obey the letter of the law but does not make changes that might restrict profits if it is not required to.

Reactors Reactor firms make changes when they feel that pressure from constituencies is sufficient such that nonresponsiveness could have a negative economic impact on the firm. For example, the firm might change to recycled paper for boxes only when the pressure from customers becomes strong enough that nonresponsiveness would lead customers to boycott its products or to simply choose a competitor's products that use recycled paper.

Anticipators Firms in this category tend to believe that they are obligated to a variety of stakeholders—customers, employees, shareholders, general citizens, and so on—not to harm them, independent of laws or pressures that restrict or regulate their actions. Firms in this category not only abide by the law, but they might take action to avoid harming constituencies, even when the constituencies might not be aware of the potential danger. For example, a firm might take steps to protect employees from harmful chemicals within the workplace even before employees suffered negative side effects sufficient for them to demand work environment changes or before safety laws are passed.

MANAGERIAL PERSPECTIVES REVISITED

PERSPECTIVE 1: THE ORGANIZATIONAL CONTEXT When it comes to managerial ethics and corporate social responsibility, the context of the organization is extremely important. While no individual manager will likely win a court case by saying "The devil organization made me do it," it is folly to ignore the tremendous impact that the organization has on individual decisions and behaviors. For example, the company may have a code of ethics, but if its culture is contrary to the code, senior managers should not be surprised when individuals act in ways that go against the code. This is perhaps one of the strongest reasons for a well-established whistler-blower system. Even if the "flow" of the company culture is in one direction, a well-established whistle-blower system can allow conscientious employees to swim against the tide. In addition, managers need to understand the general approach the company takes toward social responsibility. Trying to take an efficiency perspective in a stakeholder-orientated company or vice versa will likely lead to many incidents of frustration. The match between personal ethical and social responsibility orientation and the organization context is critical. For example, applying the tactics of a Defender in an Anticipator organization or vice versa will likely hurt rather than help one's career. While this does not mean that as an individual manager you cannot or should not try to change others around you or the entire organization, it does mean that ignoring the organizational context is naive.

PERSPECTIVE 2: THE HUMAN FACTOR A manager cannot achieve the desired ethical decisions or approach to social responsibility alone. While personal integrity and ethical decision making is critical for an individual manager, this alone does not satisfy his or her responsibility. Managers are responsible for leading their employees in ways that limit ethic lapses and increase the odds that they behave responsibly. This means, for example, that if your firm does have a code of conduct you have the responsibility of communicating, supporting, and reinforcing the standard with your subordinates. If the firm has a particular orientation toward social responsibility, as a manager you need to help your employees understand what it means and how it applies to the work they do and decisions they make. Only if the managers inculcate the ethical or social responsibility standards of the company in others can it truly have a pervasive impact.

PERSPECTIVE 3: MANAGING PARADOXES Meeting the challenges required to act ethically and in a socially responsible manner will require managing some important paradoxes. On the one hand, as an individual you may have your own personal standards of integrity, ethics, and social responsibility. On the other hand, as a manager you have a responsibility to uphold the standards of your company. What should you do when there is a conflict between the two? Do you have an obligation to correct inappropriate behaviors or blow the whistle on practices that are not in keeping with the company policies or with legal or regulatory standards? The potential paradox between personal and company standards is one of the principal challenges managers face daily regarding ethics and social responsibilities. The other major source of potential paradoxes is between tolerance and compliance. In diverse cultures encountered by firms that operate globally, differences in ethical values and judgments, as well as perspectives on social responsibility, are inevitable. Tolerance and understanding of these differences are important. However, simultaneously, companies are increasingly asking their employees and managers to abide by global standards of conduct and are developing global approaches to social responsibility. As a consequence, managers sometimes face the paradox of balancing tolerance and understanding on the one hand with integrated standards of conduct on the other.

PERSPECTIVE 4: ENTREPRENEURIAL MIND SET In Chapter 1, we discussed the need for managers to be alert in order to identify and to exploit opportunities. However, some especially lucrative opportunities may present ethical dilemmas. Therefore, managers will need to remain vigilant in balancing their personal standards and the organizational standards with the opportunities to earn large returns. They will need to understand fully how their actions will affect others, especially the organization's stakeholders.

Establishing a values-based culture should help managers remain committed to ethical practices and social responsibilities while simultaneously remaining alert to opportunities and exploiting them. Whatever decisions are ultimately made by the organization shouldn't require a compromise of managers' personal or organizational standards. In fact, emphasizing ethical practices may actually provide the organization with new opportunities because consumers and other stakeholders value such standards. Most people want to work for or do business with ethical and socially responsible organizations versus those that are not.

CONCLUDING COMMENTS

There is no universal opinion concerning managerial ethics or the social responsibility of corporations. Gray areas remain, and important questions go unanswered regardless of which fundamental perspective you adopt concerning ethical behavior or corporate social responsibility. For example, the efficiency approach argues that managers should seek to maximize shareholders' returns but must do so within the laws and ethical norms of the society. In today's increasingly global environment, a given firm may operate in a variety of societies. What if the norms of one society clash with those of another? Which societal norms should be honored?

A social responsibility approach also operates within equally large gray areas. For example, how can you calculate, let alone incorporate, conflicting needs of constituencies across countries? How can a Korean consumer's needs for low price for paper be balanced against the environmental concerns of Indonesian or Brazilian societies where large forests are being cut to produce paper? How can all of these concerns be balanced against the potential worldwide concern for the depletion of critical oxygen-providing trees?

In addition to the difficulty of determining the relative weight of different constituencies, managers face the challenge of trying to determine the weights of different groups within one category of constituencies across national borders. How are such determinations made? For example, firms may have employees in many countries, and the concerns of these employees will most likely differ. Employees in Japan may want the firm to maximize job security, while employees in England may want the firm to maximize current wages and be willing to trade off future job security. Similarly, German consumers may want firms to have high global environmental standards, and Indonesian consumers may have no such concerns. Which standards should be adopted?

The general debates concerning ethics and social responsibility have raged for generations. The purpose of this chapter has not been to resolve the debate but rather to examine the assumptions and rationales of fundamental perspectives. If there were a magic formula for meeting these challenges, there would likely be little need for bright, capable people (we could just turn the problem over to computer algorithms); nor would there be much excitement in being a manager. We hope this examination enables you to evaluate your own views, so that you will be prepared when situations arise concerning ethics or social responsibility. Perhaps then the pressure of the moment will be less likely to cause you to take actions that you might later regret. Understanding the general frameworks also helps you to better appreciate others who have differing perspectives and, thereby, interact more effectively with them.

Decision Making

From *John R. Schermerhorn, Jr. Management,* 10th Edition, 2009. Reprinted by permission of
John Wiley & Sons, Inc.

Hurricane Katrina was devastating; people lost homes, jobs, fortunes, and lives; organizations lost reputations after failing in their response capabilities. And in retrospect, it is clear that a lot of things could have been done differently to better help New Orleans prepare for Katrina and handle the killer storm's aftermath. But when things are happening "real time," it's not easy to do everything right. Information gets missed or lost or poorly used, mistakes get made, and the most well-intended decisions can go wrong or prove inadequate to the task.

Anyone who practices management knows that decision making is part of the job. They also know that quality decisions require good information, that not all decisions are going to be easy ones, and that some decisions have to be made under tough conditions. Case studies, experiential exercises, class discussions, and exam questions in college courses are intended to help students gain familiarity with the nature of decision making, the potential problems and pitfalls, and even the pressures of crisis situations. From that point on, however, only you can determine whether you will be able to step forward and make the best decisions even in difficult circumstances, or collapse under pressure.

INFORMATION, TECHNOLOGY, AND MANAGEMENT

Our society is information-driven, digital, networked, and continuously evolving. Career success requires two "must have" competencies: *computer competency*—the ability to understand computers and to use them to their best advantage; and *information competency*—the ability to utilize technology to locate, retrieve, evaluate, organize, and analyze information for decision making. How about you—are you ready?

What Is Useful Information?

This sign should be on every manager's desk—Warning: data ≠ information. **Data** are raw facts and observations. **Information** is data made useful and meaningful for decision making. In the music industry, for example, lots of data are available on the demographic profiles of customers—such as age groups buying various CDs and music downloads. Not everyone with access to this data, however, turns it into useful information for decision making. But those who do may gain competitive advantage. In the example, that might mean changing advertising because younger customers buy mostly through the Internet while older customers still shop a lot in retail stores.

The management process of planning, organizing, leading, and controlling is driven by information. Managers need good information, and they need it all the time. Information that is truly useful in management meets the test of these five criteria:

1. *Timely*—the information is available when needed; it meets deadlines for decision making and action.
2. *High quality*—the information is accurate and it is reliable; it can be used with confidence.
3. *Complete*—the information is complete and sufficient for the task at hand; it is as current and up-to-date as possible.
4. *Relevant*—the information is appropriate for the task at hand; it is free from extraneous or irrelevant materials.
5. *Understandable*—the information is clear and easily understood by the user; it is free from unnecessary detail.

Information Needs in Organizations

An important key to managerial performance in this new world is **information technology**, or IT, and the way it helps us acquire, store, process, analyze, and transmit information. And in our IT-rich world,

---

Data are raw facts and observations.

Information is data made useful for decision making.

Information technology helps us acquire, store, and process information.

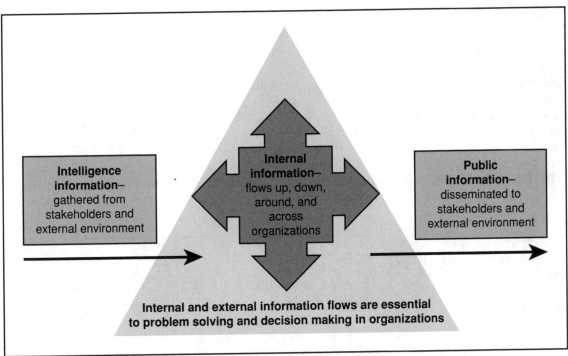

Exhibit 9.1 Internal and external information needs in organizations.

where continual advances in technologies make more information about more things available to more people more quickly than ever before, the question is: how well do we take advantage of it?

Information and the External Environment

Driven largely by IT, information serves the variety of needs described in Exhibit 9.1. At the organization's boundaries, information in the external environment is accessed. Managers use this *intelligence information* to deal with customers, competitors, and other stakeholders such as government agencies, creditors, suppliers, and stockholders. Peter Drucker once said that "a winning strategy will require information about events and conditions outside the institution," and that organizations must have "rigorous methods for gathering and analyzing outside information."

Organizations also send vast amounts of *public information* to stakeholders and the external environment. This serves a variety of purposes, ranging from image-building to product advertising to financial reporting. And the way organizations handle public information can be very strategic. When Boeing, for example, lost a contract to build a next-generation tanker for the U.S. Air Force, it published full-page newspaper ads. Why? Boeing's point was to inform the public why it believed its bid was unfairly denied and why its fierce competitors—Northrup Grumman and its European partner Airbus—should not have been awarded the contract. The ad was part of a massive public lobbying effort to gain support for having the decision overturned. The U.S. Auditor General eventually agreed with Boeing, and the Air Force reopened bidding; Boeing was given another chance.

Information and the Internal Environment

Silicon valley pioneer and Cisco Systems CEO John Chambers once pointed out that he always has the information he needs to be in control—be it information on earnings, expenses, profitability, gross margins, and more. He also says: "Because I have my data in that format, every one of my employees can make decisions that might have had to come all the way to the president. . . . Quicker decision making at lower levels will translate into higher profit margins. . . . Companies that don't do that will be noncompetitive."

Within organizations, people need vast amounts of information to make decisions and solve problems in their daily work. They need information to act individually and in teams; they need information from their immediate work setting, from other parts of the organization, and from the organization's external environment. The ability of IT to gather and move information quickly within an organization can be a great asset to decision making. It can help top levels stay informed, while freeing lower levels to make speedy decisions and take the actions they need to best perform their jobs.

How Information Technology Is Changing Organizations

In order to perform well, people in any work setting, large or small, must have available to them the right information at the right time, and in the right place. This is the function served by **information systems** that use the latest in information technology to collect, organize, and distribute data in such a way that they become meaningful as information. **Management information systems**, or MIS, meet the specific information needs of managers as they make a variety of day-to-day decisions. C.R. England Inc., a long-haul refrigerated trucking company, for example, uses a computerized MIS to monitor more than 500 aspects of organizational performance. The system tracks everything from billing accuracy to arrival times to driver satisfaction with company maintenance on their vehicles.

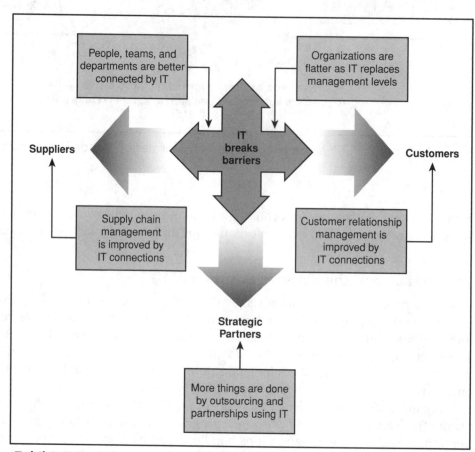

Exhibit 9.2 Information technology is breaking barriers and changing organizations.

Says CEO Dan England: "Our view was, if we could measure it, we could manage it."

Organizations are not only using IT; they are being changed by its use. Information departments or centers are now mainstream features on organization charts. The number and variety of information career fields is rapidly expanding. And, as shown in Exhibit 9.2, IT is helping to break down barriers within organizations.[8] People working in different departments, levels, and physical locations now use IT to eas-

---

Information systems use IT to collect, organize, and distribute data for use in decision making.

Management information systems meet the information needs of managers in making daily decisions.

ily communicate and share information. The new IT-intensive organizations are "flatter" and operate with fewer levels than their more traditional organizational counterparts; computers replace people whose jobs were primarily devoted to moving information. This creates opportunities for faster decision making, better use of timely information, and better coordination of decisions and actions.

IT is also breaking barriers between organizations and key elements in the external environment. It plays an important role in customer relationship management by quickly and accurately providing information regarding customer needs, preferences, and satisfactions. It helps in supply chain management to better manage and control costs everywhere from initiation of purchase, to logistics and transportation, to point of delivery and ultimate use.

INFORMATION AND MANAGERIAL DECISIONS

In a book entitled *Judgment: How Winning Leaders Make Great Calls*, scholars and consultants Noel M. Tichy and Warren G. Bennis discuss the importance of what leaders do before a decision is made, while making it, and when implementing it. Information is the center point to all three phases—information helps a leader sense the need for a decision, frame an approach to it, and communicate about it with others. As Bennis remarked in a *BusinessWeek* interview, "The source of many fatal judgments is the information pipeline. How do leaders get information that is relevant, has meaning, and is timely?"

Managers As Information Processors

The manager's job in today's IT-enriched organizations, can be depicted as a nerve center of information flows, as shown in Exhibit 9.3. Managers in this sense are information processors—continually gathering information, giving it, and receiving it. All of the managerial roles identified by Henry Mintzberg and discussed in Chapter 1—interpersonal, decisional, and informational—involve communication and information processing. So, too, do all aspects of the management process—planning, organizing, leading, and controlling. And in this regard, IT offers many advantages.

- *Planning advantages of IT*—better and more timely access to useful information, involving more people in the planning process.
- *Organizing advantages of IT*—more ongoing and informed communication among all parts, improving coordination and integration.
- *Leading advantages of IT*—more frequent and better communication with staff and diverse stakeholders, keeping objectives clear.
- *Controlling advantages of IT*—more immediate measures of performance results, allowing real-time solutions to problems.

Exhibit 9.3 The manager as an information-processing nerve center in the management process.

Managers As Problem Solvers

Problem solving is the process of identifying a discrepancy between an actual and a desired state of affairs, and then taking action to resolve it. Success in problem solving is dependent on using information to make good **decisions**—choices among alternative possible courses of action. Managers, in this sense, make decisions while facing a continuous stream of daily problems. The most obvious problem situation is a *performance deficiency*. This is when actual performance is less than desired; for example, when turnover or absenteeism suddenly increases in the work unit, when a team member's daily output decreases, or when a customer complains about service delays. Another important problem situation emerges as a *performance opportunity*. This is when an actual situation either turns out better than anticipated or offers the potential to do so.

Openness to Problem Solving

Managers often differ in their openness to problem solving, that is in their basic willingness to accept the responsibilities that it entails. What you will see in observing the behavior of others are approaches to problem solving that range from passive to reactive to proactive.

Some managers are *problem avoiders* who ignore information that would otherwise signal the presence of a performance opportunity or deficiency. They are passive in information gathering, not wanting to make decisions and deal with problems. Other managers are *problem solvers* who are willing to make decisions and try to solve problems, but only when forced to by the situation. They are reactive in gathering information and tend to respond to problems after they occur. They may deal reasonably well with performance deficiencies, but they may miss many performance opportunities.

There is quite a contrast between the last two styles and *problem seekers*. These managers actively process information and constantly look for problems to solve. True problem seekers are proactive and forward thinking. They anticipate performance deficiencies and opportunities, and they take appropriate action to gain the advantage. Success at problem seeking is one of the ways exceptional managers distinguish themselves from the merely good ones.

Systematic and Intuitive Thinking

Managers also differ in their use of "systematic" and "intuitive" thinking during decision making. In **systematic thinking** a person approaches problems in a rational, step-by-step, and analytical fashion. This type of thinking breaks a complex problem into smaller components and then addresses them in a logical and integrated fashion. Managers who are systematic can be expected to make a plan before taking action, and carefully search for information to facilitate problem solving in a step-by-step fashion.

Someone using **intuitive thinking** is flexible and spontaneous, and also may be quite creative. This type of thinking allows a person to respond imaginatively to a problem based on a quick and broad evaluation of the situation and the possible alternative courses of action. Managers who are intuitive can be expected to deal with many aspects of a problem at once, jump quickly from one issue to another, and consider "hunches" based on experience or spontaneous ideas. This approach tends to work best in situations where facts are limited and few decision precedents exist.

Problem solving involves identifying and taking action to resolve problems.

A decision is a choice among possible alternative courses of action.

Systematic thinking approaches problems in a rational and analytical fashion.

Intuitive thinking approaches problems in a flexible and spontaneous fashion.

Multidimensional Thinking

Managers often deal with portfolios of problems that consist of multiple and interrelated issues. This requires **multidimensional thinking**—the ability to view many problems at once, in relationship to one another and across both long and short time horizons. The best managers are able to "map" multiple problems into a network that can be actively managed over time as priorities, events, and demands continuously change. They are able to make decisions and take actions in the short run that benefit longer-run objectives. And, they avoid being sidetracked while sorting through a shifting mix of daily problems. Harvard scholar Daniel Isenberg calls this skill **strategic opportunism**—the ability to remain focused on long-term objectives while being flexible enough to resolve short-term problems and opportunities in a timely manner.

Cognitive Styles

Cognitive styles describe the way people deal with information while making decisions. These styles are based on a contrast of approaches toward information gathering (sensation vs. intuition), and information evaluation (feeling vs. thinking).

As the following descriptions suggest, people with different cognitive styles approach problems and decisions in quite different ways. It is important to understand our cognitive styles and tendencies, as well as those of others. In the social context of the workplace, the more diverse the cognitive styles of decision makers, the more difficulty we might expect them to have while working together.

Cognitive Styles in Decision Making

- *Sensation Thinkers*—tend to emphasize the impersonal rather than the personal and take a realistic approach to problem solving. They like hard "facts," clear goals, certainty, and situations of high control.
- *Sensation Feelers*—tend to emphasize both analysis and human relations. They tend to be realistic and prefer facts; they are open communicators and sensitive to feelings and values.
- *Intuitive Thinkers*—are comfortable with abstraction and unstructured situations. They tend to be idealistic and prone toward intellectual and theoretical positions. They are logical and impersonal, but also avoid details.
- *Intuitive Feelers*—prefer broad and global issues. They are insightful and tend to avoid details, being comfortable with intangibles; they value flexibility and human relationships.

Types of Managerial Decisions

Managers make many types of decisions while solving problems in their day-to-day work. Some decisions are quite structured and routine, while others are more unstructured and unique.

Multidimensional thinking is an ability to address many problems at once.

Strategic opportunism focuses on long-term objectives while being flexible in dealing with short-term problems.

Programmed and Nonprogrammed Decisions

Managers sometimes face **structured problems**—ones that are familiar, straightforward, and clear with respect to information needs. Because these problems are routine and occur over and over again, they can be dealt with by **programmed decisions** that use solutions already available from past experience. Although not always predictable, routine problems can at least be anticipated. This means that decisions can be planned or programmed in advance to be implemented as needed. In human resource management, for example, problems are common whenever decisions are made on pay raises and promotions, vacation requests, committee assignments, and the like. Forward-looking managers use this understanding to decide in advance how to handle complaints and conflicts when and if they should arise.

Managers also deal with **unstructured problems** in the form of new or unusual situations full of ambiguities and information deficiencies. These problems require **nonprogrammed decisions** that craft novel solutions to meet the demands of the unique situation at hand. Most problems faced by higher-level managers are of this type, often involving the choice of strategies and objectives in situations of some uncertainty.

Crisis Decisions

An extreme type of nonprogrammed decision occurs in times of **crisis**—an unexpected problem that can lead to disaster if not resolved quickly and appropriately. Terrorism in a post-9/11 world, outbreaks of workplace violence, IT failures and security breaches, ethical scandals, and environmental catastrophes are examples. Fred Sawyers knows the latter situation quite well. He was in New Orleans managing a Hilton hotel when Hurricane Katrina struck. But in what he describes as "the most harrowing week of his life," he excelled. Using common sense, quick perception, and solid hard work, Sawyers moved from decision to decision—motivating staff, keeping the damaged hotel as safe as possible, and feeding and sheltering 4,500 persons from the storm. The *BusinessWeek* article carrying Sawyers's story led with the headline: "They don't teach this in B-School." We might disagree a bit. Anyone who studies management knows that decision making is part of the job. They also know that not all decisions are going to be easy ones; some will always have to be made under tough conditions.

The ability to handle crises may be the ultimate test of a manager's problem-solving capabilities. Unfortunately, and unlike the Fred Sawyers case, research indicates that managers may react to crises by doing the wrong things—isolating themselves and trying to solve the problem alone or in a small "closed" group. This denies them access to crucial information and assistance at the very time they are most needed. Management Smarts 9.1 offers, by contrast, guidelines on effective crisis management.

It is getting more common for organizations to engage in formal **crisis management programs.** They are designed to help managers and others prepare for unexpected high-impact events that threaten an organization's health and well-being. Anticipation is one aspect of crisis management; preparation is another. People can be assigned ahead of time to crisis management teams, and crisis management plans can be developed to deal with various contingencies. Just as police departments and community groups plan ahead and train to best handle civil and natural disasters, so, too, can managers and work teams plan ahead and train to best deal with organizational crises.

Structured problems are straightforward and clear with respect to information needs.

A **programmed decision** applies a solution from past experience to a routine problem.

Unstructured problems have ambiguities and information deficiencies.

A **nonprogrammed decision** applies a specific solution crafted for a unique problem.

A **crisis** is an unexpected problem that can lead to disaster if not resolved quickly and appropriately.

Crisis management is preparation for the management of crises that threaten an organization's health and well-being.

Management Smarts 9.1

Six Rules for Crisis Management

1. *Figure out what is going on*—Take the time to understand what's happening and the conditions under which the crisis must be resolved.
2. *Remember that speed matters*—Attack the crisis as quickly as possible, trying to catch it when it is as small as possible.
3. *Remember that slow counts, too*—Know when to back off and wait for a better opportunity to make progress with the crisis.
4. *Respect the danger of the unfamiliar*—Understand the danger of all-new territory where you and others have never been before.
5. *Value the skeptic*—Don't look for and get too comfortable with agreement; appreciate skeptics and let them help you see things differently.
6. *Be ready to "fight fire with fire"*—When things are going wrong and no one seems to care, you may have to start a crisis to get their attention.

Decision Conditions

Exhibit 9.4 shows three different decision conditions or environments—certainty, risk, and uncertainty. Although managers make decisions in each, the conditions of risk and uncertainty are common at higher management levels where problems are more complex and unstructured. Former Coca-Cola CEO Roberto Goizueta, for example, was known as a risk taker. One of his risky moves was introducing Diet Coke to the market—a success story. Another of his risks was changing the formula of Coca-Cola to create New Coke—a failure; Goizueta reversed direction after New Coke flopped. When it comes to hybrid automobiles, General Motors wasn't a risk taker. Its hesitancy largely gave the market advantage to GM's Japanese rivals. The firm's vice chairman, Bob Lutz, now says: "GM had the technology to do hybrids back when Toyota was launching the first Prius, but we opted not to ask the board to approve a product program that'd be destined to lose hundreds of millions of dollars. We won't make that mistake again."

Certain Environment

The decisions just described were made in conditions quite different from the relative predictability of a **certain environment.** This is an ideal decision situation where factual information is available about the possible alternative courses of action and their outcomes. The decision maker's task is simple: study the alternatives and choose the best solution. Certain environments are nice and comfortable for decision makers, however, very few managerial problems are like this.

Risk Environment

Many management problems emerge in **risk environments**—ones where facts and information on action alternatives and their consequences are incomplete. These situations require the use of probabilities to estimate the likelihood that a particular outcome will occur (e.g., 4 chances out of 10). Because probabilities are only possibilities, they introduce risk into the decision situation. And, some people deal better with risk than others. When considering possible investments in hybrid technologies, for example,

---

A **certain environment** offers complete information on possible action alternatives and their consequences.

A **risk environment** lacks complete information but offers "probabilities" of the likely outcomes for possible action alternatives

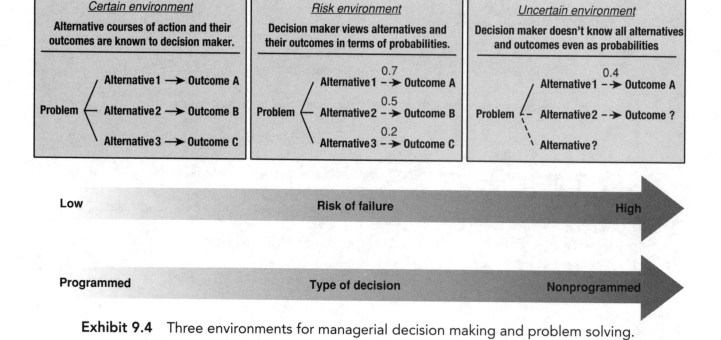

Exhibit 9.4   Three environments for managerial decision making and problem solving.

GM executives either miscalculated the probabilities of positive payoffs or didn't believe the probabilities were high enough to justify the risk. Their Japanese competitors, facing the same risk environment, decided differently and gained advantage.

Entrepreneurs and highly innovative organizations have the capacities to make good decisions under risk conditions. Also, steps can sometimes be taken to reduce risk by gathering more and better information. In the case of new products, like Diet Coke, firms often make "go or no-go" decisions only after consumer preferences are identified by extensive market testing with focus groups.

Uncertain Environment

When facts are few and information is so poor that managers are unable even to assign probabilities to the likely outcomes of alternatives, an **uncertain environment** exists. This is the most difficult decision condition. The high level of uncertainty forces managers to rely heavily on creativity in solving problems. Because uncertainty requires unique, novel, and often totally innovative alternatives, groups are frequently useful for problem solving. But the responses to uncertainty depend greatly on intuition, judgment, informed guessing, and hunches—all of which leave considerable room for error. Perhaps no better example exists of the challenges of uncertainty than the situation faced by government and business leaders during the stock market crash of October, 2008. The bank failures and dramatic world-wide stock market sell offs left all decision makers struggling to find the right pathways to deal with highly uncertain economic conditions.

An **uncertain environment** lacks so much information that it is difficult to assign probabilities to the likely outcomes of alternatives.

THE DECISION-MAKING PROCESS

Exhibit 9.5 describes five steps in the **decision-making process**: (1) identify and define the problem, (2) generate and evaluate alternative solutions, (3) choose a preferred course of action and conduct the "ethics double check," (4) implement the decision, and (5) evaluate results. All five steps can be understood in the context of the following short-but-true case.

> **The Ajax Case.** On December 31, the Ajax Company decided to close down its Murphysboro plant. Market conditions were forcing layoffs, and the company could not find a buyer for the plant. Some of the 172 employees had been with the company as long as 18 years; others as little as 6 months. All were to be terminated. Under company policy, they would be given severance pay equal to one week's pay per year of service.

This case reflects how competition, changing times, and the forces of globalization can take their toll on organizations, the people who work for them, and the communities in which they operate. Think about how you would feel as one of the affected employees. Think about how you would feel as the mayor of this small town. Think about how you would feel as a corporate executive having to make the difficult business decisions.

Step 1—Identify and Define the Problem

The first step in decision making is to find and define the problem. Information gathering and deliberation are critical in this stage. The way a problem is defined can have a major impact on how it is resolved, and it is important to clarify exactly what a decision should accomplish. The more specific the goals, the easier it is to evaluate results after the decision is actually implemented. Three common mistakes can occur in this critical first step in decision making.

Mistake number 1 is defining the problem too broadly or too narrowly. To take a classic example, the problem stated as "build a better mousetrap" might be better defined as "get rid of the mice." Managers should define problems in ways that give them the best possible range of problem-solving options.

Mistake number 2 is focusing on symptoms instead of causes. Symptoms are indicators that problems may exist, but they shouldn't be mistaken for the problems themselves. Although managers should be alert to spot problem symptoms (e.g., a drop in performance), they must also dig deeper to address root causes (such as discovering that a worker needs training in the use of a new computer system).

Mistake number 3 is choosing the wrong problem to deal with at a certain point in time. For example, here are three management problems. Which would you address first on a busy workday? *Problem*—An e-mail message from your boss is requesting a proposal "as soon as possible" on how to handle

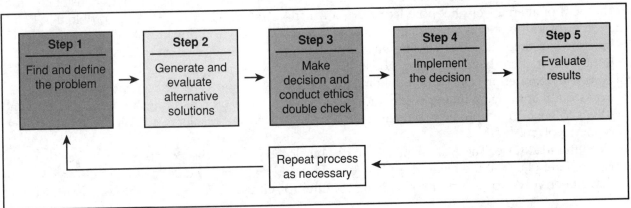

Exhibit 9.5 Steps in managerial decision making and problem solving.

The **decision-making process** begins with identification of a problem and ends with evaluation of implemented solutions.

employees' complaints about lack of flexibility in their work schedules. *Problem*—One of your best team members has just angered another by loudly criticizing her work performance. *Problem*—Your working spouse has left a voice mail message that your daughter is sick at school and the nurse would like her to go home for the day. Choices like this are not easy. But, we have to set priorities and deal with the most important problems first. In this case, perhaps the boss can wait while you telephone school to learn more about your daughter's illness and then spend some time with the employee who seems to be having "a bad day."

Back to the Ajax Case. Closing the Ajax plant will put a substantial number of people from the small community of Murphysboro out of work. The unemployment will have a negative impact on individuals, their families, and the town as a whole. The loss of the Ajax tax base will further hurt the community. The local financial implications of the plant closure will be great. The problem for Ajax management is how to minimize the adverse impact of the plant closing on the employees, their families, and the community.

Step 2—Generate and Evaluate Alternative Courses of Action

Once the problem is defined, it is time to assemble the facts and information that will be helpful for problem solving. It is important here to clarify exactly what is known and what needs to be known. Extensive information gathering should identify alternative courses of action, as well as their anticipated consequences. Key stakeholders in the problem should be identified, and the effects of possible courses of action on each of them should be considered.

A useful approach for the evaluation of alternatives is a **cost-benefit analysis**, the comparison of what an alternative will cost in relation to the expected benefits. At a minimum, the benefits of an alternative should be greater than its costs. The following list includes costs, benefits and other useful criteria for evaluating alternatives.

- *Costs:* What are the "costs" of implementing the alternative, including resource investments as well as potential negative side effects?
- *Benefits:* What are the "benefits" of using the alternative to solve a performance deficiency or take advantage of an opportunity?
- *Timeliness:* How fast can the alternative be implemented and a positive impact be achieved?
- *Acceptability:* To what extent will the alternative be accepted and supported by those who must work with it?
- *Ethical soundness:* How well does the alternative meet acceptable ethical criteria in the eyes of the various stakeholders?

Ultimately, any course of action can only be as good as the quality of the alternatives considered; the better the pool of alternatives, the more likely that any actions taken will help solve the problem at hand. A common error in this step is abandoning the search for alternatives too quickly. This often happens under pressures of time and other circumstances. But just because an alternative is convenient doesn't make it the best. It could have damaging side effects, or it could be less good than others that might be discovered with extra effort. One way to minimize this error is through consultation and involvement. It often works out that bringing more people into the decision making process brings more information and perspectives to bear on the problem, generates more alternatives, and results in a choice more appealing to everyone involved.

Back to the Ajax Case. The Ajax plant is going to be closed. Among the possible alternatives that can be considered are (1) close the plant on schedule and be done with it; (2) delay the plant closing until all efforts have been made to sell it to another firm; (3) offer to sell the plant to the employees and/or local

Cost-benefit analysis involves comparing the costs and benefits of each potential course of action.

interests; (4) close the plant and offer transfers to other Ajax plant locations; or (5) close the plant, offer transfers, and help the employees find new jobs in and around Murphysboro.

Step 3—Decide on a Preferred Course of Action

This is the point of choice where an actual decision is made to select a preferred course of action. Just how this is done and by whom must be successfully resolved in each problem situation. Management theory recognizes rather substantial differences between the classical and behavioral models of decision making as shown in Exhibit 9.6.

Classical Decision Model

The **classical decision model** views the manager as acting rationally in a certain world. The assumption is that a rational choice of the preferred course of action will be made by a decision maker who is fully informed about all possible alternatives. Here, the manager faces a clearly defined problem and knows all possible action alternatives, as well as their consequences. As a result, he or she makes an **optimizing decision** that gives the absolute best solution to the problem.

Behavioral Decision Model

Behavioral scientists question the assumptions of perfect information underlying the classical model. Perhaps best represented by the work of Herbert Simon, they instead recognize cognitive limitations to our human information processing capabilities. These limits make it hard for managers to become fully informed and make optimizing decisions. They create a **bounded rationality**, such that managerial decisions are rational only within the boundaries set by the available information and known alternatives, both of which are incomplete.

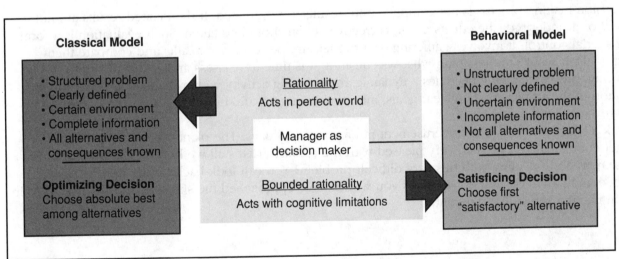

Exhibit 9.6   Differences in the classical and behavioral models of managerial decision making.

The **classical decision model** describes decision making with complete information.

An **optimizing decision** chooses the alternative giving the absolute best solution to a problem.

Bounded rationality describes making decisions within the constraints of limited information and alternatives.

The **behavioral decision model** assumes that people act only in terms of what they perceive about a given situation. Because perceptions are most often imperfect, the decision maker has only partial knowledge about the available action alternatives and their consequences. Consequently, the first alternative that appears to give a satisfactory resolution of the problem is likely to be chosen. Simon, who won a Nobel Prize for his work, calls this the tendency to make **satisficing decisions**—choosing the first satisfactory alternative that comes to your attention. The behavioral model is considered most accurate in describing how many decisions get made in the ambiguous and fast-paced problem situations faced by managers.

Back to the Ajax Case. Management at Ajax decided to close the plant, offer transfers to company plants in another state, and offer to help displaced employees find new jobs in and around Murphysboro.

Step 4—Implement the Decision

Once a decision is made, actions must be taken to fully implement it. Nothing new can or will happen unless action is taken to actually solve the problem. Managers not only need the determination and creativity to arrive at a decision, they also need the ability and willingness to implement it.

The "ways" in which decision-making steps 1, 2, and 3 are accomplished can have a powerful impact on how well decisions get implemented. Difficulties encountered at the point of implementation often trace to the **lack-of-participation error**. This is a failure to adequately involve in the process those persons whose support is necessary to implement the decision. Managers who use participation wisely get the right people involved in problem solving from the beginning. When they do, implementation typically follows quickly, smoothly, and to everyone's satisfaction. Participation in decision making makes everyone better informed and builds the commitments needed for implementation.

Back to the Ajax Case. Ajax ran ads in the local and regional newspapers. The ad called attention to an "Ajax skill bank" composed of "qualified, dedicated, and well-motivated employees with a variety of skills and experiences." Interested employers were urged to contact Ajax for further information.

Step 5—Evaluate Results

The decision-making process is not complete until results are evaluated. If the desired results are not achieved or if undesired side effects occur, corrective action should be taken. Such evaluation is a form of managerial control. It involves gathering data to measure performance results and compare them against goals. If results are less than what was desired, it is time to reassess and return to earlier steps. In this way, problem solving becomes a dynamic and ongoing activity within the management process. Evaluation is always easier when clear goals, measurable targets, and timetables were established to begin with.

Back to the Ajax Case. The advertisement ran for some 15 days. The plant's industrial relations manager commented, "I've been very pleased with the results." That's all we know. How well did Ajax management do in dealing with this very difficult problem? You can look back on the case as it was described and judge for yourself. Perhaps you would have approached the situation and the five steps in decision making somewhat differently.

The **behavioral decision model** describes decision making with limited information and bounded rationality.

A **satisficing decision** chooses the first satisfactory alternative that comes to one's attention.

Lack-of-participation error is failure to involve in a decision the persons whose support is needed to implement it.

ISSUES IN MANAGERIAL DECISION MAKING

Most management situations are rich in decision-making challenges. By way of preparation, it helps to be aware of the common decision-making errors and traps, the advantages and disadvantages of individual and group decision making, and the imperative of ethical decision making.

Decision Errors and Traps

Faced with limited information, time, and even energy, people often use simplifying strategies for decision making. These strategies or rules of thumb are known as **heuristics**. Although they can be helpful in dealing with complex and ambiguous situations, they are also common causes of decision-making errors.

Availability Bias

The **availability heuristic** occurs when people use information "readily available" from memory as a basis for assessing a current event or situation. An example is deciding not to invest in a new product based on your recollection of a recent product failure. The potential bias is that the readily available information is fallible and irrelevant. For example, the product that recently failed may have been a good idea that was released to market at the wrong time of year.

Representation Bias

The **representativeness heuristic** occurs when people assess the likelihood of something happening based on its similarity to a stereotyped set of occurrences. An example of representation bias is deciding to hire someone for a job vacancy simply because he or she graduated from the same school attended by your last and most successful new hire. The potential bias is that the representative stereotype masks factors important and relevant to the decision. For instance, the abilities and career expectations of the person receiving the offer may not fit the job requirements.

Anchoring and Adjustment Bias

The **anchoring and adjustment heuristic** occurs when decisions are biased by inappropriate allegiance to a previously existing value or starting point. An example is a manager who sets a new salary level for an employee by simply raising her prior year's salary by a small percentage amount. Although the increase may appear reasonable to the manager, the prior year's salary may have substantially undervalued the employee relative to the market. The small incremental salary adjustment, reflecting anchoring and adjustment bias, may not satisfy her or keep her from looking for another job.

Framing Error

Sometimes managers suffer from **framing error** that occurs when a problem is evaluated and resolved in the context in which it is perceived—either positively or negatively. Suppose, for example, a product that data show has a 40% market share. A negative frame views the product as deficient because it is missing

---

Heuristics are strategies for simplifying decision making.

The **availability heuristic** bases a decision on recent information or events.

The **representativeness heuristic** bases a decision on similarity to other situations.

The **anchoring and adjustment heuristic** bases a decision on incremental adjustments from a prior decision point.

Framing error is trying to solve a problem in the context in which it is perceived.

60% of the market. The likely discussion and problem solving in this frame would focus on: "What are we doing wrong?" Alternatively, the frame could be a positive one, looking at the 40% share as a good accomplishment. In this case the discussion is more likely to proceed with: "How do we do things better?" Sometimes people use framing as a tactic for presenting information in a way that gets other people to think inside the desired frame. In politics, this is often referred to as "spinning" the data.

Confirmation Error

One of our tendencies after making a decision is to try and find ways to justify it. More generally in decision making, we can fall prey to **confirmation error.** This means that we notice, accept, and even seek out only information that is confirming or consistent with a decision we have just made. Other and perhaps contrary information is downplayed or denied. This is a form of selective perception, in which we focus on problems from our particular reference or vantage point only; we neglect other points of view or information that might support a different decision.

Escalating Commitment

Another decision-making trap is **escalating commitment.** This occurs as a decision to increase effort and perhaps apply more resources to pursue a course of action that is not working. Managers prone to escalation let the momentum of the situation overwhelm them. They are unable to "call it quits" even when facts and experience otherwise indicate that this is the best thing to do.

Consider the case of a start-up "no frills" airline called Skybus. The "bus" part of the name drove the business model, with fares advertised as low as $10 for early reservations. Booking was only online, passengers retrieved their own luggage from trolleys, and food and drinks were sold on board—there were no "give aways." Skybus launched in the summer and at first filled 80% of its seats. Even though passenger traffic soon fell to "loss" levels, executives kept faith in the business model. They cut back some routes and redirected resources toward others they believed had profit potential. However, the airline failed when fuel prices soared and the economy went into recession.

Was it escalating commitment that contributed to the demise of Sky-bus? Did its executives stick with poor routes for too long or fail to admit flaws in the business model itself? Or, was it just a case of choosing a bad time to launch a new airline? It's a tough call, but the likelihood of escalation is present. It's a common decision error, perhaps one that you are personally familiar with. Management Smarts 9.2 offers advice on how to avoid tendencies toward escalating commitments to previously chosen courses of action.

Creativity in Decision Making

Lonnie Johnson is a former U.S. Air Force captain and a NASA engineer. You probably don't know him, but most likely you are familiar with something he invented—the Super Soaker water gun. Johnson didn't set out to invent the water gun; he was working in his basement on an idea for refrigeration systems that would use water rather than freon. Something connected in his mind, and the Super Soaker was born. Johnson says: "The Super Soaker changed my life." He now heads his own research and development company and, among other things, the web site says his firm has some 100 toys in development.

© Edith Heald/Corbis

A **confirmation error** occurs when focusing only on information that confirms a decision already made.

Escalating commitment is the continuation of a course of action even though it is not working.

Management Smarts 9.2

How to Avoid the Escalation Trap in Decision Making

- Set advance limits on your involvement and commitment to a particular course of action; stick with these limits.
- Make your own decisions; don't follow the leads of others, since they are also prone to escalation.
- Carefully assess why you are continuing a course of action; if there are no good reasons to continue, don't.
- Remind yourself of what a course of action is costing; consider saving these costs as a reason to discontinue.
- Watch for escalation tendencies in your behaviors and those of others.

Creativity is one of our greatest personal assets, even though it may be too often unrecognized. In fact we exercise creativity every day in lots of ways—solving problems at home, building something for the kids, or even finding ways to pack too many things into too small a suitcase. But are we creative when it would really help in solving workplace problems? Just imagine what can be accomplished with all the creative potential that exists in an organization's workforce. How do you turn that potential into actual results—the Lonnie Johnson model, so to speak?

Individual Versus Group Decision Making

Management scholars suggest that the best managers and team leaders switch back and forth among individual and group decisions to best fit the problems at hand. The "right" decision method is one that provides for a timely and quality solution, and one to which people involved in the implementation will be highly committed.

Advantages of Group Decisions

Due to their potential advantages, group decisions are well worth pursuing whenever time and other circumstances permit. Decisions that involve team members make greater amounts of information, knowledge, and expertise available to solve problems. They expand the number of action alternatives that are examined; they help to avoid tunnel vision and consideration of only limited options. Team decisions also increase understanding and acceptance by members. And, importantly, team decisions increase the commitments of members to work hard to implement the decisions they have made together.

When Group Decisions Work Best
- Individual lacks expertise or information
- Problem is unclear and hard to define
- Acceptance by others needed for effective implementation
- Time is sufficient for group involvement

Disadvantages of Group Decisions

The potential disadvantages of group decision making trace largely to the difficulties that can be experienced in group process. When many people are trying to make a team decision, there may be social pressure to conform. Some individuals may feel intimidated or compelled to go along with the apparent wishes of others. There may be minority domination, where some members feel forced or "railroaded" to accept a decision advocated by one vocal individual or small coalition. Also, the time required to make team decisions can sometimes be a disadvantage. As more people are involved in the dialogue and discussion, decision making takes longer. This added time may be costly, even prohibitively so, in certain circumstances.

Foundations
of Planning

From John R. Schermerhorn, Jr. Management, 10th Edition, 2009. Reprinted by permission of
John Wiley & Sons, Inc.

Managers need the ability to look ahead, make good plans, and help themselves and others meet the challenges of the future. The future is full of uncertainty; the likelihood is that even the best of plans will have to be adjusted and changed at some point. Thus, managers need the insight and courage to be flexible in response to new circumstances. They also need the discipline to stay focused on goals even as complications and problems arise.

WHY AND HOW MANAGERS PLAN

In Chapter 1 the management process was described as planning, organizing, leading, and controlling the use of resources to achieve performance objectives. The first of these functions, **planning,** sets the stage for the others by providing a sense of direction. It is a process of setting objectives and determining how best to accomplish them. Said a bit differently, planning involves deciding exactly what you want to accomplish and how best to go about it.

Importance of Planning

When planning is done well it creates a solid platform for the other management functions: organizing—allocating and arranging resources to accomplish tasks; leading—guiding the efforts of human resources to ensure high levels of task accomplishment; and controlling—monitoring task accomplishments and taking necessary corrective action. This centrality of planning in management is shown in Exhibit 10.1. In today's demanding organizational and career environments it is essential to stay one step ahead of the competition. This involves always striving to become better at what you are doing and to be action-oriented. An Eaton Corporation annual report, for example, once stated: "Planning at Eaton means making the hard decisions before events force them upon you, and anticipating the future needs of the market before the demand asserts itself."

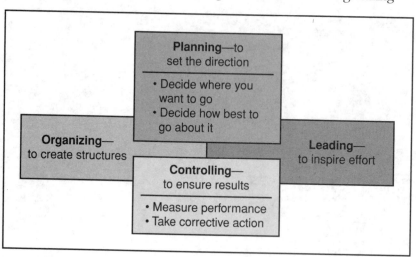

Exhibit 10.1   The roles of planning and controlling in the management process.

The Planning Process

Planning should focus attention on **objectives** that identify the specific results or desired outcomes that one intends to achieve. Planning should also create a real **plan**, a statement of action steps to be taken in order to accomplish the objectives. Furthermore, planning should result in plans being well implemented

---

Planning is the process of setting objectives and determining how to accomplish them.

Objectives are specific results that one wishes to achieve.

A **plan** is a statement of intended means for accomplishing objectives.

so that objectives are accomplished. Planning in this sense is an application of the decision-making process involves five steps.

1. *Define your objectives*—Identify desired outcomes or results in very specific ways. Know where you want to go; be specific enough that you will know you have arrived when you get there, or know how far off the mark you are at various points along the way.

2. *Determine where you stand vis-à-vis objectives*—Evaluate current accomplishments relative to the desired results. Know where you stand in reaching the objectives; know what strengths work in your favor and what weaknesses may hold you back.

3. *Develop premises regarding future conditions*—Anticipate future events. Generate alternative "scenarios" for what may happen; identify for each scenario things that may help or hinder progress toward your objectives.

4. *Analyze alternatives and make a plan*—List and evaluate possible actions. Choose the alternative most likely to accomplish your objectives; describe what must be done to follow the best course of action.

5. *Implement the plan and evaluate results*—Take action and carefully measure your progress toward objectives. Follow through by doing what the plan requires; evaluate results, take corrective action, and revise plans as needed.

The planning process as just described all seems simple and straightforward enough. But remember, planning is not something managers do while working alone in quiet rooms, free from distractions, and at scheduled times. It is an ongoing process, often continuously being done even while dealing with an otherwise busy and demanding work setting. And like other decision making in organizations, the best planning is done with the active participation of those people whose work efforts will eventually determine whether or not the plans are well implemented.

Good Planning Helps Make Us
- *Priority oriented*—making sure the most important things get first attention;
- *Action oriented*—keeping a results-driven sense of direction;
- *Advantage oriented*—ensuring that all resources are used to best advantage;
- *Change oriented*—anticipating problems and opportunities so they can be best dealt with

Benefits of Planning

The pressures organizations face come from many sources. Externally, these include ethical expectations, government regulations, uncertainties of a global economy, changing technologies, and the sheer cost of investments in labor, capital, and other supporting resources. Internally, they include the quest for operating efficiencies, new structures and technologies, alternative work arrangements, greater diversity in the workplace, and related managerial challenges. As you would expect, planning in such conditions has a number of benefits for both organizations and individuals.

Planning Improves Focus and Flexibility

Good planning improves focus and flexibility, both of which are important for performance success. An organization with focus knows what it does best, knows the needs of its customers, and knows how to serve them well. An individual with focus knows where he or she wants to go in a career or situation, and in life overall. An organization with flexibility is willing and able to change and adapt to shifting circumstances, and operates with an orientation toward the future rather than the past. An individual with flexibility adjusts career plans to fit new and developing opportunities.

Planning Improves Action Orientation

Planning is a way for people and organizations to stay ahead of the competition and become better at what they are doing. It keeps the future visible as a performance target and reminds us that the best decisions are often those made before events force problems upon us. It helps avoid the **complacency trap**—simply being carried along by the flow of events.

Management consultant Stephen R. Covey talks about the importance of priorities. He points out that the most successful executives "zero in on what they do that 'adds value' to an organization." Instead of working on too many things, they work on the things that really count. Covey says that good planning makes us more (1) results oriented—creating a performance-oriented sense of direction; (2) priority oriented—making sure the most important things get first attention; (3) advantage oriented—ensuring that all resources are used to best advantage; and (4) change oriented—anticipating problems and opportunities so they can be best dealt with.

Planning Improves Coordination and Control

Planning improves coordination. The different individuals, groups, and subsystems in organizations are each doing many different things at the same time. But their efforts must add up to meaningful contributions to the organization as a whole. When plans are coordinated among people and subsystems, there is greater likelihood that their combined accomplishments will advance performance for the organization.

When planning is done well it also facilitates control. The first step in the planning process is to set objectives and standards, and this is a prerequisite to effective control. The objectives set by good planning make it easier to measure results and take action to improve things as necessary. If results are less than expected, either the objectives or the actions being taken, or both, can be evaluated and adjusted. In this way, planning and controlling work closely together in the management process. Without planning, control lacks objectives and standards for measuring how well things are going and what could be done to make them go better. Without control, planning lacks the follow-through needed to ensure that things work out as planned.

Planning and Time Management

Daniel Vasella is CEO of Novartis AG and its 98,000 employees spread across 140 countries. He's also calendar bound. He says: "I'm locked in by meetings, travel and other constraints . . . I have to put down in priority things I like to do." Kathleen Murphy is CEO of ING US Wealth Management. She's also calendar bound, with conferences and travel booked a year ahead. She schedules meetings at half-hour intervals, works 12-hour days, and spends 60% of her time traveling. She also makes good use of her time on planes. "No one can reach me by phone and I can get reading and thinking done."

These are common executive stories—tight schedules, little time alone, lots of meetings and phone calls, and not much room for spontaneity. The keys to success in such classic management scenarios rest, in part at least, with another benefit of good planning—time management. Management Smarts 10.1 offers some good tips on developing this important management skill and competency. And, a lot of time management comes down to discipline and priorities. Lewis Platt, former chairman of Hewlett-Packard, once said: "Basically, the whole day is a series of choices." These choices have to be made in ways that allocate your time to the most important priorities. Platt says that he was "ruthless about priorities" and that you "have to continually work to optimize your time."

Most of us have experienced the difficulties of balancing available time with our many commitments and opportunities. It is easy to lose track of time and fall prey to what consultants identify as "time wasters." Too many of us allow our time to be dominated by other people or to be misspent on nonessential activities. "To do" lists can help, but they have to contain the right things. In daily living and in management, it is important to distinguish between things that you must do (top priority), should do (high priority), would be nice to do (low priority), and really don't need to do (no priority).

The **complacency trap** is being carried along by the flow of events.

Personal Time Management Tips

1. *Do* say "No" to requests that divert you from what you really should be doing.
2. *Don't* get bogged down in details that you can address later or leave for others.
3. *Do* have a system for screening telephone calls, e-mails, and requests for meetings.
4. *Don't* let drop-in visitors or instant messages use too much of your time.
5. *Do* prioritize what you will work on in terms of importance and urgency.
6. *Don't* become calendar-bound by letting others control your schedule.
7. *Do* follow priorities; work on the most important and urgent tasks first.

TYPES OF PLANS USED BY MANAGERS

I am the master of my fate: I am the captain of my soul. How often have you heard this phrase? The lines are from *Invictus*, written by British poet William Earnest Henley in 1875. He was sending a message, one of confidence and control, as he moved forward into the future. That notion, however, worries a planning scholar by the name of Richard Levin. His response to Henley is: *Not without a plan you're not.*

Managers use a variety of plans as they face different challenges in the flow and pace of activities in organizations. In some cases the planning environment is stable and quite predictable; in others, it is more dynamic and uncertain. Different needs call for different types of plans.

Long-Range and Short-Range Plans

A rule of thumb is that long-range plans look three or more years into the future, intermediate-range plans cover one to two years, and short-range plans cover one year or less. Top management is most likely to be involved in setting long-range plans and directions for the organization as a whole, whereas lower management levels focus more on short-run plans that help achieve long-term objectives.

Unless everyone understands an organization's long-term plans, there is always risk that the pressures of daily events will divert attention from important tasks. In other words, without a sense of long-term direction, people can end up working hard and still not achieve significant results. Auto industry executives know this only too well. Their firms are operating today in what used to be the far-off "future," and they have arrived here only to be in lots of trouble. Was it the inability to think long term that got them here, or was it an inability to anticipate, recognize, and adjust to changing events that led to their downfalls?

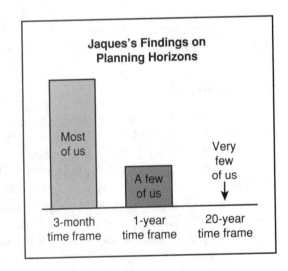

Management researcher Elliot Jaques suggests that people vary in their capability to think with different time horizons. In fact, he believes that most people work comfortably with only 3-month time spans; a smaller group works well with a 1-year span; and only the very rare person can handle a 20-year time frame. These are provocative ideas and, personally challenging. Although a team leader's planning may fall mainly in the weekly or monthly range, a chief executive is expected to have a vision extending several years into the future. Career progress to higher management levels requires the conceptual skills to work well with longer-range time frames.

Would you agree that the complexities and uncertainties of today's environments challenge how we go about planning and how far ahead we can really plan? In an increasingly global economy, planning opportunities and challenges are often worldwide in scope, not just local. And of course, the information age is also ever present in its planning implications. We now talk about planning in Internet time, where businesses are continually changing and updating plans. Even top managers now face the reality that Internet time keeps making the "long" range of planning shorter and shorter.

Strategic and Tactical Plans

Plans also differ in scope and purpose served. At the top of the traditional organizational pyramid, senior executives deal mainly with strategic plans; in the middle, managers deal with tactical plans; at lower levels, managers focus on operating plans.

Strategic Plans

When planning for the organization as a whole or a major component, the focus is on **strategic plans.** These are longer-term plans that set broad directions for an organization and create a framework for allocating resources for maximum long-term performance impact. It begins with a **vision** that clarifies the purpose of the organization and expresses what it hopes to be in the future, and it involves determining the goals and objectives that will be pursued in order to accomplish that vision.

Even though strategic plans are long term, they are also dynamic. Consider the example of Skype, the Internet telephone now owned by eBay. Skype began with the genius of its founders, Niklas Zennstrom and Janus Friis, and morphed into a company that quickly outgrew its original goals. The firm was just three years old when it was bought by eBay for $2.6 billion. That was quite a payoff for investors and the firm's founders. But it wasn't their plan to just start the company, move it fast, and sell quickly to the highest bidder. Says Zennstrom: "Our objective was to build the business." Once started, however, Skype quickly gained 54 million users and became an acquisition target. The deal was sealed after Zennstrom and Friis had a breakthrough meeting with eBay's CEO Meg Whitman. According to Zennstrom, it was an *Aha!* experience: "We went crazy on the whiteboard, mapping out ideas." The rest is business history—a strategic plan that worked so well it moved even faster than Skype's founders ever anticipated.

Tactical Plans

When a sports team enters a game or contest, it typically does so with a "strategy" in hand. Most often this strategy is set by the head coach in conjunction with assistants. The goal is clear and long term: win the game or contest. As the game unfolds, a variety of situations arise that require immediate adjustments to solve problems or exploit opportunities. They call for "tactics" that deal with a current situation in ways that advance the overall strategy for winning.

The same logic holds true for organizations. **Tactical plans** are developed and used to implement strategic plans. They tend to be intermediate-term plans that specify how the organization's resources can be used to put strategies into action. In the sports context you might think of tactical plans as involving "special teams," or as "special plays," designed to meet a particular threat or opportunity. In business, tactical plans often take the form of **functional plans** that indicate how different components of the enterprise will contribute to the overall strategy. Such functional plans might include:

A **strategic plan** identifies long-term directions for the organization.

A **vision** clarifies the purpose of the organization and expresses what it hopes to be in the future.

A **tactical plan** helps to implement all or parts of a strategic plan.

Functional plans indicate how different operations within the organization will help advance the overall strategy.

- *Production plans*—dealing with work methods and technologies;
- *Financial plans*—dealing with money and capital investments;
- *Facilities plans*—dealing with facilities and work layouts;
- *Logistics plans*—dealing with suppliers and acquiring resource inputs;
- *Marketing plans*—dealing with selling and distributing goods or services;
- *Human resource plans*—dealing with building a talented workforce.

Operational Plans

Operational plans describe what needs to be done in the short term and in response to different situations. They include both *standing plans* such as policies and procedures that are used over and over again, and *single-use plans* such as budgets that apply to one specific task or time period.

Policies and Procedures

A **policy** communicates broad guidelines for making decisions and taking action in specific circumstances. Organizations operate with lots of policies, and they set expectations for many aspects of employee behavior. Typical human resource policies, for example, cover employee hiring, termination, performance appraisals, pay increases, promotions, and discipline. Another important policy area is sexual harassment, and it's one that Judith Nitsch made a top priority when starting her engineering consulting business. Nitsch defined a sexual harassment policy, took a hard line on its enforcement, and appointed both a male and a female employee for others to talk with about sexual harassment concerns.

Procedures or **rules** describe exactly what actions are to be taken in specific situations. They are stated in employee handbooks and often called "SOPs"—standard operating procedures. Whereas a policy sets a broad guideline, procedures define precise actions to be taken. In the prior example, Judith Nitsch was right to establish a sexual harassment policy for her firm. But she should also put into place procedures that ensure everyone receives fair, equal, and nondiscriminatory treatment under the policy. Everyone in her firm should know how to file a sexual harassment complaint and how that complaint will be handled.

Budgets

Budgets are single-use plans that commit resources for specific time periods to activities, projects, or programs. Managers typically spend a fair amount of time bargaining with higher levels to get adequate budgets to support the needs of their work units or teams. They are also expected to achieve work objectives while keeping within the allocated budget. To be "over budget" is generally bad; to come in "under budget" is generally good.

Managers deal with and use a variety of budgets. *Financial budgets* project cash flows and expenditures; *operating budgets* plot anticipated sales or revenues against expenses; *nonmonetary budgets* allocate resources like labor, equipment, and space. A *fixed budget* allocates a stated amount of resources for a specific purpose, such as $50,000 for equipment purchases in a given year. A *flexible budget* allows resources to vary in proportion with various levels of activity, such as having extra money available to hire temporary workers when work loads exceed certain levels.

All budgets link planned activities with the resources needed to accomplish them. And because they are clear in identifying financial or other resource constraints, budgets are useful for tracking and control-

---

An **operational plan** identifies short-term activities to implement strategic plans.

A **policy** is a standing plan that communicates broad guidelines for decisions and action.

A **procedure** or **rule** precisely describes actions that are to be taken in specific situations.

A **budget** is a plan that commits resources to projects or activities.

ling performance. But budgets can get out of control, creeping higher and higher without getting sufficient critical attention.

One of the most common budgeting problems is that resource allocations get "rolled over" from one time period to the next without a rigorous performance review; the new budget is simply an incremental adjustment to the previous one. In a major division of Campbell Soups, for example, managers once discovered that 10% of the marketing budget was going to sales promotions no longer relevant to current product lines. A **zero-based budget** deals with this problem by approaching each new budget period as it if were brand new. In zero-based budgeting there is no guarantee that any past funding will be renewed; all proposals must compete anew for available funds at the start of each new budget cycle.

PLANNING TOOLS AND TECHNIQUES

The benefits of planning are best realized when the foundations are strong. Among the useful tools and techniques of managerial planning are forecasting, contingency planning, scenarios, benchmarking, and the use of staff planners.

Forecasting

Who would have predicted even a few years ago that China would now be the second largest car market in the world? Would you believe that by 2025 China will have more cars on the roads than the U.S. has now? Planning in business and our personal lives often involves **forecasting**, the process of predicting what will happen in the future. Periodicals such as *BusinessWeek, Fortune,* and the *Economist* regularly report forecasts of economic conditions, interest rates, unemployment, and trade deficits, among other issues. Some are based on qualitative forecasting, which uses expert opinions to predict the future. Others involve quantitative forecasting, which uses mathematical models and statistical analyses of historical data and surveys to predict future events.

Although useful, all forecasts should be treated cautiously. They are planning aids, not substitutes. It is said that a music agent once told Elvis Presley: "You ought to go back to driving a truck, because you ain't going nowhere." He was obviously mistaken, and that's the problem with forecasts. They rely on human judgment—and they can be wrong.

Contingency Planning

Picture the scene. Tiger Woods is striding down the golf course with an iron in each hand. The one in his right hand is "the plan;" the one in his left is the "backup plan." Which club he uses will depend on how the ball lies on the fairway. One of Tiger's great strengths as a golfer is being able to adjust to the situation by putting the right club to work in the circumstances at hand. Planning is often like that. By definition it involves thinking ahead. But the more uncertain the planning environment, the more likely that one's original forecasts and intentions may prove inadequate or wrong. **Contingency planning** identifies alternative courses of action that can be implemented if circumstances change.

Coke and Pepsi spend hundreds of millions of dollars on advertising as they engage one another in the ongoing "Cola Wars." It may seem that they have nothing to worry about except each other and a few discounters. But more than 50% of their revenues come internationally and it's a pretty safe bet that they have contingency plans in place to deal with any variety of global events, everything from currency fluctuations to social trends to changing politics. One thing they've had to deal with was anti-American

---

A **zero-based budget** allocates resources as if each budget were brand new.

Forecasting attempts to predict the future.

Contingency planning identifies alternative courses of action to take when things go wrong.

backlash from the Iraq war, including the emergence of new competitors Mecca Cola and Qibla Cola. These colas entered European markets riding a wave of resentment of U.S. brands and multinationals. The founder of Qibla says: "By choosing to boycott major brands, consumers are sending an important signal—that the exploitation of Muslims cannot continue unchecked."

© Volker Heick/dpa/Corbis

Scenario Planning

A long-term version of contingency planning, called **scenario planning**, involves identifying several alternative future scenarios or states of affairs that may occur. Plans are then made to deal with each should it actually happen. At Royal Dutch/ Shell, scenario planning began years ago when top managers asked themselves: "What will Shell do after its oil supplies run out?" Although scenario planning can never be inclusive of all future possibilities, a Shell executive once said that it helps "condition the organization to think" and better prepare for "future shocks."

Shell's recent planning includes a "worst-case" scenario—global conflict occurs as nations jockey with one another to secure supplies of oil and other resources; the effects are devastating for the natural environment. It also includes an alternative "best-case" scenario—governments work together to find mutual pathways that take care of resource needs while supporting the sustainability of global resources. It's anyone's guess which scenario will materialize, or if something else altogether will happen. In any event Shell CEO Jeroen van der Veer says: "This will require hard work and time is short."

Benchmarking

Planners sometimes become too comfortable with the ways things are going and overconfident that the past is a good indicator of the future. It is often better to keep challenging the status quo and not simply accept things as they are. One way to do this is through **benchmarking**, the use of external and internal comparisons to better evaluate one's current performance and identify possible ways to improve for the future.

The purpose of benchmarking is to find out what other people and organizations are doing very well, and then plan how to incorporate these ideas into one's own operations. One benchmarking technique is to search for **best practices**—things people and organizations do that help them achieve superior performance. Well-run organizations emphasize internal benchmarking that encourages all members and work units to learn and improve by sharing one another's best practices. They also use external benchmarking to learn from competitors and noncompetitors alike.

Use of Staff Planners

As organizations grow, so do the planning challenges. Cisco Systems, for example, is already planning that a lot of its growth is going to come from investments overseas. And, it wasn't too long ago that

---

Scenario planning identifies alternative future scenarios and makes plans to deal with each.

Benchmarking uses external and internal comparisons to plan for future improvements.

Best practices are things people and organizations do that lead to superior performance.

China was the big target in Asia. It still is a big one, but "big" got smaller when Cisco's planners analyzed their planning premises and projected future scenarios for both India and China. It turns out that they found a lot to like about India: excellence in software design, need for Cisco's products, and weak local competition. They also found some major things to worry about in China: centrally planned economy, government favoring local companies, and poor intellectual property protection.

In many organizations, as with Cisco, staff planners are employed to help coordinate and energize planning. These specialists are skilled in all steps of the planning process, as well as in the use of planning tools and techniques. They can help bring focus and expertise to accomplish important, often strategic, planning tasks. But one risk is a tendency for a communication gap to develop between staff planners and line managers. Unless everyone works closely together, the resulting plans may be inadequate, and people may lack commitment to implement the plans, no matter how good they are.

IMPLEMENTING PLANS TO ACHIEVE RESULTS

In a book entitled *Doing What Matters*, Jim Kilts, the former CEO of Gillette, quotes an old management adage: "In business, words are words, promises are promises, but only performance is reality." The same applies to plans—plans, we might say, are words with promises attached. These promises are only fulfilled when plans are implemented so that their purposes are achieved. The implementation of plans is largely driven by solid management practices discussed throughout the rest of this book. Among the foundation issues, however, are goal setting and alignment, management by objectives and participation.

Goal Setting and Goal Alignment

In the dynamic and highly competitive technology industry, CEO T. J. Rodgers of Cypress Semiconductor Corp. values both performance goals and accountability. He supports a planning system where employees work with clear and quantified work goals that they help set. He believes the system helps people find problems before they can interfere with performance. Says Rodgers: "Managers monitor the goals, look for problems, and expect people who fall behind to ask for help before they lose control of or damage a major project."

Goal Setting

Rodgers' commitment to goals isn't unique among successful managers. In fact it's standard practice. Here's another example. When Jim Kilts took over as CEO of Gillette he realized that the firm needed work. In analyzing the situation, however, he was very disciplined in setting planning goals or objectives. He identified core problems that were highly consequential and tagged them with measurable targets for improvement. In respect to *sales*, the company's big brands were losing sales to competitors. Kilts made plans to *increase market shares* for these brands. In respect to *earnings*, the company had missed its estimates for 15 quarters in a row. Kilts made plans to *meet earnings estimates* and raise the company's stock price.

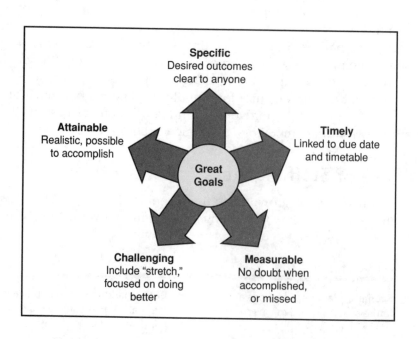

Although both Rodgers and Kilts make us aware of the importance of goal setting in management, they may make it look a bit too easy. The way goals are set can make a big difference in how well they do in pointing people in the right directions and inspiring them to work hard. The following guidelines are starting points in moving from "no goals" and even just everyday run-of-the-mill "average goals" to having really "great goals"—ones that result in plans being successfully implemented. Great goals are:

1. *Specific*—clearly target key results and outcomes to be accomplished
2. *Timely*—linked to specific timetables and "due dates"
3. *Measurable*—described so results can be measured without ambiguity
4. *Challenging*—include a stretch factor that moves toward real gains
5. *Attainable*—although challenging, realistic and possible to achieve

Goal Alignment

It is one thing to set good goals and make them part of a plan. It is quite another to make sure that goals and plans are well integrated across the many people, work units, and levels of an organization as a whole. Goals set anywhere in the organization should ideally help advance its overall mission or purpose. Yet, we sometimes work very hard to accomplish things that simply don't make much of a difference in organizational performance. This is why goal alignment is an important part of managerial planning.

Exhibit 10.2 shows how a **hierarchy of goals** or **hierarchy of objectives** helps with goal alignment. When a hierarchy of objectives is well defined the accomplishment of lower-level objectives is the means

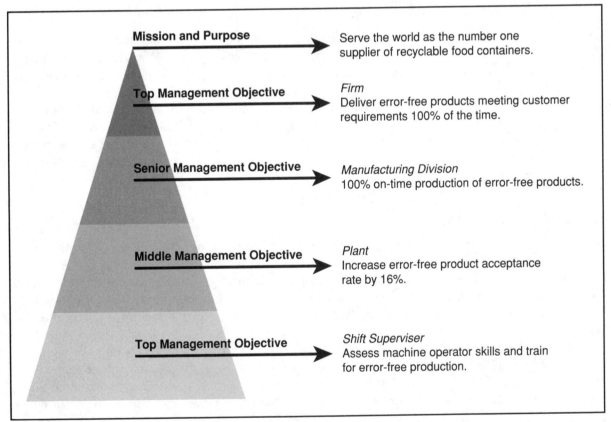

Mission and Purpose → Serve the world as the number one supplier of recyclable food containers.

Top Management Objective → *Firm* Deliver error-free products meeting customer requirements 100% of the time.

Senior Management Objective → *Manufacturing Division* 100% on-time production of error-free products.

Middle Management Objective → *Plant* Increase error-free product acceptance rate by 16%.

Top Management Objective → *Shift Superviser* Assess machine operator skills and train for error-free production.

Exhibit 10.2 A sample hierarchy of objectives for quality management in a manufacturing firm.

In a **hierarchy of goals or objectives,** lower-level objectives are means to accomplishing higher-level ones.

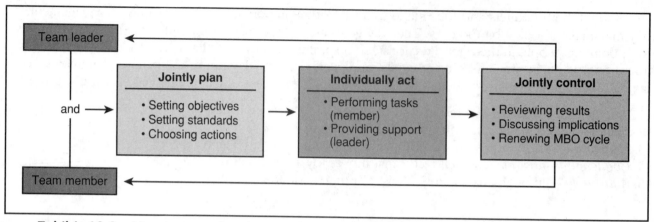

Exhibit 10.3   Management by objectives as an integrated planning and control framework.

to the accomplishment of higher-level ones. The example in the exhibit is built around quality goals in a manufacturing setting. Strategic goals set by top management cascade down the organization step-by-step to become quality management objectives for lower levels. Ideally, everything works together in a consistent "means-end" fashion so that the organization becomes "the number one supplier of recyclable food containers."

Management by Objectives

A useful planning technique that builds on the notions of goal setting and goal alignment, and that also helps integrate planning and controlling, is **management by objectives** or just **MBO.** This is a structured process of regular communication in which a supervisor or team leader works with subordinates or team members to jointly set performance objectives and review results accomplished.

As shown in Exhibit 10.3, MBO creates an agreement between the two parties regarding (1) performance objectives for a given time period, (2) plans through which they will be accomplished, (3) standards for measuring whether they have been accomplished, and (4) procedures for reviewing performance results. Of course, both parties in any MBO agreement are supposed to work closely together to fulfill the terms of the agreement.

Performance Objectives in MBO

Three types of objectives may be specified in an MBO contract. **Improvement objectives** document intentions for improving performance in a specific way. An example is "to reduce quality rejects by 10%." **Personal development objectives** pertain to personal growth activities, often those resulting in expanded job knowledge or skills. An example is "to learn the latest version of a computer spreadsheet package." Some MBO contracts also include *maintenance objectives* that formally express intentions to maintain performance at an existing level.

One of the more difficult aspects of MBO is the need to make performance objectives as measurable as possible. Ideally there is agreement on a *measurable end product*, for example, "to reduce travel expenses by 5% by the end of the fiscal year." But performance in some jobs, particularly managerial ones, is hard to quantify. Rather than abandon MBO in such cases, it is often possible to agree on performance

---

MBO is a process of joint objective-setting between a superior and subordinate.

Improvement objectives describe intentions for specific performance improvements.

Personal development objectives describe intentions for personal growth through knowledge and skills development.

objectives that are stated as *verifiable work activities*. The accomplishment of the activities serves as an indicator of performance progress. An example is "to improve communications with my team in the next three months by holding weekly team meetings." Whereas it can be difficult to measure "improved communications," it is easy to document whether the "weekly team meetings" have been held.

MBO Pros and Cons

MBO is one of the most talked about and debated management concepts. As a result, good advice is available. Things to avoid include tying MBO to pay, focusing too much attention on easy objectives, requiring excessive paperwork, and having supervisors simply tell subordinates their objectives. The advantages are also clear. MBO focuses workers on the most important tasks and objectives; and, it focuses supervisors on areas of support that can truly help subordinates meet the agreed-upon objectives. Because of the direct face-to-face communication, MBO also contributes to relationship building. By giving people the opportunity to participate in decisions that affect their work, MBO encourages self-management.

Participation and Involvement

Planning is a process, not an event, and "participation" is one of its key words. The best planning in organizations probably begins at the top of the organization or work unit, and then proceeds in a participatory fashion to actively involve others from lower levels. **Participatory planning** includes in all planning steps the people who will be affected by the plans and asked to help implement them.

One of the things that research is most clear about is that when people participate in setting goals they gain motivation to work hard to accomplish them. Whether the focus is on planning for a team, a large division, or the entire organization, involving more people creates benefits. It goes a long way toward gaining their commitment to work hard and support the implementation of plans.

This role of participation and involvement in the planning process is shown in Exhibit 10.4, and

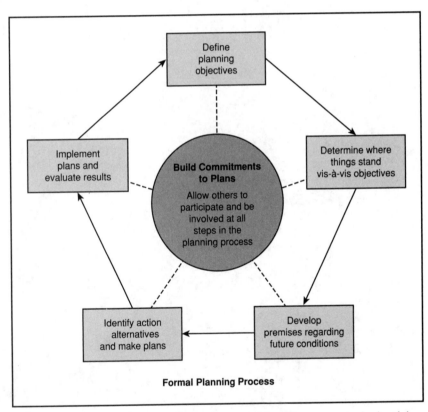

Exhibit 10.4   How participation and involvement help build commitments to plans.

there are many benefits when and if it can be followed in practice. Participation can increase the creativity and information available for planning. It can also increase the understanding and acceptance of plans, as well as commitment to their success. And even though participatory planning takes more time, it can improve results by improving implementation.

Participatory planning includes the persons who will be affected by plans and/or those who will implement them.

An example of the benefits of a participatory approach to planning is found at Boeing. Former CEO Alan Mulally faced indecision in the firm's management ranks after 9/11 left the airline industry in turmoil and new plane orders plummeted. To regain momentum he instituted a new planning approach that started with strategy sessions on Thursdays with 30 top executives. His message was to look ahead to the time when the "slump" in airplane orders would be over and plan now for a new generation of planes. Every other Thursday he added 60 new lower level managers to the process. He credits this approach with bringing to market the 787 "Dreamliner," the fastest-selling plane in the firm's history. About the benefits of engaging so many managers in the planning process, he says: "They gave us a wider perspective and could tell us if what we were planning actually worked and made sense."

Communication and Information Technology

INTERPERSONAL COMMUNICATION

Communication is the exchange of information between a sender and a receiver. The information may be something other than verbal or written messages, and the senders and receivers may be other than people. For example, an airplane instrument panel (sender) sends messages to the pilot (receiver), and a smoke detector (sender) notifies the fire department (receiver) of a fire. In today's organizations, many messages are sent by complex management information systems, where data are input from numerous sources, analyzed by computer, and then electronically transmitted to receivers.

Communication is the lifeblood of an organization; it is the thread that holds the various interdependent parts of an organization together. An organization is a stable system of patterned activities where people work together to achieve common goals through a hierarchy of assigned roles and a division of labor. These patterned activities depend on communication for coordination and integration. If the communication flows could somehow be removed from an organization, the organization would cease to exist. The patterned activities of organizations depend on the exchange of information.

The Communication Process

Symbolic Interaction

The communication process is a **symbolic interaction** between two people. For example, when a customer orders a turkey club sandwich and a strawberry milkshake at a fast-food restaurant, the customer is using words as symbols to indicate what he wants to eat. A symbol is something that represents something else. The words "turkey sandwich" are made from letters of the alphabet, but they are used to represent something made from slices of turkey and bread. The customer selected a turkey club sandwich after looking at a nonverbal representation showing a picture of the sandwich. The person behind the counter used other symbols to inform the kitchen what to prepare—"One turkey deluxe, one strawberry."

Although some symbols are quite clear, such as a hat or a chair, other symbols are much more ambiguous and difficult to explain, such as loyalty and diligence. Our ability to use symbols allows us to learn from the experience of others. People who lived many centuries ago can communicate their experiences to us symbolically through writing and art. Highly complex messages can be effectively communicated because of our ability to use symbols even though receivers have not experienced the same events as the senders. For example, someone who has never experienced a tropical storm may not know exactly what such an event might be like, but a skilled communicator who has experienced such an event should be able to describe it vividly enough for the receiver to appreciate how powerful and frightening a tropical storm can be. A symbolic presentation using words, however, is almost always only a rough approximation of what actually occurred. Even when we are communicating information about physical objects, the meaning may be ambiguous and incomplete because of our inability to find a common ground in communication.

The Communication Process

The basic elements of the communication process are diagramed in Exhibit 11.1.

1. The **source** or sender is the originator of the message and may be one person or several people working together, such as a musical group or a television news team.

Symbolic interaction
The idea that communication consists of the transmission of messages through symbols that must be properly encoded and decoded to convey the intended meaning.

2. The **message** is the stimulus the source transmits to the receiver and is composed of symbols designed to convey the intended meaning, such as words, body language, Morse code, sign language, winks, gestures, or electronic impulses.

3. The **encoding process** transforms the intended message into the symbols used to transmit the message.

4. The **channel** is the means by which the message travels from a source to a receiver, which could include personal conversations, mass media (such as radio, television, and newspapers), or electronic media (such as the Internet, fax machines, voice mail, videotape, teleconferencing, and email).

5. The **receiver** is the person who receives the message and has the responsibility to interpret it.

6. The **decoding process** involves translating the message and interpreting it.

7. **Feedback** from the receiver back to the sender is actually another message indicating the effectiveness of the communication. One-way communication does not provide an opportunity for feedback.

8. **Noise** refers to anything that disrupts the transmission of the message or feedback, which includes everything from ambiguous wording of a message to a poor telephone connection or static from a poor TV antenna.

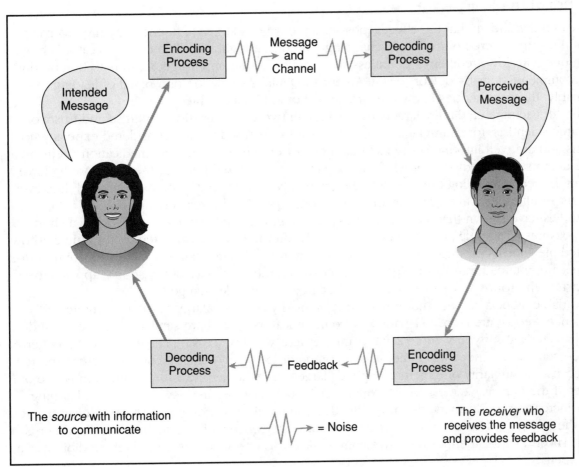

Exhibit 11.1   The Communication Process

Encoding
The process of translating the intended message into symbols that can be used to transmit the message.

Decoding
The process of translating the symbols contained in a message into meaning and interpreting the message.

The accuracy of communication depends on the successful completion of each step in the communication process. It is not enough to carefully prepare and transmit a message and then simply assume that effective communication has occurred. The encoding, transmitting, decoding, and feedback processes are all essential for effective communication. The availability of e-mail and text messaging has made communication much more convenient and rapid; however, it has also highlighted the potential for miscommunication caused by encoding and decoding errors.[1]

Persuasive Communication

Changing attitudes and swaying public opinion are important issues for many organizations, such as political parties, religious organizations, business groups, and neighborhood committees. Consequently, persuasive communication has been investigated by scholars for many years; Aristotle was one of the first to construct a basic outline of the elements of persuasive communication. In his classic work, *Rhetoric*, Aristotle identifies the three important dimensions for analyzing persuasive communication: the source, the message, and the audience.[2] Some of the characteristics associated with these three dimensions are summarized in Exhibit 11.2.

Characteristics of the Source

Extensive research has shown that the effectiveness of a message is largely influenced by the receiver's perception of the source's **credibility**. When changing attitudes, a highly credible communicator is more effective than one with low credibility.[3] Countless TV commercials attempt to get viewers to buy products because of recommendations by doctors or the American Dental Association or a panel of leading experts. Presumably, these authorities know the facts and should be listened to.

Communicators acquire credibility largely by possessing two characteristics: expertise and trustworthiness. Research scientists, for example, are more believable because they are considered experts who know the facts and are well informed. The fact that a doctor endorses a particular medication is effective both because doctors supposedly know what they are talking about and because they supposedly have nothing to gain by recommending the product. The credibility of a communicator is destroyed, however, if he or she has an ulterior motive or the recommendation appears to be self-serving.

Several studies have shown that the effectiveness of a highly credible source lasts for only a short time. When measures of attitude are obtained immediately after the persuasion attempt, the studies show that highly credible sources produce significantly greater attitude change than low-credibility sources do. If the measures are obtained four to six weeks later, however, the credibility of the source appears to have no impact; both groups show essentially equal degrees of attitude change.[4]

Another variable associated with the source is the similarity or dissimilarity of the communicator with the audience. People are more persuaded by communicators who share similar backgrounds and personality characteristics. If you want to sell a computer to a word-processing center, it may be better to get the endorsement of other users rather than a computer expert. Whether a communicator is more persuasive because of similarity or expertise depends largely on whether the issue in question is one of values or facts. If the persuasive message is a value issue, such as accepting new technology, learning new skills, or increasing productivity, the most effective communicator is one who shares similar characteristics with the audience. However, if the persuasive message concerns facts, such as which printer is the fastest and most reliable, the most effective communicator is one who possesses high credibility as a trustworthy expert.[5]

Noise
Any type of interference in the transmission of a message, either actual noise or interference within the channel.

Credibility
The degree of expertise and trustworthiness in the source.

Characteristics of the Source
Credibility: expertise and trustworthiness Similarity or dissimilarity from the receiver
Characteristics of the Message
Logical and reasonable Pleasant versus fear appeal One-sided versus two-sided arguments Primacy versus recency Overheard messages
Characteristics of the Audience
Level of intelligence Initial position

Exhibit 11.2   Characteristics of Persuasive Communication

Characteristics of the Message

In general, the most persuasive communications consist of logical, well-reasoned presentations delivered in an eloquent, organized fashion. To persuade others, messages must be reasonable and logical. However, some attitudes are not changed very easily by logic or reason because they are based on emotion and feeling.[6]

In preparing a persuasive communication, you need to know whether to present one or both sides of an issue, and if both, which side should be presented first. Should you reach a conclusion, or let the receivers draw their own conclusion? Several studies have examined the relative effectiveness of one-sided versus two-sided presentations. Most of the evidence seems to indicate that they are almost equally effective. One-sided presentations may be superior if listeners are not aware that a reasonable case could be made for the other side, yet two-sided communications were found to produce change that could withstand a counterattack.[7]

If a communicator is going to present both sides of an argument, which side should be presented first—pro or con? Studies suggest that the order of presentation does not seem to make much difference as long as both messages are presented about the same time. If there is a long time span between the two messages, and attitudes are measured immediately following the second presentation, a **recency effect** typically occurs, in which the most recent message is accepted.[8]

Messages that make the receivers feel good tend to be more persuasive. Messages that evoke happy feelings and pleasant associations seem to attract attention and evoke a favorable response from the receiver. Favorable surroundings, such as pleasant music, good food, and beautiful scenery, also contribute to the persuasiveness of communications. The persuasive effect of pleasant surroundings explains why many TV commercials use beautiful scenery and pleasant music, and people who look as if they are having fun.

However, studies have also shown that communications tend to be more persuasive when they arouse the listener's level of fear. For example, advertisements about the effects of cigarette smoking on health tend to be more effective when they specifically describe the harmful effects of cancer and emphysema. Similarly, messages about tetanus injections, safe driving standards, and dental hygiene tend to be more effective when the listeners are told specifically about possible serious consequences.[9] However, the level of arousal can be too intense if the listeners are shown vivid portrayals of accidents, disease, or other repulsive scenes. The relationship between the degree of fear and the amount of attitude change appears to be an inverted-U relationship. As the level of fear increases, there is initially an increase in attitude change. As the level of fear becomes too intense, however, people cannot cope with the problem and respond by avoiding or denying the information.[10]

Another variable influencing the credibility of a message is whether the listeners believe it was intended for them. Overheard messages tend to be very persuasive because the listeners are not worried about being intentionally manipulated; thus the source is more credible. People are also influenced by messages that appear to be censored or kept from them. The effect of censorship, whether it be movies, books, or magazine articles, generally stimulates greater interest in obtaining the censored material, which then has a more persuasive impact than if it had not been censored.

In interpersonal communication, the total message is more persuasive when both the verbal and nonverbal messages are consistent. When they are inconsistent, however, the effectiveness of the verbal message is diminished. In fact, when the verbal and nonverbal communications are inconsistent, the listeners are usually influenced more by the nonverbal behavior, such as facial expressions, physical posture, and body language, rather than by the words. Furthermore, nonverbal cues portraying emotion are recognized more easily and remembered longer than inconsistent verbal messages.[11]

Videotaped messages, such as television and video training, are generally considered the most persuasive form of mass communication because they combine the visual picture of the communicator with the verbal message. Audio messages, such as tape or radio, are generally second in effectiveness, and the printed word, such as newspapers and magazines, is third. Studies indicate, however, that the relative effectiveness of videotaped, audio, and written messages depends on the complexity of the message. Highly complex messages are more effective in a written form, which allows the receiver to reread and analyze the content of the message. Simple messages are more effectively and persuasively communicated through videotape, where they are presented in living color.[12]

Characteristics of the Audience

The effectiveness of a persuasive communication is limited by the receiver's ability to understand the message. A highly educated audience would be expected to understand complex arguments. The relationship between intelligence and persuasiveness, however, appears to be mixed. Although highly intelligent people are more receptive to communications than less intelligent people, they are more resistant to influence. Therefore, people with moderate intelligence are generally the most easily influenced by the average communication. Those with very low intelligence do not understand the influence attempt, while those at very high levels of intelligence tend to resist the influence.[13]

The initial attitudes of the receivers influence the effectiveness of persuasive communication. People tend to have a **latitude of acceptance** that includes a range of attitudes slightly more or less favorable than their own. Their latitude of rejection consists of attitudes that differ significantly from their personal position. Persuasive communications are more successful when they advocate a position that falls within the listener's latitude of acceptance. When the message falls outside the latitude of acceptance, the listeners typically respond by changing their attitudes in the *opposite* direction. The results are quite different, however, if the source is a highly credible expert. Persuasive communication has a greater impact when the expert's position is significantly different from the listener's initial position. The wider the discrepancy, the greater the distress listeners have about the differences between their opinions and the expert's. If the communicator is not an expert, the listeners are inclined to disregard such a discrepant communication: only a fool could have such a far-out position. But if the source is an expert, the wide discrepancy cannot be so easily dismissed, and the listeners are more prone to change their opinions.[14]

Latitude of acceptance
The range of attitudes or opinions that are sufficiently close
to the receiver's opinion that the receiver is willing to attend
to the message.

Supportive Communication

While the goal of persuasive communication is to change attitudes, **supportive communication** is designed to avoid defensiveness and nurture interpersonal relationships. When defensiveness occurs, people feel anger and hostility toward the other person, and communication breaks down. Defensiveness on the part of the sender results in incongruent messages, in which there is a mismatch between what the sender thinks and communicates. People are congruent when their feelings are consistent with their behavior. Defensive communicators feel irritated and angry but refuse to express their feelings and attempt to deny them. Rather than dealing with their upset feelings openly, they allow their hostility to be expressed covertly through sarcasm and insincerity. When defensiveness occurs on the part of the listener, the message is typically not received. Defensive listeners do not listen effectively, and important elements of the message are either ignored or distorted. To the extent that a defensive communication is received, it usually results in a defensive response that further aggravates the problem of ineffective communication. Defensiveness is avoided, or at least reduced, by supportive communication. This type of communication is descriptive, problem-oriented, flexible, and owned rather than disowned.

Descriptive

Supportive communication is descriptive and specific rather than evaluative or general. When people are told that their ideas or behaviors are good or bad, the evaluation process causes them to feel defensive. Evaluative statements create defensiveness and often result in arguments. For example, telling a cashier, "You did a terrible job handling that customer's complaint," would be an evaluative comment that creates defensiveness and antagonism. A descriptive comment, such as "The customer became upset because you interrupted him several times and raised your voice at him," would be less threatening and more supportive.

Descriptive communication allows the situation to be discussed without arousing the need to defend or argue. Descriptive communication consists of three elements: (1) describing the event as objectively as possible, (2) describing your feelings about the event or consequences of the event, and (3) suggesting an alternative that would be more acceptable to you.

As a general rule, communication becomes more useful and arouses less defensiveness as it becomes more specific. For example, "You are a poor cashier," is not a helpful comment because it does not indicate what behaviors need to be changed. In contrast, "You interrupted the customer three times and spoke louder each time," is a specific statement telling the cashier what was wrong.

Problem-Oriented

Supportive communication focuses on the specific problem rather than the personalities or status of the members. For example, the statement "You are too hotheaded when a customer comes in with a complaint," is a criticism of the cashier's personality. Problem-oriented communication focuses on the problem and its solution rather than on personal traits or blame. Focusing on the problem rather than personalities is particularly appropriate during performance appraisals, since employees need to understand how to improve their performance, not how to change their personalities. "You are unreliable, and we can't trust you to do your job," is a person-oriented statement that will generate defensiveness and hostility; "Your weekly reports have been late, and some of the information is so inaccurate that we can't use it" is a problem-oriented statement that helps the individual know exactly what is wrong.

Supportive communication
Communication designed to help both parties maintain open and congruent communication by avoiding defensiveness.

Problem-oriented communications also help to avoid making the listener feel inferior. The solution to a problem should be generated by a careful analysis of the problem, not by the use of status or power. Defensiveness results when one person attempts to create an impression that says, "I know and you don't," or "I am right and you are wrong," or "I have more power, so we'll do it my way." These statements are examples of win-lose conflict, where one individual attempts to win at the expense of another, or to look good by making others look inferior.

Flexible

Supportive communication is flexible, not rigid. When one person adopts a know-it-all attitude and behaves in a dogmatic manner, the other person becomes defensive, and effective communication is inhibited. "That sales projection has got to be wrong; I know it can't be that high" is a very rigid statement. A much more flexible statement is "It seems to me that the sales projection is wrong; I don't see how it can be that high." People who are dogmatic in their conversation generally prefer to win an argument rather than solve a problem, and winning is more important than building a relationship. The consequence of such rigid communication is reciprocal rigidity, defensiveness, and interpersonal conflict.

Flexible communication means that the communicator is willing to accept additional information and acknowledges that other alternatives may exist. Being flexible is not synonymous with being insecure or easily influenced; it indicates a willingness to learn and grow by considering the contributions of others. Attitudes and opinions are stated provisionally rather than as firm facts. One consequence of flexible communication is that it affirms and acknowledges the potential contribution of other people. Other individuals are encouraged to share their attitudes and opinions because they are led to feel that they can make a significant contribution to the conversation.

Owned

Supportive communication is **owned**, which means that the communicator takes responsibility for what is said. An example would be "After reviewing your qualifications, I have concluded that you have not satisfied the entrance requirements." **Disowning** communication, in contrast, is indicated by speaking in the third person or using plural pronouns, such as "We think," or "They said," or "We've heard." By attributing the source of a communication to some unknown party or external source, the communicator avoids responsibility for the message and avoids becoming invested in the communication: "The feeling of the committee is that you have not satisfied all the requirements and should not be admitted." One result of disowning communication is that the listener does not know whose point of view the message represents and often feels frustrated by not being able to pursue the problem further. Furthermore, disowned communications contain an implicit message that a certain psychological distance should be maintained rather than offering a close, interpersonal relationship.

Listening

Although listening is essential for effective communication, it is probably the most overlooked process in interpersonal communications. Reading, writing, and public speaking are taught in our educational system, and students spend many hours developing these skills, but students are usually left to falter along on their own when it comes to listening. Listening skills are developed to some extent by teaching students how to read and speak; but listening skills are different from reading and speaking skills, and students who are good at reading and speaking may still be very poor listeners.

Studies on listening indicate that most people are at best only mediocre listeners. One study found that most people remember less than half of what they hear immediately after hearing it, no matter how carefully they thought they listened. Two months after listening to a person talk, the average listener will remember less than one-fourth of what was said. Listening tests likewise indicate that people usually recall only about 25 percent of a conversation. Furthermore, when asked to rate the extent to which they are skilled listeners, 85 percent rate themselves as average or worse.[15] Clearly, listening is an important skill that needs to be more carefully developed. Effective listening comes from developing empathy and using effective listening skills.[16]

Empathy

Effective listeners have been called **active listeners**, **reflective listeners**, and **empathic listeners**. Each of these labels implies that the listener must have the ability to listen to another's message empathically. Empathy is the capacity to participate in another's feelings or ideas; it involves understanding and relating to another's feelings. Empathic listeners imaginatively project themselves into the speaker's frame of reference and comprehend the full impact of the message. **Empathic listening** involves accurately perceiving the content and also understanding the emotional components and unexpressed meanings contained in the message.

Empathic listening involves being able to reflect or restate the communicator's message on two levels. The first level is called the **expressed level of empathy**, in which the listener simply paraphrases, restates, or summarizes the content of the communication. The second level, called the **implied level**, is more advanced and involves attending not only to what the communicator expresses but also to what was implied or left unstated.

The differences between the expressed and the implied levels can be illustrated by comparing alternative responses to a student who complains about not performing very well on a test. "I read and outlined every chapter in the text and spent twenty hours reviewing my notes and still scored ten points lower than my roommate, who didn't even read all the chapters." At the expressed level of empathy, the listener responds to the content and emotion of what was expressed: "You feel frustrated because you tried so hard to learn and still didn't do as well as your roommate." At the implied level of empathy, however, the listener responds not only to what was said but also to the implied or unstated component: "You sound discouraged about trying so hard and not doing as well as your roommate. It can be very frustrating when you try so hard and not do as well as you expected. When that happens, it's easy to get depressed and feel sorry for yourself."

Good empathizers need to know when to display each level of empathy. At the beginning of an interaction, listeners need to use the expressed level. The implied level is not appropriate until a feeling of trust and acceptance has been created. If the listener continues to use the expressed level as the relationship advances, the expressed level will appear superficial and insincere. If the listener uses the implied level of empathy too early in the interaction before a feeling of trust and acceptance has been developed, the communicator may feel threatened, as though he or she were being psychoanalyzed.

Effective Listening Skills

Many listeners believe listening is just a matter of sitting back and absorbing information like a sponge. Effective listening does not just happen, however; it requires much effort and hard work.

Different situations call for different kinds of listening. In a classroom, for example, students listen to obtain information and comprehend the most important concepts. In a political debate, the public often listens to confirm previously held biases supporting their points of view. In a courtroom, the opposing lawyer listens for faults, weaknesses, and contradictions in the testimony. In building a relationship, an

---

Empathic listening
Active listening that requires you to project yourself into the speaker's frame of reference to comprehend the full impact of the message.

Expressed level of empathy
The level of understanding at which the listener paraphrases, restates, or summarizes the content of the communication as it was stated.

Implied level of empathy
A more advanced level of listening in which the listener attends not only to what the communicator expresses, but also to what was implied or left unstated.

empathic listener tries to understand the content and feeling of the message to enhance personal growth for both the communicator and the listener.

Several lists of guidelines have been proposed to explain the principles of good listening. Ten principles of effective listening are summarized in Exhibit 11.3. These ten principles identify the major differences between good and bad listeners. Good listeners look for areas of interest, overlook errors of delivery and objectionable personal mannerisms, postpone judgment until they understand the central point, listen for ideas and identify the main points, take careful notes to help them remember, are actively responsive in trying to listen, resist distractions, challenge their minds by trying to learn difficult material,

Principle	The Good Listener	The Bad Listener
1. Look for areas of interest.	Seeks personal enlightenment; entertains new topics as potentially interesting	Tunes out dry subjects; narrowly defines what is interesting
2. Overlook errors of delivery.	Attends to meaning and content; ignores delivery errors while being sensitive to any messages in them	Ignores if delivery is poor; misses messages because of personal attributes of the communicator
3. Postpone judgment.	Avoids quick judgments; waits until comprehension of the core message is complete	Quickly evaluates and passes judgment; inflexible regarding contrary messages
4. Listen for ideas.	Listens for ideas and themes; identifies the main points	Listens for facts and details
5. Take notes.	Takes careful notes using a variety of methods depending on the speaker	Takes incomplete notes using one system
6. Be actively responsive.	Responds frequently with nods, "uh-huhs," etc.; shows active body state	Passive demeanor; few or no responses; little energy output
7. Resist distractions.	Resists being distracted; has a long attention span; puts loaded words in perspective	Easily distracted; focuses on loaded or emotional works; short attention span
8. Challenge your mind.	Uses difficult material to stimulate the mind; seeks to enlarge understanding	Avoids difficult material; does not seek to broaden knowledge base
9. Capitalize on mind speed.	Uses listening time to summarize and anticipate the message; attends to implicit as well as explicit messages	Daydreams with slow speakers; becomes preoccupied with other thoughts
10. Help and encourage the speaker.	Asks for examples or clarifying information; rephrases the idea	Interrupts; asks trivial questions; makes distracting comments

Exhibit 11.3   Principles of Effective Listening

capitalize on mind speed, and assist and encourage the speaker by asking for clarifying information and paraphrasing the ideas.[17]

Making Appropriate Responses

An important element in effective listening is responding to the communicator by making appropriate responses. Some responses stimulate the communicator to discuss the issue more extensively and expand to related areas of interest. Other responses tend to restrict the topic of communication or terminate the conversation.

The appropriateness of a response depends largely on the purpose of the communication and the goal of the interaction. If the purpose of the conversation is to evaluate performance, an evaluative or confrontive response is generally best. However, if the purpose of the interaction is to help another individual solve a problem or make a decision, a reflective or probing response is generally most appropriate. Six response types have been identified that range from directive responses, which close communication, to nondirective, which tend to open additional topics for consideration, as shown in Exhibit 11.4. Each of these six responses is appropriate for different purposes.[18]

Nonverbal Communication

Face-to-face communication involves more than just the words we use. The verbal portion actually constitutes only a small part of the total message. The way in which the words are arranged and presented, including the tone, rate of speech, inflection, pauses, and facial expressions, actually provide most of the message's content for the receiver. The words themselves do not stand alone but depend on nonverbal components for their true meaning. To illustrate, the expression "Isn't this just great!" could be used as an honest expression of happiness and joy, but if it is used with the appropriate facial expression and intonation, it becomes a sarcastic comment conveying disgust and contempt. The study of nonverbal communication has identified five major variables that influence the meaning of messages. These five variables include physical distance, posture, facial cues, vocal cues, and appearance.

Physical Distance

The study of the way people structure their space and the distances between people in daily interactions is called **proxemics.** The physical distance between the source and the receiver communicates a message in itself, in addition to influencing the interpretation of what is said. We tend to stand closer when talking with people we know and like and farther away from people we do not know or do not like. Shaking hands and touching is another way to communicate to people that you like them and have an interest in them. Physical distance is also an indication of status, and subordinates tend to maintain greater distance between themselves and people of higher status. Elevation can also be used as an indication of status, particularly in some cultures, such as Tonga. People of higher status are seated on higher-level platforms than people of lower status.

Posture

The study of posture and other body movements, including facial expressions and gestures, is called **kinesics.** Posture, or body language, can be used to indicate numerous things, including liking or status. We tend to relax by leaning backward, maintaining an open-arm posture, and directly facing those we like. However, we tend to become rigid and tense around those of high status or those whom we perceive as

---

Proxemics
A study of the physical distance between two people during communication.

Kinesics
A study of the posture of people while speaking.

These six responses illustrate different ways of responding to an irate customer who states, "I ordered that part last month, and you said it would be here in a week. I think you're trying to take advantage of me."

1. Evaluative responses: Pass judgment, express agreement or disagreement, or offer advice; for example, "We are not trying to take advantage of you. You need to be patient longer." Evaluative responses are useful after a topic has been explored in depth, and it is appropriate for the responder to express an opinion.

2. Confrontive responses: Challenge the other person to clarify the message and identify points of inconsistency or contradiction; for example, "Just because we haven't been able to deliver the part yet doesn't mean we're taking advantage of you. No one else feels that way." Confrontation is useful for helping people clarify their thoughts and feelings or to think more broadly about the issue.

3. Diverting responses: Change the focus of the communicator's problem to a problem selected by the responder; for example, "Your comment reminds me of a problem I had last summer. I remember when . . ." Diverting responses often involve changing the subject and are helpful when a point of comparison is needed and the communicator needs to know that someone else has experienced a similar event.

4. Probing responses: Ask the communicator to clarify what was said or to provide additional information or illustration; for example, "Yes, our deliveries are late, but could you tell me specifically why you think we're trying to take advantage of you?" Probing responses are useful when the respondent needs specific information to understand the message or the communicator needs to respond to another topic in order to make the communication clearer.

5. Pacifying responses: Reduce the intensity of emotion associated with the message and help to calm the communicator; for example, "There's no need to think that we're trying to take advantage of you; the delay is simply out of our control." Pacifying responses are useful when the communicator needs to be reassured that discussing the message is acceptable or when the intensity of feeling being experienced is inhibiting good communication.

6. Reflective or reinterpretive responses: Reflect back to the communicator what was heard, but in different words; for example, "You're saying that we intentionally misrepresented our delivery date and are treating you unfairly." Reflective responses help communicators know they have been both heard and understood. Reflective responses should not simply mimic the communicator or be a direct restatement of what was said. Instead, they should contribute understanding, meaning, and acceptance to the conversations.

Exhibit 11.4 Six Alternative Types of Responses

threatening. Higher-status individuals are generally more relaxed in posture than those of lower status. Standing, pacing, and putting your hands on your hips are all nonverbal cues of high status. When talking to another individual, we can communicate an element of responsiveness and interest in what they have to say by making spontaneous gestures, shifting our posture from side to side, and moving closer to the individual.

Facial Cues

Although some people tend to be rather expressionless, others are very expressive and communicate many messages just using facial cues. In a job interview, for example, eye contact is an important indicator of an applicant's competence and strength of character. A pleasant facial expression also communicates a feeling of liking for another individual. We tend to maintain eye contact with people we like and avoid contact with those we dislike. High-status people tend to display less eye contact than do those of lower status. Smiling, furrowing one's eyebrows, and other facial expressions also indicate a degree of responsiveness to the communicator.[19]

Example—

"The human face provides a bewildering variety of important social signals . . . a face tells us if its bearer is old or young, male or female, sad or happy, whether they are attracted to us or repulsed by us, interested in what we have to say or bored and anxious to depart."[20]

Vocal Cues

The study of the human voice, including range, pitch, rhythm, resonance, and tempo, is called **paralinguistics**. Interpersonal attraction and concern for another individual can be expressed through vocal cues. Speaking in a pleasant tone of voice at a moderate rate of speed indicates a desire to communicate with the other individual. Anger is usually expressed in a loud, high-pitched tone of voice, while boredom is expressed with a deep, lethargic tone of voice. Lower-status people tend to have a lower voice volume than do those of higher status. Speaking loudly, rapidly, and in a moderate tone of voice generally conveys a sense of intensity and enthusiasm.

Appearance

Physical appearance, especially clothing, sends surprisingly strong nonverbal messages. High-status people often display appropriate ornaments, such as the badges and bars used in the military or police units. "Dress for success" seminars emphasize the importance of appearance in manipulating one's personal power and status in a group. For example, it is suggested that men wear long-sleeved rather than short-sleeved shirts if they want to increase their personal power and have greater influence on the outcome of a committee meeting.[21]

Although listeners may be unaware of it, they often look for nonverbal indicators as they listen to the message. The evidence suggests that women are more effective than men at both encoding and decoding nonverbal messages.[22] If the nonverbal component supports the verbal message, it can reinforce the intended meaning of the message and assist the receiver in properly decoding the message. However, if communicators say one thing but nonverbally transmit a different message, the receiver tends to give more credence to the nonverbal components. For example, if supervisors use an apathetic, monotonic voice to say, "Thanks, I really appreciate what you've done," their vocal cues destroy their intended message.

In a courtroom, jurors may ignore the testimony of a witness whose verbal testimony is inconsistent with his or her nonverbal behavior. Post-trial interviews with jurors have revealed that the testimony of a key witness may be discounted because the paralinguistic behaviors of the witness overwhelm the content of the testimony.[23]

ORGANIZATIONAL COMMUNICATION

The Effects of Organizational Structure

There is a common misperception about communication problems in organizations. The "myth of open communication" suggests that organizational problems are caused by inadequate communication, and

Paralinguistics
A study of the meaning of vocal cues during communication.

the solution is to make all information universally available. In fact, just the opposite is true. An important function of organizational structure is to *restrict* communication flows and thus *decrease* problems of confusion and information overload. Some organizational problems are solved not by increasing but by restricting the flow of communication and clearly specifying how information is to be gathered, processed, and analyzed.

Consider the situation of sixty people who gather informally in an auditorium. As long as they interact with whomever they choose, they will remain a disorganized collection of people regardless of their purpose for meeting. Unless the communication channels become organized and constraints are placed on the flow of information this group will find it virtually impossible to accomplish anything, whether they are a state legislature, a college fraternity, or a group of concerned citizens. With an unorganized group of sixty people visiting at random, the number of potential communication links between two people is $N(N-1)/2$, or 1,770. However, if they are organized into six groups of ten with a formally appointed leader, the number of communication channels is reduced to just nine in each group.

The situation is similar to that of an orchestra. If sixty musicians play whatever they want, such as they do when they are warming up, the result is unpleasant noise rather than beautiful music. To make beautiful music, the members must play exactly what they are supposed to play at exactly the right time. The same is true of communication patterns in organizations. To move from an unorganized state to an organized state requires that restrictions be placed on the flow of communication. People must use the appropriate communication channels, and only job-relevant information should be transmitted. Unrestricted communication produces noise and confusion in the organization. Without precision and timing, there may be sound but no music. Likewise, without structure and regulations, there may be conversations but no meaning.

Direction of Communication Flow

One way to analyze organizational communication is to study the direction of information flow, that is, who communicates with whom. The three most important directions of formal communication flow are downward, upward, and horizontal. Informal communication is circulated through the grapevine.

Downward Communication

Downward communication follows the organizational hierarchy and flows from higher level people to those in lower levels. The most common downward communication includes explanations of organizational policies and practices, instructions about how to do the job, the rationale for the job's importance, feedback to subordinates about their performance, and explanations of the goals of the organization. This information teaches subordinates how to perform their jobs properly and makes them feel part of the organization. However, organizational members frequently complain that the information they receive is both inadequate and inaccurate. A typical complaint is "We have absolutely no idea what's happening." Although managers usually communicate job instructions adequately, they fail to provide an adequate rationale for the job or sufficient feedback to subordinates.

A problem in downward communication is inaccuracy as the information is passed from level to level. Orders are typically expressed in a language appropriate for the next level down rather than the lowest level, where the message is aimed. Therefore, as the information travels down the organizational structure, it needs to be adapted to the members at each successive level. A classic study of downward communications in 100 organizations estimated that 80 percent of the information was lost after passing through five levels of the organization.[24]

Upward Communication

Upward communication is designed to provide feedback on how well the organization is functioning. Lower-level employees are expected to provide upward communication about their performance and the organization's practices and policies. The most common forms of upward communication include memos, written reports, suggestion boxes, group meetings, and grievances.

The most serious upward communication problem is filtered information. Since it is typically used to monitor the organization's performance, upward communication can best be described as what subordinates want the supervisors to hear rather than what the supervisors need to know. Another problem with upward communication is that organizations typically rely on lower-level members to initiate it. Instead of actively soliciting information and providing channels for receiving it, managers frequently adopt an open-door policy and assume that people who have something to say will voluntarily express it.

The higher executives advance within the organizational hierarchy, the less likely they are to know how well things are going in the company. Many executives are surrounded by "yes" people who filter information and only report good news. Successful executives need to create information channels that will keep them adequately informed.

Example—

When Yogesh Gupta became the president and CEO of Fatwire, a software company that manages business websites, he discovered that he was too far removed from his 200 employees to know what problems they were facing. To overcome this communication problem, he began holding frequent private meetings with the nine members of his management team plus periodic meetings with his 200 employees. He asks them what they think he is doing wrong and what they recommend he do differently. He looks for opportunities to publicly praise them for their feedback so they will want to make more suggestions in the future.[25]

Horizontal Communication

Horizontal communication is lateral communication between peers; it does not follow the formal organizational hierarchy. Formal bureaucratic structures do not provide for horizontal communication, and one of the challenges in creating an effective organization is providing acceptable channels for lateral communication. Adhering strictly to a formal chain of command is inefficient and creates a serious communication overload for upper-level executives. However, unrestricted horizontal communication detracts from maximum efficiency. Organizations must provide for horizontal communication channels where they are necessary while restricting unnecessary channels.[26]

In addition to helping people coordinate their work, horizontal communication among peers furnishes emotional and social support. Horizontal communication contributes to the development of friendships and informal work groups.

Informal Communication

Informal communication is called *grapevine communication*, and it exists in every organization. The **grapevine** is created by informal associations and cuts across formal lines of communication. Some of the major characteristics of grapevine information are as follows:

1. Grapevines are found in every organization, and they are virtually impossible to eliminate. It is only natural for employees to discuss matters of mutual concern, and even the closest monitoring of their conversations will not prevent them from talking. Furthermore, employees are more satisfied in organizations that have extensive informal communication.[27]
2. Information usually travels more rapidly through the grapevine than through official communication channels.
3. The grapevine is a more spontaneous form of expression, hence more intrinsically gratifying and credible than formal communication.

Grapevine
The informal communication system through which messages are passed in an organization, especially rumors and myths.

4. In situations where official censorship and filtering occur, grapevine information is more informative.

5. On noncontroversial topics related to the organization, most of the information communicated through the grapevine (estimated to be at least 75 percent) is correct. Emotionally charged information, however, is more likely to be distorted.

6. The number of people who serve as actual links in the grapevine is generally relatively small (estimated to be less than 10 percent of the group).[28]

Occasionally grapevines benefit the organization, and managers use them as a regular substitute for formal communication. For example, the grapevine can be used to test reactions to a proposed change without actually making a formal commitment. Managers have been known to leak ideas to the grapevine just to test their acceptability before implementing them.

Grapevines tend to cause trouble in organizations that are characterized by a lack of trust and confidence among managers and workers. The unfortunate irony is that organizations most in need of an effective grapevine are usually plagued by a grapevine prone to distortion. Grapevines provide a disservice when they become a constant source of false rumors. Rumors seem to spread fastest and farthest when the information is ambiguous, when the content of the rumor is important to those involved, and when the people are emotionally aroused.

Although rumors can be destructive to an organization, it has been shown that some stories and myths perpetuated in organizations contribute greatly to the organization's effectiveness by preserving valuable aspects of the organization's culture. At Hewlett-Packard Corporation, for example, feelings of job security among employees are perpetuated by a story describing how the workers at one point years ago went on a reduced workweek to avoid layoffs and preserve jobs.[29]

Communication Roles

Communication integrates and coordinates the various activities of an organization, and helps it function more effectively. If communication were eliminated, the organization would cease to exist. Studies of communication networks in real organizations have identified four communication roles that disseminate information within the organization and help it communicate with the outside world.

Gatekeepers

A **gatekeeper** is someone who controls the flow of messages between two people or two groups in an organization structure. A gatekeeper in a communication network acts like a valve in a water pipe. One function of the gatekeeper is to decrease information overload by filtering the flow of messages from one group to another. An example is a quality control clerk who collects daily reports, summarizes them, and presents them to the plant manager.

Liaisons

A **liaison** is someone who connects two or more cliques within a system without belonging to either clique. Liaisons are the cement, or the linking pin, that holds the groups of an organization together. Liaisons are somewhat similar to gatekeepers, but while gatekeepers typically govern the flow of upward communication, liaisons are typically positioned between two groups that are not arranged hierarchically. An example of a

Gatekeeper
A communication role in an organizational structure that controls the flow of information, especially between lower and upper levels in the organization.

Liaison
A communication role within an organizational structure in which an individual serves as a communication link between two groups.

liaison between a football team and the faculty is a sports writer who tells the faculty about the team and its travel schedule and tells players how they are doing in class.

Opinion Leaders

Opinion leaders fill an important role in what is called the two-step flow model of attitude change. Persuasive messages flow from the mass media to opinion leaders, who interpret the information and pass it on to the public audience. Within a group, opinion leaders are able to influence the attitudes of group members by helping them interpret new information and define situations.

Boundary Spanners

Boundary spanners are people who communicate with the organization's environment. These people are typically top executives who travel widely and enjoy many types of contact with other organizations. They help the organization gain acceptance in society and sense social changes that could influence the organization. In one sense, boundary spanners are a special type of gatekeeper because they control the communication flows by which new ideas enter the organization. Boundary spanners help the organization predict future changes and cope with its environment.

IMPROVING COMMUNICATION

Improving communication in organizations involves more accurate encoding, transmitting, decoding, and feedback at the interpersonal level, and at the organizational level, creating and monitoring appropriate communication channels. Several strategies can be used to help managers communicate more effectively.

Increasing Feedback

Adequate feedback lets communicators know whether their messages need to be revised or repeated, thus reducing the frequency and severity of misunderstanding. Feedback mechanisms are just as important for organizational communication as they are in interpersonal communication. Top managers should not issue orders or policy statements and assume they have been understood. Feedback mechanisms and reporting systems need to be established so managers know whether their messages have been understood, accepted, and followed.

Regulating Information Flow

Managers who want everyone to "see the big picture" often create a serious communication overload. Rather than trying to keep everyone involved, top-level managers need to follow the *"need-to-know" principle* when transmitting downward communication. Managers should ask whether lower-level positions need this information to perform their tasks effectively. If the answer is no, the message should not be transmitted. Another useful principle in regulating the flow of information is the *exception principle*. This principle states that only significant deviations from standard policies and procedures should be brought to the attention of superiors. As long as performance falls within the acceptable range, regular procedures are followed.

Opinion leader
A communication role in an organizational structure in which noted personalities become the opinion leaders who receive information from the mass media and interpret it for other organizational members.

Boundary spanners
Individuals who perform the role of communicating with the organization's environment by sensing environmental changes and selling the organization to the environment.

Repetition

Repetition helps listeners interpret messages that are ambiguous, unclear, or too difficult to understand the first time. Repetition also reduces the problem of forgetting. Since forgetting is such a serious problem, many managers adopt the policy of having very important messages repeated at least three or four times. Effective communicators build repetition into their presentations by expressing the same idea in different ways. A popular strategy in both writing and speaking to help the audience remember the main point is to tell them what you're going to tell them, then tell them, then tell them what you've told them.

Simplifying Language

Complex language, technical terms, and jargon make communication difficult to understand and frustrating to the listener. Complex ideas do not require complex terms to explain them. Almost every idea can be explained in relatively simple language. When it is important that listeners understand the message, communicators should make certain that the language they use is clear and easily understood.

There are times when complex language using jargon and technical terms is appropriate. When a message is communicated to an audience that understands them, technical terms and jargon are useful. Scientific research reports, for example, are written for an audience of scientists who understand the technical terms that are used. One advantage of using technical terms is that they have a precise meaning that conveys precise information without using many words. Although simple language tends to increase comprehension, complex language tends to save time and make communication more efficient for those who comprehend it.

One of the best ways to simplify an explanation is to provide an example or illustration. Complex ideas are not only difficult to understand but also difficult to remember. A simple illustration helps the listener comprehend the idea and remember it. Sometimes when listeners feel baffled and confused, the most effective thing they can do is simply ask, "Can you give me an example to help me understand that?"

Effective Timing

A useful strategy for improving communication is to manage the timing of messages so that they are received in an orderly manner. Speakers often begin to speak before the listeners are ready to listen. Many managers find that messages come to them in a disorganized fashion, and they cannot switch effectively from one topic to another as rapidly as they need to. This principle is similar to the procedure many executives use in responding to their in-baskets. Incoming mail is sorted into related topics. A similar procedure can be used, to some extent, with verbal communication where time periods are scheduled for discussing a specific topic. Organizations can schedule conferences, meetings, and retreats to focus on identified problems without the influence of other distractions.

Barriers to Effective Communication

The following are nine of the major barriers to effective communication.

Omission

The transmitted message is almost always an abbreviated representation of the intended meaning. Listeners may hear a message and feel secure thinking they understood the communication, but what they may not realize is that what they heard was neither complete nor what the sender really intended to say.

Filtering

Filtering is the manipulation of information so that selected data, especially negative comments, are either removed or altered before they are transmitted to the next individual.

Time Pressures

Limited time, which is a reality in every aspect of life, causes vital information to be distorted or deleted. Occasionally people who should be included in the formal communication channel are overlooked, creating a situation called **short-circuiting**.

Jargon

Jargon consists of abbreviated words or simplified phrases summarizing more complex concepts that convey a unique meaning to other group members. Consequently, jargon tends to increase the speed and accuracy of communication within groups and strengthen cohesiveness. But it creates a difficult barrier for members outside the group. New group members typically feel confused and alienated from the group until they master the jargon.[30]

Value Judgments

While the source is speaking, the receiver should be listening. However, many receivers assign an overall worth to the message based on small samples of it and then begin to develop a rebuttal. Effective listening requires that the listener suspend judgment until the entire message has been received, and only then evaluate the worth or accuracy of the message.

Differing Frames of Reference

Accurate communication requires that the encoding and decoding processes be based on a common field of experience that the sender and receiver may not share. For example, two people will have difficulty talking about living in the mountains of Idaho if snowy winters mean skiing, snowmobiling, and ice skating to one while the other thinks about wet feet, cold hands, icy roads, and cars that won't start.

Selective Listening

The problem of selective listening is part of the larger problem of selective perception, in which people tend to listen to only part of a message and ignore other information. We hear only what we want to hear and tend to disregard information that creates cognitive dissonance or threatens our self-esteem. We try to ignore information that conflicts with established beliefs or values.

Semantic Problems

Occasionally people who speak the same language discover that the symbols they use do not have a common meaning. Semantic problems are particularly troublesome in communicating abstract concepts or technical terms. Words such as "discounted present value," "exercise option," and "trusts" have special meanings to a finance executive that they do not have to someone in production.

Example—

Professors over the age of 50 use countless phrases that are rich with meaning to them, but not to the students they are teaching, such as Levittown, Ma Bell, like an Edsel, Great Society programs, green revolution, and Woodstock generation. Conversely, students use phrases that mean something to them but are meaningless to their older professors, such as cyber squatter, bit barfing, cookies, gigabyte, cyber hustlers, flame, Amazoned, and angry garden salad.

Information Overload

When people receive more messages than they can possibly handle, they experience communication overload. New and innovative communication channels, such as facsimile, voice mail, Internet, teleconferencing, text messaging, and electronic mail, are making communication easier, faster, and more convenient, but they are also causing a severe information overload. Organizations are being forced to create usage guidelines for the effective use of communication channels.

Reactions to Communication Overload

Organizational processes are frequently responsible for generating excessive amounts of communication. Too much communication can be just as troublesome as inadequate communication.[31] Individuals and organizations use a variety of reactions to communication overload; some are more adaptive than others. Adaptive responses focus on communicating vital information, whereas dysfunctional responses fail to solve the overload problem.

Disregarding involves ignoring what cannot be easily absorbed, which is a dysfunctional response, since information is disregarded on an irrational basis. The information that is typically ignored is usually the information that seems the most difficult to comprehend or the least pleasant to attend to.

Queuing consists of collecting the information in a pile, with the expectation of processing it at a later time. Queuing is only appropriate for recorded information such as letters, email, phone mail, and memos. Telephone calls and other verbal messages cannot be conveniently placed in a queue. Queuing, or delaying the processing of information, can be either an adaptive or dysfunctional response depending on the amount of overload. If messages continue to arrive faster than they can be processed, the queue becomes infinitely long. However, if there is adequate time between the surges of incoming messages to process them, queuing may be an effective way to respond.

Filtering involves screening information that appears to be irrelevant, and it can also be either adaptive or dysfunctional, depending on whether useful guidelines have been created for deciding what to screen. People tend to screen information that they do not readily understand or that does not make them look good.

Approximating consists of processing a sample of the information and using it to make inferences regarding the rest of the information. Approximation is typically an adaptive response because most information is highly redundant, and a random sample usually provides a good estimate of the total message.

Multiple Channels involves assigning different people or departments to be responsible for collecting and analyzing portions of the information. It is a highly adaptive response in terms of organizational effectiveness. An example of this decentralized process of handling information is to have employee complaints sent to the employee relations department, questions about stock options referred to the finance department, and issues regarding product quality submitted to the quality control department.

NOTES

1. Srivastsa Seshadri and Larry Carstenson, "The Perils of E-Mail: Communications in Nonprofits," *Nonprofit Management & Leadership*, vol. 18 (no. 1, Fall 2007), pp. 77–99.
2. Aristotle, *Rhetoric*. See also Annette N. Shelby, "The Theoretical Bases of Persuasion: A Critical Introduction," *Journal of Business Communication*, vol. 23 (Winter 1986), pp. 5–29.
3. Carl I. Hovland and W. Weiss, "The influence of Source Credibility on Communication Effectiveness," *Public Opinion Quarterly*, vol. 15 (1952), pp. 635–650.
4. H. C. Kelman and C. I. Hovland, " 'Restatement' of the Communicator in Delayed Measurement of Opinion Change," *Journal of Abnormal and Social Psychology*, vol. 48 (1953), pp. 326–335.
5. Roobina Ohanian, "Construction and Validation of a Scale to Measure Celebrity Endorsers' Perceived Expertise, Trustworthiness, and Attractiveness," *Journal of Advertising*, vol. 19, (no. 3, 1990), pp. 39–52; Roobina Ohanian, "The Impact of Celebrity Spokespersons' Perceived Image on Consumers' Intention to Purchase," *Journal of Advertising Research*, vol. 31 (February-March 1991), pp. 46–54.
6. David Kipnis and Stuart Schmidt, "The Language of Persuasion; Hard, Soft, or Rational: Our Choice Depends on Power, Expectations, and What We Hope to Accomplish," *Psychology Today*, vol. 19 (April 1985), pp. 40–45.

7. R. A. Jones and J. W. Brehm, "Persuasiveness of One- and Two-Sided Communications as a Function of Awareness: There Are Two Sides," *Journal of Experimental Social Psychology*, vol. 6 (1970), pp. 47–56.

8. N. Miller and D. Campbell, "Recency and Primacy in Persuasion as a Function of the Timing of Speeches and Measurements," *Journal of Abnormal and Social Psychology*, vol. 59 (1959), pp. 1–9.

9. H. Leventhal and P. Niles, "Persistence of Influence for Varying Duration of Exposure to Threat Stimuli," *Psychological Reports*, vol. 16 (1965), pp. 223–233; H. Leventhal and R. Singer, "Affect Arousal and Positioning of Recommendation in Persuasive Communications," *Journal of Personality and Social Psychology*, vol. 4 (1966), pp.137–146; H. Leventhal, R. Singer, and S. Jones, "The Effects of Fear and Specificity of Recommendation upon Attitudes and Behavior," *Journal of Personality and Social Psychology*, vol. 2 (1965), pp. 20–29.

10. Irving L. Janis and Semour Feshbach, "Effects of Fear-Arousing Communications," *Journal of Abnormal and Social Psychology*, vol. 48 (1953), pp. 78–92.

11. Paula T. Hertel and Alice Narvaez, "Confusing Memories for Verbal and Nonverbal Communication," *Journal of Personality and Social Psychology*, vol. 50, no. 3 (1986), pp. 474–481.

12. S. Chaiken and A. H. Eagly, "Communication Modality as a Determinant of Message Persuasiveness and Message Comprehensibility" *Journal of Personality and Social Psychology*, vol. 34 (1976), pp. 605–614.

13. Reviewed by Everett Rogers and Rekha Agarwala-Rogers, *Communication in Organizations* (New York: Free Press, 1976).

14. E. Aronson, J. Tumer, and I. M. Carlsmith, "Communicator Credibility and Communicator Discrepancy as Determinants of Opinion Change," *Journal of Abnormal and Social Psychology*, vol. 67 (1963), pp. 31–36; Marvin E. Goldberg and Jon Hartwick, "The Effects of Advertiser Reputation and Extremity of Advertising Claim on Advertising Effectiveness," *Journal of Consumer Research*, vol. 17 (September 1990), pp. 172–179.

15. Ralph Nichols, "You Don't Know How to Listen," *Colliers Magazine* (July 1953), pp. 16–17; Lyman K. Steil, "Your Listening Profile" (Sperry Corporation, 1980).

16. Valerie Priscilla Goby and Justus Helen Lewis, "The Key Role of Listening in Business: A Study of the Singapore Insurance Industry," *Business Communication Quarterly*, vol. 63 (no. 2, 2000), pp 41–51.

17. Steven Golen, "A Factor Analysis of Barriers to Effective Listening," *Journal of Business Communication*, vol. 27 (Winter 1990), pp. 25–36.

18. David Whetten and Kim Cameron, *Developing Management Skills* (Glenview, Ill.: Scott, Foresman, 1984), Chap. 5.

19. Neil C. Macrae, Kimberly A. Quinn, Malia F. Mason, and Susanne Quadflieg, "Understanding Others: The Face and Person Construal," *Journal of Personality and Social Psychology*, vol. 89 (2005), pp. 686–695; Blair, I. V. (2002). "The malleability of automatic stereotypes and prejudice." *Personality and Social Psychology Review*, vol. 6 (2002), pp. 242–261.

20. V. Bruce and A. W. Young, *In the Eye of the Beholder: The Science of Face Perception.* (Oxford, England: Oxford University Press, 1998), p. 1.

21. John T. Malloy, *Dress for Success* (New York: Warner Books, 1975).

22. Gerald H. Graham, Jeanne Unruh, and Paul Jennings, "The Impact of Nonverbal Communication in Organizations: A Survey of Perceptions," *Journal of Business Communication*, vol. 28 (Winter 1991), pp. 45–62.

23. Aaron Abbott and Adam Davis, "Pre-Trial Assessments Make Witness Testimony Pay Off," *Risk Management*, vol. 36 (June 1989), pp. 22–29.

24. Everett Rogers and Rekha Agarwala-Rogers, *"Communication in Organizations"* (New York: Free Press, 1976), p. 93.

25. Carol Hymowitz, "Sometimes, Moving Up Makes it Harder to See What Goes on Below," *The Wall Street Journal*, 15 October 2007, B1.

26. Olof Holm, "Communication Processes in Critical Systems: Dialogues Concerning Communications," *Marketing Intelligence & Planning*, vol. 24 (2006), pp. 493–504.

27. Ali D. Akkirman and Drew L. Harris, "Organizational Communication Satisfaction in the Virtual Workplace," *Journal of Management Development*, vol. 24 (no. 5, 2005), pp. 397–409

28. Harold Sutton and Lyman W. Porter, "A Study of the Grapevine in a Governmental Organization," *Personnel Psychology*, vol. 21 (1968), pp. 223-230.

29. Alan Wilkins, "The Culture Audit: A Tool for understanding Organizations," *Organizational Dynamics*, vol. 12, no. 2 (Autumn 1983), pp. 24–38.

30. Folsom, W. Davis, "Deciphering Business Jargon," *Business & Economic Review*, vol. 52 (no. 3, 2006), pp. 11–14.

31. Jose R. Goris, John D. Pettit Jr., and Bobby C. Vaught, "Organizational Communication: Is it a Moderator of the Relationship Between Job Congruence and Job Performance/Satisfaction?" *International Journal of Management*, vol. 19 (Dec 2002), pp. 664–672.

Human Resource Management

EVALUATING PERFORMANCE

Performance evaluation programs represent a significant application of motivation theory. Performance feedback, plus the evaluation process itself, contain elements of both positive and negative reinforcement. How well people perform is largely determined by whether their performance is evaluated and rewarded.

Multidimensionality of Performance

What are the behavioral requirements of effective organizations and how do organizations want their members to behave? Effective organizations require three basic types of behavior:

1. **Attracting and retaining people.** The first requirement of every organization is to attract people and persuade them to stay for at least a reasonable period of time. Every organization (other than the military when the draft is in effect) depends on its ability to attract members: the failure to attract a sufficient number of new members could prevent it from functioning effectively and could even cause it to die. High turnover and absenteeism are very costly, and as a general rule, organizations that are more successful in attracting and retaining people are more effective.
2. **Dependable role performance.** Members are assigned to perform their individual roles; they are expected to know their responsibilities and achieve minimal levels of quantity and quality performance. Organizations are more effective when workers are motivated to do their jobs well.
3. **Extra-role behaviors.** In addition to the formal task requirements, many other behaviors profoundly influence the effectiveness of an organization. These **extra-role behaviors** are also called **spontaneous and innovative behaviors**, or **above and beyond behaviors**, because they are in addition to the formal task requirements. Since an organization cannot foresee all contingencies in its operations, its effectiveness is influenced by the willingness of its employees to perform spontaneous and innovative behaviors as the need arises. Some of the most important extra-role behaviors include these:

   - **Cooperation**: assisting coworkers and helping them achieve the organization's goals;
   - **Protective acts**: safeguarding the organization by removing hazards or eliminating threats;
   - **Constructive ideas**: contributing creative ideas to improve the organization;
   - **Self-training**: improving one's skills to fill the organization's ever-present need for better-trained workers;
   - **Favorable attitudes**: expressing positive comments about the organization to other employees, customers, and the public, thus facilitating recruitment, retention, and sales.

Extra-role behaviors are voluntary actions that benevolent employees choose to perform, similar to altruism and organizational citizenship behaviors. The important insight to remember here is that performance evaluation should include more than a simple assessment of quantity and quality; there are other important behaviors that contribute to organizational success.

Role of Performance Evaluation

Why should companies evaluate the performance of their employees? Many organizations, especially smaller ones, do not have formal evaluation programs because they do not see a need for them. How-

---

Dependable role performance
The requirement that employees do their assigned jobs dependably in terms of acceptable quantity and quality performance.

Extra-role behaviors
Behaviors that are important for organizational effectiveness but are not typically considered part of an employee's formal job description, such as performing cooperative acts, making creative suggestions, and protecting the company.

ever, performance evaluation programs serve at least five important organizational functions regardless of size.

1. **To reward and recognize performance**. Performance data allows high performers to be rewarded and recognized. With merit pay programs, for example, increases in pay are tied to performance levels. Without performance data, everyone has to be rewarded equally, or rewards must be distributed subjectively—conditions that are perceived as inequitable by the recipients. Performance appraisals also provide intrinsic rewards, since outstanding performers receive positive recognition for their efforts.

2. **To guide personnel actions such as hiring, firing, and promoting**. Performance information is necessary for making rational decisions about whom to promote or terminate. When this information is not available, personnel decisions are made by subjective impressions. It is better to make careful, defensible decisions based on good performance data. Organizations that fail to have a formal evaluation program are vulnerable to costly legal challenges, because without accurate performance data, they cannot show that their personnel decisions are free from illegal discrimination on the basis of race, religion, sex, national origin, or age.

3. **To provide individuals with information for their own personal development**. Individuals need performance feedback to help them improve; accurate and timely feedback facilitates the learning of new behavior. Furthermore, most people want to know how well they are doing and where they need to improve.

4. **To identify training needs for the organization**. A well-designed performance evaluation system identifies who could benefit from training, and what abilities and skills are needed for each job.

5. **To integrate human resource planning and coordinate other personnel functions**. The information obtained from a performance evaluation is essential for individual career planning and for organizational staffing. Performance information is used to identify high potential people, who are known as "fast-track" employees. It is also used in succession planning to identify the kinds of developmental experiences employees need for advancement.

Criticisms of Performance Evaluation

In spite of its importance, the evaluation process has been severely criticized. Many people, especially low performers and people who dislike work, simply dislike being evaluated. They are opposed to having anyone evaluate their performance because they are threatened by it.

The process of evaluating performance can also be intimidating to supervisors. Some supervisors do not like to evaluate their subordinates, and they feel threatened by having to justify their evaluations. These supervisors argue that having to evaluate subordinates creates role conflict by forcing them to be a judge, coach, and friend at the same time. Many supervisors do not have adequate interpersonal skills to handle evaluation interviews. Nevertheless, evaluating the performance of subordinates is a basic supervisory responsibility, and a supervisor who lacks the skills to provide performance feedback simply cannot be a good supervisor.

On some jobs, performance is difficult to define, especially jobs that do not produce a physical product. Managers provide leadership, engineers create new ideas, and trainers present information, but these "products" cannot be meaningfully counted. So how do we know what to measure?

While some people argue that intangible products such as new ideas, leadership, and training cannot be reliably measured, in reality everything can be measured even if it is only by a subjective rating scale. If an evaluator has an opinion about an employee's performance, this attitude can be evaluated like any other attitude, regardless of how subjective it is.

Organizations need to make certain that these subjective judgments are job-related, however. Because subjective evaluations can give rise to discrimination against protected groups, the federal courts have not been willing to accept evaluation procedures that allow "unfettered subjective judgments." In some instances, organizations have been required by the courts to establish objective guidelines for evaluation, promotion, and transfer.[1]

1. Halo Effect: Sometimes one characteristic about a person, positive or negative, strongly influences all other attitudes about that person.
2. Leniency-Strictness Effect: Some evaluators give mostly favorable ratings, while other evaluators evaluate the same performance more unfavorably.
3. Central Tendency Effect: Some evaluators give average ratings to everyone to avoid sticking their necks out to identify marginal or outstanding performance.
4. Interrater Reliability: Two evaluators seeing the same behavior may disagree and give different ratings.
5. Contrast Effect: The evaluation of one employee's performance may be influenced by the relative performance of the preceding individual.
6. Zero-Sum Problem: Some appraisal systems require supervisors to balance high ratings given to some employees with low ratings given to others.
7. Numbers Fetish: An excessive focus is sometimes placed on numbers, which may be treated as though they possess unquestioned accuracy.
8. Recency Effect: Recent events are unduly reflected in the appraisal, to the exclusion of events earlier in the year.

Exhibit 12.1   Criticisms of Performance Appraisals

Evaluating performance and assigning a number to represent it often create feelings of anxiety in both the evaluator and the person being evaluated. Eight of the most frequent criticisms of performance evaluation are described in Exhibit 12.1. Although these criticisms represent legitimate problems, they should be treated as problems to resolve rather than insurmountable obstacles.

Performance Evaluation Methods

Performance evaluations occur whether or not a formal evaluation program exists. The demands to hire, fire, promote, and compensate necessitate some form of evaluation. Supervisors have always evaluated their subordinates and formed impressions about each employee's work, and these informal, subjective evaluations have influenced personnel decisions just as much as formal written evaluations. The advantage of an informal system is that it is easier to design and administer; the advantage of a formal program is that it is more unbiased, defensible, and open to inspection.

The evaluation should focus on relevant behaviors that matter to the organization. The popular proverb "what you evaluate is what you get" emphasizes the importance of evaluating behaviors that are essential to organizational effectiveness.

Example—

The importance of evaluating relevant behaviors was illustrated by the experience of a military officer who included "orderliness" as one of the criteria for evaluating a unit of clerk-typists. The officers who conducted the evaluation defined orderliness in terms of how clear and uncluttered the clerk-typists kept their desks. The clerk-typists responded by removing everything from the tops of their desks and keeping it in their desk drawers. Although the procedure was inefficient and the volume of work dramatically declined, the clerk-typists obtained high performance evaluations.[2]

Deciding what to evaluate is in part a value judgment; the personal values of those who design the evaluation system will be reflected in it. In deciding what to evaluate, an important issue is whether the evaluation should focus on outcomes (results) or behaviors (activities). For example, the performance evaluation of a salesclerk could focus on the number of products sold per hour or it could focus on the behaviors required to produce the sale, such as describing the product, arranging for financing, and making repeat calls. When asked, most people say outcomes are more important to measure than behaviors; they are primarily interested in measuring results. However, most performance evaluations focus more on behaviors than on results, especially when evaluating managers and supervisors.

The major advantage of focusing on outcomes is that attention is directed toward producing specific results. The primary objective of all employees should be to produce results, not behaviors. Unfortunately, some employees perform many of the right behaviors and still fail to produce results.

Example—

Doing the right behaviors and not achieving the outcome can be illustrated by examining the behaviors of a student writing a research paper. The right behaviors include finding references, reading articles, making notes, and studying the materials. A student can perform all these activities very well and still fail to get the paper written.

A potential problem with exclusively evaluating outcomes is that results can sometimes be achieved by unethical or undesirable means. By exerting excessive pressure on subordinates, supervisors can increase performance, but over time, excessive pressure leads to turnover, dissatisfaction, and unethical conduct. In managing people, the way it is done (behaviors) is just as important as the result (outcomes).

Good performance evaluation programs depend more on the competence of the evaluator than on the specific evaluation technique. Nevertheless, some appraisal techniques are considerably better than others, depending on the purpose of the evaluation and the nature of the work being done. The primary techniques include ranking procedures, classification procedures, graphic rating scales, behaviorally anchored rating scales, and descriptive essays.

Ranking Procedures

The objective of a **ranking procedure** is to order a group of employees from highest to lowest along some performance dimension, usually overall performance. Ranking is frequently used when making promotion decisions and occasionally used when making compensation decisions, to decide which employees should get the largest financial bonuses. However, ranking is not helpful for providing personal feedback.

Classification Procedures

Classification procedures simply assign individuals to one of several categories based on their overall performance. Many evaluation systems classify employees as "greatly exceeds expectations," "exceeds expectations," "meets expectations," "below expectations," and "fails to meet expectations." Other labels are also used, such as "superior," "outstanding," "excellent," "average," "fair," and "poor."

Graphic Rating Scales

Graphic rating scales are the most frequently used method of evaluating performance for non-managerial workers. Some of the most popular characteristics measured by graphic rating scales include quantity of work, quality of work, cooperativeness, job knowledge, dependability, initiative, creativity, and overall performance. The scales used to measure these characteristics are typically seven or ten point scales that

---

Ranking procedures
Arranging employees along a scale from best to lowest performer.

Classification procedures
Classifying employees into set categories, such as "outstanding," "excellent," "good," "average," "fair," and "poor."

Graphic rating scales
A performance evaluation method that identifies various job dimensions and contains scales that are used to rate each employee on each dimension.

are described by such words as *high* versus *low*, or *exceeds job requirements* versus *needs improvement*, as shown in Exhibit 12.2. The accuracy of graphic rating scales and their freedom from bias and subjectivity improve as the points along the scale are more accurately described in behavioral terms. Ideally, each point along the scale should be defined by a specific behavioral description.

Name of Employee _____ Job Title _____

Department _____

Rated By _____

Date _____

Instructions: Rate this employee on the basis of the actual work he or she is now doing. Read the definitions very carefully. Compare this employee with others in the same occupation in this company or elsewhere. In the space before each number, rate the employee according to the following scale.

1	2	3	4	5	6	7	8	9
Fair				Average				Excellent

[ ] 1. Quantity of Work: How does the quantity of this employees work compare with what you expect? Is this employee energetic and industrious, or does he or she waste time?

[ ] 2. Quality of Work: How does the quality of this employee's work compare with what you expect? Consider the degree of completeness and the number of errors and mistakes.

[ ] 3. Dependability and Responsibility: Habits of punctuality and attendance. Can this employee be trusted to complete work with a minimum of supervision?

[ ] 4. Initiative, resourcefulness, and leadership: Consider the employee's ability to proceed without supervision and achieve results without being told. How does this employee affect the output of coworkers? Does he or she have the ability to direct and train others, and utilize company resources and properties effectively?

[ ] 5. Judgment: Does the employee impress you as a person whose judgment would be dependable, even under stress? Is the employee likely to be excitable or hasty when making decisions in an emergency? Are decisions objective and rational, or swayed by feelings and the opinions of others?

[ ] 6. Ability, training, skill, and experience: Does the employee have sufficient job knowledge to perform satisfactorily? Does the employee need additional training on the job?

[ ] 7. Personal appearance and speech: Does the employee make a good first impression? Is the employee well-groomed, or slovenly? Does the employee have a pleasant speaking voice? Does he or she express thoughts and ideas well?

Exhibit 12.2   Illustration of a Graphic Rating Scale

<u>Cooperation and dependability</u> refer to spontaneous and innovative behaviors beyond the formal job description that contribute significantly to the effectiveness of the company, e.g., dependability, willingness to accept assignments, cooperation in working with others, initiative in seeing what needs to be done and doing it willingly.

Excellent attitude	7	Positive and enthusiastic approach to work. Always pleasant, helpful, and cooperative. A self-starter. Strives to further the company's interests.
Good attitude	6	Excellent and enthusiastic worker, willing to do more than expected. Always pleasant and cooperative unless criticized or mistreated.
Slightly good attitude	5	Performs assigned work, but seldom goes beyond the normal job expectations.
Average attitude	4	Adequate worker, but occasionally allows personal problems to influence work much of the day.
Slightly poor attitude	3	Sometimes resistive; expresses a dislike for being asked to assist others.
Poor attitude	2	Openly resistive; may even resist performing tasks that are part of the normal job. Argumentative and sometimes nasty to coworkers.
Very poor attitude	1	Occasionally acts belligerently or hostile to supervisors

Exhibit 12.3   Illustration of a Behaviorally-Anchored Rating Scale

Behaviorally Anchored Rating Scales

When the points along a graphic rating scale are clearly defined by specific behavioral descriptions, as shown in Exhibit 12.3, these scales are called **behaviorally anchored rating scales** (BARS). Research indicates that these scales are superior to regular graphic rating scales because they are more reliable, less ambiguous, and less biased; furthermore, they are more accurate measures of performance and provide better feedback to employees.[3] The disadvantage of using behaviorally anchored rating scales is that they require more time and effort to develop.

Descriptive Essays

Some performance evaluation forms simply provide a blank space for the evaluator to write a **descriptive essay** summarizing the employee's performance. New and inexperienced evaluators find this procedure extremely challenging and unpleasant; however, experienced evaluators use it quite effectively. The essay description typically identifies the employee's job responsibilities on one side of the page, and the other side of the page contains a description of how well these duties have been performed. If they wish, evaluators are free to construct and use their own scales to facilitate their essay descriptions. One of the major benefits of a descriptive essay procedure is that it provides valuable feedback to help employees improve their performance. The major disadvantage is that the information cannot be used readily to make comparisons among employees.

Behaviorally anchored rating scales
A performance evaluation method that uses scales that are anchored by observable behavior to reduce the subjectivity and bias associated with ordinary graphic rating scales.

Descriptive essays
A method of evaluating employee performance that requires evaluators to write free-form essays describing the employee's performance.

Results-Oriented Appraisals

Many organizations emphasize individual accountability through a results-oriented approach to performance evaluation. Less emphasis is placed on the activities employees perform and more emphasis is placed on the results they are expected to produce. Many labels have been attached to these results-oriented evaluations. The most popular label is **management by objectives (MBO)**.

Peter Drucker is credited with first publicizing MBO in his 1954 book *The Practice of Management*.[4] Drucker noted the advantages of managing people by "objectives" rather than by "drives." The advantages are that each manager from the highest level to the lowest level has clear objectives that reflect and support the objectives of the organization. All managers participate in the goal-setting process and then exercise self-control over their own performance; that is, they monitor their own performance and take corrective actions as necessary. To do this, their performance is measured and compared with their objectives. The measurements do not need to be rigidly quantitative or exact, but they must be clear and rational.

MBO is primarily a philosophy of management that reflects a positive, proactive way of managing, rather than a reactive way. The focus is on (1) predicting and shaping the future of the organization by developing long-range organizational objectives and strategic plans, (2) accomplishing results rather than performing activities, (3) improving both individual competence and organizational effectiveness, and (4) increasing the participation and involvement of employees in the affairs of the organization.

MBO is also a process consisting of a series of integrated management functions: (1) the development of clear, precise organizational objectives, (2) the formulation of coordinated individual objectives designed to achieve the overall organizational objectives, (3) the systematic measurement and review of performance, (4) the use of corrective action as needed to achieve the planned objectives.

MBO programs are typically implemented in three phases. The first phase focuses on evaluating managers by having them identify measurable objectives and recording how well they have achieved them at the end of a period. In phase two, MBO programs are integrated into an organization's planning and control processes so that the objectives are coordinated with the strategy and objectives of the company. Phase three fully integrates the MBO system with other organizational functions, including the development of strategic plans, budgeting and financial planning, staffing, performance evaluations, compensation, human resource development, and management training. This integration is achieved by emphasizing teamwork and flexibility during the goal-setting process, and by emphasizing individual growth and development during the performance review process.

EVALUATION PROCESS

Performance evaluations provide an excellent opportunity for supervisors to coach and mentor subordinates, regardless of the evaluation method that is used. Effective performance reviews can significantly improve employee performance and contribute greatly to their career development. Most supervisors and subordinates fail to see this as an opportunity for personal development. Good performance reviews should consist of a combination of goal setting, performance feedback, and recognition for their accomplishments.

Goal Setting

Goal setting is an important element in the evaluation process; effective supervisors help their team members set specific and measurable goals and then follow up by providing useful feedback. Individuals

---

Management by objectives (MBO)
A philosophy of management that reflects a positive, proactive way of managing. MBO requires all employees to establish written, measurable objectives that can later be used to evaluate performance.

perform significantly better when they are attempting to achieve a specific goal, such as to complete a project before noon, increase productivity by 5 percent, work for the next hour without making a mistake, maintain 100 percent attendance, or get a research paper submitted on time.

Goal Setting Theory

In 1968 Edwin A. Locke first presented a theory of goal setting and a series of studies showing the effects of goal setting on performance. Continuing research in both laboratory and field studies supports Locke's theory and shows that goal setting has a powerful impact on motivation.[5] Reinforcement theory explains why goal setting has such a powerful influence on behavior.

Some of the earliest work on goal setting was performed by Frederick W. Taylor (1856–1915) in his work on scientific management. Taylor attempted to identify appropriate goals for workers, which he called standards, using time and motion studies and a careful task analysis. Taylor's work focused on teaching workers the ideal ways to perform their tasks using the appropriate physical motions, pacing, and tools.

The basic elements of goal setting theory are illustrated in Exhibit 12.4. The goals we seek are determined by our values. After examining our present circumstances, we compare our actual conditions with our desired conditions. If we are achieving success, we feel satisfied and continue on the same course. But if there is a discrepancy, we go through a goal setting process.

Example—

Students go through the goal-setting model frequently during their educational program. Based on their personal values, students have an idea of what they want, such as graduating from college, going on to graduate school, or securing an attractive job. As they assess their present conditions, however, they often discover that their test scores are low, their class attendance is down, and their term papers are behind schedule. These discrepancies between their desired and actual conditions frequently cause students to initiate a goal setting process. They establish such goals as raising their next test score from a C+ to an A–, attending every lecture, and having a first draft of that term paper written within the next two weeks.

The process that is used to set goals seems to matter greatly in the success of a goal setting program. Supervisors need to carefully consider the maturity of their subordinates and their commitment to the organization when working with them in a goal setting program. Goal setting occurs in three ways.

- **Participative goals** allow employees to participate in the process of setting goals by providing information and contributing to the goal selection. If they believe the goals are too high or too low, they can express their opinions and try to influence the goal statements.
- **Assigned goals** are determined by management and simply assigned to the employees. In scientific management, the standards of performance are determined by industrial engineers with almost no input from the employees.

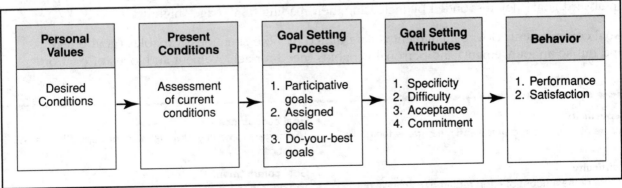

Exhibit 12.4   Goal-Setting Model

- **Do-your-best-goals** allow employees to control their own goals; management simply asks the employees to do their best, without getting involved in approving or vetoing their goals.

Applying Goal Setting Theory

The effects of goal setting on behavior are influenced by four major goal setting attributes: goal specificity, goal difficulty, goal acceptance, and goal commitment.

- **Goal specificity.** When employees are working toward specific goals, they consistently perform better than when they are simply told to do their best, or are given no instructions at all. Since do-your-best goals are only loose guidelines, they have about the same effect on performance as no goals at all. A review by Locke and his associates of field experiments using a wide variety of jobs found that 99 out of the 110 studies they reviewed concluded that specific goals led to better performance than vague goals.[6]

- **Goal difficulty.** Studies on the effects of goal difficulty have found a direct linear relationship between goal difficulty and task performance: higher goals lead to higher performance. These studies investigated a wide variety of jobs with participants ranging in age from four years to adulthood. Similar results have been observed for brief one-time tasks lasting as little as one minute, and for ongoing tasks lasting as long as seven years.[7] However, the goals should not be unreasonably difficult. When a goal is perceived as so difficult that it is virtually impossible to attain, the result is often frustration rather than achievement, and performance may be only slightly better than it would have been with no goals at all. Dreaming the impossible dream does not improve performance as much as a difficult but realistic goal. Research on the achievement motive proposed that the probability of success was one minus the probability of failure. Therefore, the optimum levels of motivation occurred when the probability of success (.5) was equal to the probability of failure (.5). Since effort is the product of the probability of success times the probability of failure, other combinations of probabilities produce lower numbers (e.g. $.3 \times .7 = .21$, which is less than $.5 \times .5 = .25$). Therefore, to obtain high performance levels, goals should be difficult and challenging, but the difficulty should not be so great that individuals believe their chances of succeeding are less than 50/50.

- **Goal acceptance.** Goal acceptance refers to the degree to which individuals accept the goal as a reasonable target to work toward. Goals are typically resisted or ignored when they are too difficult and out of reach. They can also be rejected for a variety of other reasons, such as when the employees distrust management, when they feel they are being exploited by the organization, when the goals are not fair and consistent, or when the activity is meaningless and irrelevant. Unrealistically high goals are not always entirely rejected. There is some indication that unreachable goals are reinterpreted by employees rather than rejected altogether.[8]

Example—

Employees in a training program who had been reading about 20 pages each night were told that they were expected to be reading at least 100 pages nightly. Although they considered 100 pages an absurd goal, they responded by increasing their reading to 30 pages nightly.

- **Goal commitment.** Goal commitment is determined by both situational variables (goal origin and public announcement) and personal variables (need for achievement and locus of control).

Goal specificity
A measure of how clearly defined and measurable the goals are.

Goal difficulty
A measure of the amount of effort required to achieve the goal.

Goal acceptance
The degree to which individuals accept a specific goal as a realistic target.

Goal commitment
The degree to which individuals are dedicated to reach the goals they have adopted.

Individuals need to feel that the goal belongs to them: "This is my goal." The evidence suggests that commitment to difficult goals is higher when (1) goals are self-set rather than assigned, (2) goals are made public rather than private, (3) the person has an internal locus of control, and (4) the person has a high need for achievement.[9] High levels of goal commitment can also be expected regarding goals associated with one's self-esteem. To the extent that individuals become ego-invested in achieving a goal, their level of goal commitment can be expected to be very high.

Performance Feedback

The importance of performance feedback is emphasized in learning theory. Operant conditioning explains that feedback is essential for acquiring new responses and that learning cannot occur without timely feedback. Feedback is also central to goal setting theory, since goals are meaningless when feedback is absent. There is no uncertainty about the importance of feedback, but there are questions about the most helpful way to give it.

Some recommendations for giving feedback are inconsistent with empirical research. For example, learning theory recommends that feedback occur immediately after the response for optimal learning. However, supervisors are cautioned to postpone telling employees what they did wrong until they can do so privately, to avoid public humiliation. Another popular recommendation is that supervisors should limit their feedback to positive comments and avoid criticism. Studies on discipline have shown, however, that criticism is useful and even necessary to improve performance.[10] The interesting paradox regarding criticism is that those who need it most are usually the most threatened by it and the least capable of benefiting from it. Research on the effects of performance feedback has produced these conclusions:

1. Supervisors give subordinates feedback more often after instances of good performance than after instances of poor performance. People dislike being criticized, and negative feedback creates an uncomfortable discussion. Consequently, many supervisors avoid giving negative feedback.[11]

2. When they are compelled to give negative feedback, supervisors tend to distort the feedback to make it less negative or convey the feedback in very specific terms in order to convince the subordinate that the evaluation was not biased.[12] While distorting the feedback is dysfunctional, giving specific comments is generally beneficial and helps the recipient know how to improve.

3. Supervisors are traditionally told that discussions about performance levels and pay increases should be separate. Research does not support this advice, however. Discussions about pay increases represent a significant form of feedback that clarifies and reinforces other comments about performance. Therefore, performance reviews should include information about the recommended pay increase that accompanies a given performance level.[13]

4. Feedback tends to improve performance to the extent that it indicates that prior performance levels are inadequate for reaching the goal. Therefore, negative feedback that implicitly calls for greater effort tends to improve performance more than positive feedback that endorses current performance levels does.[14]

5. Individuals who have high self-efficacy and self-esteem can respond more adaptively to criticism than can individuals who have low self-efficacy and self-esteem. People with high self-efficacy and high self-esteem are likely to use the feedback to diagnose their performance and make adaptive changes, while people who are low in these traits are inclined to coast or quit.[15]

Performance interviews are usually uncomfortable experiences for both supervisors and subordinates, but they are also significant events that have an enormous impact on employee motivation, personal development, and job satisfaction. Good performance reviews require good interpersonal skills, accurate performance information, and careful preparation. The feedback is most helpful when supervisors describe behavior in a way that is direct, specific, and nonpunishing.

Who Should Evaluate Performance?

In most instances, the immediate superior should be responsible for evaluating an employee's performance, although information can also be obtained from subordinates, peers, clients, and customers. When data come from all of these sources, the appraisal is referred to as a **360 degree appraisal**. As a general rule, performance appraisals are most accurate and useful when the evaluations come from sources closest to the person being rated.[16]

Supervisors

The hierarchical arrangement of formal authority gives supervisors the legitimate responsibility to evaluate subordinates. Generally there is a shared expectation that supervisors have the right and the obligation to evaluate performance. To behave otherwise would seem unnatural and inappropriate. Furthermore, since supervisors administer the rewards and punishments, they should be responsible for evaluating performance.

Subordinates

Although evaluations of superiors by subordinates might seem backward, they can be useful in some circumstances. Subordinates are being asked frequently to evaluate corporate officers in what are sometimes called **upward appraisals** or **subordinate appraisals**, and this information may be used to decide pay increases and promotions. There are at least three good reasons for using subordinate appraisals: (1) subordinates possess unique information about superiors that ought to be included in the evaluation process, (2) feedback from subordinates provides a powerful impetus for change, and (3) evaluations by subordinates tend to equalize the power differentials in organizations and make the workplace more democratic and responsive to human needs. Power equalization improves the flow of communication.

Subordinate evaluations of superiors have certain limitations. Subordinates can only evaluate what they observe, and so they generally evaluate their superiors based on their interactions with them. This means that supervisors are primarily evaluated on the basis of interpersonal skills rather than on organizational effectiveness. Some administrative decisions are not popular, and a desire to please their subordinates could cause managers to make bad decisions. Subordinate evaluations also have the potential to undermine the legitimate authority of supervisors and reduce their organizational effectiveness. For a two-way evaluation process to function effectively, both supervisors and subordinates must have adequate maturity to make responsible evaluations and accept feedback from one another.

Peers

In some situations, the most knowledgeable and capable evaluators are an employee's peers. Coworkers are sometimes in a better position than supervisors to evaluate each other's performance. Research on peer evaluations has found them to predict success and correlate with both objective and subjective ratings of success in numerous situations. A review of many studies examining the use of peer ratings in the military found that peer ratings were more valid predictors of leadership performance than were ratings by superiors. Peer ratings also have yielded good reliability and validity.[17] The conditions required for good peer appraisals are:

- a high level of interpersonal trust;
- a noncompetitive reward system;
- opportunities for peers to observe each other's performances.

---

360 degree appraisals
A method of evaluating employees that involves gathering performance feedback from people above them, below them, and beside them on an organizational chart.

Subordinate appraisals
Evaluating the performance of supervisors and managers by asking subordinates to evaluate their supervisor's performance.

When these conditions do not exist, the usefulness of peer appraisals is severely restricted. Peer appraisals are most frequently used among professional and technical employees in organizations that meet these conditions. The use of peer appraisals has the potential to increase the interaction and coordination among peers.

Self

People are always evaluating themselves; the question is how formally and systematically these self-evaluations should be recorded and acted on. In recent years a decline in authoritarian leadership has contributed to an increase in self-evaluations in both large and small companies. Some of the arguments in favor of self-evaluation are that self-evaluation results in:

- more satisfying and constructive evaluation interviews;
- less defensiveness regarding the evaluation process;
- improved job performance through greater commitment to organizational goals.[18]

On the other hand, the arguments opposing self-evaluations center on the fact that low agreement usually exists between self and supervisory evaluations. Because of the systematic biases and distortions that can appear, self-evaluations must be used very carefully. Self-evaluations are very valuable for personal development and the identification of training needs, but they are not useful for evaluative purposes. Asking employees to evaluate themselves for purposes of promotions or pay increases is like asking students to grade themselves. It puts individuals in the awkward and uncomfortable situation of trying to guess how biased others will be in rating themselves.

Clients

As a general rule, everyone who can observe the behaviors or outcomes of an individual should be included in the evaluation process. According to this principle, there are occasions when clients and customers ought to be asked for their observations. This information could come from casual complaints or letters of appreciation, or companies could systematically survey their clients and consumers.

Performance Interviews

Performance evaluation interviews can be uncomfortable experiences for both supervisors and subordinates. Managers complain about the difficulties they encounter in the appraisal interview, such as explaining poor performance to marginal employees, providing feedback to poor performers who think they are doing a good job, and trying to find something fresh to say about an experienced employee's performance. They are especially threatening to insecure supervisors and new employees. Some supervisors tend to postpone an interview indefinitely, which means that the employees do not receive adequate feedback on their performance. If the interview is handled poorly, feelings of disappointment, anger, and resentment may result. Rather than increasing performance and improving personal development, poor evaluation interviews can destroy initiative, creating feelings of defeat and despair. The effectiveness of evaluation interviews will be enhanced if managers and subordinates follow some simple guidelines.

1. Evaluators should develop their own styles so they feel comfortable in an interview. If the evaluator feels uncomfortable, the employee being evaluated probably will feel uncomfortable too. An evaluator should not try to copy someone else or follow a rigid format if it does not feel comfortable and natural.
2. Both parties should prepare for the interview beforehand. Employees should review their performance and document how well they have done. Evaluators should gather relevant information and compare it against the objectives for the period. Lack of preparation for the interview by either party is an obvious indication of lack of interest.

3. The evaluator should begin by clarifying the purpose of the interview. The employee should know whether it is a disciplinary session, a **contributions appraisal** (which focuses on employee results), or a **personal development appraisal**. In particular, the employee should understand the possible consequences of the interview so that he or she can prepare appropriate responses. For example, an employee's responses during a contributions appraisal can appropriately be a bit guarded and defensive, but in a personal development appraisal, such responses would greatly reduce the effectiveness of the interview.

4. Neither party should dominate the discussion. The supervisor should take the lead in initiating the discussion, but the employee should be encouraged to express opinions. The supervisor should budget time so that the employee has approximately half the time to discuss the evaluation.

5. The most popular format for the interview is the "sandwich" format—like bologna between two slices of buttered bread, criticism is sandwiched between compliments. The rationale for the **sandwich interview** format is that positive comments made at the beginning and end of the interview are intended to create a positive experience. The opening compliments should put the employee at ease and the closing compliments should leave the employee feeling good about the interview, and motivated to do better. However, most employees dislike the sandwich-interview format and report that it makes them feel manipulated.

6. An alternative format is to identify and discuss problems, then talk about future improvements, and finally express appreciation for good behaviors. This approach is very direct and to the point. The supervisor begins by saying, "There are problems I'd like to talk with you about:_____, _____, and _____." Each problem is briefly identified at the beginning before the supervisor discusses the problems in detail. An employee immediately knows what the "charges" are and does not sit in uncertainty waiting for the next bomb to fall. After the problems have been discussed by both supervisor and subordinate, the discussion focuses on accomplishments for which the employee deserves recognition. The supervisor should describe specific actions that deserve recognition, and be as complimentary as the behavior merits. The interview should not end until the supervisor and subordinate have discussed plans for future performance. Future goals and objectives should be clarified, and plans for improvement should be discussed.

Employees should be encouraged to take an active role in the performance-evaluation process. Most employees wait until their supervisor initiates action and schedules an interview. Then they sit through the interview feeling as though they are being "chewed out," manipulated, or "run over." Instead, employees should take an active role by anticipating their evaluations, collecting data about their performance, scheduling interviews with their supervisor, taking the lead in interviews to discuss their strengths and weaknesses, and asking for feedback. An active role makes the evaluation process a dramatically different experience for subordinates. Rather than dreading the interviews, subordinates consciously plan for them and anticipate the experience.[19]

The evaluation interview should focus on behaviors and results rather than on personality factors. Performance feedback helps employees achieve better results, while discussions about personality characteristics are usually dysfunctional. Because personality factors are poorly defined, discussing them usually creates unnecessary conflict. Personality changes are difficult to achieve and are usually not necessary anyway. When supervisors think a personality change is needed, what they are actually concerned about are the behaviors caused by the personality. To correct such problems, the supervisor should describe the improper *behaviors* and help the employee change his or her *behavior*. If a personality

---

Contributions appraisal
A performance appraisal that focuses on what the person has contributed to the organization. This information is used for deciding pay increases and promotions.

Personal development appraisal
A performance evaluation that focuses on helping employees develop their skills and abilities and involves a collaborative discussion.

Sandwich interview
A format for a performance evaluation interview in which negative comments are sandwiched between positive comments at the beginning and end of the interview.

change is indeed required, feedback about the specific behavior that needs to be changed is still the best approach to changing personality.

Some have suggested that appraisal interviews should include only the outstanding and poor performers, while the middle group should be excluded. Not only are the ones in the middle more difficult to evaluate, but it appears that telling people they are average is dysfunctional. Most people resent being labeled as average when they think they are members of an above-average group. Employees report a significant drop in organizational commitment when they are told that their performance is satisfactory, but below average. This suggestion, however, overlooks the important role that performance evaluations ought to play in improving performance. Supervisors should be actively involved in coaching and mentoring all employees by helping them set personal goals and advance their careers.

REWARDING PERFORMANCE

Compensation systems are an important element in organizational strategy because pay has such an enormous influence on job satisfaction, productivity, and labor turnover. Compensation also has an enormous impact on all human resource functions, especially staffing, performance evaluation, training and development, and employee relations. Consequently, compensation decisions are very important to both people and organizations.

All employers have similar compensation objectives: to attract qualified employees, to retain them, and to motivate them to perform their duties in the most effective manner. Employers want their employees to feel financially secure; but they also want them to be highly motivated. To achieve security they must provide a predictable monthly income, regardless of performance; to motivate their employees they must tie pay levels to performance. Employees are more highly motivated if at least some of their pay depends on their performance. Obviously, these two objectives are inconsistent. Achieving an appropriate balance between security and motivation, called **fine tuning**, requires an appropriate balance between base pay and incentives.

Base Pay

Employees deserve to be paid an amount that is considered just and fair. An ethical principle regarding compensation, called a **compensation maxim**, is that *employees should be compensated first according to the requirements of the jobs they perform and how well they perform them, and second by labor market conditions (supply and demand) and the organization's ability to pay.* Ethical issues concerning compensation are especially sensitive because money is such an important reason why people work. People expect to be treated fairly, and our concept of fairness is greatly influenced by such issues as why managers deserve more than laborers, why older workers should be paid more than younger workers, and whether people who need more should get more.

Example—

Although most people agree that managers deserve more than laborers, there is a growing concern that the enormous pay of chief executive officers cannot be morally justified. Fifty years ago, the average CEO received about thirty times as much as the average worker and now the multiple is about 450:1. Can their compensation be justified by the contribution they make or a scarcity of executive talent in the labor force? Most people think CEO pay is exorbitant, including many corporate board members who are trying to do a better job of tying pay to performance.

Compensation maxim
An ethical principle regarding compensation that can be examined to determine whether it is morally right or wrong.

The development of a sound wage-and-salary system involves three basic decisions. Each decision answers a critical question regarding an organization's compensation program.

Wage-Level Decision

The first decision concerns the overall level of an organization's compensation. It answers this question: How much money do members of this organization receive relative to people in other organizations who perform similar work? This decision reflects the values of the leaders of a company, and expresses their desire to be wage leaders, to be wage followers, or to pay the going market rate. In a firm that has an average profit picture for its industry, the most compelling definition of an equitable wage is usually the "going market wage," as determined by a wage survey. Both employees and managers are inclined to accept such a wage level as equitable. The primary instruments for making wage-level decisions are wage surveys conducted by the Bureau of Labor Statistics, surveys conducted by professional organizations, and surveys conducted by individual companies. Wage surveys report data regarding wages and benefits for jobs in various industries and geographic areas.

Wage-Structure Decision

The second decision concerns the relative pay of different jobs in an organization: how much money is paid for one job, relative to other jobs in the same company? People typically receive more pay if their job requires greater skill, effort, and responsibility. Companies generally use either a classification system or the point method to make decisions about the wage structure. **Classification systems** classify jobs, from simple to complex, by describing different levels of skill, effort, and responsibility, and a pay range is associated with each classification. Classification systems are used extensively in public organizations, such as the GS system used by the United States government. The **point method** involves the evaluation of the job descriptions and the assignment of points to different degrees of skill, effort, and responsibility; the pay for each job is determined by how many points it receives. The point method is very useful for determining and defending the base pay assigned to jobs that may be very different.

Individual-Wage Decision

The third decision concerns individual pay rates and incentives. It answers this question: How much money does one employee receive relative to others who perform similar work? As a general rule, employees receive more money if their performance increases or if they have been with the company longer. Companies use a variety of incentive systems to reward employees for their performance, including individual, group, and company-wide incentive systems.

These three wage decisions illustrate the kinds of wage comparisons employees make when they evaluate their wages.

Example—

Accountants in Company A compare their wages with the wages of accountants in other organizations, to see whether Company A has a higher or lower level of wages. The accountants also compare their wages with the pay of bookkeepers, computer programmers, and other members

Wage-level decision	Wage-structure decision	Individual-wage decision
How much does one company pay relative to other companies for the same jobs?	How much does one job pay relative to other jobs within the same company? How does a company justify paying some jobs more than others?	How much money should people who all perform the same job receive? What criteria, such as seniority and performance, should be used to pay one person more than another?

of Company A to learn whether the internal wage structure offers higher pay to jobs that involve more responsibility and greater difficulty. Finally, the accountants discuss their wages among themselves to determine whether each person's wage is the same, or whether differences in wages are related to productivity, seniority, education, or something else.

Financial Incentives

The effects of money on motivation depend primarily on whether pay is based on performance. Companies that use direct financial incentives, such as piece-rates or commission sales, discover that they have a greater impact on performance than any other variable. In spite of this relationship, however, it is surprising to observe how seldom pay is based on performance. For example, when employees are asked what would happen if they doubled their efforts and produced twice as much, very few say they would receive additional income. Some say their supervisors would recognize their efforts and commend them, and a few think they might eventually receive a pay increase. Most say that the consequences of doubling their effort would be negative: it would disrupt the flow of work, their coworkers would hassle them, and they would eventually be expected to work at that rate all the time without additional compensation.

Companies use a variety of incentive plans to motivate employees. Incentive compensation can be granted on the basis of individual performance, group performance, or company-wide performance.

Individual Incentives

The most popular forms of individual incentive pay include merit pay, piece-rate incentives, and commission sales. **Merit pay plans** are based on a subjective assessment of each employee's performance, and the merit pay is typically awarded by increasing base pay for the coming year. Merit pay increases are relevant to all jobs paid a fixed wage or salary. The most important requirement for an effective merit pay incentive program is the ability to measure performance against clearly defined objectives. To the extent that performance is more difficult to evaluate, the potential problems associated with tying pay to performance increase. For an effective merit pay plan to function smoothly, supervisors and managers must have the competence to evaluate employee performance and provide meaningful feedback. But even when performance can only be evaluated subjectively, most employees still believe that pay increases should be related to performance.[20]

The most direct relationship between pay and performance generally appears in the form of **piece-rate incentives**, where workers receive a specified amount of money for each unit of work. The effectiveness of piece-rate incentives has been studied for many years. Frederick W. Taylor recommended piece-rate incentives and defended them with research showing that workers paid on a piece-rate basis produced more work and earned more money. Taylor claimed that piece-rate incentive programs would increase productivity by at least 25 percent. Surveys of piece-rate plans over the past eighty years have suggested that Taylor underestimated the actual results. Most surveys have found that productivity under piece work has increased by 30 to 40 percent, and in some cases by greater than 60 percent.[21]

Although piece-work incentive systems predictably increase productivity, there is some question whether the increase is due to financial incentives alone or to other changes that accompany piece-work plans. Two variables that accompany piece-work programs are (1) changes in the design of the work and (2) higher performance goals. Before a piece-work plan is installed, a careful analysis of the job is usually conducted to ensure that it is being performed efficiently. A careful job analysis often identifies more efficient methods of performing the task. Moreover, when the task is being timed to establish pay rates,

Merit pay
Increases in an employee's basic wage level based on performance levels.

Piece-rate incentives
An incentive system that pays employees a specific amount of money for each unit of work they produce.

a goal-setting process occurs, followed by performance feedback. The question, then, is whether goal setting, measurement, and job redesign are more responsible than pay incentives for increasing productivity. Studies generally show that each factor alone has a positive influence on productivity, but that the impact is far greater when all three factors are present. Thus, incentive systems contribute to productivity increases because of improved work methods, higher performance goals with specific performance feedback, and monetary incentives that induce greater effort.[22]

An alternative to paying people for what they do is to pay them for what they are capable of doing. **Skill-based pay** encourages employees to acquire additional skills. Companies identify a list of valuable skills they would like to encourage their workers to acquire, and as the workers demonstrate mastery of each skill, they receive an increase in their base pay. Skill-based compensation plans reinforce employees for their growth and development and hopefully result in more creative ideas, organizational flexibility, and quality performance.

Another alternative, called **pay for knowledge**, provides incentives for employees to learn new information and demonstrate it by taking achievement tests. Specific dollar amounts are associated with each test, and employees receive an increase in their base pay after successfully passing each test. Pay for knowledge and skill-based pay systems are vital elements in the change strategies of organizations that experience rapid change and need to adapt to an uncertain environment.

Group Incentives and Bonuses

Although piece-work plans are typically based on individual performance, they can also be based on group production, with all members of the group sharing the money earned by the group. Group incentive plans have some important advantages over individual incentive plans, since they create greater cooperation among coworkers. This climate of cooperation usually reduces the need for direct supervision and control, since workers are supervised more by their coworkers than by their supervisors. In such a climate, slow workers are pressured by their coworkers to increase their productivity. Moreover, group incentives greatly facilitate the flow of work and flexibility in job assignments. When the normal work routine is disrupted because of unique problems such as illness or broken machines, individuals paid on a group incentive plan are willing to adapt to the problem and solve it themselves rather than complain to a manager or wait for the problem to solve itself.

Group incentives have certain limitations, however. When their jobs are independent, group members feel responsible only for their own jobs and think they should be paid individually. In this situation, group incentives provide little extra incentive to produce, since extra efforts by one worker will only result in a small increase in that worker's weekly pay. As the group gets larger, this problem becomes more severe. Thus, group incentives are most useful when jobs are interdependent, when the output of the group can be counted, and the group is small.

The powerful influence of group pressure explains why piece-rate incentives are sometimes not effective. Although many studies have shown that incentive pay systems increase productivity, other studies have found examples where groups restrict output to arbitrarily low levels. Group norms restricting productivity are very troublesome to managers, and they are particularly perplexing because they seem to be so irrational. Why should a group of workers collectively decide to restrict their productivity when they are paid only for what they produce? This behavior is not so irrational when it is examined from the workers' perspective. The problem centers on how the performance standards are established. Workers know that performance standards are somewhat arbitrary. They believe that if they consistently produce more than

---

Skill-based pay

A pay system in which an employee's pay level is partially determined by the employee's skills as a means of motivating them to acquire greater skills.

Pay for knowledge

A pay system in which an employee's pay level is determined in part by how many knowledge tests the employee has successfully completed.

the standard, the industrial engineer will return and retime the job; then they will be expected to produce more work for the same amount of pay.

Management has been guilty of retiming jobs often enough in some organizations to justify the workers' fears. Several interesting case studies have described the games played by workers and industrial engineers in setting performance standards. Since industrial engineers know that workers intentionally work slowly, they arbitrarily tighten the standards above the measured times. The workers know the industrial engineer suspects them of working slowly, so they add unnecessary and inefficient movements to look busy, which the industrial engineers expect and try to disregard.

Company-Wide Incentives

In some organizations, financial incentives are based on the performance of the entire organization. Three of the most popular forms of company-wide incentives include profit-sharing plans, Scanlon plans, and gainsharing.

Profit sharing is the most popular company-wide incentive, and in some companies the employees have been highly motivated to perform as a result of a generous profit-sharing plan. A typical **profit-sharing plan** distributes 25 percent of the pretax profit to the employees, according to an allocation formula that combines years of service and base wages. For example, in some plans, employees receive points for their base pay, such as one point for every $1000 of annual salary, and points for length of service, such as one point for every year of service. Profit-sharing money is then distributed to employees according to their percentage of the total points.

Profit-sharing plans can be either **cash plans** and **deferred plans**. Cash plans are more directly tied to performance because employees are paid annually. However, deferred plans are more popular because of tax considerations. Under a deferred plan, an employee's share of the profit is held in an individual account, where it grows without being taxed until it is received later, usually at retirement. Some deferred plans provide enormous wealth to their participants.

Profit-sharing plans generally reduce the conflict between managers and workers. Many companies claim that their plans have created a sense of partnership between employees and management, and have increased employee interest in the company. Profit-sharing plans typically increase productivity by increasing motivation; however, the impact of profit sharing is typically less than that for piece-rate plans, since each individual's profit share is not directly tied to individual productivity. Immediate rewards that are directly tied to specific individual behaviors are more effective than profit-sharing plans, especially for motivating employees who have short attention spans and cannot delay gratification. Deferred compensation plans, for example, are more effective for older workers than they are for younger workers, since retirement is not so distant.

Scanlon plans were named after their founder, Joseph Scanlon, an accountant and union steward in a steel mill. While negotiating a new labor agreement, Scanlon proposed that the percent of revenue allocated to labor costs be maintained at a fixed ratio of what it had been over the past few years. Scanlon believed that the employees would be highly motivated to increase their productivity if they knew that a fixed percent of the revenue would be paid in wages. Scanlon believed that significantly higher revenues could be obtained without an increase in the number of employee hours by motivating the employees

---

Profit-sharing plan
A program that allows employees to share in the profits of a company based on the profitability of the company and an allocation formula determining each employee's share.

Cash versus deferred plans
Profit sharing money can be distributed as cash at the end of each period or placed in a deferred fund that grows tax-free until retirement.

Scanlon plan
A company-wide incentive plan that distributes money to employees based on a fixed ratio of labor costs to revenue. As revenue increases through higher productivity and employee suggestions, the amount of money given to the employees increases proportional to the fixed ratio.

to work harder and submit suggestions of how to improve productivity. Since 1941, when Scanlon first proposed his idea, Scanlon plans have grown in popularity, and the results have shown that they tend to increase both company profits and employee wages.

Gainsharing is a company-wide incentive program similar to profit-sharing, but the bonuses are based on improved productivity rather than a percent of the profit. An effective gainsharing program requires managers to tie specific incentives to the strategic factors that determine a company's economic success, called **business drivers**. Some examples of business drivers are occupancy rates for hotels, turn-around time and vacant seats for airlines, and inventory shrinkage for retail companies. A successful gainsharing program at an oil refinery identified targeted goals for seven business drivers and promised to share the proceeds with the workers if they exceeded these goals. The goal for safety was an incident rate of 0.5, and for each accident that didn't happen the company would put $18,000 (the average cost of an accident) into the fund to be divided among employees. Gainsharing plans normally reward employees on a monthly or quarterly basis, depending on how productivity is measured, whereas profit-sharing is usually paid annually.

Bonuses

Executives and managers often participate in an additional bonus program designed specifically for them. The basic philosophy behind executive bonuses is to reward managers for good performance. When they are tied to the overall performance of a company, the bonuses are expected to create greater creativity and better cooperation among managers.

Executive bonuses are typically larger for upper-level managers than for middle-level managers, even when expressed as a percentage of salary. At upper levels of a company, a typical bonus might be 80 to 120 percent of salary. At lower levels of the company, supervisors typically receive bonuses that add only 15 to 40 percent of their salaries, if they receive bonuses at all.

The bonus plans of many companies are not carefully designed and administered. Although bonuses are intended to improve the performance of individual managers and the organization as a whole, the research evaluating bonuses does not entirely support their effectiveness.[23] Because management performance is difficult to evaluate, most bonus plans distribute money based on the manager's position rather than on the manager's performance. Consequently, these plans typically do little to motivate greater performance. Even though they are very expensive and the research evidence regarding their effectiveness is mostly negative, they are still widely used.

Fine-Tuning the Compensation Plan

In designing an effective compensation program, organizations need to find the proper balance between base pay and incentive pay, including individual incentives, group incentives, and company-wide incentives. The process of balancing the various incentives is called fine-tuning the compensation system.[24] Compensation managers must fine-tune the compensation system, just as a mechanic fine-tunes an engine. The engine needs to be adjusted for the load it must pull, the quality of fuel it will use, and even the altitude at which it will operate. Similarly, a compensation system needs to be fine-tuned to balance the employees' needs for security, equity, and motivation.

Employees who have a sizable base pay feel secure, but not motivated. However, if their total compensation consists of incentive pay without adequate base pay, several problems could develop, such as increased turnover because of inadequate security, dissatisfaction over inaccurate performance evaluations, and dysfunctional competition between coworkers.

Gainsharing
A pay-for-performance plan that shares some of the economic gains with employees according to improvements in specific performance measures.

Fine-tuning compensation
Balancing the relative percentages of base pay, individual incentives, group incentives, and company-wide incentives to create a balance between motivation and security for employees.

The fine-tuning process consists of adjusting base pay, individual incentives, group incentives, and profit-sharing, to create feelings of security and motivation. Stable base pay that provides a dependable weekly or monthly income provides security. Equity and motivation, however, are provided through incentive plans. Some organizations choose to pay large base salaries and give small bonuses, while other organizations do just the opposite.

Recognition Awards

Nonmonetary reward systems have been used effectively to improve employee attitudes, motivation, and attendance.[25] Every motivation theory agrees that praise and recognition are effective rewards. Companies have created a variety of nonmonetary reward programs to recognize employees, and some have been more effective than monetary incentives. The following illustrations demonstrate the diversity of recognition rewards.

Example—
A storage company paneled one of its walls inside the warehouse, and used it to display the photographs of the employee with the best safety record each month. The number of accidents in the warehouse was greatly reduced, and the forklift operators were pleased with the recognition they received, even though the public could not see their photographs.

Example—
Sewing machine operators receive silver stars on their nameplates if they exceed 120 percent of their production quotas every day for a week. After they get ten silver stars, they receive a purple seal. Ribbons are awarded for high-quality production, and the operators display them with pride.

Example—
A hospital gives five-, ten-, fifteen-, twenty-, and twenty-five-year service pins to recognize employees for their years of service. The pins are top-quality jewelry made with diamonds and gold that show the hospital's logo. When the price of gold increased, the hospital decided to give savings bonds rather than pins, but the administrators abandoned the idea when they discovered that the pins were far more important and valued by the employees than were the savings bonds.

Example—
To reduce absenteeism and tardiness, a small apparel manufacturer decided to give gifts of ten to fifteen dollars to randomly selected employees who had perfect attendance. At the end of each week, the names of those who had perfect attendance records were placed in a drawing. For every twenty names in the drawing, one name was selected to receive a gift. After three months, tardiness was only a third of what it had been, and absenteeism was cut in half.

Recognition awards, such as silver stars, purple seals, and photographs hung on a wall, are not inherently rewarding. Primary rewards such as food, water, rest, and the removal of pain are reinforcing because of their relationship to the innate physiology of the body. Secondary rewards such as recognition awards do not directly satisfy physiological needs. Instead, they become powerful reinforcers as people come to place value on them. Consequently, social approval, recognition, status, and feelings of pride and craftsmanship are secondary, or learned, rewards because their reinforcing properties are acquired through experience with them. Although a person may not immediately see the secondary reinforcer as a highly motivating award, over time it can become a powerful form of reinforcement. Recognition awards are often inconsequential to new employees, but as new workers observe their coworkers participate in meaningful recognition experiences, the reward comes to be a highly valued reinforcer. For example, a twenty-five-year service pin can be an extremely motivating reward, not because of its financial worth but because of the symbolic meaning associated with it. In some organizations the service pins are distributed at an annual awards banquet where the recipients are recognized individually. Employees who observe this ritual year after year come to appreciate the ceremony and see the pin as a highly valued reward.[26]

Intrinsic versus Extrinsic Rewards

Some scholars are opposed to using any form of monetary incentives to motivate workers. Indeed, they adamantly condemn all extrinsic reward programs that are designed to motivate people or change their behavior, including piece-rate incentives in industry, grades in education, and gold stars in child rearing. Their argument is not that incentives do not work, because they admit that well-designed incentive programs can have an immediate and substantial impact on behavior. Their claim is that they work for all the wrong reasons. Six of the most important criticisms of extrinsic rewards are:[27]

1. **Rewards are used to control behavior**. Rather than encourage people to direct their lives according to their personal values, rewards manipulate and control them. Rewards are effective only for people who are dependent on them, and they only work if they continue to be received.
2. **Rewards punish**. Rewards and punishment are both elements of a common psychological model that views motivation as nothing more than the manipulation of behavior. To not be rewarded, or to be rewarded less than last time, is to be punished. Therefore, all reward programs are also punishment programs.
3. **Rewards rupture relationships**. Competition for rewards within a group tends to destroy group cohesiveness. Likewise, the relationship between the person giving the rewards and the recipients is also damaged because of the unequal status inherent in the situation. The capacity of supervisors to give or withhold rewards inevitably places them in a position of power that automatically destroys feelings of equality.
4. **Rewards ignore reasons**. Successful performance is determined by both personal and situational factors, and when rewards are based strictly on performance, the uncontrolled situational factors that may have prevented success are ignored.
5. **Rewards discourage risk taking**. When people are competing for rewards, they focus primarily on customary methods that have worked in the past, and overlook new opportunities and creative insights for improving performance.
6. **Extrinsic rewards destroy intrinsic satisfaction**. The good feelings people have for performing a task or helping others are destroyed when they are given extrinsic rewards. This is the most serious and controversial criticism of using extrinsic rewards. If people who are performing a task because of the intrinsic satisfaction they get from doing it, what will happen to their motivation if they are paid for their efforts? More importantly, if the pay later ends what will happen to their motivation? Will they return to happily performing the task, or did the extrinsic reward destroy the intrinsic satisfaction? The research has produced mixed results; extrinsic rewards sometimes destroy intrinsic satisfaction, but not always.

These criticisms of extrinsic rewards are especially helpful for managers who want to strengthen the work values of their employees. The work ethic is not acquired by offering monetary incentives for good work; money may even distract employees from attending to the personal and social benefits of their labors. Feelings of pride and craftsmanship and a commitment to excellence are primarily stimulated by the intrinsic rewards of seeing the benefits that come from one's efforts and feeling that they are a reflection of one's self. Rather than using financial incentives to reward good work, supervisors need to help employees understand how their work benefits society.

Since people must be paid to work, and rewards serve many useful purposes, those opposed to the use of extrinsic rewards offer the following suggestions to minimize the damage caused by extrinsic rewards:

1. **Get rewards out of people's faces**. Encourage people to perform well without continually talking about the potential rewards. Focus on the intrinsic satisfaction of providing service and assistance.
2. **Offer rewards after the fact, as a surprise**. Rewarding excellence with unexpected rewards prevents people from feeling that they were only motivated by the rewards.
3. **Never turn the quest for rewards into a contest**. Contests reward some at the expense of others. Only have contests in which people compete against their own personal records.

4. **Make rewards as similar as possible to the task**. The best reward for good behavior is the opportunity to do it again and feel good about it.
5. **Give people as much choice as possible about how rewards are used**. If possible, let people suggest what will be given, to whom, and when.

NOTES

1. *Baxter v. Savannah Sugar Refining Corp.*, 495 F2d 437 (1974); *Brito v. Zia Co.*, 478, F2d, 1200 (1973); *Albemarle Paper Company v. Moody*, 95 SCt 2362 (1974); *Rowe v. General Motors Corp.*, 457 F2d 348, 1972; *Wade v. Mississippi Cooperative Extension Service*, 528 F2d 508 (1976).
2. Personal communication from the commanding officer.
3. John P. Campbell, R. Darvey, Marvin D. Dunnette, and L. V. Hellervik, "The Development and Evaluation of Behaviorally Based Rating Scales," *Journal of Applied Psychology*, vol. 57, (no. 1, 1973); Donald P. Schwab, Herbert G. Heneman, and T. A. DeCotis, "Behaviorally-Anchored Rating Scales: A Review of the Literature," *Personnel Psychology*, vol. 28, no. 4, (Winter, 1975), pp. 549–562.
4. Peter F. Drucker, *The Practice of Management* (New York: Harper and Row, 1954).
5. Edwin A. Locke, "Toward a Theory of Task Performance and Incentives," *Organizational Behavior and Human Performance*, vol. 3 (1968), pp. 157–189; Locke, Edwin A. and Latham, Gary P, "Building a Practically Useful Theory of Goal Setting and Task Motivation: A 35-year Odyssey," *American Psychologist*, vol. 57 (2002), pp. 705–717.
6. Edwin A. Locke, Karyll N. Shaw, Lise M. Saari, and Gary P. Latham, "Goal Setting and Task Performance: 1969–1980," *Technical Report*, GS1, Office of Naval Research, Washington, D.C., June 1980.
7. Edwin A. Locke and Gary P. Latham, *Goal Setting: A Motivational Technique That Works* (Englewood Cliffs, N.J.: Prentice-Hall, 1984); Locke, Edwin A. and Latham, Gary P, "Building a Practically Useful Theory of Goal Setting and Task Motivation: A 35-year Odyssey," *American Psychologist*, vol. 57 (2002), pp. 705–717.
8. H. Garland, "Influence of Ability Assigned Goals, and Normative Information of Personal Goals and Performance: A Challenge to the Goal Attainability Assumption," *Journal of Applied Psychology*, vol. 68, (1983), pp. 20–30; D. J. Cherrington and J. O. Cherrington, "Appropriate Reinforcement Contingencies in the Budgeting Process," *Empirical Research in Accounting: Selected Studies* (1973), pp. 225–253.
9. John R. Hollenbeck, Charles R. Williams, and Howard J. Kline, "An Empirical Examination of the Antecedents of Commitment to Difficult Goals," *Journal of Applied Psychology*, vol. 74, (February 1989), pp. 18–23; Andrew Li and Adam B. Butler. "The Effects of Participation in Goal Setting and Goal Rationales on Goal Commitment: An Exploration of Justice Mediators," *Journal of Business and Psychology*. Vol. 19 (No. 1, 2004), pp. 37–51.
10. Stephen G. Green, Gail T. Fairhurst and B. Kay Snavely, "Chains of Poor Performance and Supervisory Control," *Organizational Behavior and Human Decision Processes*, vol. 38, (1986), pp. 7–27.
11. James R. Larson, Jr., "Supervisors' Performance Feedback to Subordinates: The Impact of Subordinate Performance Valence and Outcome Dependence," *Organizational Behavior and Human Decision Processes*, vol. 37, (1986), pp. 391–408.
12. C. D. Fisher, "Transmission of Positive and Negative Feedback to Subordinates: A Laboratory Investigation," *Journal of Applied Psychology*, vol. 64, (1979), pp. 533–540; Daniel R. Ilgen and W. A. Knowlton, "Performance Attributional Effects on Feedback From Superiors," *Organizational Behavior and Human Performance*, vol. 25, (1980), pp. 441–456.
13. J. Bruce Prince and Edward E. Lawler, III, "Does Salary Discussion Hurt the Developmental Performance Appraisal?" *Organizational Behavior and Human Decision Processes*, vol. 37, (1986), pp. 357–375.

14. Tamao Matsui, Akinori Okada, and Osamu Inoshita, "Mechanism of Feedback Affecting Task Performance," *Organizational Behavior and Human Performance*, vol. 31, (1983), pp. 114–122.

15. Albert Bandura, "Self-efficacy Mechanism in Human Agency," *American Psychologist*, vol. 37, (February 1982), pp. 122–147.

16. Leanne E. Atwater and Joan F. Brett. "360-Degree Feedback to Leaders: Does It Relate To Changes In Employee Attitudes?" *Group & Organization Management*. Vol. 31 (2006), pp. 578–600.

17. Glenn M. McEvoy, Paul F. Buller and Steven R. Rognaar, "A Jury of One's Peers," *Personnel Administrator* 33 (May 1988): 94–101.

18. Edward J. Inderrieden, Robert E. Allen, Timothy J. Keaveny, "Managerial Discretion in the Use of Self-ratings in an Appraisal System: The Antecedents and Consequences," *Journal of Managerial Issues*, vol. 16 (2004), pp. 460–482.

19. Susan J. Ashford, Ruth Blatt and Don Vande Walle "Reflections on the Looking Glass: A Review of Research on Feedback-Seeking Behavior in Organizations," *Journal of Management*, vol. 29 (2003), pp. 773–799; Wing Lam, Xu Huang, Snape, Ed, "Feedback-Seeking Behavior and Leader-Member Exchange: Do Supervisor-Attributed Motives Matter?" *Academy of Management Journal*, vol. 50 (2007), pp. 348–363.

20. C. Bram Cadsby, Fei Song, and Francis Tapon, "Sorting and Incentive Effects of Pay for Performance: An Experimental Investigation," *Academy of Management Journal*, vol. 50 (2007), pp. 387–405.

21. Surveyed by Allan N. Nash and Stephen J. Carroll, Jr., *The Management of Compensation*, (Monterey, California: Brooks-Cole Publishing Company, 1975), p. 199.

22. James S. Devlin, "Wage Incentives: The Aetna Plan," Presented at the LOMA Work Measurement Seminar (April 1975).

23. J. Perham, "What's Wrong with Bonuses?" Dun's Review of *Modern Industry*, vol. 98, (1981), pp. 40–44.

24. David J. Cherrington and Laura Z. Middleton, *Human Resource Certification Preparation, Unit 4: Compensation and Benefits*, (Provo, UT: HRCP LLC, 2007) pp. 62–65.

25. Steven E. Markham, K. Dow Scott, and Gail H. McKee, "Recognizing Good Attendance: A Longitudinal, Quasi-Experimental Field Study," *Personnel Psychology*, vol. 55 (2002), pp. 639–660.

26. David J. Cherrington and B. Jackson Wixom, Jr., "Recognition is Still a Top Motivator," *Personnel Administrator*, (May 1983), pp. 87–91.

27. Alfie Kohn, *Punished by Rewards: The Trouble with Gold Stars, Incentive Plans, A's, Praise, and Other Bribes.* (Boston: Houghton Mifflin, 1993); Mark R. Lepper and David Greene, *The Hidden Costs of Rewards: New Perspectives on the Psychology of Human Motivation.* (Hillsdale, N.J.: Erlbaum, 1978).

Organizational Structure and Design

Why should you learn about organizational structure? This is a good question to ask, since organizational structure is the most abstract and difficult concept to understand in organizational behavior. The answer is very simple: poorly structured organizations contribute to employee burnout and stress; create conflict between work teams; prevent even highly motivated people from succeeding in their work; waste valuable resources, including money and time; fail to serve customers; limit the profitability of the company; and eventually threaten the organization's survival. Moreover, the most immediate and permanent way to revitalize an organization is to redesign its structure. Obviously, it is worth knowing the basic principles of organizational structure and how to adapt them to the appropriate conditions.

CONCEPTS OF ORGANIZATIONAL DESIGN

Organizations are open social systems that consist of patterned activities, and this chapter explains how these patterned activities are structured. The purpose of organizational structure is to regulate these activities and reduce the variability in human performance, or in other words, control behavior by making it coordinated and predictable.

Controlling the behavior of people in organizations is essential because organizations cannot survive if their members behave in random, unpredictable ways. Such a situation would produce chaos and disorganization. The difference between a well organized and poorly organized group is as dramatic as the difference between the beauty of an orchestra playing a symphony and the noise the musicians produce when they are tuning their instruments. To produce the necessary patterned activities and thereby create an organization, the variability in human behavior must be reduced so that people behave in predictable patterns. Although organizations vary in the amount of control they require from their members, at least some control is inherent in every organization.

The term **organizational structure** refers to the relatively fixed relationships among the jobs in the organization. The process of creating this structure and making decisions about the relative benefits of alternative structures is called **organizational design**. Creating an organizational structure involves two issues: (1) differentiation, or creating a division of labor, and (2) integration, or coordinating the different roles created by the division of labor. Therefore, the study of organizational structure examines the manner in which an organization divides labor into specialized tasks and then coordinates them. The five major design decisions that must be made are division of labor, departmentalization, span of control, delegation of authority, and coordinating mechanisms.

Division of Labor

The term **division of labor** refers to the process of dividing a large task into successively smaller jobs, called **job specialization**. All jobs are specialized to some degree, since one person can't do everything, but some jobs are considerably more specialized than others. One of the major benefits of specialized activities is that a group of people working together with a division of labor are able to produce more than they could if each member produced the entire product working alone.

Organizational structure
The arrangement of jobs and the relationships among the jobs in an organization.

Organizational design
The process of deciding on the type of structure appropriate for an organization, particularly regarding its division of labor, departmentalization, span of control, delegation of authority, and coordinating mechanism.

Division of labor
The process of dividing work into specialized jobs that are performed by separate individuals.

The key issue here is how specialized the work should be. Specialization is low when employees perform a variety of tasks and high when each person performs only a single task. The degree of specialization can be represented along a continuum.

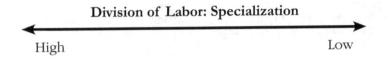

Division of Labor: Specialization

High   Low

Example—
In a word processing center, the degree of specialization is low if three typists are allowed to edit, type, and proofread the manuscripts they type. However, if each of these functions were assigned to a different individual, the degree of specialization would be high.

Deciding on the appropriate level of specialization is an important design decision because it greatly influences productivity. It is possible to create jobs that are so highly specialized that the organization suffers from a lack of coordination and at times there isn't enough work to keep everyone busy. Highly specialized jobs can also be extremely boring, yet there are definite advantages to highly specialized jobs.

Departmentalization

Departmentalization is the process of combining jobs into groups or departments. Managers must decide whether the most appropriate structure is to have a homogeneous department with similar jobs or a heterogeneous department with unrelated jobs. Jobs can be grouped according to several criteria; the most popular criteria include function, product, territory, and clientele, as illustrated in Exhibit 13.1.

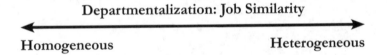

Departmentalization: Job Similarity

Homogeneous   Heterogeneous

Functional Departmentalization

Functional departmentalization involves grouping jobs that perform similar functions into the same department. For example, all the jobs associated with accounting, such as general ledger accountant, accounts payable clerk, accounts receivable clerk, and cost accountant, could all be combined into an accounting department. Organizing the departments by function would be a homogeneous form of departmentalization, since everyone in the department would share the same specialized skills. Other forms of departmentalization tend to be market-based and more heterogeneous.

Functional departmentalization is the most widely used scheme because in most organizations it is the most effective method. This explains why a typical manufacturing company is departmentalized into production, marketing, finance, accounting, research and development, and human resource departments. Most hospitals are departmentalized in terms of such functions as surgery, nursing, psychiatry, pharmacy, human resource, and housekeeping.

Departmentalization
The process of assigning jobs to units or departments according to one of these common criteria: function, product, geographical area, or clientele.

Functional departmentalization
Creating departments by grouping jobs that all perform similar functions.

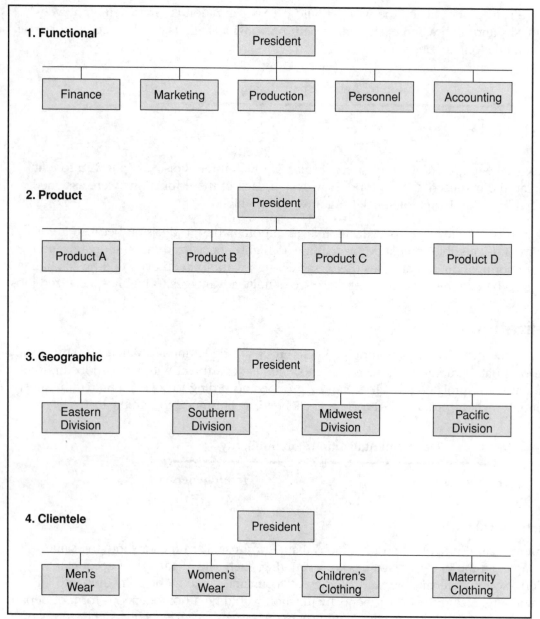

Exhibit 13.1   Bases of Departmentalization

Functional departmentalization has both advantages and disadvantages. Perhaps the most significant advantage is that it promotes skill specialization by having people work together who face similar problems and opportunities. The functional form also permits the maximum use of resources, and encourages the use of specialists and specialized equipment, thereby eliminating duplication of equipment and effort. Communication and performance are usually improved because superiors share expertise with their subordinates.

One disadvantage of functional departmentalization is that it reduces communication and cooperation between departments and fosters a parochial perspective. This narrow orientation limits managers' capacities for coordination, and encourages a short time horizon. Coordination and support across functional departments are often difficult because departments are separated both geographically and psychologically, and members come to view problems only from their limited functional perspectives.

Functional departmentalization also contributes to a problem called **suboptimizing**. Suboptimizing occurs when one department pursues its own goals and tries to look good at the expense of other departments or of the organization as a whole. Suboptimizing is particularly problematic when departments are rewarded for achieving their own goals. Although departments are expected to serve each other and they should be rewarded for the service they provide, many departmental goals can best be achieved when each department pursues its own selfish interests. Custodial departments, for example, could keep the buildings cleaner if no one used the buildings. Likewise, the accounting and human resource departments could generate better reports if managers from whom the information was obtained spent all their time completing lengthy forms.

Product Departmentalization

Product departmentalization involves grouping jobs that produce similar products, which typically occurs in large firms when it becomes difficult to coordinate the various functional departments. The members of a product-oriented department can develop greater expertise in researching, manufacturing, and distributing a specific product line. Managers have better control over the success or failure of each product if the authority, responsibility, and accountability are assigned according to products. This method is illustrated by the "brand" management structure that Procter & Gamble uses with its major products.

The product form of departmentalization has both advantages and disadvantages, and is often contrasted with the functional form of departmentalization. The major advantage is that it creates greater inter-departmental coordination and focuses the efforts of each department on producing an effective and useful product. Companies organized by product are generally customer-oriented, and their employees tend to be cohesive and involved in their work.

The major disadvantage of organizing by product is that the resources and skills of the organization are not fully employed unless the organization is extremely large. For example, a computer-driven lathe machine that is used for only one product and sits idle much of the time represents an inefficient use of capital resources. Another disadvantage is that product-oriented departments usually lead to increased costs because of duplication of activities, especially staff functions.

Geographic Departmentalization

Organizations use geographic departmentalization when they assign all the activities in an area to the same unit. This method typically occurs when organizations are geographically dispersed and a local manager is assigned to supervise both the functions and products in that area. This method is popular among retail companies that have stores located in many cities. Each store manager is ultimately responsible for recruiting, hiring, training, advertising, selling, and other diverse functions.

The major advantage of geographic departmentalization comes from minimizing problems created by distance, such as difficulties in communicating, observing, and making timely decisions. The disadvantage is that they miss the important advantages of functional and product departmentalization, which would have been superior if distance hadn't precluded them.

Customer Departmentalization

Occasionally the most effective way to combine jobs is to organize them according to the customers who are served. These advantages occur when groups of customers have distinct needs. Many universities, for

---

Suboptimizing
Where one department pursues its self-interest at the expense of the larger organization.

Product departmentalization
When departments are created by assigning all jobs that produce the same product to a department.

Geographic departmentalization
Creating departments by assigning all the jobs in the same geographical region to the same department.

example, have a separate evening class program or an executive MBA program, because the interests of these students are significantly different from those of the regular day-time students. Many department stores have separate departments for men's clothing, women's clothing, maternity clothing, and children's clothing because the customers served by each department have unique and separate interests.

Each form of departmentalization has both advantages and disadvantages. Therefore, managers are required to balance the strengths and weaknesses of each form and decide which will create the highest efficiency. In most situations, managers use a mixed strategy that combines two or more forms of departmentalization. For example, department stores combine the advantages of customer departmentalization with a functional form of organization among the staff units. The accounting, finance, human resource, and purchasing departments represent functional departmentalization, while the men's clothing, women's clothing, boys' clothing, and maternity departments represent customer departmentalization.

Span of Control

When selecting the **span of control**, managers decide how many people should be placed in a group under one supervisor; the number can vary along a continuum from few to many.

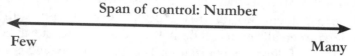

Span of control: Number

Few → Many

The span-of-control decision has a major influence on the organization's shape and structure. Organizations that use a broad span of control have relatively few hierarchical levels, while a narrow span creates a tall organizational structure, as illustrated in Exhibit 13.2. Each hypothetical structure involves thirty-one positions. A narrow span of control, with only two subordinates per supervisor, produces a tall organizational structure with five hierarchical levels. However, a span of control of five produces a flat organizational structure with only three hierarchical levels.

A narrow span of control allows for closer control over subordinates and greater personal contact between manager and subordinate. The risk, however, is that a manager with a narrow span of control comes to know only two or three subordinates very well and fails to become acquainted with others in the hierarchy. Consequently, tall organizations often inhibit interpersonal communication within the organization.

During the 1940s and 1950s, management scholars tried to prescribe the ideal span of control. One scholar calculated the geometric increase in the number of relationships a manager must supervise as the span of control increased, and concluded that the maximum span of control should never exceed three or four subordinates.[1] In actual practice, however, several organizations had spans of control greater than twenty, and the groups were supervised quite effectively. Consequently, the "ideal span of control" does not exist; the appropriate span of control varies with the nature of the tasks being performed.[2] Although a range of four to six subordinates is often recommended, a much larger span of control may be appropriate, depending on four situational variables:

1. **Contact required.** Jobs that require frequent contact and a high degree of coordination between supervisor and subordinates should use narrower spans of control. For example, jobs in medical technology often require frequent consultation of team members with a supervisor; therefore, a large span of control would preclude the necessary sharing of ideas and information that typically must occur on an informal basis.
2. **Level of subordinates' education and training.** Large spans of control are appropriate for highly skilled employees and professionals who are well trained. They generally require less supervision because they know their jobs well and they largely supervise themselves.

Customer departmentalization
Creating departments by assigning all the jobs that serve a particular group of customers to the same department.

Span of control
The number of subordinates assigned to a supervisor.

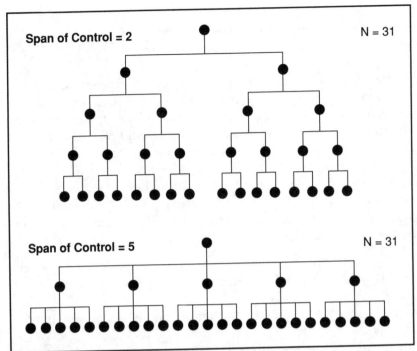

Exhibit 13.2   Span of Control: Tall versus Flat Organizational Structures

3. **Ability to communicate**. Instructions, guidelines, and policies can be communicated to employees by a variety of methods. If all the necessary instructions can be written and then disseminated, it would be possible for one manager to supervise a large group. However, as communication becomes more difficult and job-related discussions become more important, a narrower span of control is appropriate to avoid overloading a supervisor.

4. **Nature of the task**. Jobs that are repetitive and stable require less supervision and are more amenable to wide spans of control. For this reason, some field supervisors are able to supervise as many as sixty to seventy-five field hands in harvesting agricultural crops. However, when tasks are changed frequently, a narrower span of control is appropriate.

There seems to be a natural tendency for managers to adopt narrow spans of control, which increases the number of hierarchical levels. However, productivity often increases after organizations have eliminated one or more hierarchical levels of administration, so companies are often encouraged to eliminate hierarchical levels by increasing spans of control.

Delegation of Authority

The fourth design issue concerns the delegation of authority. Decentralization involves distributing power and authority to lower-level supervisors and employees. The more decentralized an organization, the greater the extent to which the rank-and-file employees can participate in and accept responsibility for decisions concerning their jobs and the activities of the organization. Decision-making authority can vary along a continuum from **centralized** to **decentralized**.

Centralized authority
Where the authority to make organizational decisions is retained by top managers in the central office.

Decentralized authority
Where the authority to make organizational decisions is delegated to lower-level managers and supervisors.

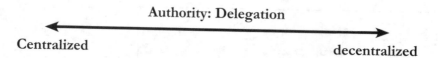

Decentralization often leads to greater organizational effectiveness, since it allows greater autonomy and responsibility among lower-level employees thereby more effectively using an organization's human resources. Supervisors in decentralized organizations typically report higher levels of job satisfaction and involvement, and they tend to be more productive because of increased autonomy and responsibility. A company that is struggling with declining sales may decide to decentralize its management structure to make it more responsive to customers and more conducive to new product development.

In spite of its benefits, however, decentralization is not universally superior and does not always contribute to greater organizational effectiveness. Some organizations have excelled with decentralized decision making while others have fared better with a centralized structure. Several weaknesses of decentralization have been identified suggesting that centralized decision making is sometimes superior.

1. Certain shared functions, especially staff functions, are more difficult to execute under decentralization.
2. Decentralization can create jurisdictional disputes and conflicts over priorities, since each unit essentially becomes an independent area.
3. Decentralization requires greater competence and expertise and greater commitment on the part of decision makers than centralized control does.
4. Decentralized decisions made by many lower-level managers create problems of coordination and integration. A decentralized organization could be very ineffective, because of inadequate coordination and integration.

To design an effective organizational structure, managers must select the optimal balance between centralized and decentralized authority. Power and authority should be decentralized to the extent that organizations use the knowledge and expertise of lower-level participants while maintaining sufficient centralization to ensure adequate coordination and control.[3] Like the other concepts of organizational design, the ideal policy depends on the situation.

Coordinating Mechanisms

Organizations need to process information and coordinate the efforts of their members. Employees at lower levels need to perform activities consistent with top-level goals, and the managers at the top need to know about the activities and accomplishments of people at lower levels. Five primary methods are available for coordinating the activities of members, and these methods vary according to the amount of discretion that workers are allowed.

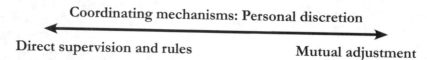

1. **Direct supervision.** All work is coordinated by supervisors through rules that are continually monitored, or by specific on-the-job instructions.

   Example—
   A landscaping crew works under the direct supervision of an architect who tells each worker where each shrub and tree should be planted. An orchestra plays under the direct supervision of a conductor who coordinates precisely when everyone plays.

2. **Standardization of work processes.** Routine jobs can be coordinated through standard operating procedures or by the technology itself that regulates the activities. Here, it is the activities that are coordinated.

Example—

Assembly line jobs are coordinated by the pace of the line. The workers know what they are required to do and they perform their assigned activities as the products move along the production line.

3. **Standardization of outputs**. When products or services must be produced according to established specifications, these specifications may serve as an adequate basis for coordinating the activities. Individual workers are allowed some discretion in performing the work, provided the output meets the required specifications. Here, it is the outputs that are coordinated.

Example—

Construction workers are mostly coordinated by the products they produce. They know how to do the job correctly so that it will pass inspection. They establish their own pace of work and to some extent they are free to vary the order of the activities they perform.

4. **Standardization of skills**. The work of highly skilled and trained employees is typically coordinated by the professional training they have received. What they do and how they do it is based on the skills they were taught in their technical training.

Example—

The work of a surgical team is mostly coordinated by having members who perform their jobs according to the ways they were trained. The members rely on each other to do what they were trained to do and this training serves to integrate their actions.

5. **Mutual adjustment**. Activities that are constantly changing and uncertain are coordinated through mutual adjustment, which consists of a constant interchange of informal communication. Here, individuals have the greatest discretion and they coordinate their work through informal meetings, personal conversations, and liaison positions, mutually adjusting to one another's needs. Employees communicate with whomever they need to communicate without regard for formal lines of communication.

Example—

Rescue teams, emergency medical technicians, and other groups that respond in crisis situations coordinate their activities through mutual adjustment. Because each situation is unique and unexpected problems arise, the team members are required to continually adjust their plans and coordinate their responses among themselves.

A crucial issue in choosing a coordinating mechanism concerns the need for information and the ways in which information is collected, processed, and disseminated. The type of information collected by a driver's license bureau, for example, is mostly routine information that can be coordinated by rules and procedures. Fashion merchandisers, however, require extensive market information, which they may obtain from a variety of irregular sources and disseminate informally to anyone who needs to know.

Coordinating mechanisms influence the degree of formalization in an organization. The term **formalization** refers to the degree to which rules and procedures guide the actions of employees. These rules and procedures can be either explicit or implicit. Explicit rules are written in job descriptions, policy and procedures manuals, or office memos. Implicit rules are often unwritten and develop as employees estab-

---

Mutual adjustment
A means of achieving organizational coordination by allowing people to coordinate their work through informal processes, mutually adjusting to each others' needs.

Formalization
The degree to which employee behaviors are guided by formal rules and procedures.

lish their own ways of doing things over time. Although they are unwritten, implicit rules often become standard operating procedures with the same effect on employee behavior as explicit rules.

In a highly formal organization, employees are required to follow strict rules and procedures that tell them exactly how to perform their work. Informal organizations have very few rules and procedures; the employees are largely free to structure their own jobs. Formal organizations tend to rely on direct supervision and standardization of work processes, while informal organizations tend to use mutual adjustment and standardization of skills. An example of a formal structure in a university would be an administrative agency, such as the student loans office, while an example of an informal structure would be an academic department, such as the sociology department.

Matrix Organizational Structures

Some organizations have combined two kinds of departmentalization, functional and product, in an effort to capitalize on the advantages of each. This dual structure, called a **matrix structure**, simultaneously organizes part of the organization along product lines and part of the organization along functional lines, as illustrated in Exhibit 13.3.

In a matrix organization, each department reports simultaneously to both product managers and functional managers who have equal authority within the organization. For example, a member of the legal department may be assigned to assist with the development of a specific product and assume the responsibility for all the legal activities associated with the development, production, and distribution of the product. This individual would report to both the product manager and the supervisor of the legal department.

Although dual structures are awkward, they can quickly create new products while retaining the benefits of a functional structure. Consequently, a matrix structure is particularly effective when environmental pressures create a demand for both technical quality (functional) and frequent new products (product). These dual pressures require a dual authority structure to deal with them. A matrix structure is particularly useful in an uncertain environment when frequent external changes and high interdependence between departments require effective linkages between departments inside the organization.

The disadvantage of a matrix structure is that it increases role ambiguity, stress, and anxiety, because people are assigned to more than one department. Matrix structures violate the principle of unity of command. The employees who work in a matrix structure often feel that inconsistent demands are made on them, causing unproductive conflicts that call for short-term crisis management. Occasionally, employees abuse the dual-authority structure by playing one manager against another, thereby generating excuses for their incompetence or inactivity.[4]

UNIVERSAL DESIGN THEORIES

The structure of an organization is determined by the five concepts explained earlier: division of labor, departmentalization, span of control, delegation of authority, and coordinating mechanisms. Different combinations of these factors can produce many different organizational structures. Which structure is the most effective? This section describes universal theories of organizational design that were meant to be ideal structures. Unfortunately, a universally superior organizational structure does not exist; the best structure depends on the situation, as explained in the next section.

Matrix organizational structure
A combination of two different forms of departmentalization, usually functional and product departmentalization.

Universal theories of organizational design
Theories of organizational design that purport to be universally appropriate for every organization. Two widely contrasting universal design theories are bureaucracy and System Four.

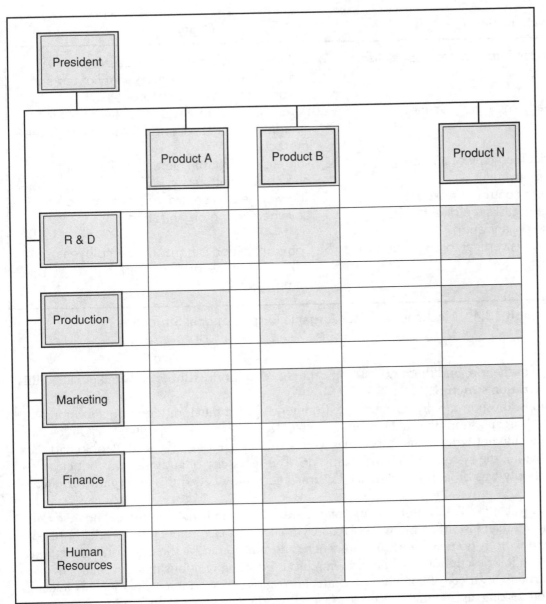

Exhibit 13.3 Matrix Organizational Structure

Mechanistic versus Organic Organizational Structures

Two contrasting types of organizational structure have been recommended as universally appropriate for every organization. These two types differ greatly in the amount of formal structure and control they advocate. Several labels have been used to describe these two types. The labels used in this book are **mechanistic** versus **organic** organizational structures.

Mechanistic and organic organizational structures were first described in a classic study by Burns and Stalker.[5] They observed twenty industrial firms in England and discovered that the external environment was related to the internal organizational structure. When the external environment was stable, the internal organization was managed by rules, procedures, and a clear hierarchy of authority. Most managerial

Mechanistic	**Organic**
1. Tasks are divided into separate, specialized jobs.	1. Tasks may not be highly specialized, and employees may perform a variety of tasks to accomplish the group's task.
2. Tasks are clearly and rigidly defined.	2. Tasks are not elaborately specified: they may be adjusted and redefined through employee interactions.
3. There is a strict hierarchy of authority and control with many rules.	3. There is an informal hierarchy of authority and control with few rules.
4. Knowledge and control of tasks are centralized, and tasks are directed from the top of the organization.	4. Knowledge and control of tasks are located anywhere in the organization.
5. Communication is vertical throughout the formal hierarchy.	5. Communication is horizontal; employees talk with whomever they need to communicate.

Exhibit 13.4   Mechanistic versus Organic Organizational Structures

decisions were made at the top, and there was strong centralized authority. Burns and Stalker called this a **mechanistic organization structure**.

Some organizations, those in rapidly changing environments, had a much different organizational structure. The internal organization was much more adaptive, free-flowing, and spontaneous. Rules and regulations were generally not written, and those that were written were often ignored. People had to find their own way within the system and learn what to do. The hierarchy of authority was not clear, and decision-making authority was broadly decentralized. Burns and Stalker called this an **organic organizational structure**.

A more recent term that is used to describe an organic structure is a **virtual workplace**; however, this term often implies more than just a flexible workplace. A virtual workplace refers to networks of people in a workplace where work is done anytime and anywhere and not bound by the traditional limitations of time, physical space, job descriptions, title, and hierarchical reporting relationships. It usually involves work that is done through a variety of communication technologies and working styles, such as telecenters, teleworking, hot-desking, and virtual offices. The virtual workplace has become an increasingly preferred workplace for many.[6]

The differences between an organic and a mechanistic organizational structure are illustrated in Exhibit 13.4. In a mechanistic structure, the work is divided into highly specialized tasks that are rigidly defined by a formal job description. In an organic structure, however, most tasks are not so highly specialized; employees are often expected to learn how to perform a variety of tasks, and to frequently adjust and redefine their jobs as the situation changes. In a mechanistic structure, communication patterns follow the formal chain of command between superiors and subordinates. In an organic structure, however, communication is horizontal, and employees talk with whomever they need to in order to do their work.

Mechanistic organizational structure
A formal organizational structure characterized by highly specialized tasks that are carefully and rigidly defined, with a strict hierarchy of authority to control them. Bureaucracy is a type of mechanistic structure.

Organic organizational structure
A type of organization structure characterized by people who work together in an informal arrangement, sharing ideas and information, and performing a variety of tasks based on whatever is needed to accomplish the group's task.

Virtual workplace
A flexible workplace where people work at any time and anyplace in informal relationships, usually with computer technologies.

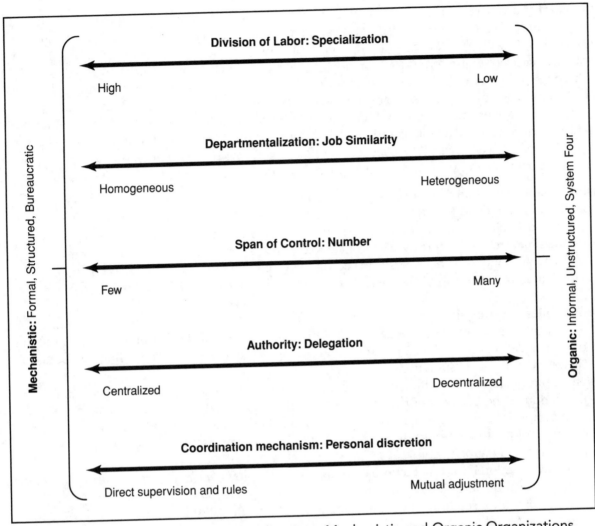

Exhibit 13.5 Structural Differences between Mechanistic and Organic Organizations

Mechanistic and organic structures differ in each of the five dimensions of organizational structure, as illustrated in Exhibit 13.5. In addition to having highly specialized jobs, mechanistic structures are characterized by homogeneous departmentalization, a narrow span of control, highly centralized delegation of authority, and coordination through direct supervision and rules. Organic structures are just the opposite: the labor is divided in such a way that the level of specialization is reduced, the jobs are organized into heterogeneous departments, there is a broad span of control, decision-making authority is widely decentralized, and work is coordinated by mutual adjustment. Deciding which structure is best depends on several environmental factors and employee characteristics, as is explained in the later sections.[7]

Bureaucratic Organizational Design

Perhaps the best description of a mechanistic organizational structure is Max Weber's description of **bureaucracy**.[8] Highly bureaucratic organizations have a very mechanistic organizational structure. Unfor-

Bureaucracy
An organizational structure that is characterized by an elaborate division of labor based on functional specialization, a hierarchy of authority assigned to different offices, a system of rules explaining how everyone is to perform, and impersonal relationships.

tunately, the word "bureaucracy" is associated with a variety of negative feelings. Many people associate bureaucracy with excessive red tape, procedural delays, and organizational inefficiency. These connotations are not consistent with Max Weber's description of bureaucracy. According to Weber, a bureaucracy was a sociological concept that referred to the rational collection of clearly organized activities. The word *bureaucracy* comes from the French word *bureau*, which means "office." In short, a bureaucracy is a collection of carefully organized offices performing specialized functions according to clearly defined rules and procedures. Weber's description of bureaucracy was intended as a description of the ideal form of a large organizational structure. The major attributes of this ideal form were rationality and efficiency. A bureaucratic structure was a well organized collection of offices that combined the efforts of many people using a system of rules and procedures. Weber's description included the following identifying characteristics.

1. **A division of labor based on functional specialization**. All tasks necessary for accomplishing the goals of the organization are divided into highly specialized jobs. Such job specialization allows jobholders to become expert in their jobs and to be held responsible for the effective performance of their duties.
2. **A well-defined hierarchy of authority**. Each officeholder in the organization is accountable to a supervisor. The authority of supervisors is based on expert knowledge and legitimized by the fact that it is delegated from the top of the hierarchy. In this way, a clearly defined chain of command is created.
3. **A system of rules covering the rights and duties of employees**. Each task is performed according to a consistent system of abstract rules to ensure uniformity and coordination of different tasks. Through a system of clearly defined rules, officeholders can eliminate any uncertainty in performing their tasks that is caused by individual differences.
4. **Impersonal relationships.** Each officeholder maintains a social distance from subordinates and clients and conducts the business of the office in a formal, impersonal manner. Strict adherence to the rules and impersonal relationships ensure that personalities do not interfere with the efficient accomplishment of the office's objectives. There should be no favoritism resulting from personal friendships or ingratiating behaviors.
5. **Promotion and selection based on technical competence**. Employment in a bureaucratic organization is based on technical qualifications, and employees are protected against arbitrary dismissal. Similarly, promotions are based on seniority and achievement. Employment in the bureaucracy is viewed as a lifelong career, designed to create loyalty and commitment.
6. **Written communications and records**. All administrative acts, decisions, and rules are recorded in writing. Since verbal conversations and discussions cannot be filed, all decisions, complaints, and administrative acts are to be written and filed. Record keeping provides an organizational memory, and written documents provide continuity over time.

Many of the characteristics that Weber recommended for an ideal bureaucracy seem quite obvious to us today because we are surrounded by organizations that have rules, a division of labor, written documents, and a hierarchy of authority. These characteristics provide an impersonal means of controlling organizations by guaranteeing that dependable work will be performed by qualified employees under the impartial direction of rational supervisors. These rational characteristics, however, were not so obvious a century ago when there were very few large organizations. Most organizations were family operated and characterized by nepotism and unfair treatment. Weber's recommendation of a rational, bureaucratic ideal was intended both to eliminate favoritism and increase organizational efficiency.

Advantages of a Bureaucracy

Bureaucracy has survived and even thrived because its advantages outweigh its disadvantages. The advantages of a bureaucracy stem logically from its ideal characteristics. At its best, a bureaucracy is a smooth-running organization in which decisions and activities are processed efficiently and all members are treated equitably. Seven major benefits have been attributed to bureaucracy, as summarized in Exhibit 13.6.

Advantages	Disadvantages
1. Technical efficiency 2. Elimination of favoritism 3. Predictability of performance 4. Job security 5. Technical competence 6. Minimum direction needed 7. Avoids impulsive action	1. Rigidity of behavior 2. Bureaucratic personality 3. Inversion of means and ends 4. Resistance to change 5. Peter Principle

Exhibit 13.6 Advantages and Disadvantages of Bureaucracies

1. **Technical efficiency**. The chief benefit of a bureaucracy is that the activities and functions have been carefully analyzed and rationally organized in a way that creates maximum efficiency. The process of dividing the labor into highly specialized jobs, assigning them to different offices, and coordinating them through a carefully designed system of rules and procedures produces what has sometimes been called **machine-like efficiency**.

2. **Elimination of favoritism**. By following the correct procedures and administering the rules impartially, clients and officeholders are treated fairly. No one is treated with special favors because of personal friendships or ingratiating behaviors. The rules and procedures are administered without regard to family, wealth, or status. This impartial treatment is consistent with bureaucratic ideals that condemn nepotism, partiality, and capricious judgment.

3. **Predictability in performance**. Strict adherence to clearly defined rules and procedures leads to greater predictability of performance. Both customers and employees know in advance the outcome of a decision. For example, if the vacation policy allows three weeks' paid vacation after five years of service, all employees with at least five years of service can expect to receive a three-week paid vacation.

4. **Job security**. By following the rules and doing what the handbook or procedures manual says they are supposed to do, officeholders are assured that they will not be fired. Such a tenure policy maximizes vocational security. Officeholders tend to view their employment in the organization as a lifelong career. Such an outlook minimizes turnover and engenders a high degree of loyalty and commitment.

5. **Technical competence**. Since officeholders are hired on the basis of their ability rather than on the basis of whom they know, they are highly trained, competent officials.

6. **Minimum direction needed**. Because a bureaucracy has been rationally designed, and the officeholders are trained experts who are expected to follow standard rules and operating procedures, very little day-to-day direction is needed to keep the bureaucracy functioning. Like a carefully designed machine that operates smoothly after it is turned on, a bureaucracy is expected to operate smoothly with little direction or added input.

7. **Avoids impulsive decisions**. Since a bureaucracy operates according to standard operating procedures, it is not possible for an impulsive idea on the part of one officeholder to immediately disrupt the entire bureaucracy. Since they must be coordinated with other officeholders, new ideas and changes cannot be implemented quickly. Although reducing the possibility of impulsive action is sometimes an advantage, it can also be a disadvantage when change is required, which explains why bureaucracies are often associated with red tape and resistance to change.

Disadvantages of Bureaucracy

Although Weber described bureaucracies as ideal structures, they are not without their problems. Over the years, several dysfunctional consequences have been identified. Some of these dysfunctional consequences are not created because the bureaucracy fails to operate properly. Instead, they are created because the bureaucracy is functioning exactly as it should; the problems are inherent to the bureaucratic structure itself. In other words, these problems cannot be solved by having the bureaucracy operate more effectively; a stricter application of bureaucratic principles would exacerbate the problems.

1. **Rigidity of behavior**. In a bureaucracy, officeholders are expected to know the rules and procedures and to follow them precisely. Bureaucracies control individual behavior by demanding strict rule compliance. However, as employees follow the rules more precisely, their behavior becomes more rigid and more insensitive to individual problems. This rigid behavior inevitably leads to conflict with clients and customers. Many times people think their personal situation represents an exception to the rule, and occasionally they are right. Wise bureaucrats know when to deviate from the rules and accept responsibility for their decisions, but bureaucrats who have been intimidated or threatened seek to protect themselves by following the rules. As the level of conflict rises, the dysfunctional consequences of a bureaucratic structure become more obvious. Instead of responding helpfully to the complaints of clients and their demands for individual treatment, bureaucrats respond by following the rules more strictly. By strict adherence to the rules in their handbooks and policy manuals, they are able to defend their actions in the face of conflict, but their client relationships suffer.

Example—

Airline passengers have been forced to remain on the planes for more than six hours after they had safely landed, because disruptive conditions prevented them from getting to their assigned gate. They were not allowed to leave the plane even though the toilets were filled, food and water were gone, claustrophobic passengers were freaking out, and mothers had exhausted their supply of diapers and formula. The airline personnel were not willing to deviate from FAA regulations in spite of obvious and intense human suffering.

2. **Bureaucratic personality**. Employees who work in bureaucratic organizations sometimes develop unhealthy personalities that are excessively power-oriented. Officeholders come to believe that moral decisions of right or wrong are defined by higher-level officers and by the rules they are expected to follow. Following the rules becomes more important than the possibly inhumane treatment required by strict rule compliance.

Example—

A pregnant student was required to walk back to her apartment in a storm because she forgot to bring her computer lab pass to show that she is registered in a computer class, even though the person at the desk recognizes her as a class member.

3. **Inversion of means and ends**. Rigid adherence to rules and regulations often results in situations where the rules become more important than achieving the organization's goals, a condition called **means-ends inversion**: the means become more important than the end. Although the rules were originally designed to further organizational success, each officeholder comes to see the rules and regulations of that office as the ultimate goal. Bureaucratic activities can become so important that they supplant the purpose for which they were created.

Means-ends inversion
Where the means of accomplishing a goal become so important that people focus on that activity rather than what the activity is intended to accomplish.

Example—
Advertising campaigns, sales incentives, and other programs are designed to increase sales. But each of these programs can come to be viewed as an end in itself, so that an elaborate awards banquet becomes so important that it dominates everyone's time and attention, and replaces efforts to achieve high sales.

4. **Resistance to change**. As noted earlier, bureaucracies are intentionally designed to resist rapid change. This resistance is created by several aspects of a bureaucracy. First, officeholders tend to avoid responsibility when they are faced with decisions they prefer not to make. By redefining the problem, most officeholders are able to say, "That's not my job." Second, bureaucrats tend to be isolated from external feedback and outside evaluation. Bureaucracies tend to focus on their own internal functioning to the exclusion of external feedback. Their failure to respond to external evaluation prevents them from making corrective adjustments. Third, bureaucracies are not designed to foster setting or accomplishing goals. Rules and procedures focus the efforts of officeholders on activities rather than outcomes. Opportunities to produce innovative products or services tend to be overlooked because of a preoccupation with bureaucratic procedures. Fourth, bureaucracies move at a painfully slow pace when making complex decisions. The delay occurs because of the number of people who must concur before a decision is made about important issues. After the decision is finally made, there is an additional delay while new rules and procedures for each officeholder are created.

Example—
After the United Auto Workers (UAW) union was created in 1935, it set the standard for other unions in negotiating high wages and plush benefits packages for its members. Known for its aggressive bargaining, it continued to bargain for better labor contracts and protective work rules even when the U.S. auto industry was challenged by foreign competition and it was clear that the auto companies could not survive with their current practices. Although it was eventually willing to accept smaller wage and benefit increases for job guarantees, the labor costs for the auto industry were still more than the auto companies could handle and the membership of the UAW has been reduced to less than a third of what it was earlier.[9]

5. **The Peter Principle**. The Peter Principle was proposed as a satirical and humorous description of the incompetence that often occurs in bureaucratic organizations.[10] This principle states that in a hierarchy, every employee tends to rise to his or her level of *incompetence*. In a bureaucracy, promotions are supposed to be based on demonstrated ability: the most competent individual at one level is promoted to the next level. The Peter Principle explains, however, that competence at one level does not guarantee competence at the next level. The skills required for a subordinate position are frequently different from those required for success at the next level. Therefore, the most competent individuals at one level are promoted from level to level within the organization until they reach their level of incompetence, at which time they are no longer considered for promotion. An example of the Peter Principle is the promotion of competent technical or sales personnel into administrative positions for which they are ill suited by temperament. According to the Peter Principle, the only effective work that occurs in bureaucracies is performed by individuals who have not yet reached their level of incompetence.

Example—
Many school districts have a "promotion from within" policy that advances the best classroom teachers to the position of assistant principal and then principal. However, the skills required to

Peter Principle
A satirical explanation for incompetence in bureaucracies, suggesting that people rise to their level of incompetence.

be an excellent teacher of children are much different from the skills needed to supervise other adult teachers. Consequently, many of the assistant principals and principals struggle in their jobs and regret being promoted.

System Four Organizational Structure

Rensis Likert proposed a theory of organizational design, called **System Four**, that is often considered the opposite of bureaucracy.[11] Likert recommended his System Four as the ideal way to design an organization: extensive research by Likert and others has supported his theory. The central premise of Likert's theory is that there are four kinds of management systems, and these systems vary along a continuum from exploitive and authoritative at one end to participative and group-oriented at the other end. The labels of these four systems and brief descriptions are as follows.

1. The **exploitive-authoritative** style, System One, is characterized by the threat of punishment, hostile attitudes, downward communication, and distrust. Top management makes all the decisions and sets all the goals.
2. The **benevolent-authoritative** style, System Two, is slightly less hostile and threatening, since top management behaves more benevolently, but all decisions, goal setting, and communication are directly under the control of top management.
3. The **consultative** style, System Three, involves greater coordination between upper and lower levels of management. The ideas and interests of lower-level employees are considered, and lower-level employees have a limited opportunity to contribute to the decision making and goal setting.
4. The **participative-group oriented** style, System Four, involves open communication, participative decision making within groups, a decentralized authority structure, broad participation in the goal-setting processes whereby realistic objectives are set, and leadership processes that demonstrate a high level of confidence and trust between superiors and subordinates.

Although Likert did not advocate a specific span of control or form of departmentalization (he admitted that these and other design decisions depended on the situation), he argued that higher-level principles should guide management decisions in the design of an organization. Likert advocated three universal principles: (1) the principle of supportive relationships, (2) the use of group decision making, and (3) the creation of high performance goals.

1. The **principle of supportive relationships** says that all employees should be treated in ways that build and maintain their sense of personal worth and importance. All interactions between superiors and subordinates must be perceived by subordinates as contributing to their personal worth and to increasing their sense of human dignity. Likert assessed the degree to which relationships are supportive by asking such questions as "How much confidence and trust do you feel your superior has in you?" "To what extent does your boss convey to you a feeling of confidence that you can do your job successfully?" "To what extent is your boss interested in helping you to achieve and maintain a good income?"
2. Likert believed that groups were universally superior to the traditional hierarchical control in decision making and leadership. System Four management involves management by groups and recognizes overlapping group membership; each supervisor also serves as a subordinate in another group at the next level above. Those who hold overlapping memberships are called **linking pins**. At each

---

System Four
A type of organizational structure that is characterized by responsibility and initiative on the part of members, widely shared decision-making authority, decentralized decision making, and goal setting by employees.

Principle of supportive relationships
A universal principle that suggests that every interaction between superiors and subordinates should be transacted in a way that builds and encourages each in the performance of their respective duties.

Linking pins
People who link different organizational units by being a member of one group and the leader of the group below.

hierarchical level, all members of a work group who are affected by the outcome of a decision should be involved in it and it is the leader's responsibility to build an effective team. This principle has important implications for design decisions, since it encourages greater delegation of authority and coordination through the mutual adjustment of self-managing teams.

3. To achieve high levels of organizational performance, Likert argued that both managers and subordinates must have high performance aspirations. However, these high performance goals cannot be imposed on employees. System Four provides a mechanism through group decision making and overlapping group memberships to set high-level goals that satisfy both individual and organizational aspirations. Likert's principle of high performance aspirations is entirely consistent with goal setting theory, and the research supporting the impact of challenging and accepted goals.

CONTINGENCY THEORIES OF ORGANIZATIONAL DESIGN

Principles of organizational design have shifted from universal design theories to **contingency design theories** that try to identify the appropriate design features for each situation. Two research studies have contributed greatly to our understanding of contingency design theories. One line of research demonstrates that differences in technology determine the most effective organizational design, while the second suggests that differences in environmental uncertainty and the demands for processing information are the crucial factors. Both of these classic studies produce the same conclusion that the appropriate organizational design depends on the environment and each study identifies an important environmental factor that we need to recognize.

Technology

The first study demonstrated that the appropriate organizational structure is determined by the kinds of technology that it uses. **Technology** refers to the organization's transformation process and includes the knowledge, skills, abilities, machinery, and work procedures that are used in the transformation process. Every organization has a unique type of technology, and Joan Woodward, a British industrial sociologist, demonstrated that an organization's technology should determine how it is designed.[12] Her research surveyed 100 manufacturing firms on a wide range of structural characteristics, such as span of control, levels of management, ratios of management to clerical workers, decentralized decision making, and management style. Her data also included measures of performance regarding economic success.

When she examined the relationships between structure and performance for all 100 companies, she found no relationships—structure didn't seem to matter. However, when she divided the companies into three categories according to their technology, she found that structure was significantly related to performance: the successful companies in each category had structures that fit their technology. The three technology groups were small-batch manufacturing, such as a printing company; mass-production, such as an assembly-line firm; and continuous-process, such as an oil refinery. In each of the three technology groupings, the successful firms had ratios and numbers that were close to the median, while the unsuccessful firms had ratios and numbers that were much higher or lower than the median. Successful small-batch and continuous-process organizations tended to have organic structures, while successful mass-production organizations tended to have mechanistic structures.

Other research has likewise shown that an organization's structure needs to match the **routineness** of its processes. Routineness refers to the degree of continuity, automation, and rigidity in the production

---

Contingency design theories
Organizational design theories that claim that the ideal structure depends on the organization's requirements.

Technology
The knowledge, tools, techniques, and actions that are used to transform organizational inputs into outputs. Essentially, technology is the organization's transformation process.

process; the technology would be considered extremely routine if the production process were totally automated and produced a consistent product. The structural variables most frequently analyzed in technology studies are the degree of centralization, formalization, and specialization, and all three of these variables are positively related to routineness. According to this research, when the technology is highly routine (1) decision making should be centralized, (2) the rules and procedures should be formalized, and (3) the process should be decomposed and performed by specialized people and equipment.[13]

Environmental Uncertainty

The second classic study, by Paul Lawrence and Jay Lorsch, demonstrated that the degree of instability and uncertainty in the environment is another important situational variable that influences organizational structure.[14] The appropriate structure depends on the level of environmental uncertainty. Research fairly consistently indicates that organic structures are more effective in uncertain environments, while mechanistic structures are more effective in stable environments.

Lawrence and Lorsch examined organizations in three industries: plastics, packaged food products, and paper containers. These three industries were selected because significant differences were found in the degree of environmental uncertainty. The environment of the plastics firms was extremely uncertain, because of rapidly changing technology and customer demand. Decisions about new products were required even though feedback about the accuracy of the decisions often involved considerable delay. In contrast, the paper container firms faced a highly certain environment. Only minor changes in technology had occurred in the previous twenty years, and these firms focused on producing high-quality, standardized containers, and delivering them to the customer quickly. The consequences of decisions could be ascertained in a short period. Between these two extremes, the producers of packaged foods faced a moderately uncertain environment.

In analyzing how these firms interacted with their environments, Lawrence and Lorsch identified two key concepts: differentiation and integration. **Differentiation** is the degree of segmentation of the organizational system into subsystems, which is similar to the concepts of specialization of labor and departmentalization. However, differentiation also considers the behavioral attributes of employees in highly specialized departments. As noted earlier, members of highly specialized functional departments tend to adopt a rather narrow-minded, department-oriented focus that emphasizes the achievement of departmental rather than organizational goals.

The consequence of high differentiation is that greater coordination between departments is required. More time and resources must be devoted to achieve coordination, since the attitudes, goals, and work orientations among highly specialized departments differ so widely. Lawrence and Lorsch developed the concept of **integration** to refer to this coordinating activity.

Lawrence and Lorsch found that environmental uncertainty was related to the amount of differentiation and integration used in each industry. For example, the firms in the container industry faced a fairly stable environment, so they did not need to be highly differentiated, and they tended to adopt a mechanistic structure. The most successful container companies were organized along functional lines with a highly centralized authority structure. Coordination was achieved through direct supervision with formal written schedules. A bureaucratic structure was consistent with the container industry's degree of environmental certainty.

In the plastics industry, however, where companies face an extremely uncertain environment, the most successful plastics companies adopted organic structures. A highly unstable environment required

---

Differentiation
The degree of segmentation or division of labor into specialized jobs. It includes the behavioral attributes brought about by creating a narrow, department-oriented focus in the minds of individuals.

Integration
The coordinating activity that is used to achieve a unity of effort among various subsystems within an organization. The five major methods of integration include direct supervision, standardization of work processes, standardization of outputs, standardization of skills, or mutual adjustment.

that these companies have a highly differentiated structure with highly specialized internal departments of marketing, production, and research and development to deal with uncertainty in the external environment. Coordination was achieved through mutual adjustment, ad hoc teams that cut across departments, and special coordinators who served as liaisons between departments. The most successful plastics firms achieved high levels of differentiation and high levels of integration to coordinate them.

Lawrence and Lorsch's study contributes to our understanding of organizational design by showing the effects of environmental uncertainty on organizational structure. When the environment is highly uncertain, frequent changes require more information processing to achieve coordination, so special integrators and coordinating mechanisms are a necessary addition to the organization's structure. These integrators are called **liaison personnel**, **brand managers**, or **product coordinators**. Organizations that face a highly uncertain environment and a highly differentiated structure may have a fourth of their management staff assigned to integration activities, such as serving on committees, on task forces, or in liaison roles. Organizations that face very simple, stable environments may not have anyone assigned to a full-time integration role.

The analysis of Lawrence and Lorsch can be extended from the organizational to the departmental level within an organization. A large firm may need to organize its production department quite differently from its research department. One department may tend toward a mechanistic design and the other toward an organic design. The differences between these two departments are due to the different environments to which the two departments must adapt.

Example—
If a marketing department of a large firm faced an extremely unstable environment because of transportation problems across international boundaries, the marketing department would need to adopt an organic structure to respond to rapid developments. In contrast, the production department may face a very stable environment that allows for long production runs of standardized products. In this case, a mechanistic structure with formal bureaucratic procedures would be most appropriate for the production department.

Information Processing

The key integrating concept that explains the relationship between environmental uncertainty, technology, and organizational structure is the way the organization processes information.[15] Information flows into the organization from various environmental sectors, and the organization must respond and adapt to this information. Rapid changes in the external environment result in a greater need for incoming information. The consequence of environmental uncertainty on managers is an increase in the flow of information that leads to a communication overload. In essence, the organization becomes inundated with exceptional cases that require individual attention. As a greater number of nonroutine demands are made on the organization from the environment, managers are required to be more and more involved in day-to-day operations. Problems develop as plans become obsolete and the various coordination functions break down. An effective organization requires a structure that allows it to adapt to such a situation.

Organic structures can deal with greater amounts of uncertainty than mechanistic structures can. Organic structures have more highly connected communication networks that permit the efficient use of individuals as problem solvers and increase the opportunity for feedback. Because highly connected networks do not depend on any one individual, they are less susceptible to information overload or saturation. But while organic structures are able to deal effectively with greater amounts of uncertainty than mechanistic structures, there are costs associated with being able to process more information. Organic structures consume more time, effort, and energy, and are less subject to managerial control. Thus, the benefits of increased efficiency and capacity to process information must be weighed against the costs of less control and greater effort and time.

Organizations in a dynamic and complex environment cannot rely on traditional information processing and control techniques where all information is communicated through a chain of command. Changes in market demand, uncertain resources, and new technology disrupt the organization's plans and require adjustments while the task is being performed. Immediate adjustments to production schedules and job assignments disrupt the organization. Coordination is made more difficult because it is impossible to forecast operations or revise standard operating rules or procedures. Organizations must obtain information that reflects the environmental changes.

NOTES

1. V. A. Graicunas, "Relationship in Organization," *Bulletin of the International Management Institute*, vol. 7 (March 1933), pp. 39–42; reprinted in Luther H. Gulick and Lyndall F. Urwick (eds.), *Papers on the Science of Administration* (New York: Institute of Public Administration, Columbia University, 1937), pp. 182–187; Arthur G. Bedeian, "Vytautas Andrius Graicunas: A Biographical Note," *Academy of Management Journal*, vol. 17 (1974), pp. 347–349; Lyndall F. Urwick, "V. A. Graicunas and the Span of Control," *Academy of Management Journal*, vol. 17 (1974), pp. 349–354.

2. Kenneth J. Meier and John Bohte, "Span of Control and Public Organizations: Implementing Luther Gulick's Research Design," *Public Administration Review*, vol. 63 (Jan/Feb, 2003), pp. 61–70.

3. Michelle A. Johnston, "Delegation And Organizational Structure In Small Businesses: Influences Of Manager's Attachment Patterns," *Group & Organization Management*, vol. 25 (2000), pp. 4–21.

4. Thomas Sy and Laura Sue D'Annunzio, "Challenges and Strategies of Matrix Organizations: Top-Level and Mid-Level Managers' Perspectives," *Human Resource Planning*, vol. 28 (no. 1, 2005), pp. 39–48; Steven C. Dunn, "Motivation by Project and Functional Managers in Matrix Organizations," *Engineering Management Journal*, vol. 13 (June, 2001), pp. 3–9.

5. T. Burns and G. M. Stalker, *The Management of Innovation* (London: Tavistock Institute, 1961).

6. F. Crandall and M. Wallace, *Work & Rewards in the Virtual Workplace*, (AMACOM, New York, NY, 1998).

7. Timothy DeGroot and Amy L. Brownlee, "Effect of Department Structure on the Organizational Citizenship Behavior—Department Effectiveness Relationship," *Journal of Business Research*, vol. 59 (2006), pp. 1116–1123; Marshall Schminke, "Considering the Business in Business Ethics: An Exploratory Study of the Influence of Organizational Size and Structure on Individual Ethical Predispositions," *Journal of Business Ethics*. vol. 30 (2001), pp. 375–390; Maureen L. Ambrose and Marshall Schminke, "Organization Structure as a Moderator of the Relationship Between Procedural Justice, Interactional Justice, Perceived Organizational Support, and Supervisory Trust," *Journal of Applied Psychology*, vol. 88. (2003), pp. 295–305.

8. Max Weber, *The Theory of Social and Economic Organization*, trans. A. M. Henderson and T. Parsons (New York: Free Press, 1947).

9. Joseph B. White and Jeffrey McCracken, "GM-UAW Deal Ushers in New Era for Auto Industry," *The Wall Street Journal*, 27 September 2007, A1.

10. Lawrence F. Peter and Raymond Hull, *The Peter Principle* (New York: Morrow, 1969); Donald E. Walker, "The Peter Principle: A Simple Put-On About Complex Issues," *Change*, vol. 17 (July-August 1985), p. 11.

11. Rensis Likert, *New Patterns of Management* (New York: McGraw-Hill, 1961); Rensis Likert, *The Human Organization* (New York: McGraw-Hill, 1967).

12. Joan Woodward, *Industrial Organization: Theory and Practice* (London: Oxford University Press, 1965).

13. C. Chet Miller, William H. Glick, Yau-De Wang, and George P. Huber, "Understanding Technology-Structure Relationships: Theory Development and Meta-Analytic Theory Testing," *Academy of Management Journal*, vol. 34 (1991), pp. 370–399; Stephen R. Barley, "The Alignment of Technology and Structure Through Roles and Networks," *Administrative Science Quarterly*, vol. 35 (March 1990), pp. 61–103.

14. Paul R. Lawrence and J. W. Lorsch, *Organization and Environment* (Boston: Harvard Business School, 1967); Paul R. Lawrence and J. W. Lorsch, "Differentiation and Integration in Complex Organizations," *Administrative Science Quarterly*, vol. 12 (1967), pp. 1–47.

15. Michael L. Tushman and David A. Nadler, "Information Processing as an Integrating Concept in Organizational Design," *Academy of Management Review*, vol. 3 (1978), pp. 613–624.

Index